Gambling and Problem Gambling in Britain

Despite a rapid increase in the availability of many forms of gambling, there has been little serious study in the literature of the likely effects. This book seeks to fill that gap by reviewing what is known about gambling in Britain and studying work on the nature, prevalence and possible causes of problem gambling. Drawing on the history of and recent British studies on the subject, including the British Gambling Prevalence Survey and a companion qualitative study, *Gambling and Problem Gambling in Britain* gives an in-depth theoretical and practical viewpoint of this subject. Areas covered include:

- Gambling in Britain since Victorian times

- Expansion of gambling in the late 20th century

- What we now know about problem gambling and its treatment

- A consideration of the future of gambling in Britain

This book will be invaluable for professionals, trainees and academics in the fields of counselling, primary care, probation and social work, as well as health and social service managers and those involved in creating policy.

Jim Orford is Professor of Clinical and Community Psychology, The University of Birmingham.

Kerry Sproston is Deputy Head of the Health Research Group, National Centre for Social Research, London.

Bob Erens is Head of the Health Research Group, National Centre for Social Research, London.

Clarissa White is formerly of the Qualitative Research Unit, National Centre for Social Research, London.

Laura Mitchell is formerly of the Qualitative Research Unit, National Centre for Social Research, London.

Gambling and Problem Gambling in Britain

Jim Orford, Kerry Sproston,
Bob Erens, Clarissa White
and Laura Mitchell

With the support of GamCare

 Brunner-Routledge
Taylor & Francis Group

HOVE AND NEW YORK

First published 2003 by Brunner-Routledge
27 Church Road, Hove, East Sussex BN3 2FA

Simultaneously published in the USA and Canada
by Brunner-Routledge
29 West 35th Street, New York, NY 10001

Brunner-Routledge is an imprint of the Taylor & Francis Group

Typeset in Times by Mayhew Typesetting, Rhayader, Powys
Printed and bound in Great Britain by Biddles Ltd, Guildford and King's Lynn
Paperback cover design by Caroline Archer

British Library Cataloguing in Publication Data
A catalogue record for this book is available from the British Library

Library of Congress Cataloging-in-Publication Data
Orford, Jim.
    Gambling and problem gambling in Britain / Jim Orford ... [et al.].
        p. cm.
Includes bibliographical references and index.
    ISBN 1-58391-922-8 (alk. paper) – ISBN 1-58391-923-6 (pbk. : alk.
paper)
    1. Gambling–Great Britain. 2. Compulsive gambling–Great Britain.
I. Title.

HV6722.G8O74 2003
363.4'2'0941–dc21   2002154927

ISBN 1-58391-923-6
ISBN 1-58391-922-8

Contents

List of figures   vi
List of tables   vii
About the authors   ix
Preface   x

1 Gambling in Britain since Victorian times   1

2 Expansion of gambling in the late 20th century   21

3 Problem gambling   50

4 The causes of problem gambling   89

5 Gambling and problem gambling in Britain: summary
   of results of the British Gambling Prevalence Survey   140

6 Exploring problem-gambling behaviour in depth:
   summary of a qualitative study   174

7 What we now know about problem gambling and
   its treatment   209

8 A nation of gamblers? The 2001 Gambling Review
   Report and beyond   234

Postscript   261
References   266
Author index   285
Subject index   292

List of figures

2.1 Consumer expenditure on gambling as a percentage of total
consumer spend, 1990–1996   31

4.1 Changes in household expenditure on gambling, 1993–94 to
1995–96   94

4.2 The dimensions of gambling accessibility   95

4.3 Evidence of arousal during horse-race betting   120

4.4 Expectancies for the emotional effects of gambling   126

5.1 Number of gambling activities engaged in within the last year   146

5.2 Number of days participated in each gambling activity in
the past week   148

5.3 Number of gambling activities last year, by age   154

5.4 Total staked (type-A activities) and sum of losses (type-B
activities) last week, as a percentage of household income,
by income group   157

5.5 SOGS problem-gambling prevalence, by sex and age   162

5.6 DSM-IV problem-gambling prevalence, by sex and age   163

5.7 Problem-gambling prevalence by type of gambling activity
in the last 12 months   166

5.8 Problem-gambling prevalence by number of gambling
activities in the last 12 months   167

7.1 Causal pathways and problem gambling   217

7.2 The development of persistent gambling according to Walker   218

List of tables

1.1 Gambling legislation in Britain in the 19th and 20th centuries: some key dates   3

2.1 The scale of the gambling industry in Britain at the end of the 20th century   24

2.2 Community expectations and experiences before and after the opening of the Niagara Falls casino   40

2.3 The regulation of gambling in Britain at the end of the 20th century   47

3.1 DSM-IV criteria for 'pathological gambling'   66

3.2 Summary of international problem-gambling prevalence estimates   75

3.3 Understanding the theory of screening   78

3.4 Vignette 1 used by Blaszczynski, Dumlao and Lange, 1997, in their study of the interpretation of gambling spend   80

3.5 Levels of gambling involvement and experience proposed by Shaffer and Hall, 1996   86

4.1 Common cognitive biases and distortions that occur during gambling   127

4.2 Examples of adequate and inadequate verbalisations produced during a thinking-aloud experiment   131

5.1 The British Gambling Prevalence Survey: response rate   143

5.2 Percentages of gamblers, and of all respondents, engaging in each of 11 forms of gambling in the last year and in the last week   145

5.3 Number of other gambling activities engaged in during the last year by those reporting each type of activity   147

5.4 Groups of gamblers identified in the British Gambling Prevalence Survey   147

5.5 Amounts staked or lost on each form of gambling in the last week   151

5.6   The relationship between multiple-interest gambling, total
       staked and sum of losses, and demographic, social and
       economic variables   153
5.7   South Oaks Gambling Screen (SOGS) and DSM-IV
       questions used in the British Gambling Prevalence Survey   159–60
5.8   SOGS scores: last-year gamblers and all respondents   160
5.9   DSM-IV scores: last-year gamblers and all respondents   161
5.10   Problem-gambling prevalence by demographic, social and
       economic variables   164
5.11   Summary of the results of logistic regression analyses   165
5.12   Problem-gambling prevalence by stake or loss on different
       gambling activities in the last 7 days   169
5.13   Attitudes to gambling experience: SOGS problem gamblers
       and non-problem gamblers compared   170
5.14   SOGS and DSM-IV problem-gambler classifications
       cross-tabulated   171
6.1   The qualitative study: sample profile   176
6.2   Factors to which increases and decreases in gambling
       were attributed   197

About the authors

Jim Orford is Professor of Clinical and Community Psychology in the School of Psychology at The University of Birmingham, Edgbaston, Birmingham B15 2TT, UK. Telephone: 0121 414 4918/7195; fax: 0121 414 4897; e-mail: j.f.orford@bham.ac.uk.

Kerry Sproston is Deputy Head and Bob Erens is Head of the Health Research Group, Clarissa White is formerly of the Qualitative Research Unit, and Laura Mitchell was formerly a researcher in the QRU, at the National Centre for Social Research, 35 Northampton Square, London EC1V 0AX. Telephone: 020 7250 1866; e-mail: k.sproston@natcen.ac.uk, b.erens@natcen.ac.uk, info@natcen.ac.uk; website: www.natcen.ac.uk.

GamCare, the National Association for Gambling Care, Educational Resources and Training, is situated at 2/3 Baden Place, Crosby Row, London SE1 1YW. Telephone: 020 7378 5200; fax: 020 7378 5233; e-mail: info@gamcare.org.uk; website: www.gamcare.org.uk. Its Director is Paul Bellringer.

Preface

The beginning of the 21st century is an intriguing and worrying time for those with an interest in gambling and gambling problems in Britain. By the turn of the century gambling was mostly being spoken of, not, as it had been by many Britons a hundred years earlier as something disreputable and destructive, but rather as a harmless entertainment to be provided by a gambling industry whose expansion and innovation were to be encouraged. The debate over possible gambling prohibition was long since dead and forgotten. The careful Home Office regulatory framework for British gambling that had prevailed throughout the second half of the 20th century, under which gambling had been permitted but not encouraged, was also rapidly being assigned to history.

In 1999 the British government set up a body to review gambling and its regulation (the Gambling Review Body), and in the same year the national voluntary organisation GamCare commissioned the National Centre for Social Research (NatCen) to carry out the first British Gambling Prevalence Survey and a complementary Qualitative Study. Kerry Sproston and Bob Erens were responsible for the prevalence survey and Clarissa White and Laura Mitchell for the qualitative work. NatCen engaged Jim Orford at The University of Birmingham to provide the academic link. This book is therefore the result of a collaboration between the School of Psychology at The University of Birmingham and the National Centre for Social Research, with the support of GamCare. At its centre are summaries of the prevalence survey and qualitative work. Those studies carried out by NatCen are placed in the context of a review of psychological, sociological, historical and other material on gambling and problem gambling with special consideration given to its relevance to Britain in the early 21st century.

The NatCen teams produced their reports for GamCare in 2001, the same year in which the Gambling Review Body produced its report for government. The Gambling Review Report recommended the abolition of the principle that demand for gambling should not be 'stimulated', which had been a cornerstone of gambling regulation, and made 176 individual recommendations, the large majority of which were in the direction of encouraging and liberalising gambling in Britain. The report was welcomed by the gambling industry. The following year the Department for Culture, Media and Sport, now given lead government responsibility for the regulation of gambling in place of the Home Office, brought out its proposals, *A Safe Bet for Success*, accepting nearly all the Review Report's recommendations.

We are going to print, therefore, at a turning point in the history of British gambling. We have tried to be as objective as possible in the presentation of evidence and review of published work. But in the end we are unable to hide our anxiety that, in the rush to liberalise gambling in the interests of encouraging business and providing a form of leisure pursuit that may be harmless for many, the downsides of gambling for many individuals and their families, and perhaps for communities and society as a whole, are being minimised and neglected.

We would like to express our thanks to all those participants in the survey and qualitative studies reported in Chapters 5 and 6, who generously gave their time in the expectation that results would be of benefit to their fellow citizens. Our thanks are also due to Paul Bellringer, Director of GamCare, for his permission to include extensive summaries of those pieces of research which previously appeared as National Centre for Social Research reports to GamCare: *Gambling Behaviour in Britain: Results from the British Gambling Prevalence Survey*, and *Exploring Gambling Behaviour In Depth: A Qualitative Study*. Many thanks are also due to Pat Evans who typed draft and final copies of the manuscript for this book.

Chapter 1

Gambling in Britain since Victorian times

Knowing where you have come from nearly always helps one understand present predicaments and disputes, and that is certainly true of gambling and the British. A bit of recent history is illuminating. The present chapter considers gambling in Britain principally from around late Victorian times to the 1980s. Chapter 2 takes up the story from then on.

This chapter draws heavily upon two books that have become standard works on the subject: Dixon's (1991) *From Prohibition to Regulation: Bookmaking, Anti-Gambling, and the Law*, and Clapson's (1992) *A Bit of a Flutter: Popular Gambling and English Society, c.1823–1961*. The former is particularly strong on changing attitudes to gambling, legislative changes, and the role of the British government. The latter is especially helpful in providing details of different forms of gambling, including some, such as betting on dog racing or private betting, which are often neglected in more general discussions of gambling. Chinn's (1991) book on working-class betting and the rise of bookmaking was also very useful, as were books by Brenner and Brenner (1990) and Reith (1999) which contain substantial historical sections, and a number of papers including one by Miers (1996).

The history of gambling in Britain over the last century is complex and fascinating, and if space allowed there are many facets that might be described and points that could be made. The historians seem to agree that the following conclusions can be drawn. First, gambling over that period has taken many different forms, which are constantly changing and developing. The second conclusion is that attitudes towards gambling are never neutral: there are at least two opposed views of gambling, one pro and the other anti, and collectively the nation's views have always been ambivalent. The third is that forms of gambling, and criticisms of gambling, have always been strongly related to social class. Lastly, they concur that recent history has seen many attempts at the control of gambling, changing with time, and varying from prohibition to legalisation and regulation; attempts to prohibit forms of gambling have repeatedly been evaded by one means or another.

Forms of gambling: varied and changing over time

Gambling in one form or another has probably always gone on, but in the second half of the 17th century the Restoration appears to have been associated with a startling rise in gambling, referred to by Reith (1999, p.58) as an "explosion" which lasted for the next hundred years. Pepys in his diary of the 1660s (1976, Vol 9, p.4, cited by Reith) referred to gambling as a "prophane, mad entertainment". Gambling took the form of private wagers on the outcome of all manner of events such as births, marriages and deaths, but particularly sporting events such as horse races, cock and dog fights, bear-baiting and prize fighting (Chinn, 1991; Reith, 1999). In 1754 *The Connoisseur* declared "there is nothing, however trivial or ridiculous, which is not capable of producing a bet" (cited by Reith, 1999, p.63). By the first half of the 19th century, with the effects of the industrial revolution, former patterns of both aristocratic and working-class recreation had declined. That period was strong on anti-gambling sentiment and saw legislation (in 1823), for example, that would outlaw lotteries for over a hundred years. It culminated in the Betting Act of 1853 which serves as a useful starting point for this brief historical review. That important Act made illegal the operating of any special 'place', such as a betting house, for purposes of off-course cash betting – legislation that was not overturned until 1960 when modern betting offices were legalised (Table 1.1 provides some key dates in 19th- and 20th-century British gambling legislation).

According to Chinn (1991), the later half of the 19th century, and particularly the 1880s, saw a marked resurgence of gambling. This he put down to several factors. Horse racing was by then much better organised and on a larger scale than before, and bookmakers, who had found plenty of ways of getting round the 1853 legislation, were more numerous, better organised and more to be trusted than previously. Sufficient working-class people now had some disposable income to spend on horse-race betting. Finally, the advent of the railways, expansion of the sporting press, and particularly the development of the telegraph, allowed people to enjoy a day out at the races, and meant that news of races, odds on the horses running, and results, could be quickly known all around the country (Chinn, 1991; Dixon, 1991; Reith, 1999). What is clear is that by the end of the 19th century, horse-race betting in Britain, which the anti-gambling sentiment and legislation of the century had strikingly failed to suppress, had become, both on-course and off it, the major form of the nation's gambling (Clapson, 1992).

Although horse-race betting came to occupy a dominant position in British gambling, many other forms of gambling have coexisted with it, their popularity rising and falling with time. Gambling on coin games was also very popular in the late Victorian and Edwardian era. The game of 'pitch-and-toss' was, according to Clapson (1992), the most popular such game. It had been played at least since the 18th century and continued to be

Table 1.1 Gambling legislation in Britain in the 19th and 20th centuries: some key dates

1808	House of Commons Select Committee on the laws relating to Lotteries	Highly critical of public lotteries
1823	Lotteries Act	Lotteries made illegal
1844	House of Lords Select Committee on Gaming	Recommended stronger police action against gambling 'hells'; and making gambling agreements unenforceable
1845	Gaming Act	Gaming debts unenforceable at law; resulted in bookmakers demanding cash from clients and a rapid growth of betting houses
1853	Betting Houses Act	Betting houses made illegal
1902	House of Lords Select Committee on Betting	Recommended legislating against street betting
1906	Street Betting Act	Acceptance of bets on streets and in other public places made illegal
1923	Select Committee on Betting Duty	Accepted the principle of legal, regulated gambling; concluded a betting tax was practicable
1933	Royal Commission on Lotteries and Betting	Argued that prohibitions on gambling should be minimal but thought betting offices should remain illegal
1934	Betting and Lotteries Act	Legalised private and small public lotteries
1951	Royal Commission on Betting, Lotteries and Gaming	Recommended that bookmakers could accept cash bets in licensed premises; but that gaming machines be illegal
1956	Small Lotteries and Gaming Act	Introduced societies' lotteries for charitable or sporting purposes
1960	Betting and Gaming Act	Legalised almost all forms of gambling including commercial gaming clubs, licensed betting offices, and gaming machines in a wide variety of venues
1963	Betting, Gaming and Lotteries Act	Consolidated the 1960 Act
1968	Gaming Act	Brought in controls on casinos; established the Gaming Board
1975	Lotteries Act	Allowed local authorities to conduct good cause lotteries
1978	Royal Commission on Gambling	Recommended the setting up of a National Lottery; and removal of some of the restrictions on betting offices
1993	National Lottery Act	Made provision for the setting up of a National Lottery
2000	Gambling Review Body set up by the Home Office	Set up to consider the current state of the gambling industry; the social impact of gambling; and the need for change to regulations and treatment for problem gambling
2001	Gambling Review Body reported to the Department for Culture, Media and Sport	Recommended abolishing the principle of unstimulated demand for casinos and other gambling establishments; the legalising of larger prizes; tighter control on machines; and the setting up of a Gambling Commission

popular up to the period between the 20th century's two world wars. The game was described to the 1844 Select Committee on Gaming by a London magistrate:

> A hole is made in the ground, or some object is placed there, and the players pitch at same with pence or halfpence; he who pitches nearest the hole or object is entitled to the first toss into the air of all the pence played with and claims every piece of money which falls with head uppermost; he who pitched second best has the second toss and so on till all the players have successively tossed, or the money is exhausted. Sometimes, young boys play for cakes, but generally for money (cited by Clapson, 1992, pp.79–80).

Another witness to that committee suggested that playing such games was particularly prevalent amongst "boys of loose habits and irregular propensities" (cited by Clapson, 1992, p.80). Nearly a hundred years later, pitch-and-toss gained notoriety as a cause of the Sheffield gang wars over the control of lucrative and illegal 'tossing rings' (Clapson, 1992). Perhaps nicely illustrating the ambivalence in attitude that surrounds almost all forms of gambling, pitch-and-toss gets a glowing reference (keeping ". . . a cool head and staking all on a single throw" being associated with manhood) in Rudyard Kipling's poem *If* published in 1910 and still, at the end of the 20th century, topping the poll as the nation's favourite poem.

In 1905, Masterman, author a few years later of *The Condition of England*, writing of the rise of gambling in the late Victorian period, said the "facts themselves are undeniable. The thing has come with a rush in almost a generation" (cited by Dixon, 1991, p.47). Part of this 'thing' was gambling on a range of sports events in addition to horse racing. These included betting on dog races, football matches, pigeon races, and games of bowls (Clapson, 1992). Dog racing had its origins in hare or rabbit coursing, popular earlier in the 19th century. Artificial quarry were substituted once the practice of using live bait was recognised as cruel, and greyhound racing boomed after World War I with the development of stadia in most British cities. They were more accessible to urban dwellers than were horse race meetings, and were artificially lit for evening racing. It was difficult, however, for the sport to overcome its earlier negative, dishonest image (hence the expression 'going to the dogs'), and it experienced some fall in popularity after World War II (Clapson, 1992).

The beginnings of organised football in Britain in the 1880s led directly to the development of companies offering football pools betting (so called because, unlike most race betting where odds are fixed before the race takes place, but like the *pari mutuel* or totalisator race betting system, all betters' stakes are pooled and prizes shared amongst winners). Always dominated by the city of Liverpool where the two biggest firms, Littlewoods and

Vernons, were situated (despite some advocates, football pools betting was never nationalised in Britain as it was in Sweden), football pools betting became immensely popular in the first half of the 20th century. By 1913 the *Morning Post* estimated that two million football coupons were issued every week, and by the late 1930s it had become a weekly 'flutter' for over ten million people nationally (Clapson, 1992). The years immediately after World War II saw the development of the 'treble chance' which offered large 'jackpot' prizes. Despite a recommendation by the Royal Commission on Betting, Lotteries and Gaming (the Willink Commission, 1949–51) that top prizes should be reduced, and the voluntary imposition of a ceiling on prizes by pools firms, it was clear that jackpots were popular and they went on rising, exceeding £100,000 for the first time in 1950 and £200,000 in 1957. In any event 'doing the pools' was by then seen as an important and largely harmless feature of national life. As the Memorandum of the Roman Catholic Church to the Royal Commission of 1949–51 put it, pools had become "a national pastime [and were] beneficial, since in many homes happy evenings are spent by the family remaining together and filling up their coupons" (cited by Clapson, 1992, p.174).

The diversity of forms that gambling can take is illustrated by two other forms described by Clapson, both popular in the first half of the 20th century but declining in popularity thereafter, and both particularly popular in the North of England on which his book focused. These were betting on pigeon racing and on crown bowling, a form of bowls popular in the North in which the green is raised in the centre falling away to the edge. Betting on cards continued to be legal in the family in private but illegal in gambling establishments until the legalisation of casinos in the 1960s. Yet other forms of gambling, which will be discussed more fully in Chapter 2 since they feature prominently in late 20th-century British gambling, are slot-machine gambling (present since Edwardian times and already big business and attracting criticism by the 1910s, 1920s and 1930s) and lotteries (illegal in all forms throughout most of the 19th century and well into the 20th, and with no national government lottery in the modern period until the very last years of the 20th century).

One could go further and include the buying and selling of stocks and shares as a form of gambling. We think that is to stretch the definition of 'gambling' rather far. For one thing there is nothing in speculating on the stock market that corresponds exactly to a stake or wager which is forfeited if the forecast is wrong. Certainly it is outwith all 19th- and 20th-century legislation on betting and gaming. It has to be admitted, however, that the boundary around the concept of 'gambling' is a fuzzy one. Certainly Clapson (1992) included extensive discussion of premium bonds since they include a prize element. Furthermore he considered that their introduction in Britain in the 1950s paved the way for the later introduction of the National Lottery. They were certainly opposed at the time, partly on the grounds that they were a form of gambling and therefore not something that should be promoted by government. As we shall see in Chapter 6, gamblers themselves hold differing opinions about what to include in or exclude from the definition of gambling.

Opposed and ambivalent views of gambling

Dixon (1991) believed that gambling was never, anywhere, defined with ethical neutrality or indifference, and Reith (1999) saw two separate traditions out of which modern ambivalence towards gambling had emerged. One was a 'tradition of licence', generally condoning all forms of play as manifestations of positive features of human nature including playfulness, gameness, composure under stressful or risky circumstances, character, and even courage, bravery and heroism (as in Kipling's poem). The opposing tradition, although the terminology has changed much over the years, ". . . has persistently regarded gambling as fundamentally problematic and condemned it as variously sinful, wasteful, criminal and pathological" (Reith, p.2). Supporters of that position had included Reformation church leaders (gambling as sinful), champions of the Enlightenment (gambling as irrational), and upholders of the capitalist work ethic (gambling as idle gain opposed to the steady accumulation of wealth through hard work). Clapson (1992) pointed out that the very term 'gambler' has mostly been used as a pejorative one. Dr Johnson stated in his *Dictionary of the English Language* in 1755 that 'gambler' was "a cant word" for gamester, a "knave whose practice it is to invite the unwary to gain and cheat them" (cited by Clapson, p.1). The verbs 'to bet' and 'to wager' meant the same thing and were less disreputable than the newer verb 'to gamble' which was associated in England with the lower class and with cheating and indulgence.

The early years of the 19th century provide much evidence of opposition to gambling. Notable was the setting up in 1808 of a Select Committee to consider the 'Evils attending Lotteries', amongst which were thought to be widespread fraud and ill-effects on the working class. The following extract from the minutes of that committee gives a flavour:

> By the effects of the lottery, even under its present restrictions, idleness, dissipation, and poverty are increased, the most sacred and confidential trusts are betrayed, domestic comfort is destroyed, madness often created, crimes, subjecting the perpetrators of them to the punishment of death are inflicted and even suicide itself is produced (House of Commons Select Committee, 1808, Appendix A, 157, cited by Miers, 1996, p.354).

There was also great concern expressed about the growth of horse-race gambling. A Reverend from Cheltenham commenting on the approach of the town's annual races in 1827 stated his view:

Gambling is . . . a vice which appears to be growing in our land; though it be a vice which is more pre-eminently destructive both of body and soul, than any other which Satan ever devised for the ruin of mankind. Every vile passion of our corrupt nature is excited and inflamed by it; envy, malice, revenge, the lust of money, pride, contention, cruelty . . . (cited by Chinn, 1991, pp.60–61).

He was accused of 'ultra-piety' by a Tory correspondent in *The Gentleman's Magazine* who pointed out that horse racing had brought prosperity to the town by giving employment and increased trade, and that suppression of the races would cause unemployment, greater rather than lesser crime, and local economic decline.

An early example of organised opposition to gambling was an association set up in 1828 in Doncaster for the 'Suppression of Gambling Houses and Gaming Tables' (Chinn, 1991). But pride of place in terms of anti-gambling organisations must be preserved for the National Anti-Gambling League (NAGL), founded in 1890, with a stated aim of:

Nothing less than the reformation of England as regards the particular vice against which our efforts are aimed . . . There is humiliation in the thought that the chosen Anglo Saxon race, foremost in the civilisation and government of the world, is first also in the great sin of Gambling (Bulletin of NAGL, 1893, vol 1, no 7, p.1, cited by Reith, 1999, p.85).

Although, looking back more than one hundred years, the anti-gambling movement of that period may appear alien and extreme, even ludicrous, it played a significant role in the development of modern gambling in Britain and commanded a great deal of support at the time (Dixon, 1991). Its opposition to gambling was largely on moral grounds of which, according to Dixon's analysis, there were three facets: it involved an appeal to chance, ". . . which is opposed to the nature and dignity of man as a rational responsible being and to the basis of ordered human society" (Social and Industrial Commission of the Church Assembly, 1950, p.17, cited by Dixon, 1991, p.48); it was inherently selfish, involving trying to gain at the expense of others; and it constituted an illegitimate method of transferring goods from one person to another, and was hence in danger of undermining the basis of capitalist society. But there were also utilitarian arguments that gambling interfered with productivity at work, and even with the nation's productivity in comparison with its growing competitors, principally Germany and the USA. One owner of an engineering works in Leeds, who sacked those he discovered to be gamblers, giving evidence to the 1902 Select Committee, stated that betting "almost entirely destroys [the employee's] usefulness as a workman, certainly if he is a skilled workman" (cited by Dixon, 1991, p.57).

The vice-president of the NAGL, in his book *Betting and Gambling*, stated his opinion that the "nation which possesses . . . the fewest gamblers must sooner or later assert its superiority" (Churchill, 1894, p.76, cited by Dixon, 1991, p.57). Furthermore, the anti-gambling movement of that period drew strength from the vibrancy of the temperance movement and the latter's apparent success in reducing excessive drinking.

In the late Victorian and Edwardian era there was widespread criticism of gambling, both in its upper-class form of betting at horse races (including considerable criticism of public figures such as Lord Rosebery who as Prime Minister was twice the owner of the Derby winner; and the Prince of Wales who moved in a 'fast racing set' and also had Derby winners in 1896, 1900 and, as King Edward VII, in 1909), and in its working-class forms of street cash betting and playing at games such as pitch-and-toss (Dixon, 1991). The movement had influential supporters. Seebohm Rowntree, the Quaker industrialist and social investigator, was one of NAGL's central members for more than fifty years. A major contribution of his was the editing of a volume of essays entitled *Betting and Gambling: A National Evil* (1905). Amongst his contributors was Ramsay MacDonald, Secretary of the Labour Representation Committee and later Labour Prime Minister. In his article, entitled, *Gambling and Citizenship*, he wrote:

> To hope . . . that a Labour party can be built up in a population quivering from an indulgence in games of hazard is pure folly. Such a population cannot be organised for sustained political effort, cannot be depended upon for legal support to its political champions, cannot respond to appeals to its rational imagination. Its hazards absorb so much of its leisure; they lead it away from thoughts of social right-eousness; they destroy in it the sense of social service; they create in it a state of mind which believes in fate, luck, the irrational, the erratic; they dazzle its eyes with flashy hopes; they make it absolutely incapable of taking an interest in the methods and the aims of reforming politicians . . . Every Labour leader I know recognises the gambling spirit as a menace to any form of Labour party (MacDonald, 1905, pp.127–128, cited by Chinn, 1991, p.179 and Dixon, 1991, p.73).

Many Labour leaders of that period were anti-gamblers. Radical noncon-formity was strong in the early British Labour party, and the view was widely held that gambling, like drinking, held back the progress of the working class. For example, in a *Clarion Pamphlet*, John Burns's 'tip to the workers' was, "Spend on books what is often given to beer; to mental improvement what is given to gambling" (1902, pp.9–10, cited by Dixon, 1991, p.74).

The NAGL met with mixed fortunes and had disappeared by the middle of the 20th century, but it is probably fair to say that it left a strong mark on British gambling for the whole of that century. Its first major campaign was directed towards betting at horse-race meetings. Its attack focused on the legal interpretation of the word 'place' in the 1853 Betting Act which stated that, "No house, office, room or other place shall be opened, kept or used for the purpose of . . . any person using the same . . . betting with persons resorting thereto" (Section 1, cited by Dixon, 1991, p.90).

Winning what appeared to be a crucial prosecution against an on-course bookmaker, it appeared that the NAGL had established in law that the betting enclosure or 'ring' at a racecourse constituted such a 'place', and that racecourse betting was therefore illegal. That would have utterly changed the nature of gambling in Britain and it was fiercely opposed by, amongst other groups, the Sporting League and the Anti-Puritan League. Only four months later, in July 1897, the Court of Appeal effectively overruled the previous judgment on the grounds that, although the enclosure was a 'place' where betting was known to go on, bookmakers did not have exclusive use of the place nor did they have any rights of possession over it.

Although that was a body blow from which arguably the NAGL never recovered (Dixon, 1991), its greatest success came a few years later in the form of the Street Betting Act of 1906 which, amongst other things, made it an offence for:

> Any person frequenting or loitering in streets or public places on behalf either of himself or of any other person for the purpose of bookmaking or betting or wagering or agreeing to bet or wager or paying or receiving or settling bets (cited by Dixon, 1991, p.141).

There had been widespread concern about 'street betting', notably on the part of the police and the Home Office, but more widely amongst the middle classes who probably knew little of the realities of such gambling and held unfounded prejudices about it (Chinn, 1991). The Select Committee which reported in 1902 and recommended legislating against street betting was a Committee of the House of Lords. Although, in an attempt to organise a balanced Select Committee it contained three racing peers as well as the President of the NAGL and three other avowed anti-gamblers, plus two neutrals, they can hardly have been expected to be very sympathetic towards the predominantly working-class street bookmaking, which they described as "undoubtedly a great source of evil . . . [and] the cause of most of the evils arising from Betting amongst the working classes" (para 18, cited by Dixon, 1991, p.117). The obviously class-based nature of the 1906 Act, only finally overturned in 1960, is reckoned by historians to be a major reason for its lack of success in practice. After World War I the police totally changed their attitude, having come to believe that the law was impossible to enforce and that attempts to do so undermined their relationship with working-class communities. The Labour Party, which in any case was moving away from its nonconformist origins, was critical of such a class-biased law. Even the

NAGL, whilst taking pleasure in its success in contributing to anti-gambling legislation, was embarrassed at the fact that it attacked working-class habits whilst leaving upper-class gambling untouched.

An intriguing sub-plot in this story of the development of modern British gambling concerns the uncomfortable compromise that Rowntrees and their equally anti-gambling competitors Cadburys were obliged to adopt in their role as owners of successful newspapers. As already noted, part of the growth in popularity of betting in the late 19th century had been the rise of the racing press both in the form of dedicated sheets or papers (many of them very ephemeral) and the racing pages of wide circulation national newspapers which were to become such a feature of British gambling throughout the 20th century. So dependent did such newspapers become on racing news that both Quaker firms had no choice but to include such news in their own papers. Public libraries, it is interesting to note, continued to act as censors by 'blacking out' racing pages in their reading rooms up to the 1930s, and even in some places such as Wolverhampton until the 1950s (Chinn, 1991).

From World War I onwards the NAGL, and the anti-gambling movement in general, was in decline. But significant skirmishes continued. One, of particular interest because of the prominence of the National Lottery in British gambling at the very end of the 20th century, was the proposal towards the end of World War I to introduce premium bonds in order to help finance the war effort. Since premium bonds are now uncontroversial and are mostly considered to be a form of saving rather than gambling, it is hard now to appreciate the strong feelings aroused by the proposal (Dixon, 1991). A Select Committee considered the matter carefully and reported in 1918 that the introduction of premium bonds would constitute too sharp a break with existing gambling legislation and would meet with strong opposition from the anti-gambling movement. The NAGL (1918, p.3, cited by Dixon, 1991, p.180) considered the proposal to be "one of the most powerful and insidious attempts which have been made yet to entrench gambling in the national life".

The NAGL had few other successes and finally folded in the late 1940s after a number of years of decline and disorganisation (Dixon, 1991; Collins, 1996). Rowntree finally shifted support to the Churches' Committee on Gambling which under the generally highly regarded leadership of the Reverend Gordon Moody, later became the Churches' Council on Gambling (Chinn, 1991; Dixon, 1991).

Although they appear not to have been prime targets for the attentions of the NAGL, two other forms of gambling attracted criticism in the early years of the 20th century and both have significance for us now. The first, the football pools, is important because of the place of football as a national sport and more generally the close association between gambling and sports of various kinds. According to Dixon there was considerable middle-class disappointment that football, which had been seen by many as a healthy counter-attraction to drinking for the working classes, should have become a source of gambling. A leader in the *Manchester Evening News* in 1905 complained that:

> Recently a very insidious form of gambling has made its presence known in the North of England, and unless some means can be found for stopping this undoubted evil we are afraid the future of football will be as bad as horse racing has become (Clapson, 1992, p.164).

Both the Football Association and the Football League made efforts to rid the game of betting and what they saw as betting's harmful effects. In 1907 the FA had passed a rule that any club official, referee, linesman or player who was proved to have taken part in coupon football betting would be permanently suspended from taking part in football or football management. A fear was that there would be temptation to rig matches: indeed a famous episode was the rigging of a match between Manchester United and Liverpool in 1915. A Chairman of the FA in the 1920s stated, "if betting gets hold of football, the game is done for" (cited by Clapson, 1992, p.168). As late as 1935 the Football League forbade clubs to put advertisements for the pools in their programmes or at their grounds, and even tried to withhold the publication of match fixtures until two days before kick-off so that pools coupons could not be prepared in advance.

Another form of gambling, which in this case appears to have gone largely unnoticed by the anti-gambling movement of the early 20th century, but which has become of great significance in more recent times, is machine gambling. What is perhaps surprising in this case, to those who may have thought that concern about machine gambling only arose later in the century, is the fact that voices of concern were being raised much earlier on. Even before World War I there was confusion about whether machines that took money and gave prizes contravened the law because they were games of pure chance. The diversity of types of machine already in operation were causing the police difficulty even then (Clapson, 1992). In 1927 the Lord Chief Justice stated that the slot machine, "was a pest and a most mischievous pest, because it operates on the minds of young persons and corrupts them in their youth" (cited by Clapson, 1992, p.88). In 1932 the Chief Constable of the Metropolitan Police told Parliament that, "By far the most troublesome form of gaming [in] recent years is the automatic gaming machine of the 'fruit' variety" (cited by Clapson, 1992, p.85).

The class-based nature of British gambling

A theme that runs through the historical accounts of gambling in Britain is that of social class. One late Victorian view was that the working class had been comparatively free of gambling and that the danger lay in the upper classes setting a bad example and passing on the gambling habit to lower-class people. The historians' consensus is that that view merely reflected ignorance of working-class forms of gambling, and that class differences were largely to do with the forms taken by gambling. Reith (1999) suggests that a clear social stratification had already emerged by the 18th century with upper-class private clubs such as Whites and Crockfords at one end, and the playing of cards and dice in unlicensed ale houses and coffee shops ('hells') and the playing of lotteries, at the other. It is an interesting question whether class differences in forms of gambling remain today. It might be expected that the rich and the poor will always find different ways to gamble. Certainly Clapson (1992) was able to describe, for the early part of the 20th century, class divisions even within what might appear to be the same forms of gambling. For example, within dog racing it was a case of 'whippets for workers, greyhounds for gentry', and in the world of pigeon racing he drew a distinction between the superior long-distance racing clubs that met in hotels and the short-distance, pub-based type.

As we have already seen, much of the public concern about gambling that peaked at the end of the 19th century and early in the 20th was about the dangers of working-class gambling, and in the event it turned out to be more possible to legislate against working-class forms of gambling. The concerns, now easily recognised as patronising, included a lack of confidence in the judgement of working-class people to choose their own recreation sensibly, concern that poorer people unlike the better off could not afford to lose, and a fear of the idleness of the poor should they win (Brenner and Brenner, 1990; Dixon, 1991). A letter from the then Metropolitan Police Commissioner to the Home Office in 1911 typifies such sentiments:

> The man who can afford to lose . . . need not be the object of our concern; contrary to the recognized principle, what is now required is one law for the rich and another for the poor. The poor have no grievance as to this. It would be for their protection against themselves . . . (cited by Dixon, 1991, p.132).

Chinn's (1991) view was that class divisions in attitudes to gambling, and particularly in attitudes towards bookmakers, remained deeply entrenched right up to the time he was writing. These differences reflected, in his judgement, nothing less than a clash of views between two opposing interpretations of life, one the basically working-class attitude which judged people in a down-to-earth way, the other a superior middle-class view that passed judgement on bookmakers and their punters based on little knowledge of working-class life in general or of bookmaking in particular.

Perhaps because of the recent history of anti-gambling sentiments and agitation, and because of the class prejudice that has attended investigations and legislation about gambling (and even racial prejudice directed towards Jewish bookmakers – Chinn, 1991), recent historians have mostly been at pains to defend working-class gambling (and by implication all gambling) against charges of irrationality, excess, the creation of poverty through losing, and the inducing of idleness through winning. Late 19th and early 20th century social investigations by Booth, by Rowntree and by Bell, concluded that there was no direct causal link between gambling and poverty (Brenner and Brenner, 1990; Dixon, 1991; Clapson, 1992). Drawing on earlier historical work by McKibbin (1979) and by Mott (1973), and on the autobiographical evidence and oral testimonies that he collected, Clapson (1992) concluded:

> Gambling can be seen as a moderate, economistic and expressive form of recreation . . . In an unequal society, most people had a good idea of the odds facing them, and of how the dice were loaded, and they spent their time and money as best they could. Their regular and moderate betting was part of a continually evolving culture in which leisure and economy were and are fundamental to people's lives (p.210).

Chinn (1991) also concluded, on the basis of the historical evidence available plus personal accounts of earlier 20th century betting that he collected, that working-class betting was largely for very small stakes (the 'penny punter' and the 'threepenny flutter' for example) and was rationally and carefully controlled. He followed McKibbin (1979) in concluding that much working-class betting was "fairly regular, prudent, usually considered" (p.163, cited by Chinn, 1991, p.178). It could not lift people out of poverty but it could offer the prospect of being able to afford a good night out, a luxury item, or a present for the family. It was "the only possibility of making a decision, of a choice between alternatives, in a life otherwise prescribed in every detail by poverty and necessity, and always the object of other people's decisions" (Pilgrim Trust, 1938/1985, p.99, cited by Chinn, 1991, p.178). Some picked horses with a pin, but others took great care in making selections. Chinn (1991) supported the suggestion that gambling, as a result of all the studying, calculating, note taking and communicating that was involved, encouraged literacy as well as arithmetical ability amongst people who had had otherwise relatively little education.

Legislation and changing attitudes to gambling in Britain in the 20th century

The Street Betting Act of 1906 built on the bias against popular gambling enshrined in the 1853 Betting Act. It had already been recognised that total prohibition was impossible, and therefore the intention was to localise betting to racecourses or other sporting venues (although credit betting by letter, telegram or telephone remained legal, Dixon, 1991). It represented the high watermark of gambling prohibition in Britain and the 20th century saw a steady retreat from that position.

The 1906 Act was always controversial. At a meeting in Manchester in October 1906 the maverick Liberal MP Horatio Bottomley proclaimed his intention to rouse Englishmen against "the prevailing wave of puritanical and namby-pamby, goody-goody legislation [which] struck at those fundamental principles of self-reliance and robust manhood which made the English race what it was" (cited by Clapson, 1992, p.32). As he might have predicted, the 1906 Act was conspicuously unsuccessful in stamping out off-course cash betting. Both Chinn (1991) and Clapson (1992) provided rich detail of the reality of 'street betting' in the years between the 1906 Act and the Betting and Gaming Act of 1960 which finally legalised betting offices. In fact the expression 'street betting' gives only a very imperfect impression of the many inventive ways in which the Act was circumvented. Much betting did take place literally in the street with bets being taken in back alleys or closes or anywhere where the bookmaker, 'tout' or 'runner' was safe from police surveillance or could easily escape if warned of police approach. Bookmakers had their territories or 'pitches' which were often passed on from father to son or even sold. But according to Chinn and Clapson much so-called 'street' betting took place in pubs, at work, in domestic houses, newsagents, tobacconists, fish and chip shops and other shops that doubled as betting 'offices', as well as at the offices of book-makers ostensibly engaged only in legal credit betting but in fact also engaging in illegally taking cash bets. One of Clapson's oral testimonies, from a man in Salford, included the following:

> The 'office' was in the rear room of a terraced house in each case, complete with a telephone and 'blower' . . . A simple cover over a back yard led to a door with a 'window' cut in, this window was just a hole with a removable shutter/cover and it had a small shelf on the inside. Bets were placed by knocking on the shutter if not open, and handing in the bet through the opening . . . look-outs ('dogger outs') were placed at strategic points to warn of police activities, these were usually assisted by enthusiastic local youngsters. The bookie usually had a 'mug' whose main job was to be caught by the police with nominal evidence only (Clapson, 1992, p.49)

Chinn's written accounts included the following from a Birmingham resident:

> a gentleman by the name of W. who owned a greengrocer's shop at Dogpool. The procedure was to eye up the outside of the shop, looking to see if any uniformed police were about, or strangers – we knew all

the locals in those days; when it was 'all clear' we walked into the shop – if it was clear of customers we walked straight through to a shed in the back-yard where we handed in the coppers, wrapped in our betting slip (Chinn, 1991, p.123).

The impression given by these accounts is that cash betting, illegal for over 50 years in the early part of the 20th century, was very widely available in working-class districts throughout the country. Of particular concern to critics of this state of affairs were women betters (cash betting was by all accounts much more attractive to women than, for example, active involvement in gambling on games such as pitch-and-toss) and the involvement of children, both as betters themselves and as messengers and assistants for adult betting. The Betting and Loans (Infants) Act had been passed in 1892, "to render Penal the inciting of Infants to Betting or Wagering or to borrowing money" (cited by Chinn, 1991, p.169), but many thought the measure had been unsuccessful. In 1947, for example, the *Gateshead Times* reported that police keeping watch on a particular house over a period of three days had observed 117 men, 159 women and 105 children between the ages of 5 and 14 enter the house and reappear a few minutes later (cited by Chinn, 1991, p.170). Bookmaking was on such a scale that it was of significance in terms of employment. In 1936 a writer in *The Economist* estimated that 66,000 people were directly dependent on bookmaking, and the Royal Commission report of the early 1950s estimated the figure at 80,000 (Chinn, 1991, p.228). There appear to have been marked regional differences in the exact form taken by illegal cash betting, with betting 'offices' more common in Northern Ireland and the north of England, and betting on the street more common in southern England. Chinn (1991), however, thought the idea of 'two betting Englands', north and south of the River Trent, was an over-simplification, pointing to the existence of many illegal betting shops in Birmingham, Brighton and elsewhere.

The 1906 Act made available a maximum fine of £10 for a first offence, £20 for a second, and £50 or imprisonment for a maximum of six months with hard labour for a third or for any offence involving a person under 16 years of age. Growing police frustration, with widespread accusation of police collusion and corruption, is described in absorbing detail by Dixon (1991). By the late 1940s the Police Federation was telling the Willink Commission, "We have achieved nothing except perhaps the arrest and conviction of many hundreds of otherwise ordinary respectable citizens who perhaps abide by every law in the land except the Betting Act of 1906" (cited by Clapson, 1992, p.66). The evidence suggests that the people convicted were mostly bookmakers' 'runners' or even 'mugs' or 'dummies' (and sometimes individual punters although they were not the target of the 1906 Act), and that the Act had probably inadvertently had the effect of pushing the bookmakers themselves out of the law's reach. The large majority of fines were first offences only. For example in 1931 of 586 convictions in Birmingham, 570 were first offences, 14 second, only 2 were third offences and no-one had been previously convicted more than twice (evidence to the 1932-33 Royal Commission, cited by Dixon, 1991, p.146).

The main thesis of Dixon's book was that, once it was clear that total prohibition of gambling in Britain was not supported and that even the partial prohibition of the 1906 Act was unworkable, an alternative way of accommodating gambling had to be found. Since neither nationalisation of gambling nor complete decriminalisation ever commanded much support (although the Tote and more recently the National Lottery are partial forms of nationalisation, and there were some calls in the late 1950s and early 1960s for the decriminalisation of street betting rather than the setting up of licensed betting offices), the answer had to be some form of administrative regulation, implying licensing, registration and taxation. The 55 years following 1906 witnessed slow but steady progress towards the acceptance of such regulation along with the normalisation of gambling and a withering away of the moral, anti-gambling sentiments of the late Victorian and Edwardian era.

Three Committees and Commissions which reported during those 55 years chart the changes that took place. The first was a Select Committee (the Cautley Committee) set up in 1923 to "consider the question of imposing a duty on betting and to report whether such a duty is desirable and practicable" (Dixon, 1991, p.199). The word 'desirable' was probably too advanced for the times and the Committee preferred to report simply that such a duty was 'practicable'. The matter was still highly controversial. Winston Churchill, the Chancellor of the Exchequer who introduced a duty in 1926, referred to "the numbers of eminent holders of my office who have looked longingly on the project, and touched it and thought about it, and passed it by" (cited by Dixon, 1991, p.188). Snowden, the Labour Chancellor who abolished the duty in 1929, had "confessed to a feeling of dismay amounting to horror that the country should have come to such a pass that recourse should be had to legalizing and making respectable. . . the second greatest curse of the country" (cited by Dixon, 1991, p.189, the first presumably being drink). In recommending a duty the Cautley Committee took, according to Dixon, a much more sympathetic view of working-class male gambling (the Committee continued to express concern about gambling by women) than had prevailed in earlier years, believing that gambling was not in itself immoral or sinful. Dixon emphasised the importance of this change:

The significance of accepting administrative regulation must not be underestimated. It meant that, for the first time, a certain amount of everyday working-class gambling was officially regarded as legitimate and as compatible with the overriding interests of control. Distinctions were being made between levels of gambling activity and amongst working-class gamblers. Specifically, this meant that moderate betting by working-class male adults had become acceptable to an extent which would have seemed unthinkable twenty or thirty years before (Dixon, 1991, p.209).

In the event Churchill's betting duty was, as he himself admitted, a fiasco. For one thing it fell foul of inter-departmental Government conflict between Customs and Excise who appreciated the opportunity for gaining revenue (Churchill estimated at least £6 million per annum although in practice it was never as much as half that amount) whilst the Home Office, under the 'Puritan Home Secretary' Jix, saw the prospect of increased betting and rising crime and dug its heels in. It refused to countenance the legalisation of cash betting or *de facto* decriminalisation. Hence collecting the duty had to contend with the obvious fact that much of the activity it might have wished to tax was in fact illegal and the distinction between what was legal (cash betting on-course and credit betting off-course) and what was illegal was not always easy to make. Furthermore, all sorts of details had been neglected, probably through sheer ignorance of the actual nature of betting e.g. how could bets between individuals be distinguished from betting with bookmakers? (the former not taxable); were hedged bets taxable?; were 'doubles' and 'accumulator' bets to be counted as one transaction or more than one? (Dixon, 1991, p.290). Government was cautious about taxing gambling for many years thereafter.

Two Royal Commissions, one before World War II, the second after it, are of significance. The first, the Royal Commission on Lotteries and Betting, 1932–33, adopted, as Dixon saw it, a liberal and pragmatic philosophy arguing that prohibitions on gambling should be minimal. But the time was still not right for fully endorsing administrative regulation. Licensed off-course betting offices, legalised in Ireland in 1926, were thought to be a retrograde step, and it was thought wrong to use taxation to generate revenue. The Commission report was notable for its intriguing, but totally impracticable proposal (not in any case unanimous) that registered bookmakers should be permitted to receive cash bets in special 'deposit boxes' at a registered office, thus obviating the need for direct contact between bookmaker and punter (Dixon, 1991, p.325). The subsequent Betting and Lotteries Act of 1934 therefore failed to deal with the increasingly confused and unacceptable state of off-course betting, dealing instead with large and foreign lotteries (making it illegal to advertise or bet on the Irish Hospitals Sweepstake which had become very popular in Britain – Clapson, 1992) and the rise of off-course Tote clubs, an unforeseen development following the legalisation of the on-course Tote in 1928. Indeed Dixon made the point that debate in that period showed that betting on horse racing was losing its place as the overriding topic. The gambling question was beginning to diversify into issues involving football pools, totalisators, charity sweepstakes, and dog racing. The picture was starting to become one that is much more recognisable to us now.

By the time of the Royal Commission on Betting, Lotteries and Gaming, 1949–51, World War II had hastened changes in national attitudes on all manner of subjects. Legal football coupons betting and urban on-course betting on dog racing had both become more popular, and changing the law on off-course betting was long overdue. Dixon saw the new Commission as taking a much more relaxed view about the dangers of gambling compared to its predecessor of the early 1930s:

> . . . it was discounted as a significant source of crime, serious social problems, or harm to individual character. Gambling was regarded as an unremarkable feature of everyday life which was much less distinct from other leisure activities and about which gamblers were much less naïve than anti-gamblers suggested . . . The problem of gambling was identified as being, not everyday participation, but rather the excessive, abnormal behaviour of certain individuals (Dixon, 1991, p.331).

By that time, problems initially experienced with betting offices in Ireland had been cleared up – all the Commissioners visited the Republic at least once to see for themselves – and the licensed betting office was the model proposed. But a further nearly ten years were to pass before the Betting and Gaming Act of 1960. Opposition to the idea of legalised betting offices was not totally dead, and included, at first, opposition both from small bookmakers who feared increasing domination by large bookmaking firms (the 'big fish') or an eventual Tote monopoly, and the racing lobby who saw betting offices as a threat to racing and who recommended a Tote monopoly (consistent with a long-standing suspicion of bookmakers in many middle- and upper-class racing circles). The 1960 Act was, in the spirit of administrative regulation, both liberalising and controlling. Gambling was to be legalised and regulated but not encouraged. One consequence was the requirement that betting offices should not be positively attractive. As the Conservative Home Secretary of the time, Butler, put it, "the House of Commons was so intent on making 'betting shops' as sad as possible . . . that they ended up more like undertakers' premises" (Dixon, 1991, p.339).

The 1960 Act also licensed gaming clubs and thereby inadvertently created a decade of casino gambling which Government and the industry have been living down almost ever since. According to the Gaming Board the 1960 Act was ". . . intended to provide a relatively small relaxation in the control surrounding gaming [but which] result[ed] in an uncontrolled proliferation of casinos and other gaming with attendant malpractices and criminal involvement . . ." (Gaming Board, 2000, p.63). It took little time to realise the mistake, and the Gaming Act of 1968 followed shortly. Other than the 1993 Act that brought the National Lottery into being and hence may have had far-reaching effects on Britons' gambling behaviour and attitudes, the 1968 Gaming Act was the most important single piece of legislation setting the scene for gambling in Britain in the late 20th century. Because of the mistakes of the legislation in 1960, the main purpose of the 1968 Act was the control of crime; as the Home Secretary of the time stated, it was to clean up gaming and to contain it. The three instruments of control were to be: the Gaming Board (the regulator), the licensing magistrates, and the regulatory powers of the Secretary of State at the Home Office. The general view is that in those aims the 1968 Act was largely successful.

By the time of the 1976–78 Royal Commission on Gambling, the last of the 20th century, chaired by Lord Rothschild, legalised gambling was well entrenched, its regulation was considered largely satisfactory, and relaxation of some of the restrictions on betting offices (but not the introduction of television sets) was considered appropriate. Furthermore the Commission found that a good case had not been made for greater control on the grounds of the problem of compulsive gambling (Dixon, 1991). Nor was there considered to be a strong case that the scale of illegal race betting had again become a problem since the reintroduction of a duty in 1966. Altogether, according to Dixon, the philosophy of the Rothschild report was that:

> Commercialised gambling was considered primarily, not as a social problem, but rather as a business which (in providing entertainment for which people paid) was not structurally different from other types of leisure and recreation. Everyday gambling was 'normalized': it was treated as an acceptable part of everyday life, rather than as a marginally deviant activity (Dixon, 1991, p.341).

The following Betting, Gaming and Lotteries (Amendment) Act of 1984 allowed relaxation of restrictions on betting offices including, contrary to the Commission's recommendation, the provision of television sets for showing live or recorded racing and other sports events. As Dixon said, this ". . . accorded well with the neo-conservative enthusiasm for deregulating and encouraging business" (p.351). The 1984 Act and the Rothschild Commission Report were in his view much more important than they appeared to be, and did not receive the public discussion that they warranted. They represented, as he saw it, an abandonment of the principle of administrative regulation which it had taken so long to establish:

> What the smart new betting shops and their sophisticated technology symbolize is the decline of a strategy which allowed people to gamble,

but attempted to restrict commercial exploitation of their activities. It was an expression of a paternalism which was part of the social/liberal democratic philosophy which dominated British politics from the Second World War to the 1970s: its method was close administrative regulation. . . This [the new normalised view of gambling] provides a challenge to the Home Office orthodoxy. . . in which gambling continues to require close regulation (Dixon, 1991, pp.354–355).

In particular Dixon foresaw the undermining of what had become a fundamental aspect of British public policy on gambling in the middle decades of the century, namely the principle that gambling facilities should only be provided at a level that met 'unstimulated demand'. Although he recognised the naivety of thinking that demand, stimulated and unstimulated by market provision, could be easily distinguished, he nonetheless concluded that the principle had ". . . worked as a rough and ready rule of thumb for the legalization of popular gambling and the control of its commercialization in the 1960s and 1970s" (p.353). Dixon was accurate in his prediction as we shall see in the following chapter where we pick up the story in the last decades of the 20th century.

Chapter 2

Expansion of gambling in the late 20th century

International growth in gambling

There can be no escaping the fact that the last years of the 20th century have been extraordinarily good ones for the gambling industry around the world. As Fisher and Griffiths (1995) put it, "the last decade has witnessed an unprecedented de-regulation of gambling in numerous jurisdictions throughout the world" (p.239). In Canada, the National Council on Welfare stated, "in less than a generation, gambling has become a multi-billion dollar industry . . ." (1996, cited by Room et al, 1999). From Australia the Productivity Commission's report on gambling began by saying, ". . . even by Australian standards, the recent proliferation of gambling opportunities and the growth in the gambling industries have been remarkable" (APC, 1999, p.xv). That report includes a graph showing a rise in total expenditure on gambling in Australia from around 4.5 billion Australian dollars in 1987–88 to approximately 11 billion in 1997–98, expenditure having more than doubled in real terms in a decade. Much of the growth had come from gaming machines which accounted for more than 50 per cent of expenditure in the late 1990s compared to less than a third in the late 1980s, without displacement of expenditure on other forms of gambling which on the whole maintained their previous growth trend.

Many authors have referred to the recent rapid growth in gambling in the USA (e.g. Rose, 1991; Goodman, 1995; Christiansen, 1998; Shaffer et al, 1994; Castellani, 2000). Total gambling turnover was reported to be $639 billion in 1997, with total net expenditure of $51 billion, and payment of gambling taxes $17 million (Christiansen, 1998). Goodman (1995) wrote about the growth in machine gambling in the USA, changes in the operation of lotteries towards bigger prizes and more frequent draws (he cites the move in New Hampshire from a twice-yearly draw 30 years ago to the present daily draw), the spread of casinos from isolated areas to riverboats and thence to the centres of cities, and plans for the use of interactive TV for gambling. Shaffer et al (1994) referred to an "extraordinary proliferation" of gambling in the USA in the later 1980s and early 1990s, in particular increased access to gambling provided by development of casinos and state-sponsored lotteries. By 1998 it could be said that US citizens in that year had made 161 million trips to casinos and almost three in every ten households had made at least one visit, despite the fact that casinos had been illegal in almost all the states of the US for much of the 20th century (KPMG, 2000). Separate legislation allows American Indian tribes to operate gambling facilities in the USA. According to Frey (1998) such facilities existed in 24 US states and American Indian leaders had maintained that they had been economically very beneficial.

In Japan, casinos as such are not legal, but it is fascinating to see how this restriction has been circumvented. According to KPMG (2000) Japan has its own type of gaming hall, of which there were 18,000 in the country, housing over 4 million gaming machines of which 'pachinko' is the most common. In that game, instead of paying for each play, balls are rented for a fee for a session, and can be won or lost during the course of play, those remaining at the end of a session being converted into a ticket showing the win. Tickets can then be exchanged for non-cash prizes, commonly household or electrical goods, but often 'special' prizes such as a small piece of gold or silver. Although it is illegal for the operator to buy back the prize directly, the latter can be exchanged for money by designated dealers outside the hall who then sell the prizes back to the operator. Fisher and Griffiths (1995) commented that Japan had the largest number of gambling machines of any country in the world.

The story of increased liberalisation and expanded opportunities for gambling in the late 20th century has been repeated around Europe. In Spain, for example, gambling by any means was legalised only as recently as 1977 and machine gambling was legalised in 1981. Besides traditional casino games, sports betting, and lotteries, machine gambling became especially popular, according to Becoña et al (1995), with nearly half a million machines installed in leisure centres, casinos, bingo halls and almost every bar and restaurant in the country within a few years. Cayuela and Guirao (1991) reported total spending on gambling in Spain increasing from 562,000 million pesetas in 1980 to over three times that amount for the following year, and thereafter a steady increase to almost double that figure by 1988.

Meyer (1992) reported a seven- to eight-fold increase in amusement arcades offering machine gambling in West Germany between 1974 and 1989. In The Netherlands, according to Hermkens and Kok (1991), opportunities to gamble rose greatly between the early 1960s and late 1980s, including growth in machine gambling (with a very confused legal situation), the spread of casinos, the permitting of off-track betting (with a leading commercial role being played by Ladbrokes), and the commercialisation of bingo. The tax take from gambling rose, according to those authors, from 3 million guilders in 1962 to 9 million in 1973 and to 100 million in 1987. In Sweden, where there has been a tradition of gambling being offered by a small number of state-owned companies, total gambling turnover rose from 20 billion SEK in 1991 to 30 billion in 1998, a rise well above price inflation (Rönnberg et al, 1999).

France was one Western European country that was slow to permit the widespread public locating of gambling machines, but, once committed, the industry grew in six years from nothing to one with a turnover of almost 3 billion French francs (Fisher and Griffiths, 1995). There is also said to be a gambling boom occurring in Eastern European countries such as the former East Germany and Poland, and in Russia. Kassinove et al (1998) reported that lotteries and casinos, once prohibited, were now widespread in major cities in Russia. In St Petersburg and Moscow, for example, lottery and scratchcard vendors could now be found selling their goods at most subway stations, and casinos were common, often located in hotels.

Growth of gambling in Britain

Britain has partaken in a big way in this international growth trend. As Bellringer (1999) has put it:

> In the space of a few years the availability of gambling has greatly increased . . . It is quite remarkable that in such a short space of time gambling has been catapulted from an activity that you had to seek out to one that appears to be available everywhere (pp.9, 11).

Bellringer graphically describes how opportunities to gamble are now available in most high streets in the form of betting offices, amusement arcades and bingo clubs, as well as in corner shops, supermarkets, post offices, cafes and pubs, newsagents, railway or bus stations and cinemas and leisure centres which provide opportunities to buy National Lottery (NL) tickets or football pools coupons and/or to play gambling machines. In addition, casinos, race courses, dog tracks and other sporting venues are available without much difficulty, and places such as motorway service areas, theme parks and fairgrounds are also likely to provide opportunities for machine gambling. Furthermore, it may not be necessary to leave home at all in order to gamble, since agents may call at the door to sell and collect football pool coupons, telephone betting is available to those who have obtained clearance to open an account with a bookmaker, and the internet already has hundreds of gambling sites available to those with credit cards.

Table 2.1 provides an overall summary of the vast scale of the gambling industry in Britain as it was in the last months of the 20th century. The figures are taken from a report on *The Economic Value and Public Perceptions of Gambling in the UK*, commissioned by Business in Sport and Leisure (BISL), which represents 'a number of major leisure companies and

Table 2.1 The scale of the gambling industry in Britain at the end of the
20th century – UK gaming activity in 1998 in £m – (a summary of
industry figures in KPMG report for Business in Sport and Leisure,
2000, Figure 6.2)

	Amount wagered	Gross gaming yield[1]	Net revenue[2]	Contribution to profit[3]
On-course bookmakers	711	157	157	72
Off-course bookmakers incl. machines	7,464	1,648	1,108	392
On-course Totes	230	51	52	12
National Lottery	5,376	2,688	538	108
Small lotteries	134	88	36	0
Football pools	370	255	151	30
Casinos incl. machines	18,547	479	375	66
Bingo incl. machines	2,450	678	447	80
Premium Bonds	517	0	0	0
Amusement centres and seaside arcades	2,320	471	378	20
Machines in clubs	1,253	251	47	0
Machines in pubs and other	2,750	583	450	88
Total	42,121	7,349	3,736	867

[1] After subtracting winnings
[2] After subtracting tax, duty, licences, levies and good causes
[3] After adding ancillary income and subtracting other operating charges

their advisors in the sport and leisure industry', and produced by KPMG (2000). Their figures have been supplemented with some information from the Gaming Board report for 1999/2000. Some of the figures shown are known with greater precision than others, a fact that reflects the piecemeal and inconsistent way in which gambling has developed and been regulated in Britain. The principal regulatory body was the Gaming Board for Great Britain which was established by the Gaming Act of 1968. Although its remit had been a broad one – to ensure that 'gaming and lotteries' are run fairly and in accordance with the law; that those involved in organising gaming and lotteries are fit and proper to do so and to keep gaming free from criminal infiltration; and to advise the Secretary of State (at the Home Office) on developments in gaming and lotteries – its coverage of modern day gambling in fact has been only very partial. It considered and made recommendations about applications for licences to run casinos and bingo clubs, and hence it had a complete picture of the number of such clubs operating in the country at any time, as well as a well-informed overview of how such venues were being operated and what the current issues might be. In the case of gaming machines, the Board issued certificates to those who wished to sell, supply and maintain machines, but had to rely upon the relevant gambling trade association (the British Amusement Catering Trades Association, BACTA) for estimates of the actual number of machines in operation.

Even in the case of casinos, however, estimating the amount of money staked or wagered is not straightforward. The basic statistic for measuring casino activity is what is called the 'drop' or the amount of money exchanged for chips, but there is no simple relationship between that figure and the total amount staked. For one thing chips may not always be used in play (what is known as 'false drop'). A much bigger factor, however, is the recycling of winnings whereby an initial holding of chips may be used for playing a number of times (Creigh-Tyte, 1997; KPMG, 2000). For this reason the KPMG report estimated the total amount of money wagered in casinos in 1998 by multiplying up total house takings by a factor of 40 (since house take in British casinos is approximately 2.5 per cent). A further complication is that industry estimates for amounts spent in casinos, bingo clubs and betting offices all included money spent on gaming machines which are permitted to be sited in those venues. This has the result of over-estimating expenditure on casino games, bingo and sports betting, and under-estimating amount spent in playing gaming machines.

The single most evident way in which the Gaming Board's overview of British gambling is incomplete is in terms of the NL which was completely outside its remit (Gaming Board, 2000). That reflects, as we shall see, the very different view held by the UK government regarding the NL in comparison with other, more traditional forms of gambling. On the other hand the Board has been responsible for registering charities and societies that wish to run their own lotteries (if the proceeds of any single lottery exceed £20,000 or if total annual proceeds are greater than £250,000) as well as for registering all local government authorities who wish to run lottery schemes (of which there are currently very few).

A final complication in estimating the total amount of gambling that goes on in Britain, is what to leave out. Although there is general agreement that 'gambling' is to be equated with the activities shown in Table 2.1 this leaves out of the picture a number of categories that might be included. One of these is private betting which, as we shall see in Chapter 5, exists on quite a large scale but which is obviously outside the purview of the Gaming Board or the gambling industry, and which makes no obvious contribution to the national economy. Similarly, internet gambling, of great interest to the Gaming Board and to the government, was unregulated and difficult to estimate. A different case is presented by premium bonds, a form of government savings bond which pays out draw prizes for some in place of interest for all. The KPMG report (2000) included just over £500,000 'wagered' in the form of premium bonds in 1998, on the grounds that, whilst the purchase of the bond itself could not be considered a stake, the interest which is foregone by the purchaser could be thought of as a gamble for a higher return. Because holding premium bonds was thought by the present authors not to be generally considered as gambling, those figures have not been included in Table 2.1, nor were premium bonds included in the British Gambling Prevalence Survey to be reported in Chapter 5. As we saw in Chapter 1, however, many people thought of premium bonds as gambling when they were first mooted as a way of raising national revenue, and as we shall see later in this chapter when considering the National Lottery, and in Chapter 6 when reporting the results of interviews with gamblers, the question of what constitutes gambling is for many people still an open one.

All those complications aside, there can be no doubting that gambling in Britain is big business. The industry's own estimate (KPMG, 2000) was that the total amount wagered in the UK in 1998 was over £41 billion or, after winnings are deducted, a total take by the industry of £7.3 billion. Once VAT, and various duties, licences and levies and contributions to good causes were deducted – the contribution of NL takings to 'good causes' being the single largest item – net revenue to the industry was estimated at £3.7 billion. Once operating charges had been deducted, the industry's own estimate of its total profits for 1998 was £867 million, the most profitable sectors being off-course bookmaking at just under £400 million, and gaming machines and the National Lottery at just over £100 million each (the figure for gaming machines being an under-estimate for reasons stated earlier).

KPMG (2000) calculated that the annual per capita spend, net of winnings, on all gambling activities in 1998 was between £100 and £150 in the

UK, and was very comparable to the USA (although it appears that their calculations did not include certain forms of gambling such as gambling on machines outside casino halls, and gambling in bingo clubs). The only other two countries where a comparable figure could be calculated were Australia, with an annual per capita spend almost twice as high as that in the UK and USA, and New Zealand where the spend was equivalent to less than £100.

The National Lottery and its effects

Undoubtedly the biggest event of the last decades of the 20th century in British gambling was the inauguration of the National Lottery (NL). Britain in fact was a relatively late starter being virtually alone amongst Western countries in having no national state lottery by the early 1990s. Despite the earlier role of public lotteries in funding public works, such as raising funds for London's water supply and for building the British Museum, they had been illegal since the last public lottery in 1826. Small charitable lotteries were legal from the 1930s onwards. The 1978 Royal Commission on Gambling had recommended a national lottery but it was not until 1992 that the Conservative Party general election manifesto promised that one would be established. The National Lottery Act was passed in 1993. There has been no effective political opposition to the NL. The election of a Labour Government in 1997 was quickly followed by the publication of *The People's Lottery* White Paper policy statement, and the Labour Party in office was as enthusiastic as the previous Conservative government. The first weekly lotto game was held in November 1994, with the first National Lottery Instants scratchcards introduced in the following March. A second, mid-week, lotto draw was introduced in February 1997, and a further game, Thunderball, was introduced in 1999 (Miers, 1996; Creigh-Tyte, 1997; KPMG, 2000).

The view of the last two British governments of the 20th century was that, provided certain controls were exercised (e.g. a minimum age, no door-to-door or street sales, and no games that involve interactive play), then the NL represented a harmless, even 'tasteful', form of leisure pursuit providing very suitable means of raising money for national causes which otherwise might have a lower priority call on public funds. Indeed, Miers detected an intention to promote the lottery as hardly constituting gambling at all:

> The National Lottery will be of a different nature from the kind of gambling which is legislated for by the Home Office under existing gambling laws. It is intended to be addressed to a different market and not to be thought of as gambling in the same way. In that respect, the fact that it is absolutely a matter of chance, and there is no skill

involved in the decision which the individual player takes, is a critical one (National Heritage Committee, 1993, cited by Miers, 1996, pp.366–367).

The foregoing quote begs a number of questions about the nature of gambling, the real or imagined involvement of skill, and the potential of lotto games and scratchcards for inducing addiction to gambling. These matters will be taken up in later chapters. For the moment the important point to note is that the lottery has been widely supported in Britain as a benign institution from which everyone can benefit and which is quite unlike other forms of gambling. The Gaming Board, part of whose remit involved ensuring that gambling is not infiltrated by criminal elements, was therefore considered quite inappropriate as a regulatory body. Instead, a unique operating and regulating system was set up under which a licence to operate the NL is awarded to a single private operator which, because of its monopoly position, is regulated by a small, non-ministerial government department – the Office of the National Lottery or OFLOT (responsibility for regulation moved to the National Lottery Commission in 1999). Creigh-Tyte (1997) pointed out that this mix of a private supplier and public regulator was unusual, most other state lotteries around the world being run under a public-supplier – public-regulator system. What is certain is that the way the NL is run is highly newsworthy in Britain. The operator licence came up for renewal in 2000, and the ins and outs of the decision, involving questions of how much profit the operator should make and accusations that tendering rules had been broken, gained high media attention for much of that year.

The success of the NL exceeded all expectations. In 1995–1996 and 1996–1997 ticket sales (the on-line draw plus Instants scratchcards) reached totals of £5.2 billion and £4.7 billion respectively. Research published by OFLOT (1996, cited by Creigh-Tyte, 1997) suggested that almost two-thirds of the adult population had played the lottery within the last week, that around 30 million Britons were regular players, and that the number of outlets selling tickets exceeded 24,000. Research conducted for the licensed operator (Camelot) in 1999 suggested a figure of 71 per cent playing the lotto game in the previous week. Immediately on its inauguration, the NL became a high profile feature of national life in Britain. Not only are there are several sales outlets on every high street, as Bellringer (1999) noted, but the draws are featured and advertised on prime-time, main channel television. Indeed, New Year 2001 was seen in on the main BBC channel (BBC 1) with a programme entitled 'The National Lottery New Year's Stars' which, ". . . welcomes the New Year with a draw that it is hoped will make more millionaires in one night than ever before".

Creigh-Tyte (1997) compared absolute and per capita sales of tickets for national lotteries in 13 European countries, Canada, Australia, New

Zealand and the USA. The UK National Lottery was one of the largest in absolute terms (by 1998 the largest of any individual lottery in the world according to KPMG, 2000), but not the largest in per capita terms. The $125 US equivalent spent per capita in the UK was exceeded by Austria (the largest per capita spend at $164), Norway, Denmark and Ireland. The majority of countries had per capita spends lying between $85 and $125, with Portugal, Italy, Spain and The Netherlands (the lowest at $13) having lower rates.

What has been happening, meanwhile, to other forms of British gambling? A major issue during the debate that preceded the setting up of the NL was the extent to which spending on the lottery would represent either 'a new income stream' or simply a redirection of existing discretionary spending. Specifically the question arose to what extent spending on the lottery would be a diversion of expenditure on other forms of gambling. Football pools gambling was expected to be particularly affected, and although dire forecasts that the lottery would kill off football pools within a matter of weeks proved to be exaggerated, pools betting certainly declined after the start of the NL (Miers, 1996; Forrest, 1999). The detailed analysis of the history of football pools in Britain and the kind of gambling that they have offered, carried out by Forrest (1999), shows quite clearly why that has happened, and at the same time provides some insights into motives for gambling (a subject taken up in Chapter 4). Until the late 1940s pools companies had been many, and prizes small, but with the introduction of the 'treble chance' in 1946 a new feature was introduced into the British betting market, namely a long-odds, high-prize product, with prizes by the 1990s sometimes exceeding £1 million depending upon the pattern of soccer results. Until the NL started, the football pools had a monopoly on that type of gambling in Britain. In another way, too, the pools resembles the lottery: many pools players (in fact the majority according to pools companies), rather than making choices on any basis to do with the likely performance of particular teams, choose simply on the basis of the numbers allocated to different matches (Forrest, 1999).

A number of relaxations to the regulations governing pools gambling were conceded by the government at the time of the NL's inauguration, some minor changes were made to the pools game in order to bring it more in line with the NL, and one pools company successfully exercised its right to apply to the lottery regulator for a joint-venture licence to use the NL retail network to market its own soccer-based lottery game (Easy Play, which lasted only one season). Despite these changes, turnover reported by the then three football pools companies (the number of companies reduced rapidly after the introduction of the treble chance game in the 1940s) declined steadily after the introduction of the NL. In fact turnover declined by 12 per cent in the football season during which the NL was launched, and by 1996–97 the cumulative decline had reached nearly 60 per cent, with gross revenue down from over £900 million to around £400 million per annum. By 1997 the largest pools company had reduced its workforce to one quarter of its pre-lottery level (Forrest, 1999). The NL appears to have had competitive advantage, amongst other things in its more efficient use of modern technology for collecting wagers, its higher rate of return to players, and its broader appeal, for example to women and younger people.

The effect of the NL on other forms of gambling is less clear. The Bingo Association of Great Britain reported a significant decline in attendances in the year or two immediately following the launch of the NL (Miers, 1996), and the Gaming Board (2000) reported a decrease of 21 per cent in the numbers of licensed bingo clubs over the five years between 1995 and 2000. According to KPMG (2000) the industry's own view was that sales of scratchcards, rather than the main NL game, may have impacted on bingo the most. In fact the number of bingo clubs had been in decline since the peak in the mid-1970s and that part of the industry successfully underwent a restructuring towards fewer, larger clubs, and total amount staked in licensed clubs continued to rise steadily through the 1990s (Gambling Review Body Report, 2001).

There is also a case that horse racing betting may have been affected. In the year following the start of the NL there was a 1.5 per cent fall in betting turnover instead of the projected 6.2 per cent growth (Miers, 1996). But the number of betting offices had been in decline for at least 20 years, from about 12,500 in the late 1970s to around 8,400 in the late 1990s (KPMG, 2000), and there had been other changes since the NL started, including evening and Sunday betting.

Other sectors appeared not to have been reduced as a result of the NL. Indeed society, charity and local authority lotteries, regulated by the Gaming Board, continued to show a considerable increase, including a sharp increase of just over 100 per cent in stakes in 1995–96 (Creigh-Tyte, 1997). Since football pools is one of the smaller sectors of the British gambling industry, and some of the larger sectors such as casinos, gaming machines, and sports betting have probably remained stable or continued to expand, it seems likely that overall the NL has added 'new money' to gambling turnover. This conclusion is supported by data reported by Creigh-Tyte (1997) and reproduced here as Figure 2.1. For the nearly five years of the 1990s prior to the introduction of the NL, total betting and gaming spending was running fairly consistently at about 0.8 per cent of total consumers' expenditure. In the first quarter of 1995, non-lottery betting and gaming had fallen to its lowest percentage of consumer expenditure for five years, but by the last half of the following year it had picked up to be as high as it had been at any time in the 1990s. As Figure 2.1 shows, the addition of the Lottery raised total betting and gaming expenditure to around 1.4 per cent of total consumers' expenditure.

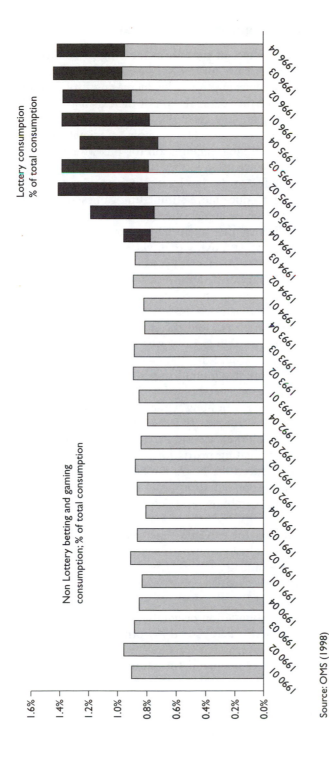

Source: OMS (1998)

Figure 2.1 Consumer expenditure on gambling as a percentage of total consumer spend, 1990–1996 (reproduced with permission from Creigh-Tyte, 1997, Figure 1)

The deregulation of gambling in Britain

But the most significant effect of the NL in the long run is likely to be an enhancement of the historically quite new, positive view of gambling as a harmless form of leisure consumption, plus increasing proliferation of new forms of gambling and further deregulation of the existing ones. This likely 'ratcheting up' effect on gambling generally was noted by both Miers (1996) and by Creigh-Tyte (1997). Miers, for example, predicted further liberalisation of all forms of gambling. One reason for this would be the government's increasing dependence upon lottery funds, which experience in other countries suggested tended to decline after a period of initial enthusiasm, leading to pressure to introduce more stimulating games and in other ways to remove restriction. For example state governments in the USA had responded to the public's waning interest by promoting lotteries that were increasingly interactive or fast moving (e.g. video lotteries and 'keno'), and the German lottery includes interactive games ('speil' games), all of which at the time of writing could not be approved under British NL regulations.

Referring to this 'ratcheting up' effect as governments 'chasing their losses', Goodman (1995) illustrated how state governments in the USA might start 'upping the ante'. He told the story of how Iowa rapidly escalated its riverboat casino gambling. Iowa was the first US state to legislate for modern riverboat casinos, and the first facility opened in 1991 with strict rules limiting bets to $5 and maximum losses to $200 per excursion. Within a year of Iowa's legislation, neighbouring Illinois and Mississippi had legalised their own riverboat gambling without Iowa's restrictions and with a larger number of games available. By 1994 Iowa had, as a result, removed betting and loss limits, allowed riverboats to operate around the clock, legalised new games, eliminating restrictions on the amount of boat space devoted to gambling, reduced the hours the boats were required to cruise, and at the same time responded to appeals from the racing industry by lowering taxes on race gambling and legalising gambling machines at the tracks.

Indeed the main reason for expecting increasing deregulation of gambling, for which there was already much evidence, is the demand from other sectors of the gambling industry for 'a level playing field'. Before the UK NL started, the Gaming Board was observing:

> The promotion and stimulation of gambling necessary if the [National] Lottery is to be a success is regarded [by other suppliers] as difficult to reconcile with the Government's established policy, under which the Board operates, that the demand for gambling should not be unduly stimulated (Gaming Board, 1994, para 8, cited by Miers, 1996, p.369).

The following year the Board stated:

Many of the gaming associations and organisations with which the Board deals have made representations to it about the adverse impact the National Lottery is having upon their businesses. They express particular concern about the way in which the National Lottery is able to promote its activities aggressively whilst they are strictly circumscribed in what they do . . . the Lottery has greater freedom to advertise than most other gambling activities. The Board believes that all this is having, and will continue to have, consequences for the areas of gaming for which it is responsible. There will continue to be pressures from the rest of the gaming industry seeking change to compensate for the impact of, and freedoms given to, the National Lottery (Gaming Board, 1995, paras 1, 19, 120, cited by Miers, 1996, pp.368, 370).

Miers referred to:

. . . the government's failure to recognise the implications of its promotion of a national and massively advertised new gambling opportunity offering prizes far in excess of those available elsewhere . . . the way in which the government has permitted the Lottery to be marketed is having precisely the effect of driving other sectors of the commercial gambling market to seek the relaxation of the rules under which they operate (Miers, 1996, pp.364, 368).

Many of the instances of lifting of restrictions on gambling which occurred in the last years of the 20th century can be attributed, not solely to the NL, but to a general policy, pursued by Conservative governments over a number of years and continued by the Labour government, to reduce regulations that restrict the operating of businesses, including gambling businesses, but, ". . . they surely are given a greater urgency by the impact of the Lottery" (Miers, 1996, p.370). There have been many instances. Football pools promoters, for example, in compensation for the likely effects of the NL on their trade, negotiated liberalisation of the rules under which they had operated for many years: reducing the minimum allowable age of participation to 16, permitting newsagents to collect stakes as well as to distribute coupons, introducing jackpots, and allowing rollovers.

In other sectors of the British gambling industry deregulation continued in a piecemeal but steady fashion largely unopposed by the Gaming Board. Many of these changes, each apparently small but in total significant, were possible under the 1994 Deregulation and Contracting Out Act which enabled the government to relax, without further legislation, some of the controls and restrictions in the 1968 Gaming Act. Despite setting up, early in 2000, an Independent Review Body to design a new regulatory structure for the gambling industry (the Gambling Review Body – see below and Chapter 8), the Home Office said that meanwhile it "will seek to continue to proceed with sensible and uncontroversial derestrictions of the legislation relating to gaming using the Deregulation Act powers . . ." (Gaming Board, 2000). With minor exceptions, the Gaming Board, which met regularly with representatives of different sectors of the gambling industry in meetings that sound remarkably amicable, and which expressed little concern and awareness of the possible effects of the deregulations upon rates of gambling problems, indicated that it was, "generally content with all the proposals" (Gaming Board, 2000, p.4).

In the casino sector, for example, changes were brought in: to allow application for casino membership by post and similar means, rather than only in person as previously; to permit limited advertising in newspapers, magazines, etc., giving factual information about casinos; to allow casinos to close at 6.00 a.m., rather than 4.00 a.m., every day of the week except Sunday; and to increase the number of jackpot gaming machines permitted in casinos from six to ten (unlike the so-called 'amusement-with-prizes' or AWP machines, and 'all-cash' machines, that were permitted in other locations, jackpot machines offered maximum prizes of £1,000 in casinos, £500 in bingo clubs and £250 in other clubs). Another significant development in casino gambling was the diversification of games that can be played, plus changes to existing games described by the British Casino Association and the Gaming Board as 'minor'. In addition to new games introduced in 1995 ('casino stud poker' and 'super pan 9'), three new games were proposed in the year 1999–2000: 'casino brag' (a three-card game played against the bank), 'big six' (a spin-the-wheel game with a straightforward staking and payout structure) and 'sicbo' (in which betting takes place on the outcome of three dice being thrown). Other variations that were proposed include a simplified version of roulette, a change to the layout of the dice table to allow additional bets, an accumulator jackpot feature to be added to casino stud poker, and a further small change to the rules of blackjack (Gaming Board, 2000, p.18). Even more significant, when it comes to the potential for gambling addiction, were proposals for an electronic version of roulette called 'touchbet roulette' which would be played at electronic terminals while a player watches an individual screen showing a recording of play going on at a normal roulette table. Bets can be placed, and any winnings credited, at the terminals. The Gaming Board indicated that it was content in principle with all these proposed changes.

It is clear, furthermore, from the gambling industry's own report, that the casino sector aspired to greater derestrictions still. There is reference, for example, to: "the inability of casinos to promote themselves effectively [which] allows a public perception to perpetuate which is more likely to be based on film and television images of Las Vegas or James Bond" (KPMG, 2000, p.10); the "house advantage in casinos [being] very low, of the order of 2.5 per cent" (p.65) compared to that pertaining in casinos in the USA; restrictions on number of fruit machines which therefore represent less than

10 per cent of casino gaming revenue compared with, for example, over 80 per cent in French casinos; the fact that live entertainment is forbidden in British casinos unlike, for example, in France where casinos "are expected to provide entertainment of a quality that adds to the attractiveness of or culturally enhances the area" (p.10); and restrictions on the location of casinos in 'permitted areas' only in the UK, a degree of restriction that applies only in some other countries such as France. On this last point, the Gaming Board agreed in 1999 to change its policy which had previously been to object to the award of new casino licences in permitted areas where there was already one or more casino. The Board was now persuaded that more than one casino could operate "successfully and in a compliant manner", even when demand appeared to be satisfied by existing casinos. Although the Board was of the view that this change offered no risks to its regulatory objectives, it did represent a significant shift, in a direction corresponding to the interests of the gambling industry, away from the principle of refusing a new application unless 'unmet demand' could be demonstrated.

In the bingo sector also, a number of changes, all in the direction of lifting previous restrictions, had either taken place in the last few years before the Review Body reported or were in process without any serious objection from the Gaming Board or government. These include: the use of debit cards to pay for bingo gaming; the use of an automated teller machine operating only on debit cards; abolition of controls which limited the amounts which might be charged per two-hour period; abolition of the requirement to give licensing justices 14 days' notice of changes to charges, so that bingo clubs could react flexibly when they believed alterations should be made; permission for bingo clubs to deploy both AWP and up to four jackpot gaming machines; a proposal to bring forward from 2.00 p.m. to noon the hours on Sunday during which bingo may start to be played; an increase in the prize bingo maximum total take and prize limits from £60 to £120; and in the case of restrictions on 'multiple bingo' (a form of bingo played across the country at several clubs simultaneously) to remove all limits on prize levels and allow greater flexibility in the prize structure (Gaming Board, 2000).

In the gaming machine sector the British Amusement Catering Trades Association (BACTA) was seeking certain changes to the legal controls over payment systems for playing machines, which in the light of an understanding of the ways in which forms of gambling have addiction potential (see Chapter 4) must be counted as very significant indeed. These are: removal of the requirement that machines should be able to accept payment only for a single play, allowing instead for machines which accept only £1, and in the future £2 coins for multiple plays; machines to be permitted to accept bank notes; and electronic and other non-monetary methods of payment; and (probably most significant of all) removal of the requirement that a machine pay out before accumulated winnings could be replayed (Gaming Board, 2000). Consistent with its general attitude towards derestriction of gambling, the Gaming Board stated that it had no objections in principle to these proposals. To its credit, the Parliamentary Deregulation Committee had expressed concern about any further piece-meal relaxations of controls relating to gaming machines (the committee's concern was referred to by the Gaming Board as a "difficulty"), and the Home Office had indicated that it hoped to conduct a public consultation on these proposals.

The permitting of AWP machines in licensed betting offices is another development in British gambling in recent years, and what the industry has said about such developments as diversification into betting on sports other than horse racing and dog racing, more 'spread betting' (see below) and more placing of bets by telephone, implies that these developments would be welcomed (KPMG, 2000).

Internet gambling

One aspect that was causing uncertainty and consternation at the turn of the century, in Britain as elsewhere, was the impact of rapid technological change, and especially the likely future of internet gambling (both placing bets via the internet and, more particularly, playing 'virtual' games operated solely on the internet). In 1999 the evidence was that only a very small proportion of British gambling was conducted via the internet (Sproston et al, 2000; and see Chapter 5), but it was widely expected that this would grow rapidly in the space of a few years. One estimate was that internet gambling in 2001 would contribute just over £21 billion to global gambling turnover of £638 billion (KPMG, 2000). Because such gambling would be unregulated, unlicensed, and would pay little or no tax, this prospect was naturally alarming to the Gaming Board and to the rest of the established gambling industry.

KPMG in their 2000 report devoted a chapter to technology and the future for gambling, including not only the growth of the internet but also developments in telecommunications such as more sophisticated mobile telephones, and the prospects for digital interactive TV. They examined the pros and cons of five models of internet gambling regulation: Caribbean, Australian, Scandinavian, British, and that being pursued in the USA. A number of countries in the Caribbean (but also other small jurisdictions such as Gibraltar and Alderney) were capitalising on the revenue potential of licensing internet gambling sites with very little regulation for operators. True to form, Australia was thought to be following the path of licensing and regulation but with greater control and hence a higher level of per-ceived probity. The Scandinavians were taking a more controlling approach by prohibiting gambling on internet sites other than those licensed in their own country; the USA was attempting total prohibition; and the British were waiting to see what happened.

The Gaming Board in 1999 conducted its own assessment of opinions about how internet gambling should be regulated, sending out letters to 22 organisations and individuals, half of whom were part of the gambling industry. Although the British position of retaining the status quo for the time being might look attractive, in fact none of those who gave their views to the Gaming Board thought it was a tenable position, and most thought there was a great urgency to put regulation in place. The gambling industry was particularly concerned that the British approach was restricting competition and would have the effect of displacing spending to overseas suppliers (KPMG, 2000).

In fact the legal position, like so much about gambling, was complicated and sometimes unclear. It was not illegal for individuals to gamble on the internet from their own homes (although the legality of doing so at an internet cafe was less clear), but providing some forms of gambling service via the internet was illegal. For example, whilst a bookmaker accepting a bet via the internet using a credit account, or accepting a football pool entry in the same way, were perfectly legal, British promoters could not offer virtual casino, bingo or machine gambling on the internet. In the case of lotteries there is a very thin line between using the internet simply as a means of communication by which one person offers another a lottery ticket and a second person agrees to buy, which is legal, and running a lottery entirely by computer via the internet, which amounts to selling tickets by means of a machine which is illegal. Meanwhile overseas operators, since it is a global market, were free to operate and even, within limits, to advertise. Not surprisingly, British operators were already starting to set up legitimate opportunities abroad from which they could take bets from anywhere including Britain (Gaming Board, 2000).

In preparing its own report on the matter, the marketplace arguments appeared to carry most weight with the Gaming Board:

> If the market develops and matures without British involvement, it will be too late to recover and make an impact. Inevitably, British companies will look for overseas opportunities themselves (. . . this is starting to happen) and once established abroad they will not return later. In short, there is a need to act quickly if a valuable commercial opportunity is not to be missed for ever. Such a missed opportunity would conflict with the Government's stated aim of making Britain a leader in e-commerce (p.111).

The Board rejected the Scandinavian model as being unworkable (it would be very difficult to stop individuals gambling via offshore sites; British courts would have no jurisdiction over such sites; service providers could not easily block such sites; nor could banks easily recognise such sites and refuse to honour payments to them), and appeared not to have thought prohibition even worthy of consideration. Thus the Board's preference was to legislate as quickly as possible to permit, regulate and tax internet gambling, certificating and licensing to be the responsibility of the Gaming Board. Any non-licensed British-based internet gambling operation would thereby be illegal. The Board saw no reason why licensed sites should not be allowed to offer gambling to overseas residents, nor why credit cards should not be used if they were being used commonly for internet gambling throughout the world (even though debit cards, but not credit cards, could be used in casinos in Britain).

It is clear, then, that the Gaming Board, like the gambling industry that provided a large proportion of the opinions on which the Board drew, was largely influenced by neo-liberal global marketplace considerations, besides which the possible impact on the incidence and prevalence of problem gambling accounted for very little. The Board thought that domestically run and regulated internet gambling, ". . . would be very attractive to British gamblers" (p.114), but this was seen as a virtue because they, ". . . would then have no wish or need to resort to off-shore alternatives" (p.114). It was acknowledged that there were concerns about under-age and problem gambling, but all that the Board could say on that account was that operators should be required to impose, "relatively modest, daily spending limits on their customers", and that sites should have, "effective means of denying access to children and young persons" (p.114). Compared to the attention given to how people might have access to opportunities for internet gambling, how competition might be stimulated, and unfair overseas competition met, the Board gave no detailed attention whatever to how the young and otherwise vulnerable might be protected.

Spread betting

Spread betting was another newcomer, again illustrating the point that forms of gambling are forever changing and developing. It started as a form of betting on aspects of financial markets (e.g. the state of the FTSE 100 index in a particular month), and although it has become a way of betting on the outcome of sporting events, such betting facilities are offered by specialist companies (e.g. IG Index and City Index) and spread betting has been regulated quite separately from other forms of gambling, by the Financial Services Authority (Gambling Review Body Report, 2001). The unique quality of spread betting, and hence the fear that it may be particularly dangerous, lies in the fact that the gambler's potential loss can be far greater than the amount of money staked. The way it works is that the spread betting company offers a 'spread' (e.g. that Australia will score between 280–300 runs in a particular innings in a cricket match against

England). The better may 'buy' for £1 per run at 300, in which case £1 will be won for every run that Australia scores above 300, and £1 will be lost for every run that they fall short under 300. Likewise one might 'sell' for £1 per run at 280, in which case £1 would be won for every run under 280 and £1 lost for every run over 280. The different outcomes, singularly or in combination, on which spread betting can be offered are almost limitless. The volume of spread betting in Britain may yet be comparatively small, but figures supplied by the IG Group to the Gambling Review Body (2001) suggested a strong upward trend (turnover of nearly £6 million in 1998, doubling to £12 million in 1999, and almost doubling again to £23.6 million in 2000).

The benefits and costs of gambling

Before examining the problem of addictive gambling, which will be the main subject of later chapters, first let us consider the overall balance of benefits and drawbacks to gambling, and in particular the argument of the gambling industry that it provides a valuable service to individual players and to society as a whole. Since no research using that cost–benefit approach has been carried out in Britain we need to look at some key studies from countries such as Canada and Australia. A particularly thorough before–after study of the opening of a casino in Niagara Falls in Ontario Province, Canada, carried out by Room and his colleagues is a good example. Turner et al (1999) interviewed just over 1,000 residents of the Niagara Falls area just prior to the opening of the casino in late 1996, and Room et al (1999) reported a comparison of pre-opening data obtained from those living in Niagara Falls City, with post-opening interviews with over 1,000 Niagara Falls residents a year later (about half of whom had also been included in the pre-opening sample). As a further control, results were compared with those obtained from samples of residents of Ontario Province generally (the large majority of whom lived in areas other than Niagara Falls).

By factor analysing a large number of opinion statements, Turner et al (1999) concluded that most residents' expectations about the opening of the casino fell into the three main groups shown in Table 2.2: expected social problems, environmental problems, and economic benefits. Niagara Falls was in the special position of being a medium-sized city which had experienced an economic downturn with the closure of several big plants, and which was well situated to attract outside visitors including many from across the border in the USA. In some other smaller communities in North America where less thorough studies of casino opening had been carried out, high initial enthusiasm for a casino had been found to waver after the opening (Turner et al, 1999). In Niagara Falls, as Table 2.2 shows, overall enthusiasm remained high. On the whole, however, compared to expectations prior to the opening, both harms and benefits were endorsed by

Table 2.2 Community expectations and experiences before and after the
opening of the Niagara Falls casino (based on results reported by
Turner et al, 1999, and Room et al, 1999)

	Prior expectations 1996 (%) (N = 677)	Actual experiences 1997 (%) (N = 1076)
Social problems and disruption		
People who live in Niagara Falls will move away because of the casino (agree)	28	16*
The number of serious crimes (increase)	77	44*
The number of people on welfare or other social assistance (increase)	24	18
The number of marriages and families breaking up (increase)	50	42*
The number of young people who will be in trouble with the law (increase)	63	35*
The number of people who become addicted to gambling (increase)	87	90*
The kinds of tourists visiting the Niagara region will change (yes)	65	58*
Economic and amenity benefits		
The variety of stores and services (increase)	85	64*
The variety of entertainment (increase)	87	39*
Property values (increase)	66	46*
The amount of money going to stores and local business (increase)	84	65*
The number of jobs (increase)	93	88*
The average personal income of residents (increase)	56	49*
Environmental problems		
The level of traffic congestion (increase)	98	88*
The amount of litter on the streets and lawns (increase)	59	17*
The size of crowds in public places (increase)	90	64*
The noise levels (increase)	71	32*
Disturbances caused by people who have been drinking (increase)	72	31*

* difference significant $p<0.01$

fewer residents a year after the casino had opened. For example, fewer
people thought that crimes had increased, marriages and families broken
up, and young people been in trouble with the law, than had been expected.
The same was true for traffic congestion, litter, crowding, noise and
drinking disturbances. Equally, fewer people reported economic benefits
such as improved stores and services, entertainment and property values,
and increases in numbers of jobs and incomes, than had expected such
benefits.

The one negative expectation, endorsed by an even larger proportion of residents a year later, was that there would be an increase in the number of people who became addicted to gambling. There was further evidence that the casino had actually had such an effect. The proportion of the local population gambling in a casino in the year after the opening (43 per cent) was almost four times what it was the previous year (11 per cent) and this change was significantly greater than the change for Ontario residents as a whole. The numbers of regular attenders had also increased: 3.6 per cent in Niagara Falls reporting going to a casino two or more times a month after the casino had opened locally, compared to less than 1 per cent before the opening and in the province as a whole. Several indicators of problem gambling were used, and all showed an increase from before to after the opening. The proportion of the sample with a score of two or more on a short, five-item version of the South Oaks Gambling Screen (SOGS: see Chapter 3 for a discussion of this and other problem gambling screening questionnaires), which gives a reasonable indication of numbers of people with gambling problems, rose from 2.5 per cent to 4.4 per cent. There were also significant increases in those reporting that family members or friends had talked to them about their gambling, and in the proportions experiencing problems with the gambling of other members of their families (5.0 per cent up to 7.5 per cent), and the gambling of friends (14.0 per cent up to 20.5 per cent). Comparison data suggested that there had been no province-wide increases of these kinds in the same period.

Room et al (1999) concluded that problems arising from the opening of the new casino arose not in the public arena but rather in "the arena of private life, behind curtains rather than out on the street" (p.1465). Public support for the casino had not waned, and local officials and business people were particularly positive. The economic development officer for the city was quoted as saying, "the interest on an international basis in Niagara Falls and the region just took off once the announcement of the casino was made", and the Mayor's view was, "it's never been as vibrant and the atmosphere has never been as optimistic". According to a local businessman, even "traffic problems had not materialised like they said" (Turner et al, p.67). On the economic side, however, Room et al's (1999) conclusion, based on results shown in Table 2.2 and calculations of slight increases in employment that had resulted (unemployment down from 7.5 per cent to 6.2 per cent, and somewhere between 1,200 and 2,200 new jobs created for local people in connection with the casino compared with more than 6,000 that had been promised), was that the net increase in jobs that had occurred was not at the projected level. Room et al (1999) were critical of economic models that had been used for estimating the benefits to a community from a new gambling outlet (e.g. the model of Ernst and Young, 1994) which make the assumption that none of the share of the local economy attributable to a casino would otherwise have been devoted to other purposes, and which do not factor-in the costs to the community of negative impacts such as those arising from increased problem gambling, additional policing, or effects on other businesses. They quote the British Columbia Gaming Policy Review (1994, p.14) as saying, "Most of the analysis done respecting specific ventures is done by the industry itself and tends to ignore or understate costs."

Also of interest here is a report by Giacopassi et al (1999) of interviews held with 128 key individuals in seven US cities with new casinos. Overall the view of their informants was positive about the casinos, but this varied considerably from city to city (some were thought to have benefited less, for example because they were larger cities and the effects were less noticeable or because of competition from neighbouring cities), outcome by outcome (overall, people were more persuaded of the economic benefits and more uncertain about possible effects on crime), and particularly depending upon which group the informant represented. Local mayors and business people were most positive, as might be expected, and social service providers least so. Most negative were that minority who indicated that they knew of someone who was a problem gambler and whose life had been ruined by the experience. Most of that group were opposed to the casinos and saw them as a threat to community well-being.

The Productivity Commission (APC, 1999) report on *Australia's Gambling Industries* considered the costs and benefits of gambling to a society in minute detail. Indeed their report on all aspects of Australian gambling is so thorough that it must be counted as a key document in the modern literature on gambling worldwide. Looking first at what that report said about the possible benefits of gambling, the interesting point is made that consumers of most products are assumed to purchase them because they personally gain from their consumption, whilst in the case of gambling advocates have typically pointed to benefits in terms of income and job generation, both directly and indirectly related to gambling, and to the contribution made to taxation (the British KPMG, 2000, report is a good example: it estimated that the British gambling industry as a whole paid £1,840 million in 1998 in the form of tax, duty and licences). The Australian report took the opposite approach, arguing that the latter kinds of benefit from gambling were likely to be small and were often exaggerated. The 'production side' economic benefits were largely illusory, they concluded, principally because resources associated with the gambling industry were mostly diverted from other industries (the same point is made by Creigh-Tyte, 1997, and by Room et al, 1999), and hence that changes in the size of the industry would have little impact on Australia's GDP, overall levels of consumption, or labour market outcomes over the long term. Particularly suspect were thought to be assumptions about the indirect effects of growth in the gambling industry on other businesses: contraction of other business might be as likely as expansion.

Two ways in which gambling might be of economic benefit were considered by the report: spending by tourists, and the reduction of unemployment. Casino gambling particularly attracts tourists. The Australian Casino Association estimated that overseas visitors accounted for 25 per cent of casino revenue in 1997-98. In Britain KPMG (2000) stated that over a third of the amount wagered in British casinos was by foreign nationals. In the Niagara Falls example, attracting tourists was a prime objective of opening a casino. In the round, however, calculations carried out for the Productivity Commission and submissions made to it indicated that the net income benefits were small. Regarding the possibility of reduced unemployment, the report referred to there being little evidence that unemployment rates are significantly affected by economic development policies such as the establishment of new gambling industries, although there might be a beneficial local effect in depressed areas where labour is comparatively immobile.

Paradoxically it was those benefits of gambling which might be thought to be most intangible and not amenable to costing on which the Productivity Commission report attempted to put a figure. They argued that spending on gambling by those who do not have a gambling problem is spending on a consumer benefit (although their own national survey found that most regular gamblers considered that their gambling made no difference to how enjoyable life was, and only about a quarter considered that it made their life a little more enjoyable) and they went on to use the economic concept of 'consumer surplus' to calculate the overall amount of benefit that this represents for the community. Consumer surplus refers to the difference between what a consumer pays for a product and the amount that he or she would be prepared to pay rather than do without it. Put another way, it is a measure of the degree to which consumers are paying less for a product than its real value to them. This can only be calculated if there is some basis for knowing how sensitive (or 'elastic' to use another economic term) demand for the product is to changes in price. If the price elasticity of demand for gambling is comparatively low, as submissions to the Commission by the gambling industry tended to suggest, indicating that consumers would be prepared to pay more for the product, consumer surplus would be relatively high, and the industry could be said to be responding to a 'need'. If on the other hand, as much of the literature reviewed by the Commission suggested, elasticity was higher, indicating that reductions in gambling would be comparatively great if price were to rise, then the estimate of consumer surplus would be that much lower.

All the evidence on which it could draw suggested to the Commission that the price elasticity of gambling for non-problem gamblers lay between a higher estimate of 1.3 and a lower estimate of 0.8 (elasticity of 1.0 means that a doubling in price would produce a halving of consumption; an elasticity of 2.0 would mean that if price were to double consumption would decrease to a quarter). The final figure needed to calculate consumer surplus is the amount of total expenditure on gambling that is attributable to non-problem gamblers as opposed to those with problems, a figure calculated for Australia at 65 per cent (the nature and extent of problem gambling and the costs associated with it will be discussed in detail in Chapter 3). On the basis of all these calculations, the Commission came out with a final estimate of between 2.7 billion and 4.3 billion Australian dollars as their estimate of the overall national consumer surplus benefit of gambling as a desired form of entertainment.

Although that represents a brave attempt to quantify the benefits of gambling, the reasoning behind it seems to the present authors, who are not economists, to be tortuous and somewhat suspect. Apart from the fact that the calculation rests upon a crucial parameter that can only be estimated very approximately (the elasticity of demand), the whole idea of consumer surplus as an estimate seems to be clever but hardly convincing. A major flaw when dealing with a 'product' like gambling, which we shall see in the following chapter has a propensity to cause addiction, is the admittedly arbitrary separation of people into those whose gambling is purely 'recreational' (and whose 'need' for gambling can be claimed not to have been artificially stimulated) and those with problems whose continuing need has been at least partly created by the marketing of the product itself.

To the figures cited above the Productivity Commission added 3.8 billion Australian dollars transferred to government in the form of tax, and subtracted an estimated loss for problem gamblers of between 1.1 billion and 1.9 billion Australian dollars. Problem gambling and its costs, which represent by far the biggest downside to gambling according to the Commission report, are the subjects of the following chapter of the present book. But mention should be made here of other impacts on communities. One conclusion was that crime associated with the industry was no longer a significant issue (they considered petty crime committed inside casinos and other gaming venues, street crime in the vicinity, money laundering, and the involvement of organised crime) now that gambling was legalised and regulated rather than illegal as formerly.

A less tangible but often mentioned negative impact is the effect on the atmosphere of a hotel, bar or club in which gaming machines have been installed, and the possible 'crowding out' of other forms of entertainment. For example, in its submission to the Commission, the Jazz Co-ordination Association of New South Wales, having surveyed the impact of gaming machines on its own industry, asked:

> Is it part of the image Sydney wishes to project that its only pub recreation is gambling? Local music is a vibrant presence in the world's great cities. On present trends, Sydney will soon have none (Productivity Commission, p.9.16).

On the other hand, licensed and registered clubs are very popular in Australia and provide a variety of services to their local communities. Gambling is now a vital component of the operation of most such clubs in most Australian states. Furthermore some people are of the view that gambling venues constitute beneficial community resources over and above the gambling opportunities they provide. Amongst statements given in the course of other Australian studies cited by the Productivity Commission were the following:

> . . . EGM [electronic gaming machine] venues have almost achieved the status of community centres – pleasant places to go to meet and socialise with friends . . . It is also apparent that the comfort and ambience of such venues is very attractive and that good food, in particular, is an incentive.

> The *impression* is that it [EGM usage] is largely a new audience, that it is a previous 'stay at home' audience which is now a 'going out' group. This appears to be especially so in the case of the unemployed, women, the newly retired and elderly . . . migrants and the disabled for whom there are very few non gambling based community social and cultural alternatives . . . (Australian Productivity Commission, p.9.17).

There may be costs of gambling which are 'external' in the sense that they are experienced by people who are neither part of the gambling industry nor are they necessarily gamblers. For example some people may feel badly that society condones gambling, and may feel regret or frustration that gambling is expanding, seeing this as a sign of a degenerating society. Equally, however, some people with libertarian ideals may feel unhappy if gambling were banned or too tightly controlled. Some people feel that the expansion of gambling is changing the norms and social ethos of society in a direction of which they disapprove.

The quantification of those possible community impacts, and whether they were on balance negative or positive, was beyond the ingenuity of even the Productivity Commission. In fact the only costs to which the Productivity Commission could put any sort of figure were the private and social costs of problem gambling (see Chapter 3 for details). These lay, according to the Commission, somewhere between 1.1 billion and 5.2 billion Australian dollars annually. Subtracting these figures from the estimates of the benefits from gambling discussed above, produced estimates for the net annual benefits of gambling to Australia annually ranging from a low of as little as $150 million to as much as $5.2 billion. The crudeness of these estimates (despite the thoroughness with which the Australian report considered all the arguments, gathered all its evidence and made all its calculations) hardly needs any further pointing out. What the report's argument and figures do make quite clear, however, is the fact that gambling remains a problematic and controversial topic for society. The trends in the provision of gambling opportunities and people's expenditure on gambling show gambling to be in the ascendant at the turn of the century in countries such as Britain and Australia and elsewhere, but public awareness of the drawbacks of gambling remains as alive as public appreciation of its benefits (see Chapter 8).

Regulation

The Australian Productivity Commission report found regulatory policies in Australia to be, ". . . complex, fragmented and often inconsistent" (p.xxxix). The situation has been widely thought to be incoherent and inconsistent in Britain also. The legislation and regulatory framework governing gambling in Britain is certainly complex, largely as result of the labyrinthine history of British gambling and attempts to control it. What is not in dispute is that gambling should be subject to regulation. The Gaming Board for Great Britain (2000) stated its view that gambling had to be regulated for two reasons: susceptibility of gambling to fraud, money-laundering, other criminal activity and malpractice, because of the large amounts of money involved; and the fact that gambling could be addictive for some individuals, causing damage to themselves and those near them. For these reasons gambling was regulated in all developed countries, regulatory systems having three objectives in common, (1) that gambling should be crime-free, (2) that players should know what to expect and should not be exploited, and (3) that there should be protection for children and vulnerable people.

Gambling constantly poses a dilemma for government, which is faced with trying to reconcile the benefits of gambling and its potential and actual harms. As a result there is a constant struggle to get legislation right and to strike an acceptable balance (see Chapter 1 and especially Table 1.1). Sometimes legislation designed to correct a pre-existing anomaly has itself been responsible for too violent a swing of the pendulum, the new balance has been thought to be in the wrong place, and new corrective legislation has quickly been required. A notorious example of this in Britain was the Act of 1960 and the corrective legislation of 1968 which soon followed. Not, however, that Britain is totally crime free even now when it comes to gambling: KPMG (2000) cited 92 court proceedings against unregistered amusement machine traders and 41 proceedings against unregistered bookmakers between 1995/6 and 1998/9 for example. Recent years, also, have seen much media attention in Britain given to bribery in connection with the influencing of results of prominent sports fixtures on which a great amount of money has been wagered.

What is notable is the neglect in all recent British legislation of any efforts explicitly to prevent problem gambling by individuals. The

Table 2.3 The regulation of gambling in Britain at the end of the 20th century (reproduced with permission from KPMG report for Business in Sport and Leisure, 2000, Figure 8.1)

Organisation	*Responsibilities*
Home Office	Social policy and legislation necessary to regulate betting and gaming
Gaming Board for Great Britain	Regulator for casinos, bingo, gaming machine suppliers, and larger society and local authority lotteries; responsible for ensuring operators act fairly and industry is free from crime
HM Customs & Excise	Collect gambling duties from bookmakers, casinos, pools promoters, bingo clubs, and the National Lottery
Department for Culture, Media and Sport	National Lottery
Police	Vet potential employees and directors in the gaming industry on behalf of the Gaming Board; investigate illegal gaming and betting
Local authorities	Register small lotteries; issue permits for amusement machines in unlicensed premises; examine accounts of pools companies
Licensing magistrates	Issue licences, after due process, for casinos, bingo, clubs, and bookmakers' shops; grant permits to bookmakers
Horserace Betting Levy Board	Collects levies from bookmakers to provide financial support to racing
National Lottery Commission	Ensures probity of the National Lottery and interests of the players; maximises money to good causes; licenses operators and individual games; responsible for compliance

containment of gambling and the probity of its operation have been the emphasis. Hence, of the two main justifications for regulation – crime and problem gambling – it was really only the former that had been of much interest to government. As the KPMG (2000) report noted, the Gaming Board appeared to have no powers to assess or contain problem gambling.

The gambling industry itself, as might be expected, was more concerned that the regulatory framework of the last few decades was unnecessarily and unfairly restrictive of their business. Table 2.3, taken from the KPMG (2000) report, summarises the responsibilities of the different organisations involved in regulating British gambling at the turn of the century, which in their view had resulted in an uneven pattern of regulation. It noted for example the existence of as many as five types of gaming machine with their different regulations, the different rates of duties and levies payable in the different sectors of the industry, and restrictions on advertising thought to be unfair in the light of the freedom of the NL to advertise. The general view of the industry, made plain at many points throughout the KPMG (2000) report, was that the industry was subject to far too much unnecessary 'interference', and that aside from matters to do with the law, supplying opportunities for gambling in response to consumer demand "is best left to market forces" (p.80). Furthermore, the report argued, regulation should as far as possible be left to the industry itself: self-regulation already existed in a variety of forms such as the British Horseracing Board, the Jockey Club and the National Greyhound Racing Club.

Specifically, industry recommendations included: free advertising of gambling; no barriers to the new entry of firms offering gambling; the abolition of the idea of 'permitted areas' for casinos; the reduction of the present system of 'demarcation of offering' whereby suppliers are limited to offering one or a small range of forms of gambling; and the setting up of a single Gaming Regulator which, unlike the Gaming Board, would have responsibilities across all forms of gambling. Needless to say, all of these recommendations, if acted upon, would have the effect of increasing the public's opportunities for and access to gambling. Dismantling the system of demarcation between different forms of gambling was a particularly radical suggestion and one with utterly uncertain consequences. Although the system had already been partially dismantled, particularly due to the siting of gaming machines in such locations as casinos and bingo clubs, by and large it was still the case that gambling venues were specialised. The KPMG (2000) report cited the chairman of the British Horseracing Board as believing that legalised betting in the nation's 30,000 pubs and clubs would raise turnover and help solve racing's financial problems; and a well-known BBC commentator and columnist (Robin Oakley) as saying that restrictions on the retail of betting products was "akin to having a law which said that Marks and Spencer can open their shops, but only if they restrict themselves to selling socks" (*The Spectator*, 15 April 2000, cited by KPMG, 2000, p.83). KPMG (2000) themselves said: "It could be argued that mature consumers should be allowed to exercise choice over where and when, and with what basket of other products, they consume gambling products" (p.83).

The 2000–2001 Gambling Review Report

At the very beginning of the 21st century an official look was being taken, yet again, at the state of gambling legislation and regulation in Britain. In December 1999 the Home Secretary announced the government's plans to establish a Gambling Review Body. The Home Office Minister responsible for gambling policy said at the time:

Much of our current gambling legislation is over 30 years old. Social attitudes have changed and the law is fast being overtaken by technological developments. The Government wants to get rid of unnecessary burdens on business, while maintaining protections necessary in the public interest. We believe there is now a good case for a comprehensive review of British gambling legislation. Reform would raise important issues and the social and economic impact would have to be carefully assessed (cited by the Gaming Board, 2000, p.3).

There can be no doubting the significance of the report of the Gambling Review Body for British gambling in the early 21st century. For that reason we highlight its recommendations, and immediate press response to them, and make our own comments on them, in the final chapter. Before that, we turn our attention to exploring the nature of problem gambling (Chapter 3), and its possible causes (Chapter 4), and in Chapters 5 and 6 we summarise the results of two important studies carried out by the National Centre for Social Research – the first British Gambling Prevalence Survey (Sproston et al, 2000) and an in-depth qualitative study of problem gambling (White et al, 2001).

Problem gambling

Modern historians of British gambling have been motivated to correct what is now recognised as an altogether negative, moralistic, and often class-prejudiced view of gambling, but in the process might be accused, in turn, of painting rather too rosy a picture of what gambling was like. Historical accounts have sometimes attempted to arrive at a single view of the subject, often that of a harmless but inappropriately maligned pleasure, to put in the place of former, now discredited one-dimensional, anti-gambling views (see Chapter 1). The more accurate view might be that gambling has in the past given rise to a wide diversity of experiences, and continues to do so, and that one view of gambling cannot do justice to that diversity.

Even in those historical accounts there is a recognition that the truth about gambling may be more complicated. Clapson (1992, p.61), for example, stated that no causal link between gambling and poverty was ever established, "Except in extreme cases . . .", and Rowntree, whilst emphasising 'primary poverty' which was the real enemy and target of social reform, recognised the existence of what he called 'secondary poverty' caused principally by excessive drinking or gambling. Chinn (1991), Clapson (1992) and Reith (1999) all give examples of accounts and testimonies of people whose family lives were marred by excessive gambling.

The fact of individual problem gambling

As early as the mid-19th century there were celebrated cases, usually of 'respectable' middle-class background, whose lives had been harmed by gambling. They were made much of by anti-gambling campaigners. Such were David Hoggart, whose character was ruined by a fondness for 'raffles, cards and dancing', and William Palmer, whose betting debts had led him to murder his wife, his brother and his best friend (Chinn, 1991, p.66, p.74). To complete the picture of British gambling in the first half of the 20th century, we have, to put alongside accounts of gambling as an activity well integrated with neighbourhood life, autobiographies such as that of Garratt (1939) (cited by Chinn, 1991), whose father's excessive gambling spoilt family life. One of Clapson's (1992) informants, Sheila H, recalled the effects of her father's gambling on pitch-and-toss and various card games at a location called the 'Hollow':

> If my father had a good day in the 'Hollow' he would not go to work the next day. If he had a bad day in the Hollow then he would take it out on my Mother, Brother and myself. Many's the time we have trudged through the streets looking for lodgings (Clapson, 1992, p.83).

In his book, *Labour, Life and Poverty*, the sociologist Zweig (1948/1975) described what he saw as five different types of gambler at dog-race meetings in the late 1940s. One group was what he called the 'unhappy types', the poorest, most desperate, who shouted loudest, and whom he saw as most likely to neglect their families' well-being (Clapson, 1992). Chinn, too, acknowledged:

> . . . it is likely that each community could point to families and individuals demoralized by the activity, and it is not surprising that many working-class people viewed any form of betting as disreputable . . . (Chinn, 1991, p.175).

The fact that many individual people get into trouble with their gambling is the subject of this chapter and much of the rest of this book. We shall refer to this by using the generic term 'problem gambling'. Others have preferred terms such as 'compulsive gambling', 'pathological gambling', 'excessive gambling' or 'gambling addiction'. Although all these terms are used by and large synonymously, we shall later look at some of the operational definitions and distinctions that have been employed.

The idea that gambling can get out of control for some people, becoming very troublesome in the process, is certainly not a new one. In an article in the *American Journal of Psychology* for 1902 Clemens France unearthed a number of descriptions of problem gambling from much earlier periods. Among early historical witnesses to the fact of problem gambling were the Englishman, Cotton (1674), whose description of gaming as "an enchanting witchery . . . an itching disease . . .", is well known, and the Frenchman, Barbeyrac. In the latter's three-volume work, *Traite du Jeu*, published in 1737, Jean Barbeyrac had this to say:

> I do not know if there is any other passion which allows less of repose and which one has so much difficulty in reducing . . . the passion of gambling gives no time for breathing; it is an enemy which gives neither quarter nor truce; it is a persecutor, furious and indefatigable. The more one plays the more one wishes to play . . .

The Russian novelist Dostoevsky is often referred to as the most famous of all 'compulsive gamblers'. There have been a number of case studies of the writer, mostly by psychoanalysts, one of the most often quoted being that by Squires published in the *Psychoanalytic Review* in 1937. Amongst the many sources he drew upon were Dostoevsky's own letters and his second wife's diary. From the latter's account of the year in which they married, Squires concluded that Dostoevsky was "powerless in the clutches of his terrific gambling mania, which blunted his sense of moral responsibility as effectively as extreme alcohol addiction could" (p.372). Stripped of the glamour that surrounds the life of a world renowned writer, Dostoevsky's life story contains moments that compare with the experiences of the most obscure man or woman who has struggled with a gambling problem.

Problem gambling in fiction

One place where the dangers of gambling have been well represented, or at least where the picture of gambling is a very mixed one, is in fiction. Chinn (1991), Dixon (1991) and Clapson (1992) each referred to the subject of gambling in fiction, and Knapp (2000) wrote a whole book on the topic devoting a chapter to each of several notable examples. Nineteenth-century fictionalised accounts of problem gambling include Edgar Allan Poe's short story *William Wilson* (1839) which, using the device of a split-personality, depicted the conflict between "the evil gambler, wastrel, and reprobate pitted against the amenable, conscious-driven, and righteous young man" (Knapp, 2000, p.73). A classic is Dostoevsky's own *The Gambler* (1866). The narrator, Alexei, an inveterate roulette player, illustrates a number of features of problem gambling that have been the subject of much more recent research: the heightened emotions experienced during gambling, the difficulty in leaving go of the idea that there is some order to the pattern of wins on the roulette table, and the feelings of guilt associated with excessive gambling (Knapp, 2000). Late 19th century English novels include *A Dangerous Friend, or Tom's Three Months in London* by Leslie (1890, cited by Dixon, 1991), and *Esther Walters* (Moore, 1895, cited by Clapson, 1992). Novels from the first half of the 20th century, cited by Clapson (1992) include Arlen's *The Green Hat* (1924), Spring's *Shabby Tiger* (1934), and Greene's *Brighton Rock* (1938) which depicted protection rackets and racetrack violence. But the most notable work of English fiction from that period is Walter Greenwood's *Love on the Dole* (1933), and in particular the character of the bookmaker Sam Grundy. Chinn (1991) described Greenwood's portrayal of the bookmaker in some detail, taking the author to task for painting such a negative portrait of a greedy, exploitative, upwardly mobile bookie who was also involved in pimping. Chinn argued that this portrayal fitted the stereotype held by the middle classes that was in reality as little true of working-class life in Salford in the 1920s, where the story was set, as it was of any other British working-class area at the time. Clapson (1992), on the other hand, whilst recognising that Grundy's character represents an unflattering stereotype, conceded that it was partly the response of a working-class writer who had lived amongst the poor and was frustrated by their conditions, seeing some bookmakers as villains who profited from poverty.

Problem gambling has also featured much in film, to which Dement (1999) devoted a whole book. He reviewed no less than 151 films on the subject that had appeared between 1908 and 1998. Dement picked out *Fever Pitch* (1985, directed by Brooks), *The Gambler* (1974, directed by Reisz) and *The Great Sinner* (1949, loosely based on Dostoevsky's novel *The Gambler*) as providing probably the most detailed and accurate portrayals of problem gambling. Dement expressed strong views on how problem gambling should be portrayed in film, and was particularly concerned about films' endings. Many endings were, in his view, "dishonest" or "unrealistic" because they showed the gambler having a big win. He particularly took *Fever Pitch* to task on those grounds since otherwise it was one of the most important Hollywood films dealing with the subject of 'compulsive gambling', and everything leading up to the ending was informative and valuable. Technical advisers to the film included Custer (of Custer and Milt, 1985) and several other notable experts. Possible reasons for the ending, in which the central character has a series of big wins, were the expectation that gamblers would not go to see the film if it was just about 'losers', or simply that Hollywood required a happy ending.

Notable amongst the many other films mentioned by Dement are *The Lady Gambles* (1949), one of only three films that focused on problem gambling amongst women, and *Parenthood* (1989), one of a small number focusing on the effects of problem gambling on others, in this case the effects on the central character's father (family members have supporting roles in many other films of course).

The recognition of problem gambling

In the early 20th century Stekel (1924) recognised gambling as one of the 'manias' and some psychoanalysts recognised comparatively early on that gambling could take a compulsive form (e.g. Bergler, 1958). But it was not until the 1960s that British psychiatrists started to write of their experiences of being consulted by people whose gambling was out of control. Notable amongst these was Moran (1970, 1975) who took a special interest in what he called 'pathological gambling'. In addition to the sheer amount of the gambling activity, indications were the person's concern about its excessiveness, the strength of desire for and preoccupation with gambling, a feeling of loss of control, and harms thought to be caused by gambling in economic, social and psychological spheres of life. According to Moran these harms included: debt, loss of employment and friends, eviction, criminality, marital and family problems, depression and attempted suicide. Barker and Miller (1968) were other British clinicians who treated 'compulsive gambling' and provided brief case summaries that give an idea of the extent of the personal problems that could be associated with gambling.

One such case was a man whose problem was 'the horses':

> He had gambled in 'betting shops' for more than 2 years and had lost over £1,200. Initially he ascribed his gambling mainly to boredom, but he had recently gambled to repay his debts, which exceeded £100. His usual practice was to spend all his salary (£15 to £30 per week) in a betting shop on Saturdays. He invariably reinvested his winnings on horses and returned home with nothing so that his wife and children went without food, clothes and fuel . . . Matters came to a head when he put his own money and the complete pay packet of a sick friend (who had asked him to collect his pay) on one horse and lost £40. This resulted in 18 months probation. His gambling had been causing serious marital difficulties and was affecting the health of his wife and his eldest son. He was referred for treatment by his doctor (pp.288–289).

Another was a man in his early thirties, married with two children, who had recently been jailed for 18 months for obtaining money by fraud for gambling on fruit machines. His wife, who had to work throughout their marriage to support their family and repay his gambling debts, vividly portrayed the situation thus:

> Over the last few years we have had a monster living with our family – a monster in the shape of a 'fruit-machine'. Practically every penny my husband earned went into that machine and while it consumed, we starved. He was obsessed by it. Frequently we were without food, fuel and light (pp. 287–288).

Of crucial significance in raising awareness that gambling could be harmful for some individuals was the development of the self-help organisation Gamblers Anonymous (GA). GA was slower to develop than Alcoholics Anonymous, upon which it was closely modelled, perhaps because gambling remained illegal longer than drinking in the USA (Castellani, 2000). But once it started in Los Angeles in 1957 it developed rapidly. GA then spread to Northern Ireland in 1962 and thence to mainland Britain in 1964 (Bellringer, 1999). A number of studies describing the harmful effects of problem gambling were based on studies of GA members in other countries notably the USA. For example, Lesieur (1984) reported in his book, *The Chase*, the results of lengthy interviews with 50 men with 'compulsive gambling' problems in the USA, most but not all of them members of GA. He particularly noted how the development of compulsive gambling affected a man's relationship with his work. He described how compulsive gamblers might work part-time, overtime, sometimes two jobs at once, in order to gamble or pay gambling debts; would often borrow from close friends at work, get advances in pay, steal money and items for ready cash, and in other ways exploit fellow employees, the boss, customers and business associates; would often leave jobs so they would not have to pay debts; and would commonly be simultaneously holding loans from a number of different sources, not uncommonly six or more sources at one time. According to Lesieur a compulsive gambler developed a similar kind of 'exploitative' financial relationship with his family. This took a variety of forms including using entertainment money, funds from part-time jobs, and overtime money; borrowing from parents or in-laws; lying to his spouse about the true extent of earnings; referring to 'bills' or 'deductions' from wages which in reality did not exist; 'borrowing' from family resources such as savings and life insurance; selling or pawning his own or family members' possessions; hiding loans; and finally when all else fails using money that is required by the family for essentials. As one respondent put it:

> Sold my tools, sold my car, sold my camera, sold my wrist watch. Sold personal things, antiques that I brought from Europe. I sold them for gambling. A stamp collection. Yes, I sold everything (p.69).

Ladouceur et al's (1994) study of 60 GA members in French-speaking Canada is another that paints a picture of how serious the adverse impacts of problem gambling can be upon finances, work and crime. Over half of the participants in that survey had been spending more than $1,000 a month on gambling, and 83 per cent had had to borrow money during the past year in order to gamble. Sixty-two per cent had borrowed money from relatives or friends, and 20 per cent from 'loan sharks'. Both lateness and absence from work were very frequent, and in addition more than half reported that they had often been irritable at work and frequently had difficulties in concentrating due to the pervasive nature of thoughts about gambling. Over a third had stolen money from their employers in order to gamble, nearly half of these more than once. A third had already lost jobs because of gambling problems and others had nearly done so. Altogether two-thirds reported having engaged in illegal acts of one kind or another in order to finance their gambling, including falsifying documents or forging signatures, embezzlement, signing cheques without sufficient funds, filing false income tax returns or neglecting to pay income tax, making false statements to insurance companies, non-violent theft, violent theft, shoplifting, and fencing stolen goods.

Effects on family relationships are often highlighted in descriptions of problem gambling. In their book, *When Luck Runs Out*, Custer and Milt (1985) devoted a chapter to 'compulsive gambling' in the family, stating:

> . . . compulsive gambling . . . spreads out and affects every person with whom the compulsive gambler is closely involved – his wife, his children, his siblings and parents, his other relatives, his friends and business associates . . . It is the nature of emotional disorders that when one member of the family is afflicted, the effects are felt by all the others. There are few, however, in which the impact is felt with such severity as in the case of compulsive gambling (Custer and Milt, 1985, pp.122–123).

Although problem gambling is most often depicted as harmful to family, employers and others who are affected by excessive gambling, it has been recognised that when gambling is out of control it also harms the gambler's own mental and even physical health. In their report of a study of over 200 members of GA in the USA, Lorenz and Yaffee (1984) described a 'syndrome' in which emotional and psychosomatic problems were associated with a desperate need for money, and feelings of guilt and depression. The most common symptoms, each reported by 30 per cent or more, were: depression; knotted stomach, loose bowels, constipation or colitis; insomnia; feeling faint, dizzy; clammy or sweaty hands, or perspiring heavily. In their later Canadian survey, Ladouceur et al (1994) reported that more than two-thirds of respondents indicated experiencing depressive moods, insomnia and/or headaches or stomach aches, at least once a week, attributed to gambling.

Reviewing the evidence from a number of studies, both Dickerson (1990) and Blaszczynski and Farrell (1998) have concluded that problem gambling is associated with a significantly higher rate of both depression and attempted suicide than are found in the general population. Some of the studies reviewed involved samples of GA members (e.g. Frank et al 1991, cited by Blaszczynski and Farrell, 1998), people being treated for problem gambling (e.g. Moran, 1969, cited by Blaszczynski and Farrell, 1998), or those telephoning a gambling crisis hotline (Sullivan, 1994, in New Zealand). Other studies have found elevated rates of suicide for both residents and non-resident visitors in US towns known for gambling (Las Vegas, Reno and Atlantic City: Phillips et al 1997, cited by Blaszczynski and Farrell, 1998), or have compared rates amongst problem gamblers and others in a general population survey. Cunningham-Williams et al (1998) reported a study of the latter kind carried out in St Louis as part of the large US Epidemiologic Catchment Area Study of mental disorders in the general population. Compared to non-gamblers, problem gamblers had a significantly higher rate of depression and psychosomatic symptoms.

Blaszczynski and Farrell (1998) were able themselves to examine all the case records of suicides in which reference was made to gambling behaviour from the coroner's office in the state of Victoria, Australia. Forty-four such cases (thirty-nine men and five women) were identified from the years 1990 to 1997. Although the results can of course say nothing about actual rates of gambling-related suicide, the detailed examination of these records helps make the case that out-of-control gambling can be a major contributory cause of suicide as has been so widely assumed. In seven of the forty-four coroner's records, suicide notes made specific reference to a chronic gambling problem and one to a gambling-related financial crisis as the precipitating factor. In a further two instances relatives or significant others reported that gambling had been a direct contributing factor. In the remainder of the cases there was sufficient descriptive evidence, either in the form of heavy gambling immediately preceding the suicide and/or the presence of severe gambling-related financial debts, to strongly suggest a major role for gambling. All had some financial difficulties and many substantial gambling debts. Losses in excess of $10,000 over a few months were not uncommon and three had been declared bankrupt and two had been forced to sell homes. There were records that eight had engaged in some type of illegal activity to support gambling, including stealing from parents, fraud, stealing from a club, a joint business venture or from employers. One case of a man known to have gambled in the period immediately prior to his suicide was described as follows:

> . . . on the 20th October 1995 Mr . . . a 34 year old married Vietnamese engineer was found hanging in the garage by his neighbour. According to the Police investigation report, Mrs . . . stated that her husband had lost approximately $13,000 in three lots of $3,000, $4,000 and $6,000 at the casino over the nine months prior to his death. This resulted in marital friction, with his wife being forced to take out a loan to cover their commitments. On the 30th September his wife visited her parents in the United States of America leaving him on his own. She stated that she left him $500 cash and that he would also have received his monthly salary of $1250 during her absence. Bank records revealed that on the 5th October he withdrew $500 from an ATM at the casino, on the 9th he withdrew and lost $1,000 and on the 11th absented himself from work and withdrew another $240 at the casino's ATM. He made a further withdrawal of $700 but it was unclear where this was spent. The remaining balance in his joint account was $7.00 on the evening of his death. There were indications that his job was stressful, that he had been overlooked for promotion and that he was jealous over the relative success of his brother. While these may potentially be compounding factors, it was considered that gambling and financial problems were of paramount importance in his death (Blaszczynski and Farrell, 1998, p.98).

None of this research can be completely conclusive on the question of whether problem gambling is a direct cause of depression, suicidal thoughts, attempted suicide and successful suicide. Research in this area is particularly difficult for many reasons including the very selective nature of some of the samples (e.g. problem gamblers in treatment) and the very incomplete nature of records such as coroners' records. Nevertheless the descriptions provided by Blaszczynski and Farrell and the consistency of other evidence can be taken as strong support for the existence of a causal link, in individual cases, between the development of problem gambling and subsequent suicidal thoughts and attempts. Furthermore, from what is known about the experience of developing a gambling problem, and from all accounts of problem gamblers themselves and from others who have lived with them or helped them, such a link is only to be expected. Blaszczynski and Farrell put it thus:

> Intuitively, it is reasonable to predict a strong causal relationship between excessive gambling and risk for suicide. Impaired control and the process of chasing losses . . . invariably exposes gamblers to a series of repetitive psychosocial crises. These may take the form of escalating gambling-induced severe financial difficulties, fear of disclosure of debts and/or criminal offences, marital discord and possible termination of employment due to absenteeism or reduced productivity . . . Under conditions of intense emotional distress, turmoil and sense of hopelessness, suicide is often considered as the only optional solution to their predicament (p.94).

Much the same problems in establishing cause and effect surround the question of the link between problem gambling and the committing of crimes. Numerous case studies and descriptions of GA or treatment samples attest to the likelihood of a causal link, and again what is known of the experience of problem gambling and its associated financial difficulties would strongly support such a link. But it has to be admitted that the link may not always be a straightforward one. For one thing some of the crimes committed by people who develop problems with gambling may be committed before the latter develops. And for other problem gamblers their gambling may not be the only cause of crime (the same argument for the existence of a variety of causal pathways had been accepted in the case of the link between drug misuse and crime e.g. Hammersley et al, 1989). This issue has particularly been looked at by Meyer and Stadler (1999) in Germany. They compared the self-reports of crime given by 300 problem gamblers in treatment and 274 non-problem gamblers recruited from army members and directly at casinos, gaming arcades and pubs in different German cities. The former were much more likely to admit having ever committed a crime, committed a crime in the last 12 months of gambling, and to have ever been convicted. A multivariate statistical procedure known as structural equation modelling showed that a causal model in which the degree of problem gambling (or 'addiction' as Meyer and Stadler called it) significantly predicts the extent of criminal behaviour provided a good fit to the data. They did not test other possible models, however, and admitted that other causal pathways were possible.

What is much more convincing, however, is the nature of the offences which contributed most to the difference between the crime rates of problem gamblers and controls. Whereas a number of types of events showed comparatively little difference between the two groups (e.g. consumption of soft drugs, driving under the influence of alcohol, travelling without paying, burglary), other types of self-reported offence showed a six-fold or greater difference between the groups. This was the case for fraud, embezzlement, theft in the family, and theft from non-family members (38 per cent, 22 per cent, 21 per cent and 7 per cent of treated problem gamblers admitted to these four offences respectively in the last 12 months of regular gambling, compared to 6 per cent, 1 per cent, 2 per cent and 1 per cent respectively for the non-problem gamblers). These are of course just the kinds of offences that would be expected to follow from the development of out-of-control gambling and which have been described in detail in case studies and in GA or treatment samples. Less dramatic differences were found in the case of some other kinds of crime (e.g. 23 per cent versus 16 per cent for theft at work, 13 per cent versus 9 per cent for shoplifting, and 11 per cent versus 4 per cent for receiving stolen goods).

Incidentally Meyer and Stadler reported the interesting fact that there were approximately 30,000 registered bannings from German casinos (they do not say over what period of time), of which more than half were on the request of the gamblers themselves (machine gambling, often in casinos, was the commonest form of gambling associated with problems in their research on crime). The fact that problem gamblers themselves often ask to be banned from gambling venues is well known to anybody who has met many problem gamblers, and is an important indication of the addictive-like nature of the problem which can create an intense conflict between the out-of-control urge to gamble and awareness of the desirability of controlling gambling in order to reduce or prevent the harms that it is causing.

Young people and problem gambling

In most of the studies of problem gambling based on GA or treatment samples the typical problem gambler has been a man in his middle years, with average ages of samples around 40 years. Contrary to the view that problem gambling is largely an adult problem, however, there is now much expert opinion and evidence to suggest that teenagers might be particularly vulnerable to the development of gambling problems. In Britain this has particularly come to light because of the permissiveness of the legislation of the 1960s which allowed gaming machines to be located in a wide variety of settings, many of them easily accessible to young people. Moran was one of the first to draw attention to the problem. He noted, first, the appearance of newspaper reports such as the following:

> 'There is not a minute when the machines are not on my mind. It is their lights and the noises. Most of all the flashing lights. I dream about them and can't get them out of my head. I feel as though I am losing my sanity. The machines should be banned – they are bad, bad, bad'. Suicide note left by a young man in North London who had spent £2000 on fruit machines before he died (*Daily Express*, 4 March 1987, cited by Moran, 1987, p.16).

One of the first surveys of young people and gambling in Britain was Moran's (1987) survey of the head teachers of 30 secondary schools in four London boroughs. Problems related to pupils' behaviour were associated with reported fruit-machine gambling, and the latter was considerably higher in schools which had a greater number of machines and more amusement arcades in their localities. He concluded, as others have done, that the Trade Code of Practice excluding children from access to fruit machines, was evidently not effective. Head teachers' reports suggested that consequences for some children could be very disturbing. One head teacher was quoted as saying:

> Once the habit is established, there is a serious interference with school work and truancy often occurs. This leads to a situation in which the children even resort to extortion, in order to continue to play on the machines. This has led to violence in the playground. Often, the most serious effects are on the home. Parents are distraught because money is stolen from the family and from friends. Ultimately, domestic relationships are eroded because all sense of trust is lost, as a consequence of the incessant stealing and lying (p.12).

Since then, Griffiths, in the form of a book and a series of papers, is one who has done much to raise awareness about the phenomenon of problem fruit-machine gambling amongst young people in Britain. In his 1990 paper he reported the results of informal discussions and observations conducted between himself and a group of eight 'self-confessed addicted adolescent fruit-machine gamblers' at their local amusement arcade. The average age of the group was 19 years but all of the group reported beginning fruit-machine playing by the age of 11. Five of the group claimed that they were addicted at the age of 13 and all acknowledged being addicted to machines by the age of 15. A number of serious problems had been experienced:

By far the major problem, which was apparent in all eight cases, was the constant need to play and spend all their own (and others' borrowed) money at every available opportunity . . . This had left them all in debt at some time in their adolescent lives and had forced two of them to seek help from Gamblers Anonymous. All of the group wishes they could stop gambling, and the assertion that 'fruit machines should be banned' because they are 'deadly' and 'life-destroyers' was re-iterated a number of times during the course of the discussion (Griffiths, 1990, p.123).

Elsewhere Griffiths (1993a) has reported the results of a study of 19 'former adolescent fruit-machine addicts' contacted through the organisation Parents of Young Gamblers, a self-help group set up in the 1980s for parents concerned about the excessive gambling of their adolescent children. Fifteen were young men and four women, and the average age was 19 years. Among the statements quoted by Griffiths are the following:

While I was playing fruit machines there were no good experiences, only bad, such as stealing money from my family and robbing chip shops, phone boxes and tills in shops (male, aged 17).

. . . any dinner, bus fare money went into fruit machines during school hours. When I started my full time job . . . as a cashier, my weekly wages (£75) went . . . in a few hours. I needed more money therefore I stole from the cash till . . . I am now going to court (female, aged 16).

In the case of one 18 year old who took part in this small survey, participation led to regular contact over a six-month period between Griffiths and both the young man and his mother, resulting in a very valuable case study (Griffiths, 1993b). Yeoman and Griffiths (1996) also reported the results of an analysis of nearly 2,000 police reports of contacts with juveniles during a one-year period in one town in south-west England. Of these contacts, 72 (3.9 per cent), 67 male and 5 female, were identified as having some association between the offence recorded and gambling-machine playing. Brief case descriptions include the following two:

Male (14 years old). Lives with mother, father and brother. Home conditions excellent. Burglary with two juveniles and an adult where property was stolen from a mail box. He was involved in school burglaries and handling stolen property . . . Family indicate theft from home over 2.5 years both of their property and selling his clothes – in excess of £150 – to play fruit machines.

Female (14 years old). Lives with mother and stepfather. Suffers lack of supervision. Family violence when mother and father drink heavily.

> Missing person. Left home because of heavy drinking by family and ensuing violence. Spends all day at the arcades and some nights. As a result has been involved in theft and handling.

Concern about problem gambling and young people has in no way been confined to the UK. For example, Jacobs (1989) suggested that large numbers of legally under-age young people who lived within easy access of casinos in the USA were gaining access to gambling, and that slot-machine playing was the most popular form. He concluded from his own and others' evidence that legal controls on juvenile gambling were being widely flouted in the USA at that time, and furthermore that parents were very often aware of their children gambling and in many cases appeared to condone or encourage it, for which there might be a number of explanations. Perhaps parents believed that legal sanctions would be effective in discouraging any really serious gambling amongst teenagers? Perhaps under-age gambling was simply dismissed as being harmless amusement. Perhaps there was a lack of awareness amongst adults about the role they might be playing in fostering child and teenage gambling. Or perhaps the situation simply reflected delayed awareness on the part of parents and others that teenage gambling was becoming a problem. As we shall see later in this chapter, concern about young people and problem gambling has been widespread, not just in the UK and USA, and as a result a number of surveys of young people and gambling have been carried out.

Can gambling be addictive?

It is clear then that gambling, for some people, gets out of control and is associated with serious problems in a number of areas of life. But is gambling for those people an addiction? The history, mostly quite recent, of ideas around that question is intriguing. That history is well described by two writers, Collins (1996) writing mainly about Britain, and Castellani (2000) writing principally about the USA. Collins's main thesis was that 'pathological gambling' had been a surprisingly late-comer on the scene when compared with apparently similar forms of mental health problem such as alcohol or drug addiction. Gambling as a form of pathology or addiction had only really been taken on by what he termed the 'psy professions' or the 'psy sciences' following the listing of pathological gambling as a distinct disorder by the American Psychiatric Association in its *Diagnostic and Statistical Manual* (DSM) and the World Health Organisation in its *International Classification of Diseases* (ICD) in the 1980s and 1990s. Since then interest had mushroomed, but before that there had been remarkable silence on the subject on the part of the mental health professions. That could certainly not be put down to lack of awareness of gambling as a source of social problems in 19th century Britain. Nor could it "be attributed to a shy or reticent psychiatry" (p.84), in the early 20th century, either, since psychiatry recognised a large number of 'manias' (of which erotomania, dipsomania, pyromania, kleptomania and toxicomania were just some), not to mention a whole range of 'personality deviations and neurotic reactions' (Collins refers to psychiatry's 'baroque nosologies'). Maudsley in 1868 mentioned gambling as one of a number of possible causes of insanity but not as a form of insanity in itself. Kraepelin and later Bleuler both referred to 'gambling mania' early in the 20th century but this was not taken up by others and scarcely appears in mid-century textbooks of psychiatry. The psychoanalytic literature is a possible exception (e.g. Fenichel, 1945; Freud, 1961) and particularly the specialised work on the subject of Bergler (1936, 1958). But Bergler's 'unconscious desire to lose' theory (see Chapter 4) never achieved wide support and according to Collins, Bergler remained the only thorough-going specialist, and the subject received little attention even from psychoanalysts.

Collins speculated about the causes of the late emergence of the 'pathological gambler' and the silence on the subject that had previously existed. One strand was the decline of moral arguments against gambling of the 19th and very early 20th centuries, and their replacement in Britain by a climate favourable to licensing and regulation after World War II, and eventually to a neo-liberal view of gambling as part of the leisure market which functioned best with as little restriction as possible (see Chapter 1). A further possible reason for the invisibility of pathological gambling, according to Collins, was the almost complete lack of accurate statistics: he cited the 1978 Royal Commission on Gambling's conclusion that "There is . . . a serious lack of quantitative information about certain classes of gambling" (Collins, 1996, p.88). Another possible factor alluded to by Collins, and in our view one of the most important, was the difficulty the mental health professions had in seeing gambling, which involved the ingestion of no substance, as similar in kind to substance addictions such as 'alcoholism' and drug addiction.

Castellani (2000), too, wrote about the types of discourses that have dominated presentations about problem gambling in the USA, and about the alliances that have been part of the emerging picture in that country. To a greater extent than in Britain gambling remained illegal and was largely seen as a morally and legally illegitimate activity well into the second half of the 20th century. It is against that background that Bergler's 1958 classic *The Psychology of Gambling* should be seen. His attempt, according to Castellani, was to make a complete break with the past by viewing gambling problems "within the new and powerful discourses of medicine and psychiatry" (p.24). It was important, therefore, to construe problem gambling as non-rational, but also as non-criminal since the discourse of law had been amongst the dominant discourses of the past. Hence Bergler's insistence that his book was about a kind of gambling 'neurosis', specifically an unconscious wish to lose. It was not about immoral behaviour nor about crime, but rather about 'psychopathology'.

Much more significant, in the longer term, however, were the mutually supportive developments of GA and professional treatment services in the USA. In 1971, Custer, whose achievement in gaining national and international acceptance of the idea of 'pathological gambling' is widely acknowledged, was director of an alcoholism treatment programme in Ohio when he was approached by members of the local GA group asking for professional treatment for some of their members. Custer attended GA meetings and met members and saw "desperate people, in great pain, suffering, helpless and hopeless and, from a psychiatric standpoint, these were people we would regard as emergencies" (Custer and Milt, 1985, p.217). As a result he started the first of a number of in-patient gambling treatment facilities in the USA. Of even greater significance, Custer is credited (e.g. by Dickerson and Baron, 2000) with achieving the inclusion of pathological gambling in the first edition of the American Psychiatric Association's DSM which, rightly or wrongly, has now become the gold standard for assessing and counting problem gambling.

Castellani saw two sides emerging in the now out-in-the-open debate about gambling in the USA. On one side were the gambling industry (supported by federal and state governments who remained virtually silent on the question of problem gambling) and the criminal justice system (which refused to countenance the idea that 'pathological gambling' was a form of insanity: e.g. the case of *Torniero v. the United States*, 1983, which provided the framework for Castellani's excellent discussion of gambling discourses). On the other side (arguing that pathological gamblers were suffering from an illness and therefore required treatment) were GA, the addiction treatment field including the new gambling treatment speciality, and national and local councils on compulsive gambling (the National Council on Compulsive Gambling, later to change its name to the National Council on Problem Gambling, which started with GA help in the USA in the early 1970s).

The inclusion of 'pathological gambling' in the American Psychiatric Association's DSM and WHO's ICD has probably done more than anything to increase the visibility of problem gambling in the 'psy professions and sciences' (Collins, 1996). The third edition of DSM was the first to include 'pathological gambling'. It was conceived of as a disorder of impulse control (along with kleptomania, pyromania, and 'explosive disorders') whose essential features were described as a "failure to resist an impulse, drive, or temptation to perform some act . . . an increasing sense of tension before committing the act . . . [and] . . . an experience of either pleasure, gratification or release at the time of committing the act" (American Psychiatric Association, 1980). There were two criteria in DSM-III, both of which had to be satisfied. First, the individual needed to be "chronically and progressively unable to resist impulses to gambling". Second, gambling had to "compromise, disrupt or damage family, personal and vocational pursuits", as indicated by at least three of seven possible harms (arrest, debts, family disruption, borrowing, inability to account for loss of money, loss of work, needing another person to provide money to relieve a desperate situation). This represented a fairly plain and straightforward set of criteria reflecting problem gambling as a behaviour that is difficult to control despite the fact that it is causing trouble in a number of life domains.

Unfortunately such a comparatively straightforward definition did not fit easily with the way psychiatry, health insurance, and the legal system worked in the USA (Castellani, 2000) and a radical change occurred between 1980 when DSM-III was published and 1987 when the revised version (DSM-III-R) appeared. The revised criteria had been specifically modelled on alcohol and drug dependence. Hence, whilst harm remained in the form of three items about social, educational, occupational, leisure, financial and legal difficulties, 'pathological gambling' was now considered to be a form of 'dependence' and the criterion of impulsiveness was replaced by six items to do with preoccupation, gambling more than intended, the need to increase the size or frequency of bets, restlessness or irritability if unable to gamble, chasing losses, and repeated efforts to cut down or stop (Lesieur and Rosenthal, 1991). At least four of the total of nine criteria were required to be satisfied for a diagnosis. As Lesieur and Rosenthal noted, all criteria, with the exception of 'chasing losses', had their counterpart in the diagnostic criteria for alcohol, heroin, cocaine, or other forms of drug dependence. This move, based on appeasing powerful professional groups, deliberately sought the advantages of equating pathological gambling with addiction to substances. It was as if gambling could only be admitted as a potential addiction by claiming that it mimicked addictive drugs. That was a pity since the result was that the most influential definition of problem gambling rested on a limited and increasingly outmoded definition of addiction which gives a prominent place to 'neuroadaptation' as indicated by such 'symptoms' as tolerance and withdrawal (Orford, 2001).

The current version of DSM is the fourth, which appeared in 1994. The basic idea of a substance-like addiction was retained, as was the basic checklist approach to making a diagnosis: under DSM-III-R rules, four out of nine of the individual criteria had to be present; in DSM-IV, five out of ten. There were, however, substantial changes to the individual criteria. Two had been dropped (frequent gambling when expected to meet social or occupational obligations; continuation of gambling despite the inability to pay mounting debts or despite other significant social, occupational, or legal problems that the person knows to be exacerbated by gambling), new criteria had been added (numbers 5, 7, 8 and 10 – see Table 3.1), and all the rest had been rephrased (e.g. 'restlessness or irritability if unable to gamble',

Table 3.1 DSM-IV criteria for 'pathological gambling' (reproduced with permission from the Diagnostic and Statistical Manual, American Psychiatric Association, 1994, p.618)

A.   Persistent and recurrent maladaptive gambling behaviour as indicated by five (or more) of the following:

   (1)   Is preoccupied with gambling (e.g. preoccupied with reliving past gambling experiences, handicapping or planning the next venture, or thinking of ways to get the money with which to gamble)

   (2)   Needs to gamble with increasing amounts of money in order to achieve the desired excitement

   (3)   Has repeated unsuccessful efforts to control, cut back, or stop gambling

   (4)   Is restless or irritable when attempting to cut down or stop gambling

   (5)   Gambles as a way of escaping from problems or of relieving a dysphoric mood (e.g. feelings of helplessness, guilt, anxiety, depression)

   (6)   After losing money gambling, often returns another day to get even ('chasing' one's losses)

   (7)   Lies to family members, therapists or others to conceal the extent of involvement with gambling

   (8)   Has committed illegal acts such as forgery, fraud, theft, or embezzlement to finance gambling

   (9)   Has jeopardised or lost a significant relationship, job, or educational or career opportunity because of gambling

   (10)   Relies on others to provide money to relieve a desperate financial situation caused by gambling

B.   The gambling behaviour is not better accounted for by a Manic Episode

had become, 'is restless or irritable when attempting to cut down or stop gambling'). The changes appear to have been based on representations that top clinicians in the field had made to Lesieur and Rosenthal, the principal architects of the DSM criteria, and a single rather doubtful piece of research in which those authors had compared the results, item by item, of a questionnaire given to 220 'pathological gamblers' and 104 substance misusing controls (Lesieur and Rosenthal, 1991). The full set of DSM-IV criteria of pathological gambling is shown in Table 3.1.

It may seem strange to many that such an influential operational definition as DSM should have undergone such rapid transformation in such a short period of time, and that it has been constructed in such an apparently haphazard fashion. On the other hand it will not surprise those who have watched a very similar process taking place in the cases of alcohol and drug dependence (Orford, 2001). In the case of 'pathological gambling' there is the added twist of whether it belongs in the section of the Manual devoted to addictions or under the heading of impulse control disorders. In DSM-IV a compromise had been reached whereby the criteria for pathological gambling were based on those for substance addiction, but were placed in the section on impulse control disorders. This has led to an unnecessary and largely arid debate about whether 'pathological gambling' is one thing or the other. The undisputed fact is that many people experience gambling as to some degree out of control and find it difficult to curtail their gambling despite the harm that it is causing. Whether one calls this 'addictive', 'impulsive', or indeed 'compulsive' (to use a word that was favoured by GA and which is still in common usage to refer to problem gambling) is almost arbitrary since there is no universally agreed precise definition of those terms, and they are all terms which problem gamblers use to describe their gambling.

Since the neuroadaptation theory of substance addiction has been a leading model, albeit a limited one, for thinking about problem gambling, it is worth considering the twin ideas of withdrawal symptoms and tolerance in more detail. With respect to withdrawal symptoms the findings of Wray and Dickerson (1981) are often cited. They reported that 30–50 per cent of a sample of GA members described disturbances of mood or behaviour on ceasing to bet. The most commonly reported symptoms were irritability, restlessness, depressed mood, poor concentration and obsessional thoughts. Rosenthal and Lesieur (1992) compared the gambling 'withdrawal symptoms' of the same two groups of people included in the study, mentioned above (Lesieur and Rosenthal, 1991), that was used to make decisions about which items to include in the DSM-IV list. Of the 220 men and women (26 per cent were women unlike Wray and Dickerson's sample all of whom were men) 'pathological gamblers', all of whom met DSM-IV criteria (which at that time had the status of proposed criteria), 87 per cent stated that they felt restless and irritable in the first days or weeks of stopping gambling and substantial numbers experienced psychosomatic withdrawal-like symptoms including insomnia (50 per cent), headaches (36 per cent), upset stomach or diarrhoea (34 per cent), loss of appetite (29 per cent), physical weakness (27 per cent), heart racing or palpitations (26 per cent), shaking (19 per cent), muscle aches or cramps (17 per cent), difficulty breathing (13 per cent) and sweating (12 per cent). Of the 104 controls, all of whom were receiving treatment for alcohol/or drug dependence and who gambled at least occasionally, only 6 per cent stated that they felt restless and irritable when attempting to cut down or stop gambling, and the percentage reporting the individual psychosomatic gambling withdrawal-like symptoms was never greater than 2 per cent. Impressive though these results are, there is of course a degree of circulatory involved since feeling restless or irritable when trying to cut down or stop gambling is one of the criteria contributing to the diagnosis of 'pathological gambling' which members of the gambling group had to meet to be included. Rosenthal and Lesieur (1992) also cited a German study by Meyer (1989) which reported withdrawal-like symptoms amongst gambling machine and roulette players.

A smaller but in some respects tighter study was reported by the present first author and colleagues (Orford et al, 1996). We also compared problem gamblers with a group of people undergoing treatment for problem substance use (all alcohol in this case), with 16 in each group. To be included the gamblers had to acknowledge at least two of 13 possible harmful effects of gambling (e.g. 88 per cent said their financial position had been adversely affected, 69 per cent family relationships, 69 per cent self-respect, and 50 per cent their ability to keep out of legal trouble). On a questionnaire measure of 'attachment', the gamblers as a group were equally attached to their gambling as the drinkers were to drinking. When asked how often they had experienced 28 possible symptoms (14 psychological and 14 physical) that might have occurred 'first thing in the morning during a period of heavy drinking or gambling', the problem drinkers obtained a higher mean score for psychological symptoms and a very much higher score for physical symptoms. In terms of individual symptoms, the only physical symptom which did not show a significant difference between the groups was 'headaches' and of the psychological symptoms the ones that were most nearly equal for the two groups were: feeling miserable or depressed, feeling as if you were going mad, and smoking more. Note that, unlike in the Rosenthal and Lesieur (1992) study, we compared problem gamblers' symptoms when gambling with problem drinkers' symptoms when drinking, which is a stricter test than that used by Rosenthal and Lesieur. Our definition of what constituted a 'withdrawal symptom' was also tighter, since the requirement was that symptoms be experienced first thing in the morning during a period of heavy gambling (or drinking) rather than over a period of days or even weeks when trying to stop or cut down. Our participants were also interviewed about their experiences; the results of which suggested that when symptoms that look as if they might be withdrawal symptoms occurred, their timing rarely corresponded to what would be expected of withdrawal symptoms. They often appeared to be related not so much to the recent cessation of gambling, but rather to the recent experience of loss, feelings of indecision about continued gambling, or worry and preoccupation about debts and other gambling-related harms (Orford et al, 1996).

Others have agreed that such symptoms need not be attributed to drug-like withdrawal. For example Elster (1999) cited Peck (1986, p.464) who wrote, "Compulsive gamblers are never relaxed, but the restlessness, irritability, paranoia, hypersensitivity at this stage [the final stage of 'desperation'] increase to the point that sleep and eating are disturbed." Elster concluded that there was therefore no reason to attribute such feelings to quitting gambling. Even Rosenthal (of Rosenthal and Lesieur, 1992) wrote that:

> In my experience withdrawal has been relatively insignificant both in the course of treatment and as a diagnostic criterion. There may be depression when the person stops gambling. This may be an underlying depression against which the gambling had defended. Alternatively, it may be that once the individual stops gambling he realises how

destructive his behaviour had been (Rosenthal, 1989, p.104, cited by Elster, 1999, p.216).

Tolerance, similarly, is controversial. A number of writers on the subject had assumed that it occurs and that the phenomenon is parallel to the tolerance that occurs to the effects of certain psychoactive drugs. For example in gambling, according to Lesieur (1984, p.44, cited by Elster, 1999, pp.215–216) this has, "an uncanny similarity to 'tolerance' among alcohol, barbiturate, and narcotics addicts. Once the 'high' of a five-hundred-dollar event has been reached, the two-dollar bet no longer achieves the desired effect." Cornish (1978, p.203, cited by Elster, 1999, p.216) similarly referred to, "the possibility that habituation to certain levels of excitement may occur as a function of experience, so that it becomes necessary to raise one's stakes in order to recapture the same subjective quantity of 'thrill'". But in fact tolerance is likely to be a very complex phenomenon in the case of gambling and it is even more difficult to study than are supposed gambling withdrawal symptoms. For one thing escalation of gambling could take a variety of different forms: playing more frequently, for larger stakes, or against higher odds, to name just three possibilities (Elster, 1999). Furthermore, when escalation does occur, it is very difficult in practice to separate any real tolerance or habituation to the excitement or 'high', from the need to escalate gambling in order to chase losses or repay debts (Elster, 1999), or indeed from increases in disposable income which may come about with increasing age. Not surprisingly, there have been no satisfactory studies of tolerance and gambling.

In fact whether problem gambling matches up to the criterion of addiction as defined by tolerance and withdrawal is probably beside the point. As Lea et al (1987, p.270 cited by Elster, 1999, p.208) stated, "the issue of whether [gambling] can properly be labelled an addiction will probably not be resolved until the nature of addiction in general is better understood". Although tolerance and withdrawal were once thought to be the essential hallmarks of drug addiction, that is no longer the case. Although they appear as individual criteria in DSM and ICD checklists for drug dependence, their presence is not essential for such diagnoses. This is partly because the drug addiction scene of recent years has become more varied, with a big part now being played by drugs such as cocaine and the amphetamines which do not produce such obvious tolerance and withdrawal as heroin, and partly because theories of addiction have moved on, placing much more emphasis now upon positive incentive motivation and much less upon drive-reduction motivation created by withdrawal and the relief of withdrawal symptoms by further drug taking (Jaffe, 1992; Orford, 2001).

No wonder, then, that there is confusion about whether problem or pathological gambling can be an addiction. This confusion is reflected in the writings of Walker who is one who has considered the question carefully and been sceptical about it. In his book *The Psychology of Gambling* (1992) he wrote, "If pathological gambling is an addiction, then we must show that it operates through the same physiological processes as drug addictions and fulfils the same functions for the addictive individual" (pp.180-181). Elsewhere he expresses uncertainty about whether gambling can even be addictive in a broader sense: ". . . until gambling can be shown to have the properties of a psychological addiction, the efforts to generalise theories of addiction to include gambling are likely to remain futile" (Walker, 1989, p.198). In his book, however, he referred to ". . . growing evidence for a unitary structure underlying a range of psychological addictions . . . Whether such a theory will apply to heavy gambling remains to be seen" (1992, p.184). Others, including the present first author, have argued for the existence of a group of 'excessive appetites' (Orford, 2001) or 'behavioural addictions' (Griffiths, 1996), including drug addiction, alcohol dependence, problem gambling and binge eating, which share the common characteristics of out-of-control behaviour which is difficult to modify despite the harm that it is causing. Excessive gambling has even been referred to as a 'pure' addiction for the simple reason that it does not involve the ingestion of a substance (Custer and Milt, 1985, cited by Walker, 1992).

Not only has confusion and controversy reigned over the meaning of addiction, but it has also not been difficult for the legal profession to pick holes in the DSM definitions. Castellani (2000) recounts, for example, how the insanity defence of Torniero was damaged by cross-questioning of expert witnesses about the apparent inconsistency of DSM-III (which was then in force) on the question of whether pathological gamblers were *unable* to resist or simply showed a *failure* to resist impulses to gamble. One expression was used in the introduction to the diagnosis, the other in the first line of the actual criteria. Although the distinction may be too fine a one for clinicians to argue about, it is of course crucial in law. One expert witness admitted that the inconsistency was simply a mistake of drafting.

In an article, 'Problem gambling: one view from the industry side', Bybee (1988, cited by Castellani, 2000), who was a licensed attorney and consultant in Las Vegas and in his career had been a regulator of the gaming industry in Nevada, president of a casino hotel in New Jersey, a legal representative for several casino operators in Nevada, and a lobbyist for casinos in New Jersey, took the concept of 'pathological gambling' to task on a number of grounds. Castellani noted that, as well as preferring the term *problem* gambling to *pathological* gambling, Bybee used such terms as 'over-indulgence' and 'abhorrent behavior'. Amongst Bybee's points was the argument that people with gambling problems often had other problems as well, and hence it was unreasonable and unjust to the gambling industry to pigeonhole people as 'pathological gamblers'. The second point was that labelling people's problems as 'pathological gambling' implied that their excessive gambling was not their fault or responsibility. By examining the literature put out by a prominent gambling treatment facility (the Brecksville Program for the Treatment of Compulsive Gambling at Cleveland Veterans Administration Medical Center), Bybee suggested that treatment professionals were taking an Alice-in-Wonderland approach, making it up as they went along, not only to the advantage of their clients but also of themselves and their careers. He pointed, for example, to the apparent inconsistency in the statement that 'pathological gambling' was an illness and therefore "not the gambler's fault that he or she has lost control of gambling", and the statement that when it came to treatment:

> The victim must be willing to do most of the actual work. The professional is, at best, a teacher and advisor; no one can assume responsibility for anyone else's gambling. So, although we believe that the gambler has an illness that is out of control, we do not treat the problem with traditional medical methods. The gambler is expected to become fully responsible for this treatment and his life in general (Brecksville Program brochure, p.304, cited by Castellani, 2000, pp.129-130).

Bybee certainly put his finger on a matter that has intrigued and perplexed students of addiction. It is a paradox, and one that is very familiar to AA, GA and all who get involved in trying to treat or help people with addictive behaviours, that people can voluntarily take control over forms of behaviour that previously seemed so out of control that they threatened to ruin or shorten their lives. This is as true of the most uncontroversial addictions, such as addiction to heroin or nicotine, as it is to problem gambling.

Others have expressed serious reservations about the diagnostic approach to problem or 'pathological gambling', whilst not rejecting the idea that for many people gambling can be seriously out of control. Dickerson (1990) recognised that the inclusion of 'pathological gambling' in the DSM system had been a major factor encouraging the development of treatment and research, but also recognised the conceptual and operational difficulties in trying to create an objective, diagnostic category. He preferred a broader concept of 'excessive' or 'problematic' gambling, lying on a continuum from less to more problematic, categorised by the frequency of gambling, the harmful effects, and particularly the degree of impaired control over gambling (Dickerson and Baron, 2000).

McConaghy (1991) also pointed out the arbitrariness of drawing a line between those whose gambling problems were sufficient for a diagnosis and those whose problems fell below the line. He described, for example, the case of a 65 year old woman who sought help and was successfully treated for a gambling problem although she did not satisfy DSM-III-R criteria.

She believed her gambling had been excessive for 15 years and had become a "real problem" in the previous 18 months. She had "become fascinated" by slot machines which she had played at a club in her late thirties but had only more recently had the opportunity to play regularly once her children had left home. The amount of her losses had gradually increased, until recently when she had been playing machines six days a week, often taking US $100 at a time and staying all afternoon, losing about $2,000 a year and $600 in the previous month. She still had sufficient money for household expenses but would have preferred to spend the money helping her children financially and giving her grandchildren gifts and she frequently felt guilty about this. Her husband was now retired, and himself played bowls for several hours several times a week, and he was not complaining about her gambling. At follow up a month after treatment she described a "huge improvement". She had been playing machines no more than once a week, taking $30 at a time and only staying an hour and a half.

The DSM criteria have been found by many to be too restrictive in practice. One common solution has been to distinguish 'pathological gambling' (most serious) from 'problem gambling' (less serious) (e.g. Shaffer et al, 1997). Becoña's (1993) solution was to employ three categories associated with a decreasingly severe threshold for definition. Four or more symptoms on the DSM-III-R list resulted in a diagnosis of 'pathological gambling' in accordance with others' usage. Two or three of these symptoms were sufficient for 'problem gambling'. Finally, if a person had one or no symptoms on this list but spent more than 25 per cent of personal income or dedicated two or more hours a day to gambling, he or she was considered an 'excessive social gambler'.

Controversy continues, therefore, about exactly how to define problem gambling, whether it can be thought of as an addiction like dependence on a drug, and even about the best term to be used to describe it. That the phenomenon exists, however, is no longer in dispute. There are individuals whose gambling is so excessive, and so out of control, that they and their families experience serious social, financial and/or legal harm as a result. How many such individuals and families there are is another question.

Estimating the prevalence of problem gambling

Recent years have seen attempts in a number of countries to estimate the prevalence of problem gambling. More studies of this kind have been carried out in the USA than in any other country and the US studies were summarised by the National Research Council (NRC, 1999) drawing on a meta-analysis carried out by Shaffer et al (1997) of 120 studies carried out in various states and provinces of the USA and Canada. No fewer than 25 different sets of questions had been used in those studies, although many were based upon the DSM criteria, and one – the South Oaks Gambling

Screen (SOGS) – had been used far more often than any other scale, to the extent that it had become "the de facto standard operationalization of pathological and problem gambling for adult populations" (NRC, 1999, p.68). SOGS was developed by Lesieur and Blume (1987) based on the DSM-III-R criteria. The 20 items include questions about going back another day to win back money lost, gambling more than intended, being criticised by others over gambling, feeling guilty about gambling, having difficulty stopping gambling, and losing time from work because of it. No less than half the items, however, refer to borrowing money to gamble from various sources (household money, spouse, other relatives or in-laws, credit cards, etc.). In most of the surveys this questionnaire has been administered over the telephone.

The restrictive nature of the criteria for 'pathological gambling', apparently omitting many people with significant gambling problems, has led most survey researchers to adopt two levels of definition. Five or more affirmative answers to the 20 SOGS questions have generally been taken as an indication of 'pathological gambling' and three or four as an indication of 'problem gambling not amounting to pathological gambling'. Shaffer et al (1997) referred to these two groups combined as representing 'disordered gambling'.

The US National Research Council (1999) identified twelve studies using SOGS carried out with adults in different states in the USA, all carried out in the 1990s, which produced figures for 1-year prevalence (i.e. respondents were asked about gambling problems occurring at any time in the previous twelve months). Estimates for pathological and problem gambling combined ranged from 1.2 to 4.9 per cent (median 2.9 per cent). Figures were obviously smaller if the estimate was confined to pathological gambling (ranging from 0.5 to 2.1 per cent, median 0.9 per cent), but larger if based only on those respondents who gambled at all in the last year (ranging from 2.7 to 10.0 per cent, median 4.4 per cent, 10 studies). Although from a policy standpoint it is recent problem gambling that is most relevant (NRC, 1999), several earlier surveys had asked solely about lifetime prevalence, a figure which obviously includes people who believe they have had problems in the past but not recently. Estimates of lifetime prevalence of pathological and problem gambling combined ranged from 2.3 to 12.9 per cent (median 5.4 per cent, 15 studies).

All those studies were confined to individual US states. Three national studies have been attempted in the USA. One was carried out in the 1970s at a time when many forms of gambling now available in the USA were illegal, and before DSM criteria and the SOGS questionnaire had been developed (Kallick et al, 1979). That study estimated only the lifetime prevalence of what was referred to as 'probable compulsive gambling'. That figure was estimated at 0.8 per cent, with a further 2.3 per cent identified as 'potential' compulsive gamblers. The second national US survey was conducted much more recently by the National Opinion Research Center (NORC, 1999) commissioned by the National Gambling Impact Study Commission. The authors of that report took the view that SOGS, based on DSM-III-R, had been overtaken by the publication of DSM-IV, and in addition had deficiencies as a scale for estimating population prevalence (see below). Consequently they developed a new scale – the NORC DSM Screen for Gambling Problems (NODS) – based on DSM-IV. This was a somewhat cumbersome seventeen-item scale with between one and three items corresponding to each of the DSM criteria. It produced a score out of 10, those scoring 5 or more being referred to as 'pathological gamblers', 3 or 4 as 'problem gamblers' and 1 or 2 as 'at-risk gamblers'. A further complication in that study was that NODS questions were only put to those who either acknowledged ever losing $100 or more in a single day of gambling, or ever having been behind at least $100 across an entire year of gambling at some point in their lives.

Yet another controversial aspect of that study was the attempt that was made to correct for the likely underestimate obtained from a random population survey. The basic survey was carried out by telephone with 2,417 adults, which is actually a rather small number for estimating a problem affecting a small percentage of the population (for example they found only three past-year pathological gamblers by that method). It has also been pointed out that people with gambling problems are more likely than others to be missed by such methods (Walker, 1992; Lesieur, 1994; APC, 1999). NORC attempted to correct their figures by drawing a supplementary 'patron' survey of 530 people contacted directly at lottery ticket outlets, casinos in Nevada and New Jersey, riverboat casinos, American Indian reservation casinos, pari-mutuel locations, and locations with video lottery terminals. Using a complicated method of weighting, the estimates based on the telephone survey were adjusted upwards. The past year combined pathological and problem gambling prevalence estimate was 0.5 per cent based on the telephone survey alone, and 1.3 per cent after adjustment (the figure for the patron survey alone was 10.2 per cent), which is still much lower than the median 2.9 per cent from studies reviewed by NRC (1999).

Another, similarly sized, national US telephone survey was reported by Welte et al (2001). The survey was conducted with those of 18 years and older between August 1999 and October 2000. For comparative purposes it had the advantage of using the SOGS (as well as a scale based on DSM-IV). One-year prevalence of 'pathological gambling' (five or more positive SOGS answers) was estimated to be 1.9 per cent and of 'pathological' plus problem gambling 5.5 per cent.

Using the most cautious figure of 2.9 per cent as the best estimate of the 1-year prevalence of combined pathological and problem gambling amongst US adults, NRC (1999) estimated there to be approximately 5.7 million US citizens of 18 years or older who were currently or had been

Table 3.2 Summary of international problem-gambling prevalence estimates (according to SOGS threshold 5 or more)

	N	1-year adult prevalence %	Confidence interval	Source of information
Sweden 1997–98	7,139	0.6	0.4–0.8	Rönnberg et al (1999)
USA 1977–97	Mean of several state surveys	1.1	0.9–1.4	APC (1999)
USA 1999–2000	2,638	1.9	not stated	Welte et al (2001)
New Zealand 1991	3,933	1.2	0.9–1.5	Abbott and Volberg (1996)
Spain 1991–94	Mean of 4 regional surveys	1.6	1.4–1.7	Becoña et al (1995)
Australia 1999	10,500	2.3	1.9–2.7	APC (1999)

within the last 12 months people with gambling problems. Although that represents only a small minority of the population, the absolute number is spectacularly large. By comparing this figure with figures from the best national survey data on alcohol and other drug problems, they were able to show that, although the gambling figure of 2.9 per cent was less than one third the estimate of the 1-year prevalence of alcohol dependence and abuse amongst US adults (9.7 per cent), the gambling figure was not far off the estimate for drug dependence and abuse (3.6 per cent).

Similar surveys have been carried out in New Zealand, Australia and Sweden, as well as in most of the provinces of Canada and a number of the regions of Spain. Results of national studies using a common threshold of five plus on SOGS are summarised in Table 3.2. The Swedish study (Rönnberg et al, 1999) is of particular interest to us, being the first national prevalence study to be carried out in a European country. A random sample of 8,500 15–74 year olds, stratified for sex, age (five groups) and education (three groups) was recruited using the Swedish National Register. The main sample was supplemented with an extra 1,000 randomly chosen 15–17 year olds and 500 randomly chosen people born outside Sweden (because there was reason to believe that gambling prevalence might be particularly high in those groups). An attempt was made to reach all selected participants by telephone, which produced a 68 per cent response rate. The remainder were sent a questionnaire through the post, which produced an additional 4 per cent. It is interesting to note that, although the numbers were small, prevalence was significantly higher amongst those who received the postal questionnaire. One explanation is that a higher rate of problem gambling is to be found amongst those who are the more reluctant to take part in such a survey.

Rönnberg et al referred to those scoring three or more on SOGS as 'problem gamblers' (which produced a 1-year prevalence of 2.0 per cent), and all those scoring 5 or more as 'probable pathological gamblers' (a prevalence of 0.6 per cent). Results of asking participants how much they spent on gambling in the previous month (Rönnberg et al showed some awareness of the problems involved in asking people such questions – see below) was that an average of 194 SEK (the equivalent of 21 Euros) was said to have been spent on gambling. The distribution of spend was very skewed, however, with the majority reporting spending 100 SEK or less and, at the other end of the scale, 3 per cent reported spending 1,000 SEK or more (equivalent to 30 per cent of expenditure by the whole sample on gambling).

Until the British Gambling Prevalence Survey, which will be summarised in Chapter 5 of the present book, there had been no national or even regional adult problem gambling prevalence survey in Britain. It had only been possible to make rough estimates, and the best of these had been made back in the 1970s when the national gambling scene was a very different one (e.g. Dickerson, 1974; Cornish, 1978).

An interesting later survey, confined to British casino patrons, was reported by Fisher (1996, 2000). The survey was commissioned by a consortium of five of the largest casino firms operating in the country, and a representative sample of 40 casinos in London and the provinces were involved (only those London casinos at the 'top end' of the market were excluded on the grounds that their customers would not be typical; even then more than half of those interviewed at London casinos were not British nationals). Fisher used a scale of ten questions based upon DSM-IV, with response options of 'never', 'once or twice', 'sometimes' and 'often' for each item. 'Often' was required for a positive score for all items except the last three (committed illegal acts to finance gambling; jeopardised or lost a significant relationship, educational or job opportunities because of gambling; been bailed out financially by others) for which 'once or twice' was sufficient. Fisher rejected a diagnostic approach and the term 'pathological gambling', preferring to view problem gambling as lying on a continuum. She referred to those scoring five or more of the ten items as 'severe problem gamblers', and those scoring three or four (provided at least one of the last three items was included) as 'problem gamblers'.

On that basis Fisher estimated 2.2 per cent of British casino patrons to be severe problem gamblers and an additional 5.2 per cent problem gamblers. Careful reading of her report is necessary, however, to appreciate how those figures were arrived at. In fact, of the 1105 people interviewed in the casinos, 7.7 per cent scored as past year severe problem gamblers and an additional 8.6 per cent problem gamblers. Fisher then used what the respondents said about how frequently they visited casinos to adjust those figures downward. The argument was that those who visit casinos more frequently were more likely to be available to be approached for an interview, and on that basis the results from the less frequent attenders were given greater weight. That is a not unreasonable argument, but there is a need to be careful when interpreting results. It might be more accurate to say that of those people present in British casinos at any one time around 16 per cent might be expected to have gambling problems (8 per cent severe), whilst the best estimate of the figure for all those who frequent British casinos at any time in a single year is around 7 per cent (2 per cent severe).

Criticisms of prevalence studies

The methods involved in these prevalence studies have been criticised on a number of grounds. One of the most frequently voiced criticisms has been that the SOGS, despite its widespread use in population surveys, is an inappropriate technique for such studies because it was validated by checking how well it discriminated a clinical sample of problem gamblers and a control group (Dickerson and Hinchy, 1988; Walker, 1992; Walker and Dickerson, 1996). Specifically, the criticism is that the rate of false positives (those who are mis-classified as problem gamblers when really they are not) may be very large in a general population survey, even though the *percentage* of false positives is quite low. In the original validational work the false positive rate amongst the non-problem gamblers was 7 per cent. In a case-control study, with roughly equal numbers of 'cases' and controls, that is an acceptably low percentage: the large majority of positives will be true positives i.e. 'cases' who scored positive on the test. But in the general population, where the real percentage of non-problem gamblers may be in the region of as high as 97–99 per cent, a false positive rate of 7 per cent means that as many as two out of every three people who score positive on the test will actually be false positives (Walker, 1992). Hence the estimated prevalence rate may be much exaggerated. Table 3.3 explains this effect and some of the terms are those used, such as 'sensitivity' and 'specificity'.

In their prevalence study in New Zealand, Abbott and Volberg (1996) attempted to overcome such problems by using a two-stage design in which a large general population telephone survey using SOGS was followed by quite lengthy face-to-face interviews with all those who scored as 'pathological gamblers' in the telephone survey plus a sample of those who had scored negative. After comparing the results of the interviews, using DSM-III-R criteria, and the telephone test results, Abbott and Volberg concluded that the telephone-administered SOGS had actually performed rather well. Sensitivity was calculated to be 0.86, specificity 0.72.

Unfortunately Abbott and Volberg appear to have got themselves into some deep statistical waters as a result of using what otherwise sounds like a sensible two-stage procedure. Gambino (1999) pointed out that a bias had

Table 3.3 Understanding the theory of screening (based on information provided by Johnson et al, 1997, Gambino, 1999, and Rönnberg et al, 1999) (PG = problem gamblers, NPG = non-problem gamblers, TPs = true positives, FPs = false positives, FNs = false negatives, TNs = true negatives)

		(1) Validated on a small clinical sample with equal proportions of PGs and NPGs and good sensitivity and specificity			(2) Used in a large population survey, assuming sensitivity and specificity remain the same and the true prevalence of PG is 1%		
		True status			True status		
		PG	NPG	Total	PG	NPG	Total
Status according to the test	PG	95 (TPs)	5 (FPs)	100	95 (TPs)	495 (FPs)	590
	NPG	5 (FNs)	95 (TNs)	100	5 (FNs)	9,405 (TNs)	9,410
	Total	100	100	200	100	9,900	10,000

Sensitivity
TPs/(TPs + FNs)   = 95/100 = 0.95   = 95/100 = 0.95

Specificity
TNs/(TNs + FPs)   = 95/100 = 0.95   = 9,405/9,900 = 0.95

Positive predictive value
TPs/(TPs + FPs)   = 95/100 = 0.95   = 95/590 = 0.16

Negative predictive value
TNs/(TNs + FNs)   = 95/100 = 0.95   = 9,405/9,410 = 1.00

True prevalence
= 100/10,000 = 1.0%
Estimated prevalence
= 590/10,000 = 5.9%

been introduced into their calculations by the selection of respondents for the second stage. Had it been possible to interview everyone at the second stage (obviously an impossibility) then Gambino's estimate was that both false positives and false negatives would have been greater. If false negatives had been substantially greater, the sensitivity of SOGS would have been considerably lower than Abbott and Volberg's estimate of 0.86, which would be a factor leading to *under*-estimating prevalence, partly offsetting the likely much increased false positive rate in a whole population sample (which decreases the 'positive predictive value' of the screening test and inflates the estimate of prevalence).

   This controversy does suggest a number of things. First it is evident that the epidemiological study of problem gambling is by no means a straightforward business, and many problems remain. Another, more positive, conclusion is that the classification errors produced in a large survey by a scale such as SOGS (and there are always such errors in epidemiological work) cannot be assumed to be solely in the direction of a large number of false positives and hence an over-estimate of prevalence, but might also be expected to be in the direction of a large number of false negatives contributing to an under-estimate of prevalence. There are, of course, other reasons for believing that prevalence figures might be under-estimates, if it can be assumed that people with gambling problems are more likely to be in debt and have their telephones cut off, might otherwise be unavailable for screening or interviewing, might more likely be in hospital or prison, or might simply be more inclined than other people to under-report the extent of their gambling (Walker, 1992; Lesieur, 1994; APC, 1999).

A large part of the difficulty about validation of methods for estimating the prevalence of problem gambling is the lack of an agreed 'gold standard' against which to validate scales such as SOGS. With hindsight, Abbott and Volberg's (1999) view was that their face-to-face interviews, which were carried out by trained interviewers who were not clinicians, was an alternative, but not necessarily more valid, assessment of problem gambling than the SOGS questionnaire. Their conclusion, like Gambino's (1999), was that more than one measure of problem gambling should be used simultaneously.

A number of alternatives to SOGS exist including scales based on DSM-IV criteria (e.g. Fisher, 1996; NORC, 1999; Sproston et al, 2000) and GA's '20 Questions'. Johnson et al (1997) even reported that just two questions, which they called the 'Lie/Bet Questionnaire', were alone highly sensitive and specific in the detection of problem gambling. The two items were based on the DSM-IV criteria two and seven: 'Have you ever felt the need to bet more and more money?' 'Have you ever had to lie to people important to you about how much you gambled?' Dickerson and Hinchy (1988) favoured the use of the following six questions: (a) losing more than can afford six or more times; (b) losing more than planned on four or five of the last five sessions; (c) usually or always chases losses; (d) betting causes debts; (e) I want to stop or cut back; (f) I've tried stopping. Holding strongly to the view that gambling problems exist on a continuum, and that any one estimate can only be arbitrary, they produced four separate estimates of the prevalence of excessive gambling in the Australian Capital Territory. At level one it was necessary to bet once or more a week and report either or both of (a) and (b). If in addition at least one of (c), (d), (e) or (f) were present then this qualified for level two; with at least two of those items, level three was reached; and with at least three of those four questions, level four. As a result their prevalence estimates ranged all the way from 0.25 per cent (level four only) to 1.73 per cent (levels one to four combined).

Table 3.4 Vignette 1 used by Blaszczynski, Dumlao and Lange, 1997, in their
study of the interpretation of gambling spend

Vignette 1

You recently decided to gamble $120 on your favourite form of gambling. You initially
won $60 but then following a bad run of luck, lost $100. Feeling tired, you decided to
leave and return home.

How much did you spend on gambling?

Walker and Dickerson (1996), like Rönnberg et al (1999), were of the
view that prevalence studies should also include a detailed assessment of
people's expenditure on gambling. This matter will be taken up later in
Chapter 5 when we discuss the British Gambling Prevalence Survey. For
the moment suffice it to say that assessing a person's spending on gambling
raises yet further problems as Blaszczynski et al (1997) have nicely illustrated. Suspecting that the apparently simple question 'How much do you
spend gambling?' might be open to a variety of different interpretations,
they presented a sample of 181 medical students with five case vignettes
describing various scenarios of wins and losses during a gambling session.
The first of these is shown in Table 3.4. The students were asked a number
of questions about each vignette, including the key question, 'How much
was spent gambling?' Around two-thirds of the students (64 per cent in the
case of the vignette 1 for example) interpreted 'spent' in terms of net
expenditure (i.e. in the case of vignette 1, $40, calculated by subtracting
($120 + 60 – 100) from the initial investment of $120). Quite a number (17
per cent for vignette 1) interpreted it to mean initial investment (i.e. $120).
Smaller numbers calculated the figure by considering the initial amount
invested as a loss together with losses incurred during the session less any
winnings (i.e. $120 + 100 – 60, or $160), or simply the loss during the
session ($100). Only five students interpreted spend as turnover i.e. invest-
ment plus winnings (or $180). Further complications were introduced in
other vignettes which involved uncertainty about the definition of a session
(the gambler went away and came back to continue gambling later) or
involved incidental expenses such as travel or eating which were included as
spending on gambling by some students. Needless to say, unless questions
about spending are made very precise, further uncertainty will be introduced if the form of gambling or the time period to which questions refer
are not specified.

Women problem gamblers

The sex ratios amongst problem gamblers found in these surveys are of
particular interest since they show that very sizeable minorities of detected

problem gamblers, and occasionally even a majority, are women. The US NRC (1999) report, for example, found that amongst 18 studies carried out in the USA, the median percentage of women amongst problem and 'pathological' gamblers was 38 per cent. This is despite the fact that the popular stereotype of problem gambling has been that it is an almost entirely male preserve, and despite the fact that studies have almost always found samples of problem gamblers in treatment to be overwhelmingly male (e.g. between 86 per cent and 93 per cent in five US states according to Volberg, 1994, cited by Crisp et al, 2000). It seems likely that women's and men's gambling take somewhat different forms, in that women and men may be motivated to gamble by different factors (Trevorrow and Moore, 1998), and that women and men with gambling problems may have different treatment needs. It may even be the case that a scale such as SOGS, perhaps based on the stereotype of a male problem gambler, is less sensitive to the forms of gambling problems experienced by women (NORC, 1999).

Hraba and Lee's (1996) random household telephone survey of 1,000 adults in Iowa, USA, is just one of a number that illustrate sex differences in the form of gambling. Overall, men reported more gambling than women, but this was due to the greater 'scope' of their gambling rather than the differences in gambling frequency or quantity. A higher percentage of women than men reported any recent bingo gambling (38 per cent versus 22 per cent), and very slightly more women than men reported recent casino gambling (28 per cent versus 25 per cent). Men, on the other hand, more frequently reported betting on games in public (40 per cent versus 19 per cent), sporting events in which people participated themselves (25 per cent versus 9 per cent), other sporting events (40 per cent versus 24 per cent), and betting on the stock market (35 per cent versus 19 per cent). The most frequently reported form of gambling for both sexes was a lottery (75 per cent of men and 73 per cent of women). In Rönnberg et al's (1999) Swedish study too, women reported more often playing 'fast lotteries', 'bingo-lotto', and bingo, with men reporting most forms more frequently than women, and higher expenditure overall. Rates of last year 'probable pathological gambling' were 0.9 per cent for men and 0.2 per cent for women.

Trevorrow and Moore (1998) suggested that along with a normalisation of gambling in Australia had come a 'feminisation' (or at least 'andro-gynisation'). Their particular concern was machine gambling in the state of Victoria which a previous study (Brown and Coventry, 1997, cited by Trevorrow and Moore, 1998) had suggested was now more common in women than men. In their own study of women recruited in machine gambling venues, around local shopping complexes, or from recreational areas of a suburban university, they identified a group of women who were spending considerable amounts of time and money on machine playing, and often scored as problem gamblers on SOGS, gambling more money than intended, chasing losses, feeling guilty, experiencing criticism from others about their gambling, arguing with others over money used to gamble, and 'borrowing' from housekeeping money to support their gambling habit. Crisp et al (2000), also reporting from Victoria, Australia, found that as many as 46 per cent of individuals who sought help from one of a number of publicly funded problem-gambling counselling services in Victoria during a 12-month period between 1996 and 1997, were women. Compared to men who had sought help from the same services, women reported significantly smaller amounts of debt, and were less likely to report legal problems or problems in the workplace associated with gambling. In contrast, they were more likely to report problems of a psychological kind and to have physical symptoms associated with gambling. Women clients were positive for only slightly (but significantly) fewer DSM-IV criteria (an average of 5.8 compared with men's 6.1). Women were more likely to report playing gaming machines or bingo (although the latter was only a minority pursuit), but were less likely than men to report placing bets in betting offices, on course at the races, or playing cards.

Adolescent problem gambling

The factor that is most strikingly associated with the prevalence of problem gambling is age. Although there has been some attention given to the dangers of problem gambling for adults of retirement age (McNeilly and Burke, 2000), all the evidence so far accumulated shows that it is adolescents who are particularly at risk. In Britain a number of surveys of young people and gambling were reported in the late 1980s and early 1990s following Moran's (1987) early survey of head teachers. Because some machine gambling has been legally available to children of any age in the UK, and because this form of gambling appears to have particularly great addiction potential, British surveys, unlike those in the USA, have focused upon this form of gambling. These studies were reviewed by Griffiths (1990, 1995a) and by Fisher and Griffiths (1995). Particularly large surveys were carried out by the UK National Housing and Town Planning Council (1988) and by the Spectrum Children's Trust (1988) and by Graham (1988), Lee (1989), Rands and Hooper (1990), Walton (1990) and Huxley and Carroll (1992) (all cited and reviewed by Griffiths, 1995a). All were questionnaire studies carried out with school children in age groups ranging from between 10 and 13 years to 15 or 16 years old. All found that the experience of gambling was a common one for adolescents and that substantial minorities reported experiencing problems associated with their gambling. The National Housing and Town Planning Council (1988) study was the largest and the most nationally representative, and its findings were typical. It involved nearly 10,000 school children aged 13 to 16 years from 17 different schools in six different local education authorities. Sixty-four per cent of pupils reported gambling at some time in the last 12 months, and 14 per cent gambling weekly. Seventeen per cent reported financing gambling by using lunch money, 7 per cent by stealing, and 6 per cent truanting.

Only one substantial British study (Fisher, 1992, 1993a) of adolescent gambling from that period used a standard scale to estimate the prevalence of problem gambling. Fisher's samples consisted of the 467 11–16 year olds who were present on the morning of the survey in the one local authority secondary school serving a single seaside town (where the accessibility of 'amusement arcades' to young people was particularly great). For that study Fisher adapted the DSM-IV criteria (at that time the nine criteria proposed by Lesieur and Rosenthal, 1991, rather than the ten finally included in DSM-IV) so that they would be suitable for adolescents (what she called the DSM-IV-J). Of all the children surveyed, 62 per cent reported gambling at some time in the last 12 months, 17 per cent gambling at least weekly, and 5.6 per cent satisfied four or more of the DSM-IV-J criteria, thus scoring in the 'probable pathological gambling' range. Harmful consequences of gambling, each reported much more frequently by those with gambling problems, included truancy, stealing, trouble with parents and/or teachers, borrowing money, using lunch money, irritability, and poor school work. Gambling on fruit machines was the commonest form of regular gambling, two-thirds or more of those with gambling problems saying that in a usual week they spent an hour or more in an 'amusement arcade' and spent £5 or more.

A few years later Fisher (1999) reported the first prevalence study of adolescent problem gambling in England and Wales. That study is particularly significant here since it complements the British Gambling Prevalence Survey to be summarised later in this book, but which was confined to those of 16 years of age or older. Fisher's study involved 9,774 pupils in two year groups (year 8 or 12–13 year olds, and year 10 or 14–15 year olds) in 114 local authority schools (46 per cent of all schools approached, a figure that might have been higher had the sponsors not required the survey to be carried out in May and June (of 1997), a particularly difficult time of year for schools). For that study further modifications were made to the DSM-IV-J. Of the nine criteria included in her earlier study (Fisher, 1992, 1993a), one had been dropped (the original number nine: 'Needed another individual to provide money to relieve a desperate financial situation produced by gambling') and a new one had appeared ('Often spends much more money on gambling than intended'). In addition the questionnaire was now cast in a multiple response (MR) form, each question having four response options: never, once or twice, sometimes, often (different questions requiring different level of response in order for the criterion to be met). Fisher referred to the resulting scale as the DSM-IV-MR-J.

A further feature of that study, which constitutes a possible limitation, was that the prevalence of problem gambling, according to DSM-IV-MR-J was assessed twice, separately, once referring to fruit-machine gambling, and secondly referring to National Lottery scratchcards. The possibility of problem gambling in relation to other gambling forms appears not to have been assessed, presumably on the grounds that fruit machines and scratch-cards were most likely to give rise to problems for adolescents. The resulting prevalence estimate may therefore be a slight under-estimate. Furthermore, in view of the association between problem gambling and truancy, found in Fisher's study as in nearly all others, prevalence estimates based on those present in school are likely to be slight under-estimates for that reason also (although in Fisher's study, where four or more pupils were absent from a class, up to two follow-up visits were arranged to try to complete the dataset).

The prevalence estimate for problem gambling on fruit machines and/or National Lottery scratchcards in the Fisher (1999) study was 5.6 per cent, a figure identical to that reported in her earlier study based in one small town (Fisher, 1992, 1993a). This is probably to be interpreted as 1-year pre-valence since five of the twelve DSM-IV-J items specify 'in the past year', six are phrased in the present tense (e.g. 'do you . . .') and one might be interpreted as being both current and lifetime (Gupta and Derevensky, 1998). Of the problem gamblers, 62 per cent had a problem with fruit machines, 17 per cent with NL scratchcards, and 21 per cent with both. Of those identified as problem gamblers, 50 per cent reported spending school dinner money or fare money to gamble, 43 per cent stealing from the family to gamble, and 27 per cent stealing from outside the family to gamble.

In addition, a small number of studies have focused upon the involve-ment of British adolescents in playing NL games. Fisher and Balding (1996, cited by Fisher, 1999) found that 15 per cent of a national sample of 7,200 12–15 year olds had spent their own money on the NL during the week prior to the survey. Pugh and Webley (2000), reporting a study of 256 pupils aged 13–15 years in four schools in one English county, carried out in 1995 within the first year of the operation of the NL, found that over half had already participated in the NL draw game (56 per cent) and NL scratchcards (54 per cent), substantial numbers (24 per cent and 17 per cent respectively) playing those games weekly. Although some had tickets pur-chased for them, the large majority had been sold tickets illegally (it is illegal to sell NL draw or scratchcard tickets to those under 16 years of age). Of those who had purchased tickets or scratchcards for themselves, only 6.3 per cent and 6.6 per cent respectively claimed ever to have been refused at a point of sale. In Fisher's (1999) national prevalence study, carried out two years later, there was a suggestion that retailers were challenging young people more often. Even so the reported success rate for attempted under-age purchases of NL products was 56 per cent, and was very similar for draw tickets and scratchcards.

The message that adolescents are particularly prone to problem gambling comes across just as strongly, if not more strongly, from the larger number of studies carried out in the USA and Canada. Those studies have been reviewed on a number of occasions (Jacobs, 1989; Shaffer and Hall, 1996; NRC, 1999). Summarising the results from five such surveys from the USA (involving a total of over 2,500 students) and one from Canada (involving over 1,500 students), Jacobs (1989) found a median 9 per cent of students for whom gambling was reported to have harmed family relationships, 9 per cent reporting that they had committed illegal acts to obtain gambling money or to pay gambling debts, 5 per cent who would like to stop gambling but who could not or who believed gambling was out of control, and 5 per cent who met GA or DSM-III criteria for 'compulsive' or 'pathological' gambling. If percentages are based upon only those who had any experience of gambling (roughly half the total number) then they obviously appear greater still. For example, a median 20 per cent of those who had gambled at all in the previous 12 months said they would like to stop but could not or believed their gambling was out of control. Dealing in drugs, working for a bookmaker, selling sports cards, and shoplifting, were among the more frequent illegal means used by high-school students for obtaining money to gamble or to pay gambling debts. Since the large majority of high-school students represented in these surveys were under 18 years of age, the gambling activities reported by them would themselves have been illegal. More than a third reported their first experience with gambling for money before 11 years of age, and three-quarters or more before they were 15. Jacobs concluded that as many as seven million juveniles might have been gambling for money with or without adult awareness or approval in the USA at that time, and that more than one million of them were probably experiencing serious gambling-related problems.

Shaffer and Hall (1996) conducted a meta-analysis of twelve reports of nine separate studies of adolescent problem gambling in the USA or Canada reported between 1985 and 1994. A number of different sets of criteria and questionnaires had been used including the GA 20 questions, the DSM-III criteria, a version of SOGS modified for adolescents (SOGS-RA, Winters et al, 1993), and the Massachusetts Gambling Screen (MAGS) used by Shaffer et al (1994). In an effort to bring order to the terminological and methodological diversity in the literature, Shaffer and Hall suggested the use of a system of levels of gambling involvement and experience, shown here in Table 3.5. Using this system, their meta-analysis suggested with 95 per cent confidence that the prevalence of level 3 or 4 gambling (which they refer to elsewhere as 'serious problem or pathological' gambling) amongst North American adolescents lay between 4.4 per cent and 7.4 per cent. In addition, again with 95 per cent confidence, the prevalence of level 2 gambling ('at risk or in-transition' gambling) lay between 9.9 per cent and 14.2 per cent.

Table 3.5 Levels of gambling involvement and experience proposed by
Shaffer and Hall, 1996

Levels of gambling involvement and experience	Operational definition
Level 0: Non Gambling	Has never gambled
Level 1: Non-Problem Gambling	Gambles recreationally and does not experience *any* signs or symptoms of gambling-related disorder
Level 2: In-Transition Gambling	Gambler who experiences symptoms or displays signs of gambling problems as a function of gambling activity; may be progressing either *toward* more serious or intense symptoms (i.e. progression) or *away* from these symptoms (i.e. during recovery)
Level 3: Gambling-related Disorder with Impairment	Gambler who meets diagnostic criteria (e.g. DSM-IV, MAGS, SOGS) as impaired in biologic, sociologic or psychologic domains
Level 4: Impaired Gambler who Displays Willingness to Enter Treatment	Gambler who satisfies level 3 requirements and, in addition, displays interest in entering the health-care domain (with or without existing obstacles)

That review was brought up to date by the National Research Council
(1999) which reviewed no less than thirty-three studies of adolescents and
college students conducted in the USA and reported between 1985 and
1997. By that time SOGS (in various versions) and other DSM-based
instruments (again various versions) had clearly emerged as the main
instruments used for studying prevalence. Ten reports produced an estimate
of past-year level 3 gambling (referred to in the NRC report as 'pathological gambling'). Apart from one low estimate of 0.3 per cent, all estimates lay between 4.3 per cent and 9.5 per cent, with an overall median of
6.1 per cent. Authors of the NRC report observed, as did Jacobs (1989),
that, by prevailing operationalisations, the proportion of pathological
gamblers amongst adolescents in North America could be more than three
times that of adults. Since then studies have continued to appear. For
example Westphal et al (2000) reported a past-year level 3 (pathological
gambling) prevalence of 5.8 per cent amongst 12,066 grade 6 to 12 school
students in Louisiana.

Two studies from Canada are of additional interest because they
examined the possibility of variation in rates of problem gambling by age
within high-school samples. Gupta and Derevensky (1998) administered the
DSM-IV-J to 817 12–17 year olds in four high schools in central city or
suburban Montreal. They found an overall prevalence of pathological

gambling (i.e. meeting four or more criteria) of 4.7 per cent, with an additional 3.3 per cent who could be described as problem gamblers (meeting three criteria). Ladouceur et al (1999a) used SOGS with 3,426 12–18 year olds in eight schools in the Quebec and Charlevoix regions. They reported a prevalence of pathological gambling (i.e. a SOGS score of five or more) of 2.6 per cent, with an additional 4.8 per cent scoring three or four. Neither study found an increase in problem gambling with age during the teenage years. If anything the reverse was the case. Ladouceur et al did point out, however, that Quebec has one of the highest school drop-out rates in the Western world and substantial numbers of the older students would have been missing from school when the survey was carried out. The safest conclusion, therefore, is that there is little evidence of much variation in prevalence across the teenage years.

Although theirs was not a prevalence study, Moore and Ohtsuka (1997) reported the results of a survey of just over 1,000 young people of average age 17 years, drawn from six schools, plus volunteers from first-year students at four campuses at one university, all in the western suburbs of Melbourne, Australia. Twenty-nine per cent reported often trying to win back money lost in gambling; 14 per cent having gambled more than was meant at times; 8 per cent sometimes trying to keep the amount gambled secret from family and friends; 5 per cent wanting to cut down the level of gambling but finding it difficult to do so; 4.5 per cent having on occasions taken time off school or work to gamble; and 3 per cent endorsing the item, 'to some extent, I have a gambling problem'.

Overall, then, the evidence from a number of countries including Britain that adolescents, including quite young teenagers, probably experience gambling problems at a rate just as high as adults, and probably higher, is impressive. Notes of caution have been sounded, however, by Stinchfield and Winters (1998) who questioned the appropriateness of adapting adult screening methods such as SOGS or DSM-IV-based questions for use in adolescent surveys, and by Ladouceur et al (2000) who presented some evidence that such questions are often misunderstood, especially (but not only) by adolescents. Both called for work to verify whether existing findings reflected a truly high rate of adolescent problem gambling or whether they were partly due to measurement artefact.

Several of the authors of the relevant reports cited above have commented, on the other hand, on the hidden nature of this problem, the likelihood that the problem has grown as opportunities to gamble have increased in the late 20th century, and the continued and surprising neglect of the problem. In the USA, Jacobs (1989) noted that there had been virtual silence in professional, scientific, government or lay domains on the subject of the potentially harmful effects of teenage gambling up until the 1980s. Even in the mid-1990s Shaffer and Hall (1996) were noting that the prevalence rates of problem gambling amongst adolescents were very similar to the prevalence rates of substance abuse amongst youth, although there was no comparison in the amount of attention that had been focused on the two kinds of problem. In her prevalence study in England and Wales, Fisher (1999) reported that in the week prior to the survey 48 per cent of all pupils surveyed had taken alcohol, 30 per cent had played fruit machines, 23 per cent had smoked cigarettes, 18 per cent had played NL scratchcards, and 10 per cent had taken illegal drugs. The proportion who had felt bad in the past year about the amount they had gambled on fruit machines was second only to the proportion who had felt bad about the amount of alcohol taken (22 per cent versus 23 per cent; 19 per cent had felt bad about the amount smoked, and 8 per cent about the amount of drugs taken).

We are left in no doubt, then, that there is such a phenomenon as problem or out-of-control gambling. It is prevalent in large numbers of people in several countries where surveys have been carried out and seems to be particularly prevalent amongst young people. In the following chapter we look at the results of research and theorising about the possible causes of this problem gambling which, by all accounts, gives rise to great distress for those affected by it.

Chapter 4

The causes of problem gambling

Opportunities to gamble have increased greatly in Britain and in many other countries. Government and public attitudes, although still somewhat ambivalent, are more favourable towards gambling than they once were. At the same time large numbers of people, albeit a minority, experience problems controlling their gambling which harms their lives and affects people around them. So much is established. To what, then, might we attribute this 'problem gambling' which represents the dark side to gambling – the cost, probably the major cost, of gambling to individuals, families and society as a whole?

There has been much speculation on this question and many theories. Very little is conclusively proven but, as this chapter attempts to show, some possible causes have been studied more intensively than others, and some conclusions can be drawn with greater confidence than others. One conclusion can be stated confidently at the outset: problem gambling has no single cause but is always the result, even for a single person, of a number of factors in combination. That statement follows, not only from research on the many factors of different types that might cause problem gambling, but also from what is known about the origins of all manner of problematic or deviant forms of behavioural conduct, including alcohol or drug problems (Jessor and Jessor, 1977; Hawkins et al, 1992; Orford, 2001). We are certainly dealing here with a form of behaviour that is multi-factorial in its origins. No uni-factor theory of the causes of problem gambling will do.

This chapter will consider in turn a number of different kinds of explanation for problem gambling, beginning with those that consider problem gambling as a product of the gambling environment, including the sheer accessibility of gambling and the nature of gambling activities themselves, and finishing at the other end of the scale with biological explanations.

Availability, accessibility and ecology

One of the most obvious explanations for problem gambling, and one for which there is much evidence, is that people get into trouble with gambling because it is a dangerous activity that has potential to create loss of control, and therefore the more people are exposed to opportunities to gamble the more gambling problems there will be. This is essentially the same kind of argument that says that there will be more illicit drug use at those times and in those areas where illicit drugs are relatively easy to obtain; or that alcohol problems are more prevalent when the national consumption of alcohol rises; or that tobacco-related deaths are greater in number when the price of cigarettes is lower. It is the 'supply' of the product that puts people at risk. The fault lies in the product as much as in the person that uses it. Gambling is one of many risks to which people are exposed, and the greater the exposure the more prevalent the problem. In direct contradiction to such explanations are person-centred theories which suppose that there is a constant minority of people who are personally vulnerable. Such individuals would have gambling problems irrespective of the availability of gambling, and if gambling was not available at all they would have other equally if not more troublesome problems. In his review in the 1970s, Cornish (1978) concluded that there had up to that time been an almost total reliance upon person-centred forms of explanation in the gambling field, and that this had resulted in a neglect of the importance of availability and 'ecologic opportunity' as he termed it.

A number of researchers have noted a correlation, across geographical areas, between the availability of gambling opportunities and the prevalence of problem gambling. The National Gambling Survey reported by the Australian Productivity Commission (1999) found a positive correlation, across the eight states and territories in Australia, between per capita expenditure on gambling (excluding lotteries) and a number of indices of problem gambling. New South Wales and Victoria with an annual per capita expenditure on gambling of over $800, at the higher end, scored consistently higher on each of these indices than Tasmania and Western Australia, at the other end, where annual per capita expenditure was less than $400. Similarly, Volberg (1994, cited by APC, 1999) compared problem-gambling prevalence rates among five US states with differing histories of accessibility, and found that those with a longer history of legally available gambling had significantly higher levels of problem gambling. Walker and Dickerson (1996) presented a table comparing Australia, New Zealand and Canada showing Australia to have the highest level of expenditure on gambling as a proportion of personal consumption and also the highest prevalence of problem gambling (SOGS scores of five plus), with New Zealand intermediate for both expenditure and problem gambling, and Canada lowest for both.

Another way of looking at the availability-prevalence link is to explore whether rates of problem gambling have increased during a period of time when opportunities to gamble have risen, as availability theory would predict. Although the last years of the 20th century should have given plenty of scope for such an analysis since opportunities to gamble increased so dramatically in Britain and elsewhere during that time, in fact there is not a great deal of evidence to go on because of the rarity of studies using the same method for estimating prevalence on more than one occasion. The US National Research Council review (NRC, 1999) included an analysis of results of such studies carried out in six US states in the late 1980s or 1990s. Such meta-analyses, combining the results from several individual studies, are important because results from any one study may be unreliable due to differences in response rates at different times, differences in sampling procedure, or for a host of other reasons. In the case of all six studies, prevalence estimates (in all cases using some variant of SOGS) were made in two separate years with intervals between the two estimates varying from two to ten years. In four cases the two survey dates straddled the intro- duction of significant new legal gambling opportunities (e.g. the opening of riverboat casinos, the inauguration of a state lottery, or the establishment of American Indian casino gambling). In only two of those studies was it possible to compare past year prevalence (in the other three, only lifetime prevalence had been estimated on the first occasion), but comparisons could be made of lifetime prevalence in all cases.

Apart from Connecticut, where American Indian gambling had been established with the opening of a large casino between the two surveys in 1991 and 1996, and where the prevalence of 'pathological' gambling (referred to by NRC as level 3 gambling) had gone down (from 2.7 per cent to 1.2 per cent), all other estimated changes (including level 2 gambling in Connecticut) showed changes in an upward direction. In Iowa, for example, where riverboat casinos were opened and slot machines permitted at the state's race tracks, the estimated lifetime prevalence rate of problem gambling (levels 2 and 3 combined) appeared to have increased between 1988 and 1995 from 1.7 per cent to 5.4 per cent. In the remaining two cases of repeated surveys (New York and South Dakota) no major new forms of gambling had been introduced, although it is safe to assume that national trends had resulted in a general increase in the availability of legal gamb- ling. In New York the estimated prevalence of problem gambling (levels 2 and 3 combined) went up from 4.2 per cent in 1986 to 7.3 per cent in 1996, whereas in South Dakota there was a smaller decrease from 2.8 per cent in 1991 to 2.3 per cent in 1993.

Despite the small number of studies, and some contrary findings, NRC's overall conclusion was that "the changes observed in those studies, however, was consistent with the view that increased opportunity to gamble results in more pathological and problem gambling" (p.84). Volberg (1997, cited by Ladouceur et al, 1999b) noted that increases in prevalence found in these studies were greater the longer the period between surveys. She suggested that after three or more years following the introduction of new gambling opportunities, the evidence was that the prevalence of pathological gambling increased.

Ladouceur et al (1999b) reported the results of a similar exercise carried out in Quebec province in Canada in 1989 and again in 1996. Again SOGS was used, and again only lifetime prevalence was estimated. Prevalence of problem gambling (NRC's levels 2 and 3 combined) increased from 3.3 per cent to 4.5 per cent, and for 'pathological' or level 3 gambling alone, from 1.2 per cent to 2.1 per cent, representing an estimated increase of 38,000 Quebec adults suffering from 'pathological' gambling over the seven year period.

In Britain there has been no directly comparable study, although Shepherd et al (1998) posted a questionnaire, including items based on DSM-IV criteria, to a random sample of 2,000 GP patients in the county of Cambridgeshire in October 1994, just prior to the start of the National Lottery (NL), and again 6 and 12 months after the start of the NL. Unfortunately response rates were low and the analysis of change across the three times was based on only 206 participants. Although with such small numbers it would have been impossible to show any significant change in the numbers of people who scored as 'pathological gamblers', it was possible to show that the mean DSM score was significantly greater, both at 6 months and at 12 months after the start of the NL, compared to the month before the start. NL draw tickets had been bought by 89 per cent of the sample at 6 months and 50 per cent purchased an NL scratchcard, the numbers being slightly greater still at 12 months. There was a significant positive correlation between mean DSM score and average number of NL tickets purchased per week at 6 months, and average number of scratch-cards per week at both 6 and 12 months.

More convincing is an analysis of Family Expenditure Survey (FES) data for the last full year before the start of the NL (1993–94) and the first full year after the start (1995–96) (Grun and McKeigue, 2000). Although this was not, therefore, a specialised gambling survey, and no estimate of the prevalence of problem gambling using scales like SOGS or one based upon DSM-IV was possible, household members were asked to record their outlay on several different forms of gambling separately (bearing in mind all the difficulties of recording gambling spend which were discussed in the previous chapter). These are data collected annually by the Office for National Statistics involving 10,000 households across the UK. In each household adult members complete a two-week expenditure diary. In place of a problem gambling prevalence estimate, two indicators of excessive behaviour at the household level were reported: spending more than £20 a week, and spending more than 10 per cent of household income. The results showed sizeable increases in gambling and expenditure on gambling. In 1993–94, 40 per cent of households were gambling and mean household gambling expenditure was £1.45 a week or 0.5 per cent of household income. In 1995–96 75 per cent of households were gambling and mean gambling expenditure had risen to £3.81 a week or 1.5 per cent of household income. The proportion of households spending more than £20 a week rose from 0.8 per cent to 2.5 per cent, and the proportion spending more than 10 per cent of their income on gambling had risen from 0.4 per cent to 1.7 per cent. Most, but not all, of this change was due to spending on the NL, supporting Creigh-Tyte's (1997, see Chapter 2) conclusion that spending on the NL was largely 'new money' as far as gambling was concerned.

Grun and McKeigue concluded that their results were in keeping with the 'single distribution theory', of gambling, which had been successfully applied to the study of alcohol consumption and alcohol problems (e.g. Colhoun et al, 1997; but challenged by Duffy, 1986, both cited by Grun and McKeigue, 2000). That theory maintains that the extent of a behaviour like gambling (or drinking) in the population is distributed along a continuous, but markedly skewed, frequency distribution curve of the kind shown in Figure 4.1. The large majority of the population are moderate in their consumption (or even abstinent as the majority of households were in relation to gambling according to the 1993–94 FES data) with ever-decreasing proportions of people expending or consuming greater and greater amounts. The important part of the theory is that the distribution curve behaves like a single entity with changes in the average consumption affecting the whole distribution. Specifically the theory predicts that any change that increases the average level of gambling in a population will inevitably increase the numbers in the tail of the curve and hence the prevalence of excessive or problem gambling. Between 1993–94 and 1995–96, as Figure 4.1 shows, the whole household gambling distribution curve shifted to the right (the higher expenditure end of the distribution): more households were gambling, more money was spent by the population as a whole, and more households were gambling large amounts of money.

If that model is valid it has profound implications for public health and gambling. The whole nation is responsible for contributing to the conditions that help create larger numbers of gambling problems. The more we as a whole society enjoy gambling, and the more we spend on it, the more people there will be who suffer the ill-effects in the form of problem gambling. Problem gambling is as much the fault of all of us, including government and the gambling industry, as it is of the minority of problem gamblers themselves.

Another indication of the possible relationship between availability of gambling opportunities and the prevalence of gambling problems is the apparent rise in the numbers of people seeking help for gambling problems following the introduction of new gambling opportunities. Such increases have been reported in Germany, Holland, and New Jersey, USA (studies cited by APC, 1999). Gamblers Anonymous (GA) in Britain reported a 17 per cent increase in calls in the year after the start of the NL (Mintel, 1995, cited by Shepherd et al, 1998). Across both the states of the USA (Lester, 1994) and across states and territories in Australia (APC, 1999) it has been

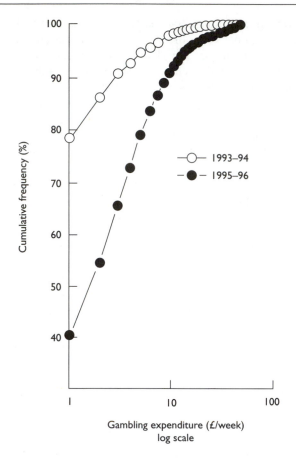

Figure 4.1 Changes in household expenditure on gambling, 1993–94 to 1995–96 (reproduced with permission from Grun and McKeigue, 2000)

found that GA is more developed in those states where there is more opportunity to gamble. Across the 48 contiguous US states Lester found a significant correlation between the number of chapters of GA to be found in the state and the number of separate forms of gambling that were legally available in the state (from states such as New York and Nevada with much gambling and many GA chapters, to those such as Arizona and Utah with few opportunities to gamble and very little presence of GA). Similarly the Australian Productivity Commission found a positive correlation between annual per capita expenditure on gambling and the number of GA groups per million adults (with ten times the concentration of GA in high-spending New South Wales compared to low-spending Western Australia).

The Australian Productivity Commission report (1999), which studied the issue of availability of gambling as thoroughly as it did almost every

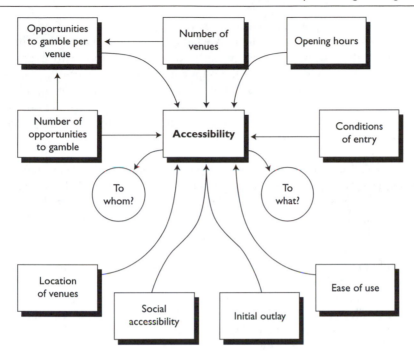

Figure 4.2 The dimensions of gambling accessibility (reproduced with permission from Australian Productivity Commission, 1999, Figure 8.2. Copyright Commonwealth of Australia)

other facet of the subject, pointed out that the accessibility of gambling had a number of dimensions to it and was not simply a question of the number of forms of gambling that were legal or the number of machines, casinos or other gambling outlets in a region or a country. As Figure 4.2 suggests, accessibility is also a matter of the spatial location and distribution of gambling venues (a given number of outlets dispersed evenly across an area might afford greater overall accessibility for the whole population than the same number concentrated in one area for example), the number of opportunities to gamble at any given venue, opening hours, restrictions on entry or lack of them, whether gambling can begin with a small outlay or requires a relatively high initial stake, and how attractive and inviting the venue is to a wide range of people including women, young people and members of different ethnic groups.

A further, important aspect of the ecology of gambling consists of the 'structural' characteristics of the gambling activity itself. In his review, Cornish (1978) paid particular attention to such characteristics which he concluded rendered different gambling activities differentially attractive and some more prone to give rise to problems than others. He referred to:

. . . forms of gambling which offer participants a variety of odds and/ or stake-levels at which to make bets, and hence choose the rate at which their wins or losses multiply are likely to appeal to a greater variety of people . . . When the opportunity to use longer-odds bets or higher stakes in order to multiply winnings or recoup losses rapidly is combined with a high event-frequency and short payout-interval, participants may be tempted to continue gambling longer than they might otherwise do (Cornish, 1978, p.168).

The range of odds and the range of the possible stakes – what Weinstein and Deitch (1974) called 'multiplier potential' – was just one of the structural variables which Cornish considered important. Others, which together make up structural 'profiles' of the different forms of gambling, include the interval elapsing between betting and paying out (the payout interval), the degree of active involvement of the bettor and the amount of skill involved, the probability of winning an individual bet, and average winnings per unit amount staked (the payment ratio). The Royal Commission on Betting, Lotteries and Gaming (1951), which recommended that fruit machines should be illegal, and later Fisher and Griffiths (1995) too, were of the view that gambling machines incorporated a number of structural features that made them particularly risky:

> Slot machines are fast, aurally and visually stimulating and rewarding, require a low initial stake, provide frequent wins, require no pre-knowledge to commence play, and may be played alone . . . structural characteristics of slot machines which are designed to induce the player to play and/or to continue playing are likely to play an important role. Such characteristics include frequent payout and event intervals, arousing near miss and symbol proportions, multiplier potential, bettor involvement and skill, exciting light and sound effects, and significant naming (Fisher and Griffiths, 1995, pp.240, 241).

There is now wide acceptance that 'event frequency' is a key variable, with forms of gambling that allow the opportunity for rapid cycles of stake, play and determination having particularly great potential for causing problem gambling (Cayuela and Guirao, 1991; Rönnberg et al, 1999). Griffiths (1993a, 1995a) has described in greater detail the ways in which the gaming machine industry has used various inducements over the years to entice people to play and to keep on playing fruit machines. Machines have progressively been developed so as to pay out frequently thus providing regular reward and at the same time ensuring that loss periods and opportunities for reflection on one's state of finances are short, and that winnings can be re-gambled almost immediately. It is also thought to encourage continued play if fruit-machine gamblers think that skill is involved. Although Griffiths

(1995a), who researched fruit-machine playing extensively, concluded that there is very little skill involved in playing such machines, players often think that there are a whole variety of skills involved, and the introduction of such features as 'hold' and 'nudge' buttons (whereby a symbol in a winning position or thought to be to the player's advantage can be held stationary, or a reel can be moved manually after automatic play is over) undoubtedly encouraged that impression. According to Griffiths (1995a) this had the further advantage to the industry of enabling the legislation of the time to be circumvented, re-defining machine playing as an act of skill and therefore outwith the current definition of gambling.

A further element, the psychology of the 'near miss', was studied by Reid (1986) who noted that some commercial gambling activities, notably fruit machines and scratchcard lotteries, were designed to ensure a higher than chance frequency of near misses e.g. two winning symbols in the middle, payout line on a fruit machine with a third in view just above or below the payline. Reid theorised that a near miss could produce some of the excitement of a win, and in that way a player was not so much constantly losing but constantly nearly winning. Moran (1995) referred to near misses as 'heartstoppers'. A related theory is that the near miss increases frustration and energises further gambling. Another way in which a 'near miss' can be engineered by design was by arranging that the first reel to stop carried a larger proportion of winning symbols than the second, with the third and last to stop carrying the smallest proportion. Hence the player was more likely to see a winning symbol early. Strickland and Grote (1967, cited by Cornish, 1978) carried out an experiment with a modified gaming machine and showed that the result was indeed that players stayed at the machine significantly longer than if winning symbols occurred relatively late in the display. Lotteries, such as the British NL, provide ample opportunities for experiencing near misses. Not only that, but, as Miers (1996) pointed out, the NL prize structure makes sure that the 'winning experience' is something that many players have an experience of, even if their wins are tiny in comparison to the much publicised jackpots.

Many adolescent machine gamblers reported to Griffiths that they were attracted to the 'aura' of the machine, including the accompanying music, lights and colour, and other sound effects. The latter include the sound of coins falling with a loud clatter into metal payout trays, and sometimes loud buzzes or the playing of musical tunes after a win. As Griffiths (1995a) pointed out, other people in the vicinity always hear about those who are winning, but never about those who are losing. This is similar, he said, to the 'ploy' used by Las Vegas and Atlantic City casinos who bang loud gongs to let the punters know when someone has 'beaten the house'. Anything which creates a 'suspension of judgement' (Cornish, 1978, cited by Griffiths, 1995a) is likely to encourage continued play. An example would be the use of tokens rather than real money. Even the names given to gaming machines were identified by Griffiths (1995a) as structural features likely to further encourage play. He found that names of fruit machines fell into a number of categories. The most common referred to money in their names, giving the impression that the machines were places where a player could gain money rather than lose it (e.g. *Action Bank*, *Cashpoint*, *Cashline*). The second category were those suggesting that skill was needed (e.g. *Skillcash*, *Fruitskill*), and a third category gave the impression that the odds of winning were fair (e.g. *Fortune Trail*, *Silver Chance*).

In this section evidence has been considered for the theory that problem gambling has, as one of its causes, the ways in which opportunities to gamble are made available to people, especially the volume of gambling opportunities and the accessibility of gambling, but in addition the ways in which gambling is presented and structured to make playing more attractive and enticing. We agree with the conclusion of the Australian Productivity Commission (1999) who, after very careful study, concluded:

> While causation is hard to prove beyond all doubt, the Commission considers that there is sufficient evidence from many different sources to confirm a significant connection between greater accessibility, particularly to gaming machines, and the greater prevalence of problem gambling (p.824).

The UK Gambling Review Report (2001) was also convinced:

> A central question for us has been whether increasing the availability of gambling will lead to an increase in the prevalence of problem gambling. The weight of evidence suggests that it will do so (para 17.7)

Social groups at risk

Are some social groups more at risk than others? Survey evidence on prevalence, reviewed in Chapter 3, has already suggested two such groups: adolescents and males. Beyond those two factors – sex and age – the research evidence is thin, and few findings have been replicated enough to be confident about the conclusions. Two additional factors, however, do stand out as receiving repeated support: parental gambling, and the use of alcohol, tobacco and other substances.

Parental gambling

It is often observed by those who offer counselling or treatment services for problem gamblers that the rate of parental problem gambling is very high and represents a significant risk factor. Bellringer (1999), for example, lists amongst childhood experiences contributing to the development of a gambling problem: "Gambling has been an approved and accepted activity by one or both parents or by other significant adult family members" (p.39).

Evidence that problem gambling is associated with parental gambling comes from both clinical and community studies, and from several countries. Two clinical studies involved patients at special centres for the treatment of alcohol or other drug problems in the USA, both finding a relationship (Lesieur et al, 1986; Gambino et al, 1993). Of 83 patients questioned by Gambino et al, for example, 24 per cent reported that a parent (more often father than mother) had a gambling problem, and they were three times as likely as other patients to score five or more on lifetime SOGS. They extended their investigation to ask about problem gambling amongst grandparents. The latter was less often reported (by 10 per cent), but those who reported grandparents with gambling problems were even more likely to score five plus on SOGS (12 times as likely as other patients).

Such studies alone provide rather weak evidence since the samples are highly selective. They are supported, however, by survey data collected for the Australian Productivity Commission (1999). The latter reported a parental problem-gambling rate of 2.3 per cent amongst those who themselves had gambling problems in the previous year, compared to a rate of 0.4 per cent amongst those without such problems. An additional interesting finding was a greater relative risk of having a gambling problem if a sibling was reported to have such a problem (3.3 per cent compared to 1.2 per cent). The APC report also cited a study of a South Australian prison population which found even greater relative risks (32 per cent of problem gamblers in prison reporting having a father with a gambling problem compared to 3 per cent for non-problem gamblers; with 18 per cent and 3 per cent being the equivalent figures for having a sibling with a gambling problem) (Marshall et al, cited by APC, 1999, p.7.26). In her study of gambling in British casinos, Fisher (1996) reported a significantly higher rate of reported parental problem gambling (33 per cent) amongst her group of severe problem gamblers compared to the less severe problem gamblers and social gamblers (4 per cent and 7 per cent respectively). Rönnberg et al (1999) also found a significantly higher (but still low at 6 per cent) rate of reported parental gambling problems amongst those who scored as problem gamblers themselves in the Swedish prevalence survey.

Studies of adolescent gambling, naturally enough, have focused in more detail on the possible influence of parental and family gambling. In Montreal, Canada, Gupta and Derevensky (1997, 1998) have reported two studies, one of 477 9–14 year olds, the other of 817 12–17 year olds. In the former study 81 per cent of those who had gambled (who were in a majority even at the youngest age) reported gambling with family members, and between 70 per cent and 80 per cent gambling at home irrespective of age group. The proportion reporting gambling at friends' homes increased substantially with age, from around 20 per cent in the youngest age group to around 60 per cent in the oldest. Of interest was the finding that only 20 per cent of the young gamblers in their sample indicated that they were fearful of being caught gambling by a parent or authority figure, the percentage being highest (44 per cent) amongst 9–10 year olds, declining to 10 per cent amongst 13–14 year olds (Gupta and Derevensky, 1997). In their second study, of older adolescents, they reported 65 per cent gambling with family members (including parents, siblings, and extended relatives such as grandparents, aunts, uncles and cousins), that figure declining from 78 per cent amongst 12–13 year olds to 53 per cent amongst 16–17 year olds. The overall percentage of those reporting gambling primarily at home was 66 per cent, a figure that declined significantly with age, whilst the percentages reporting gambling in other locations such as friends' homes, arcades, bars, casinos and corner stores increased significantly. Those who scored as 'pathological gamblers' on the DSM-IV-J were more likely to report having a father with a gambling problem, and the same was true for having a mother with such a problem.

The influence of parents is also highlighted in British studies of adolescent gambling. Wood and Griffiths (1998) who gave questionnaires to over 1,000 11–15 year olds in nine schools, reported significant positive correlations between adolescent and parental (as reported by the adolescents) participation on both the National Lottery and scratchcards. Of those participants who took part in the NL, 71 per cent reported having tickets bought for them by their parents, and the equivalent figure for scratchcards was 57 per cent. In her national prevalence study of 12–15 year olds in England and Wales, Fisher (1999) asked young people a number of questions about their parents' gambling and the latter's attitudes towards their children gambling. Participants were more likely to report playing the NL draw with their parents than with anyone else, and the same was true for scratchcards. Significantly more of those who had made their own (and therefore illegal) purchases reported that their parents approved or 'didn't mind' if children of their age spent their money on the NL, and the same was true for those who registered as problem gamblers on the DSM-IV-J compared to others. Those identified as problem gamblers were more than three times as likely as others to say they thought their parents gambled 'too much', and they were significantly more likely to report that their parents had gambled on each of the nine different forms of gambling that were asked about.

Friends' gambling

This focus on parental influence in the research literature on gambling contrasts with that on other adolescent 'problem behaviours' such as smoking, drinking and drug taking where, although there is a correlation with parental behaviour, the emphasis has tended to be on the influence of friends (e.g. Orford et al, 1974; Jessor and Jessor, 1977; Farrell et al, 1992). It is difficult to know whether this represents a real difference, with parents being less aware of the dangers of gambling and even approving of under-age gambling, particularly in the case of forms such as the NL which may scarcely be perceived by parents as gambling at all (Wood and Griffiths, 1998), or whether it simply reflects the particular interests of those who have carried out the research. When friends' influence is looked for, evidence in support of it is usually found. For example, in her earlier study of fruit-machine gambling amongst 11–16 year olds at one English seaside school, Fisher (1993a) found 40 per cent reporting that they usually played machines with friends compared to 9 per cent with parents and 12 per cent with other family members. Playing with friends increased significantly across the age groups she studied and playing with parents decreased significantly. In her later national prevalence study she reported that, unlike the NL draw and scratchcards, fruit machines were more likely to be played in the company of other young people than in any other kind of company (Fisher, 1999). The US National Research Council (1999) also reported a number of studies of adolescent gambling in the USA finding an association between personal gambling and peer gambling. In a smaller sample of adults in the south-west of England, Coups et al (1998) found friends' lottery play to be the strongest single correlate of NL play amongst a number of variables.

Smoking, drinking and drug-taking

The second hypothesis about which groups of people are more likely to be problem gamblers, which has received consistent support, predicts that the extent of a person's gambling is positively correlated with the extent of involvement with other potentially problematic or addictive activities such as tobacco, alcohol and drug consumption. Many studies attest to this relationship amongst adolescents. For example, Griffiths and Sutherland (1998) found that higher proportions of 11–16 year olds who reported gambling once a week or more, smoked cigarettes (23 per cent versus 18 per cent of others), drank alcohol regularly (72 per cent versus 58 per cent) and took illegal drugs (21 per cent versus 13 per cent). In studies in New York state, Barnes et al (1999) found that adolescents who were abstainers from drinking were more likely not to have gambled at all in the last year, and in the case of male participants, for whom the relationship between drinking and gambling was stronger, those who were the heaviest drinkers were most likely to have gambled weekly or more often.

The relationship is also clear when it is problem gambling rather than merely gambling per se or regular gambling that is considered. In her earlier study of pupils at a single school Fisher (1993a) found that 'pathological gamblers' were more likely to visit pubs, and in her later national pre-valence study (Fisher, 1999) she found that problem gamblers were signi-ficantly more likely than other young adolescents to have smoked cigarettes (47 per cent versus 22 per cent), taken alcohol (73 per cent versus 46 per cent) and taken illegal drugs (28 per cent versus 9 per cent) in the previous week. The same has been found in North America (e.g. Gupta and Derevensky, 1998; Ladouceur et al, 1999a; Westphal et al, 2000). Gupta and Derevensky (1998), for example, found a regular increase in the proportions of adolescents smoking, drinking and using drugs across four groups: non, occasional, regular and problem and 'pathological' gamblers. To cite just one of their findings: daily cigarette smoking was reported by 7.4 per cent, 7.8 per cent, 18.9 per cent and 32.3 per cent of those four groups respectively. Other North American studies which came to the same general conclusion were reviewed by Giacopassi et al (1998). In their US national population survey, which covered alcohol as well as gambling, Welte et al (2001) found a very significant degree of association between 'pathological gambling' and alcohol dependence.

Another type of study which has been popular, and which supports the link between gambling and substance use, is one that examines the co-occurrence of gambling and substance problems amongst adults receiving treatment. Reviews of such studies carried out by Rosenthal and Lorenz (1992, cited by Giacopassi et al, 1998) and by Crockford and el-Guebaly (1998, cited by NRC, 1999) have found high rates of lifetime substance use disorders (varying from a quarter to almost two-thirds) amongst 'patho-logical gamblers' in both community and clinical samples. Conversely, the NRC (1999) review concluded that a number of studies had found that people in treatment for a drug or alcohol problem were three to six times as likely to be problem gamblers as were those from the general population. Rosenthal and Lorenz (1992) estimated in their review that one fifth of patients being treated for alcohol or drug problems had at some time had problems with gambling. It should be borne in mind that almost all this work had been carried out in North America, mostly in the USA. It is very unlikely, however, that such results are confined to that part of the world. Kyngdon and Dickerson (1999) cited an Australian study (Dickerson et al, 1995) which found that regular machine gambling was associated with heavy alcohol consumption, and the New Zealand survey of Abbott and Volberg (1992) found an association between problem and 'pathological' gambling and the consumption of harmful amounts of alcohol. A study in Cataluña, Spain (Martínez-Pina et al, 1991) found a significantly higher rate of alcohol dependence amongst a group of casino gamblers who met SOGS criteria for 'pathological gambling' than amongst a 'clinical control group' matched for age and sex.

Although the link between gambling and substance use appears to be well established, the reason for the association is more controversial.

Increased use of alcohol and other substances might be a response to the problems created by gambling excessively, although that seems unlikely to be the whole explanation particularly in early adolescence. The possibility that intoxication might facilitate gambling or heavier gambling is a serious contender which will be considered later when looking at explanations of gambling that focus on people's decisions about gambling and the rewards obtained from it. An explanation that has received widespread support, particularly in relation to adolescent gambling, is that a greater degree of involvement in gambling, along with higher levels of consumption of tobacco, alcohol and other substances, is part of a constellation of youthful behaviours, also positively correlated with fast driving, failure to wear seat belts, and delinquent behaviour generally, and negatively with more con-formist behaviours such as religious observance. These non-conforming or deviant youthful behaviours are partly a reflection of the developing per-sonality of a young adult and partly a reflection of the social milieu which a person inhabits (e.g. Jessor and Jessor, 1977; McGee and Newcomb, 1992). These signs of 'behaving badly', which cluster together, have been expected more of boys than girls, and carry certain risks for young people, but are things that it is expected young people will grow out of in time, and which may not be too harmful unless they persist or are taken to extreme.

Income, education and ethnic group

Although the evidence is clearest in the case of parental gambling and substance use, they are of course not the only risk factors that have been considered. Amongst others, those that are most often referred to include income, education, ethnicity, and the age at which gambling first took place.

Regarding income, there is some consistency in the finding that people with lower incomes spend a higher proportion of them on gambling. A number of studies carried out shortly after the inauguration of the UK NL are examples. Miers (1996) cited figures from a small study reported by LeGrande (1995) showing an average weekly spend on the lottery of £1.50 for those in socioeconomic groups A and B in comparison with £2.20 by those in groups D and E. Although that difference is not great, it rep-resented a sizeable difference in proportion of disposable income (0.3 per cent versus 2.6 per cent). Miers noted that OFLOT's Advertising Code of Practice specifically forbade advertising that exploited people, "falling into any. . . recognisable social category" (1994). In their study of residents in one English county, Shepherd et al (1998) found a significant negative correlation between household income and the weekly number of scratch-cards purchased. Those with incomes under £20,000 a year bought more scratchcards and lottery draw tickets than those with higher incomes. Although the difference only approached statistical significance in the case of scratchcards, differences by proportion of household income spent would be much greater. In their study of national household expenditure before and after the introduction of the NL, Grun and McKeigue (2000) found that the increase in proportion of income spent on all gambling had been greatest amongst households with income less than £200 a week. In that low income group the average percentage of income spent on gambling increased from 0.6 per cent to 2.1 per cent, and the proportion of households spending more than 10 per cent of their income on gambling had increased five-fold to 3.2 per cent (compared to 0.3 per cent amongst those with incomes of £400 a week or more). In absolute terms, however, it was the better-off who were spending more on gambling: just over 3 per cent of those with incomes of £400 a week or more reported gambling more than £20 a week compared to around 1 per cent of those with incomes of £200 or less. The finding that those with more income spend more on gambling may apply even to young adolescents. Pugh and Webley (2000) reported that 256 13–15 year olds from schools in one English county had an average weekly disposable income of £12 (most had pocket money and more than half had jobs) of which 22 per cent on average was spent on gambling of all kinds. Participation in the NL draw and scratchcards were both significantly correlated with disposable income.

If, as seems likely, it is expenditure as a proportion of income, rather than absolute expenditure, that is associated with problem or 'pathological' gambling, then it is to be expected that household income will be negatively correlated with having a gambling problem, and there is some preliminary evidence that this is indeed the case. The US NRC (1999) review found 17 prevalence studies carried out in the USA between the 1970s and 1990s which showed a breakdown by household income (most usually above and below $25,000 per year). The NRC conclusion was that these studies, ". . . showed some tendency for lower-income persons to be overrepresented among pathological and problem gamblers" (p.97).

In terms of educational attainment, Shepherd et al (1998) found significant differences in the numbers of scratchcard and draw tickets purchased per week by educational level; those with 'ordinary level' exam passes or less buying significantly more of both kinds of ticket than those with 'advanced level' exam passes or higher. In their study of an adult sample in the South-West of England Coups et al (1998) also found a significant negative correlation between NL play and level of education. Rönnberg et al (1999) found Swedish adults with university education reported less gambling expenditure than others.

The relationship between gambling and ethnic group remains unresearched in Britain, but has received some attention in the USA. The NRC (1999) review found 18 prevalence studies which were able to make a comparison between ethnic groups and in every case there was an association between being a member of a minority ethnic group and problem or 'pathological' gambling. The relationship pertained for both those referred to as African Americans and Hispanics. Welte et al (2001) found the same in their national US survey, with significantly raised prevalence figures for black, Hispanic and native American groups. Studies of adolescence have produced some mixed findings. For example, Westphal et al (2000) found the highest prevalence of 'pathological gambling' amongst the Hispanic group (9.4 per cent) in their sample of Louisiana adolescents, with the lowest rate for Caucasians (5.6 per cent) and intermediate rates for other groups (African Americans 7.7 per cent, Native Americans 6.5 per cent). On the other hand Barnes et al (1999), in their studies in New York state, found less gambling amongst black than white young people in one study and little relationship in the other. Rönnberg et al (1999) found a higher rate of problem gambling amongst Swedish survey participants born outside Sweden.

Age at which gambling started

Evidence is generally in support of the long-held hypothesis (e.g. Custer, 1982, cited by Fisher, 1996) that starting gambling early in childhood or adolescence puts young people at greater risk of subsequent gambling problems. In the USA the NRC (1999) review concluded that the evidence "weakly supported" (p.113) the hypothesis. In Britain there have been a number of studies in support. Griffiths (1990) found that adolescents addicted to fruit machines reported beginning gambling significantly earlier than those who were not addicted (9.2 versus 11.3 years). In her study of pupils at one school, Fisher (1993a) found a small but significant negative correlation between the age of commencing fruit-machine playing and 'pathological gambling'. In her later study of attenders at British casinos (Fisher, 1996) she reported a significant association between problem gambling and reporting starting gambling at age 14 or younger (reported by 64 per cent of severe problem gamblers, 50 per cent of problem gamblers, and 16 per cent of social gamblers).

In this section a number of factors have been noted which, in the present state of knowledge on the subject, have the strongest claims to be considered as risk factors for problem gambling. These factors are: having had a parent(s) who gambled; having started to gamble at an early stage; being young; being male; being a regular smoker and/or heavier user of alcohol and other drugs; and having a relatively low income. Before proceeding to consider other types of explanation for problem gambling, we should enter a number of cautions about so-called 'risk factors' (NRC, 1999; APC, 1999).

First, correlation does not equal causation. This is obvious in the case of the correlation with substance use which could be either a cause or an effect of problem gambling, or neither – both might be a reflection of a third variable. But the caution might also be relevant to a variable such as age of commencing gambling, since research has relied upon retrospective reports by adolescents or adults, and recollections may be affected by the development of problem gambling. Second, apparent risk factors might be unique risk factors for problem gambling (e.g. starting to gamble at a very young age might be a specific risk for problem gambling and not for problems of other kinds) or it might put people at risk in a number of ways (e.g. having a parent with a gambling problem might put someone equally at risk for a later drinking problem as for a gambling problem, although Gambino et al's 1993 results suggested that was not the case). Third, the way in which risk factors relate to one another, and the pathways through which they might influence gambling, need to be considered very carefully. For example, might maleness be a risk factor for problem gambling because boys start gambling earlier than girls, or because parents tolerate their gambling more, or because they receive more peer group support for gambling, or because gambling is more available to them in other ways? A complete model of risk factors for problem gambling would also specify the point in the sequence of development of a problem at which a risk factor had its influence: for example, parents' gambling might be important at an early stage, and alcohol and drug use at a later stage.

Finally, we have to face the complexity of the phenomenon of gambling. Is it one thing or many? Do we need one model of how problem gambling develops or several? A number of writers have suggested that the psychology of different forms of gambling may be quite distinct: for example German-style slot machines and roulette play may appeal to two very different groups of German gamblers (Kroeber, 1992); and Australian poker-machine playing and off-course sports betting might be quite different kinds of habit (Cocco et al, 1995).

Are there positive personal-social functions of gambling?

In total contrast to the epidemiological survey, questionnaire or interview type of research that has given rise to the identification of possible risk factors, are studies that have observed gamblers or groups of gamblers in an effort to understand what positive functions gambling might be serving for them. These have tended to be observational, or even participant-observational studies of gamblers in action. Rosecrance (1988) referred to these studies as 'sociological'.

Ideas emerging from studies of that kind in the USA, reviewed and cited by Rosecrance (1988), include the following suggestions: that gambling might serve a function for society by providing a safe outlet for the relief of frustrations and tensions without threatening society's institutions directly (Devereux, 1949); that gambling, involving taking a chance, represented a pleasurable alternative to the routine and boredom of industrial life (Bloch, 1951); and that gambling represented a milieu in which gamblers could appear to exercise control, show composure and make apparently rational decisions, uncover information (e.g. about horses) and 'beat the system' (Zola, 1963; Herman, 1976; Scott, 1968). Zurcher (1970) introduced the idea of an 'ephemeral role' to describe the opportunity that poker playing provided participants for temporary satisfactions unavailable in everyday roles.

Goffman (1967), the most famous sociologist of them all, who worked as a blackjack dealer and croupier in the Nevada casinos, concluded that the gambler, by engaging in risk taking, could demonstrate character strength in a way unavailable to most people in ordinary life. Players could exhibit valued traits such as courage, gameness, integrity and composure. Rosecrance cited Frey (1986, p.56) who observed that, "people don't want to admit it, but a great part of gambling is consistent with the American way. We admire people that take risks". Newman's (1972) observations of betting shops in London's East End also suggested that gambling provided an opportunity for exercising intelligent choice, the experience of control, the opportunities to discuss with others, and to appear knowledgeable. Griffiths (1995a) considered the idea of 'gambling as play', and the possibility that common children's games such as marbles or card-playing might be precursors to gambling. Amongst other things, games, according to Griffiths, "provide the opportunity to prove one's superiority, the desire to challenge and overcome an obstacle and a medium by which to test one's skill, endurance and ingenuity" (p.47), and gambling might be the same. The way in which the positive functions of gambling had been neglected was a recurring theme in accounts of recent British gambling history, summarised in Chapter 1 (e.g. Chinn, 1991; Dixon, 1991; Clapson, 1992).

It is often suggested that gambling is a social activity and serves the important function of aiding socialising. One set of authors who supported that view were Ocean and Smith (1993) who based their findings on a year and a half of participant observation by one of them at a casino in Edmonton, Canada. Data were collected mainly through first-hand observations while working as a blackjack dealer, informal talks with players and casino staff, and, "tuning into the players' table conversations" (p.323). Their conclusions concerned regular casino players for whom the casino became 'encompassing', almost akin to Goffman's (1961) 'total institution', where players could watch television, eat, meet friends, gamble and, thanks to a recently obtained liquor licence, drink as well. As one player explained, on hearing of the new licence, "Wow, guys can stay here all day. They've got everything here!" (p.324). It was observed that regular players would often stay in the casino even after losing all their money, remaining to watch others play, to give advice to friends, or to borrow money to get back into the action. Strong group norms pertained in the casino and players bonded with other regulars in a number of ways, for example by combining to play against the house or providing emotional support to a player who had lost heavily. Participation could help boost self-esteem for those who conformed to the group norms and who were respected for their skill, knowledge and bravado. Because 'role dispossession' was a common experience, whereby roles in outside society were left behind on entering the casino, and everyone was potentially of equal status, Ocean and Smith concluded that being a regular gambler in the casino they studied, at least, was particularly attractive to those of lower ascribed status in the outside world – those of lower socioeconomic status, immigrants, ethnic minorities, the less well educated, and the physically disabled, for example.

In Britain, Fisher's (1993b) observations in one 'amusement arcade' containing fruit machines suggested that such a venue might serve very different functions for different people. She worked for a time in the arcade as an unpaid cashier in the 'change box'. Regular players were aware of her research interest and sometimes invited her to accompany them on their round of play. Findings were presented in the form of a typology of six different types of young machine player. The types of player that she described indicate what she believed to be the dominating motivation of the type but she emphasised that those motivations were by no means mutually exclusive, and elements of each type were relevant to all. Her study has become a classic in the British literature on gambling and is worth describing in some detail.

The 'Kings', as she called them, were the most highly regarded and had mastered fruit machine playing skills to a far greater extent than others. In fact Fisher referred to their status as being that of 'quasi professional' players. Although part of a group, who might share winnings or losses at the end of a session, Kings tended to keep themselves to themselves during play in order to exploit opportunities to move from one machine to another in order, as they believed, to maximise their winnings. Although psychologists such as Griffiths (1990) have questioned whether choosing to play a machine that has not recently paid out, memorising the reel sequences ('knowing the reels'), and use of play features such as 'hold' or 'nudge' buttons or using the 'gamble' feature, really adds a skill element to playing gambling machines, as opposed to merely creating the illusion of skill, Fisher's Kings were clearly of the view that there were skills to be learned, and Fisher appears to have been convinced: ". . . it seems unlikely that players would persistently spend so much time, effort and money on the enterprise if it did not increase the odds in their favour" (1993b, p.457). Expertise was shared with mates and even made available to other players, usually in return for 10 per cent of winnings. For example:

I'm quite good. I expect some of the kids would say it's big-headed saying that, but I'm pretty chuffed at the way I've learned it like, you know, 'cos it's quite hard. I mean if I said to you – put a machine in front of you and said, like, 'Give you two weeks to learn the reels', you probably wouldn't be able to do it. I'd say I learn a machine's reels in about six weeks (p.460).

The Kings attracted a band of followers, boys aged around 9 to 11 years, whom they called 'slaves' and whom Fisher refers to as the 'apprentices'. They provided the Kings with services such as fetching food and drink and moving a King's cigarette from one ashtray to another, but the main service they provided to the Kings appeared to be that of an appreciative audience. Whilst the Kings displayed emotional composure, their apprentices showed spontaneous exclamations of praise for a win and rationalisations for losses (e.g. castigating the machine). Kings would even leave winnings for apprentices to collect. It was particularly entertaining, according to Fisher, to see a King simultaneously play several machines, and win simultaneously on several, whilst continuing to maintain a state of apparent emotional disinterest. In short, Kings demonstrated 'good gamesmanship', playing the technical game well and managing their money and emotions well:

We don't go mad, like, we usually have a tenner each, like. We might go down and blow the lot plus another tenner each, like. But that's what happens on a Saturday like. But we wouldn't stay down there trying to win it back. That's pointless 'cos once you're forty quid down you've got no chance. So you leave it 'til next week – you go down with a tenner – you might only spend a fiver of that and end up walking out with fifty, like, you know (p.462).

Although Fisher noted that repeated playing of machines in this way could result in losing huge amounts of money relative to income, the Kings did not perceive themselves as 'addicts' or having gambling problems; quite the contrary in fact since their status was based on rationality and self-control.
     'Action Seekers', in contrast, were primarily motivated by thrill and excitement, particularly marked in machine playing, Fisher observed, because the cycle of wagering, anticipation and outcome, with its associated emotions, was so short:

It's some sort of, not challenge, but (*thinks*) not knowing what's going to happen next – suspense – that's the word I was looking for. 'Cos you put your money in and you don't know what's going to happen, but you'll find out any second now (p.467).

For such adolescents the excitement was further enhanced by the opportunity afforded by the arcade to escape from the attentions of controlling adults and to adopt an adult demeanour:

> Yeah, you go down the arcade and you fink 'Right, I'm out of that (*being treated like a child*), let's go and have a gamble. It makes you feel older.

> There are no parents there and it's dark and smoky. It's the Gang's Turf – you can say 'Fuck off' and smoke (p.468).

'Rent-a-Spacers' were teenage girls with few playing skills who gambled on machines mainly to gain access to the arcade where they could socialise with friends:

> If you look around at all the boys and girls in an arcade, the boys will all be playing, while the girls will all be standing around watching, being 'girlie' and giggle and things like that. [Are they there to get to know the boys?] In some ways, yes. I mean, if you like a boy and you think 'Oh, I'll follow him tonight', and you know where he'll be, you would go into an arcade and stand and watch him play his game (p.466).

Unlike other types, Fisher identified two groups of young problem gamblers. The first she called 'Machine Beaters'. Unlike Kings, they resented others watching them play, concentrating alone on what became an obsession with beating the machine. They were unable to sustain the self-discipline shown by the Kings, invariably chasing their losses in an attempt to beat the machine, and frequently evidencing frustration by, for example, cursing or kicking a machine. The inevitable losses lead to self-deprecation and remorse:

> Well you do regret it, when you've lost, you regret it – walking home, you think 'Christ how did I do it?' The next day you feel your head's buzzing and you go down to the bank and get a five and you're off again (p.465).

Fisher cited one young man who spent much of the first year of his college course in the arcade, spending an estimated £10 a day and in total £800 in savings plus weekly income from a part-time job; others whose pre-occupation with beating the machine led to unsociable or illegal actions such as spending school dinner money, selling possessions, or theft; and one young man whose parents bought two fruit machines and sited them in his bedroom in the hope that he might spend less money in the arcade (partly successful because his main orientation was to beat the machine wherever it was and whether or not he was winning money).

The other problem type Fisher termed 'Escape Artists', who were gambling principally to escape from overwhelming problems at home and/or school. For them the attraction lay in both the game and the venue. The machine itself was a source of non-human interaction (referred to by Griffiths, 1990, as an 'electronic friend'); the absorbing nature of inter-action with the machine meant that problems were temporarily forgotten; and some players expressed a temporary feeling of power or control when playing.

There was also support in Fisher's findings for the idea of the arcade as a 'cultural space', in this case for young people with few other areas in their town which could provide such opportunities. Although many adolescents in her single school survey (Fisher, 1993a) described the unpleasant aspects of arcades including smoking, the risk of losing too much money, and such unwanted occurrences as getting involved in a fight, being made to feel uncomfortable by a stranger, being offered money by a stranger, being offered drugs, being approached by a stranger asking them to steal, or being offered goods for sale (see also Huxley and Carroll, 1992), many of the things that young people said about arcades supported the view that they served a social function. Of eight possible reasons for visiting arcades, the most frequently endorsed (by 58 per cent) was 'to meet friends or hang around', although 'to play machines' was a close second (56 per cent). When the 11–16 year old participants were asked to write in their own words what they liked or disliked about arcades, most of the favourable comments referred to them as good places to meet friends and to enjoy the 'fun' atmosphere (e.g. "a good place to meet your friends and a good laugh", female 16 years). Many also reported that there was 'nowhere else to go'.

Fisher considered findings from studies such as her arcade research to be a corrective to the tendency of research to focus on psychological or econ-omic explanations, and to emphasise the 'social problems' side of gambling. She was suspicious of terms such as 'compulsive gambler' or 'pathological gambler' but in her paper used the words 'addict' and 'addiction' since they were terms used by the players themselves. A number of her observations supported earlier writings on the social functions of gambling. Her obser-vations of the emotional composure shown by the Kings supported Goffman's (1969, cited by Fisher, 1993b) and a number of other writers' conclusion that gambling afforded players the opportunity to show 'char-acter': approval from the peer group including admiration for a display of courage and composure in the face of losses.

As a final note to this section on the possible positive functions of gambling, for individuals and for society, it is interesting how well rep-resented in writings of that kind are authors who themselves had a personal or family background in the world of gambling or who had worked for a while at a gambling venue. Goffman and Rosecrance are examples from the USA, and Chinn and Fisher from Britain. They certainly give the impression of having got closer to the action than has usually been the case for researchers in other traditions.

Psychodynamic and personality theories

The ideas just described focus on the personal-social functions that gambling can serve as a consequence of the social milieu in which it is set. In the present section a different set of explanations is considered which centre on factors intrinsic to the individual personality of the gambler. The oldest of these are the psychoanalytic theories which go back, according to Rosenthal's (1987) review, at least to Simmel (1920) and Freud (1928/1961). Psychoanalytic views of gambling are complicated, partly because they have developed and changed in a number of different directions over the years, and partly because it is an accepted concept in psychoanalysis that behaviour is usually 'over-determined', having multiple meanings and functions, both conscious and unconscious. Freud's essay, "Dostoevsky and Parricide", about the Russian writer who himself had a gambling problem, and whose book, *The Gambler* (1866), is described by Rosenthal (1987) as, "the finest and certainly the best known case history of a pathological gambler in or out of literature" (p.45), is often quoted. Freud introduced the idea that a gambler might gamble out of a sense of guilt, losing at gambling being particularly effective as a form of self-punishment. The main sources of a sense of guilt, unknown to the gambler, were murderous Oedipal impulses towards the father. Gambling also relieved guilt because, like all addictions, it was a substitute for masturbation which itself gave rise to guilt.

Freud's ideas were most fully developed by Bergler. He first put forward his view, that 'real' or neurotic gamblers had an unconscious wish to lose, in an article in the 1930s. There followed several further publications and popularization in several magazines such as *Reader's Digest* in the 1940s, and the theory of the unconscious wish to lose was later adopted by Gamblers Anonymous. Bergler was impressed by the excessive gambler's almost fanatical belief in the possibility of success: "his illogical, senseless certainty that he will win" (1958, p.15). He was struck, as others with very different theoretical positions have also been, by the selective nature of reminiscences, the dwelling on success, and the relative forgetting of numerous failures. Bergler concluded that the motivation for 'real' or excessive gambling must be unconscious. The fanatical, and illogical belief in success was like the child's feeling of omnipotence or megalomania. Growing up involved replacing these feelings with the 'reality principle' largely instilled by parental figures. Gambling offered the perfect rebellion against this principle, because in gambling chance rules, and the virtues of honesty, logic, reason, and justice – all virtues that parents had taught – conferred no advantage. Hence gambling revived old childhood fantasies of grandeur and, more important, "it activates the *latent rebellion* against logic, intelligence, moderation, morality, and renunciation" (p.18, his emphasis). It enabled the individual:

. . . to scoff ironically at all the rules of life he has learned from education and experience . . . Since the child has learned these rules from his parents and their representatives . . . his rebellion activates a profound unconscious feeling of guilt (p.18).

It was this unconscious rebellion against parents that was responsible, in Bergler's view, for the neurotic wish to lose, because, like all acts or feelings of rebellion against parents, whether conscious or unconscious, it produced feelings of guilt and an unconscious tendency to self-punishment. Although Bergler seems to have been unaware that motivation can change greatly with the development of a behavioural excess such as gambling, his was a persuasive argument for one particular kind of expressive motivation. It is of interest that it is the 'wish to lose' part of Bergler's formulation that has been best remembered, although it is by no means the most prominent part of the theory expounded in his book, and it is probably the aspect of his ideas which fits least well with observations made by others about problem gambling.

Other psychoanalytically based theories, reviewed and cited by Rosenthal (1987), include: the idea that the feeling of omnipotence associated with gambling may be an attempt to ward off depression (Greenson, 1947); that gambling is a response to the helplessness of losing a parent or the break up of a marriage (Bolen and Boyd, 1968); identification with a favoured relative who gambles (Bolen and Boyd, 1968); or that gambling feeds the grandiose fantasies of power and success of the narcissistic personality, which compensate for a low sense of self-worth (Taber, 1982). There are a number of obvious limitations with these and other psychoanalytic ideas about problem gambling. All are based upon highly selected clinical samples, often merely one or a very small number of 'cases' (Bergler is an exception), and almost always predominantly or entirely male. Furthermore there has been no consideration given to the way in which certain forms of gambling might appeal to certain personalities, nor to the possibility that forms of personality seen clinically might be consequences rather than antecedents of problem gambling.

Personality disorders

Mainstream psychiatry in the USA, heavily influenced by the Diagnostic and Statistical Manual (DSM) of the American Psychiatric Association, has more recently taken a diagnostic approach to the question of whether certain personalities are particularly vulnerable to problem gambling. The key question from that perspective is whether 'pathological gamblers' (to use the DSM term) are also diagnosed as having 'personality disorders'. The National Research Council (1999) in the USA found very few studies that had linked 'personality disorders' with pathological gambling, and most of those studies were limited to small clinical samples.

One of the most thorough was Blaszczynski and Steel's (1998) study of 82 people receiving treatment for their excessive gambling. Using a standard questionnaire for diagnosing 'personality disorders' they found that no less than 76 of the 82 participants met diagnostic criteria for at least one of the 11 types of 'personality disorder' which they listed in their paper, with the average number of such disorders per patient being 4.7. The most common disorders were those falling in Cluster B which includes: 'antisocial', 'borderline', 'histrionic', and 'narcissistic' disorders. The rates of 'personality disorder' found in that study are admitted by the authors to be exceptionally high and may partly have been due to the questionnaire approach that they used. They contrasted their results with those of a study of 40 problem gamblers receiving treatment (Specker et al, 1996) which used a standard, structured interview and found only 25 per cent of the sample to have diagnosed 'personality disorder'. Blaszczynski and Steel pointed out that the rate found by Specker et al may have been lower on account of the comparatively recent onset of gambling problems in that study and the comparatively low achieved participation rate (60 per cent).

Relevant studies of general population samples scarcely exist. One study, carried out in a single mid-west US city in the early 1980s, but only reported in the late 1990s, found that problem gamblers were over six times more likely than non-gamblers to meet criteria for 'antisocial personality disorder' (ASPD) (Cunningham-Williams et al, 1998). The NRC review of this work concluded that it was at an early stage and that in future research of this kind would need stronger designs, more rigorous methods, and replication.

At least as interesting as the tentative findings of such research are the assumptions they embody about the nature of problem gambling, the nature of personality, and the link between the two. Quite apart from the assumption that personalities can be categorised, and clear distinctions drawn between those that are 'disordered' and the rest that are presumably 'normal' – all of which is highly controversial and roundly criticised from both within and without psychiatry – such studies often contain the assumption that antisocial or other 'personality disorders' are long-standing, possibly originating in childhood or even having genetic origins, and that they therefore pre-date and are *antecedents* of problem gambling. That is, of course, only an assumption, and an equally convincing argument could be made that signs of difficult or deviant personalities are a *consequence* of the development of a gambling problem, particularly since the latter often have their beginnings in adolescence. Although some authors working in the diagnostic psychiatry tradition, such as Blaszczynski and Steel (1998) are careful not to make explicit the assumption that 'personality disorder' precedes problem gambling and is causative of it, such an idea is inherent in the diagnosis of ASPD which is assumed to have its origins in childhood (NRC, 1999). This kind of assumption is sometimes found in an explicit and stark form (e.g. Kroeber, 1992), but similar assumptions in less explicit and extreme form are often made, usually without the backing of solid research findings.

Personality traits

Psychologists with an interest in personality and gambling have taken a somewhat different approach based upon personality traits. Traits are assumed to lie on a continuum, with scores on a measure of a trait being distributed according to a 'normal' or inverted bell-shaped curve. That approach shares with the psychiatric diagnostic method the assumption that aspects of personality can be measured by fairly simple means (usually questionnaires in this case), and often carries the same assumption that positions on traits are long-standing and are likely to pre-date the development of gambling problems.

In fact the trait approach has not met with a great deal of success. One of the most often tested hypotheses is that problem gamblers are high on the trait of 'sensation seeking'. The latter was defined by Zuckerman (1979, p.10, cited by Walker, 1992, p.94) as the "need for varied, novel and complex sensations and experiences, and the willingness to take physical and social risks for the sake of such experience". The hypothesis that problem gamblers would be high on this trait is based on the simple, but plausible, notion that gambling enhances the sensations associated with arousal and would therefore be more attractive to high-sensation seekers (Brown, 1986). Those who have viewed the evidence for the sensation seeking hypothesis have concluded that it has not received consistent support (Walker, 1992; Coventry and Brown, 1993, cited by Coventry and Norman, 1998). Although there are supportive studies, some show no difference in sensation seeking between groups and there are even some studies showing problem or regular gamblers to be lower on sensation seeking than the norm.

Two other personality traits that Walker (1992) found had been used in several studies of problem gambling were 'extraversion' and 'locus of control'. Extraversion, popularised by the work of Eysenck (e.g. 1967), might be thought to be associated with gambling because more extraverted people are less easily aroused psychophysiologically and might therefore be expected to enjoy the arousal associated with gambling more than introverts. In fact the studies of extraversion reviewed by Walker (1992) were almost evenly divided between those that found problem or regular gamblers to be reasonably high on extraversion, low, or indistinguishable from other people in that respect.

Locus of control had fared somewhat better: half the studies reviewed by Walker (1992) found no difference between problem or regular gamblers and other people, but the remainder found the gambling groups to be higher than normal on external locus of control, with no studies finding the opposite. External locus of control is defined as holding the belief that rewards are "the result of luck, chance, fate, as under the control of powerful others, or as unpredictable because of the great complexity of the forces surrounding [one]" (Rotter, 1966, p.1, cited by Walker, 1992, p.98). A person with such beliefs might be expected to be relatively attracted to gambling, so Walker reasoned, whilst those with a comparatively internal locus of control, believing that rewards are largely contingent upon their own actions, would find gambling relatively unattractive. Unfortunately for that theory, Carroll and Huxley (1994) later found the opposite amongst young machine players in England, 'dependent' players scoring as more *internally* controlled than non-dependent players. This was consistent, Carroll and Huxley argued, with the orientation of the former towards skill in playing the machines.

A further trait that has been popular in this kind of research since Walker (1992) wrote his review is 'impulsivity', defined by Barratt et al (1981, p.286, cited by Castellani and Rugle, 1995, p.277) as "a personality trait that is characteristic of individuals who act hastily or are impatient . . . Typical questionnaire items on impulsiveness scales are: I make up my mind quickly; I act on the spur of the moment . . .". Because relatively impulsive people may be comparatively sensitive to reward rather than to punishment, they might be expected to be relatively encouraged by gambling wins and less discouraged than others by gambling losses (Breen and Zuckerman, 1999). Impulsivity and gambling is also of particular interest to those who believe that problem gambling is best categorised, within psychiatric nosology, as an 'impulsive control disorder' (e.g. Vitaro et al, 1998). A number of studies have reported positive findings for impulsivity but they represent a very mixed bag of research designs. They include a study predicting extent of gambling in the late teens from impulsivity earlier in the teenage years (Barnes et al, 1999; Vitaro et al, 1998); a correlation between impulsivity and 'pathological gambling' amongst a volunteer sample of college students (Langewish and Frisch, 1998); an association between impulsivity and within-session 'chasing losses' on a computer game simulating gambling (Breen and Zuckerman, 1999); a finding of higher scores on impulsivity amongst treated 'substance abusers' with gambling problems compared to those without (McCormick, 1993); and higher impulsivity amongst treated 'pathological gamblers' than amongst treated alcohol or cocaine misusers (Castellani and Rugle, 1995).

This approach to understanding problem gambling is beset with difficulties and at best should be thought of as being at an early stage of development, and at worst a blind alley. Allcock (1986, p.262, cited by Griffiths, 1995a, p.15) thought the trait approach, "a naive over-simplification and a fruitless direction for research", and Griffiths (1995a) concluded that the utility and value of such studies remained doubtful. Apart from the assumptions inherent in the whole trait approach, which many consider unwarranted, there are a number of other difficulties. For one thing there is acknowledged overlap between some of the leading ideas such as sensation seeking, extraversion, and impulsivity, and a number of different measures exist for the same trait. Furthermore, the literature is a small one and still largely consists of a number of unrelated studies which vary in the ages of the participants, whether the index gambling group consists of problem gamblers, regular gamblers or simply gamblers, whether the sample is all male or includes women, the type of gambling, and the location of the research. A particular personality trait might be more important at an early or late stage in the development of a gambling problem but not at other stages, might be more important for men than for women or vice versa, or might be significant in the case of some forms of gambling and not others. Furthermore, traits such as sensation seeking (the same goes for impulsivity, and locus of control) have often been found on close study to consist of a set of inter-related components rather than a unitary construct, and hypotheses should therefore be more specific than they have often been. For all these reasons, Walker (1992) concluded, perhaps rather generously, that it might be too early to dismiss the hypothesis that personality traits such as sensation seeking and extraversion (and we might add impulsiveness) were related to gambling.

Theories based on reward or reinforcement

Operant conditioning or learning based on reward

Unlike personality or personal-social theories or those based upon a diagnostic psychiatric view, behavioural theories focus little on differences between individual people and much on the process of becoming more heavily involved in gambling as a result of one's experiences of it. The central idea is that people become 'conditioned' or 'learn' the habit of gambling as a consequence of the rewards (or 'reinforcement') obtained through gambling. That is the basic notion behind the form of learning known as operant or Skinnerian conditioning. Much of Skinner's and other learning theorists' early work was based on experiments with animals such as pigeons learning to peck at coloured panels or monkeys learning to press levers to obtain rewards in the form of food. So closely does gambling seem to resemble operant experimental procedures used with animals that a behavioural learning analysis seems an obvious contender for explaining, at least in part, how gambling might become a problem (Cornish, 1978; Griffiths, 1995a; Knapp, 1997; Elster, 1999; Orford, 2001). Knapp (1997, p.130) stated "no other contemporary public policy issue provides such an isometric fit with the principles of behavior analysis as gambling. . .". He pointed out that introductory psychology textbooks very frequently give gambling, particularly machine gambling, as an illustration of the principles of operant learning.

There are a number of features of operant learning theory which between them might go a long way to explaining the paradox inherent in problem gambling – that the behaviour persists despite apparently producing more harm than good for the person concerned. The first is the point that it is *probabilities* that are affected in learning. It is not a matter of one response becoming totally dominant to the exclusion of others, but rather of certain acts gradually becoming more probable, thus providing an explanation for the insidious development of strongly habitual behaviour such as problem gambling. The second feature is the 'gradient of reinforcement': behaviour may have both immediate, rewarding consequence, as well as harmful or punishing longer-term outcomes, but it is the *immediate* consequences that are the most important in shaping habitual behaviour.

The third important feature of operant learning concerns the partial nature of much reinforcement: *inconsistent* reward results in behaviour even more strongly conditioned than that produced by consistent reinforcement. It is often pointed out that the financial rewards from gambling (the 'wins') are paid out on a 'reinforcement schedule' corresponding to one termed by Skinner a variable-ratio (VR) schedule which he found led to particularly persistent behaviour on the part of experimental animals even when the behaviour was no longer successful in leading to reward (in learning theory terms it was 'resistant to extinction'). In his general work, *Science and Human Behavior*, Skinner wrote, "the efficacy of such schedules in generating high rates has long been known to the proprietors of gambling establishments" (1953, p.104, cited by Knapp, 1997, p.131). Under VR schedules, not only is behaviour not rewarded every time it occurs, but it is not even regularly rewarded after a certain number of responses (e.g. after every fifth or tenth pull of a lever, which would correspond to a fixed-ratio or FR schedule). The probability of reinforcement does depend on the number of pulls of the lever, but the ratio of pulls to rewards is made variable: it is predictable that reward will come, but not when.

In fact, as Knapp (1997) carefully pointed out, gambling operates on a reinforcement schedule that is similar in some respects to VR, but is different from it in a respect that is probably of the utmost importance. In the VR schedule, the probability of reward increases with each successive response since the last reward was given. Although, as we shall discuss later in the section on cognitive processes, gamblers often believe that the latter is true (the 'gambler's fallacy'), gambling truly corresponds to a random ratio (RR) schedule of reinforcement under which the overall likelihood of a payout remains constant. This makes financial reward even less predictable: the more you play the greater the chance of having a win, but you don't know when, and the chances of a win on the next play do not increase the greater the run of losses. RR may be thought of as a special case of a VR schedule. The latter according to Knapp (1997, p.132), ". . . whether in a laboratory setting, as part of a gaming device, or as an aspect of a natural environment, leads the organism under its control to respond at high rates for relatively little reinforcement, and to persist in long periods of responding when no payoff is forthcoming".

Operant theory based on VR (RR) reward schedules fits well with the often-repeated observation that problem gamblers are very likely to have experienced 'beginner's luck' in the form of a big early win in their own personal histories of gambling (Moran, 1970; Dickerson, 1974; Cornish, 1978; Custer and Milt, 1985). Although, once established, these intermittent reinforcement schedules are very effective in maintaining behaviour, even in the face of repeated failure to achieve reward, it is comparatively difficult to establish behaviour in the first place using such schedules. It is much easier if behaviour is 'shaped' early on by building in a favourable history of reinforcement or 'enriching' an otherwise sparse programme of reinforcement. Early experiences of winning would serve this purpose very well. Although there is surprisingly little concrete evidence for the early win hypothesis (but much anecdotal evidence), it fits well with the learning theory explanation.

Emotional rewards from gambling

So far our discussion of a behavioural approach has rested on the assumption that the sole reward from gambling is financial. But numerous writers on the subject have argued that emotional rewards are just as important, have reported the emphasis that gamblers often put upon the excitement associated with gambling, and have suggested that an increase in arousal may be one of the most important, perhaps the most important reward from gambling behaviour (e.g. Lesieur, 1984; Carroll and Huxley, 1994; Griffiths, 1995a). Most agree that gambling is like a 'drug' in this respect, and that emotional regulation may be much more important than financial gain for understanding gambling. Hickey et al (1986) used a set of questions known as the Addiction Research Center Inventory, validated with groups of drug takers, and applied them to a group (admittedly rather small and selective) of problem gamblers, concluding that the pattern of responses was most like that associated with the taking of amphetamines. Most of the 30 regular fruit-machine players (playing at least once a week) studied by Griffiths (1995b) also reported feeling excitement during playing as opposed to before or after playing. In his report of interviews with 50 compulsive gamblers, Lesieur (1984, p.44) wrote:

> *All* compulsive gamblers (and many non compulsive gamblers) talk of the action aspect of gambling. It is described in terms of 'getting my

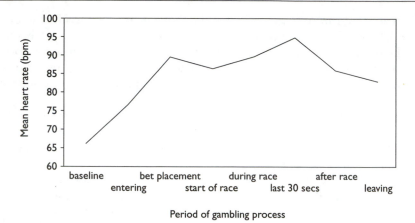

Figure 4.3 Evidence of arousal during horse-race betting (reproduced with permission from Coventry and Norman, 1997, Figure 1)

rocks off', 'adrenalin flowing', and most often compared to sexual excitement. . . Each win is described in terms of being a 'high', and each loss is a 'downer' or 'depressing'. These are *emotional* rather than purely economic terms and states.

In fact, early psychophysiological studies conducted under laboratory conditions found no evidence for an increase in arousal with gambling, but since Anderson and Brown (1984, cited by Griffiths 1995b) raised the question of ecological validity and found that regular gamblers showed substantial increases in heart rate when gambling in a real casino, reliable increases in cardiovascular activity have been observed during gambling-machine playing in a number of studies (Leary and Dickerson, 1985; Coulombe et al, 1992; Huxley, 1993; Carroll and Huxley, 1994; Griffiths, 1993c, 1995b; Coventry and Hudson, 2001). The same phenomenon has been demonstrated for horse-race betting by Coventry and Norman (1997) whose results are summarised in Figure 4.3.

Quite apart from the pleasurable arousal or excitement associated with the uncertainty of winning or losing, gambling settings, as pointed out earlier, contain multiple stimuli which, simply because they are arousing, may have reward value in themselves independently of financial reward. Since such events as race commentaries and spinning reels are present on all occasions, whether a win or a loss is the result, it may be more correct to think of the rewards of gambling being delivered on a schedule that combines fixed-interval (FI, in which emotional reward arrives reliably with every gamble) and VR/RR (the much less reliable financial reward), as suggested by Dickerson (1979).

Discussions of what precisely are the emotional rewards of gambling can become quite complicated. For example, Lesieur and Rosenthal (1991) reported finding evidence for two quite different motives for early involvement in gambling, 'action seeking' and 'escape seeking', referred to by Elster (1999) as pull and push motives respectively. The fact that most of the literature has highlighted the former may be related to it being more common, according to Lesieur and Rosenthal, among male gamblers. They reported finding that more than half the women problem gamblers they interviewed stated that they initially viewed gambling as a means of escaping from problems in their home lives, in their pasts or in relationships. Those who gambled as an escape frequently described their gambling as an 'anaesthetic' which 'hypnotised' them, a phenomenon described by Jacobs (1993) as a dissociative state akin to a memory blackout, trance or out-of-body experience. Of a sample of 121 'compulsive gamblers', over two-thirds said that they, at least occasionally and in many cases more often, "felt like they were in a trance", and "felt like a different person", and half "felt outside themselves watching themselves as in a dream" (Jacobs, 1993). Lesieur (1984, p.46) suggested that an important mechanism for mood regulation might be distraction since, once engaged in gambling, the gambler "becomes oblivious to his surroundings and concerned with the action itself", and Reith (1999) unearthed many anecdotal accounts of experiences when gambling, including taking on a different identity, timelessness, separation from the rest of life, disassociation, intense concentration, and even feelings like vertigo. Diskin and Hodgins (1999) set up an experiment in which video lottery terminal (VLT) players in Alberta, Canada, were required to respond when lights came on which were placed at either side of the terminal at which they were playing. 'Pathological' VLT players were slower to respond to lights than were occasional players, and were more likely afterwards to agree with the statements that they had "taken on a new identity", and "lost all track of time".

The subject of emotional rewards from gambling can become very complicated indeed. Although the idea that gambling induces arousal has been very popular, account needs to be taken of a number of complicating factors. One is individual differences (some may gamble for excitement, others for its 'anti-depressant' effect); emotional rewards from gambling may be very different for different forms of gambling; the value placed on arousal may change from time to time or setting to setting (as 'reversal theory' has it, it may be pleasant when one is in a pleasure-oriented, or 'paratelic' state, but unpleasant when in a task-oriented, or 'telic' state); gambling might in some circumstances be a way of 'turning off' a state of unpleasantly high arousal induced by anticipation of gambling (a kind of 'behavioural completion mechanism'); and rewards from gambling might be expected to change as a problem-gambling 'career' develops, with earlier excitement turning into later desperation (Lesieur, 1984; Custer and Milt, 1985; Cocco et al, 1995; Sharpe et al, 1995; Coventry and Norman, 1998).

Classical conditioning or conditioning by association

Whatever the nature of the primary reward from gambling – whether financial or some kind of emotional reinforcement – a complete behavioural account of gambling rests not solely upon the operant reinforcement of behaviour by its consequences, but also on a multitude of conditioned associations with cues that precede or accompany the different phases of the activity and its aftermath. If an activity becomes at all regular or frequent, numerous opportunities arise for conditioning of formerly neutral cues. Experimental studies with both animals and humans have repeatedly shown how activity-specific and setting cues, that in themselves have no intrinsic capacity to produce rewarding effects like those produced by the activity itself, can become conditioned stimuli through a process of classical, Pavlovian, conditioning, thus acquiring the capacity to motivate further activity (Glautier, 1994). This is what is otherwise termed incentive conditioning or incentive learning (Wise, 1994; White, 1996). Behaviour then comes to be as much under the control of stimuli or 'cues' accompanying an activity as of the consequences of behaviour. Some of these 'discriminative stimuli' are closely linked to the activity itself. The graphic account of the characteristic 'stimuli' of the gambling casino provided by Dostoevsky in his autobiographical novel *The Gambler* is a good case in point:

> With what trembling, with what faintness of heart I hear the croupier's cry . . . With what greed I look . . . at the little columns of gold when they are scattered from the croupier's shovel into piles glowing like fire, or columns of silver a yard high lying stacked round the wheel. Even while approaching the gambling hall, two rooms away, as soon as I begin to hear the clinking of money being poured out, I almost go into convulsions (cited by Minihan, 1967, p.319).

A more modern example of the same thing is given by David, a 'fruit-machine addict' described by Griffiths.

> Although winning money was the first thing that attracted me to playing fruit machines, this was gradually converted to lights, sounds and excitement. I always received a great thrill from new machines with new ideas and new lights and sounds (David, cited by Griffiths, 1993b, p.393).

As well as the lights and sounds he spoke of, other associated cues are to do with the time and setting in which activity usually takes place, such as a particular time of the week or of the day, being with a particular group of friends or being in a particular place.

Conditioning by association is such a ubiquitous and fundamental process that it is almost certainly of importance in the development of a gambling habit, but a real test of its occurrence requires a demonstration that arousal occurs for gamblers specifically in the presence of cues that have been associated with gambling but which in themselves have no primary reinforcing value. The first study to provide such a demonstration was reported by Sharpe et al (1995). They compared three groups in Australia: problem gamblers (who met DSM-III-R and SOGS criteria for 'pathological gambling'), high-frequency social gamblers (gambling at least once a week), and low-frequency social gamblers (never having gambled more than once a month). Gambling in all cases referred to machine gambling (Australian 'poker machines'). Psychophysiological responses were taken before and during four 'tasks': a neutral task, watching a horse-race video, watching a poker-machine video, and imagining winning at poker-machine playing. Three types of recording were made: heart rate (HR), skin conductance level (SCL, which measures hand perspiration), and frontal electromyography (EMG, recorded from the frontal area of the brain).

Results were most clear-cut in the case of SCL recordings: problem gamblers showed more arousal than the other groups when watching a poker-machine video and when imagining winning. Results on HR and EMG were less clear-cut. Nevertheless, as the authors of that report stated, ". . . the importance of the present results are that they represent the first empirical demonstration of the relationship between autonomic arousal and problem gambling in the absence of gambling behaviour" (p.1539). Sharpe et al were surprised to find no differences in reactions between the high frequency and low frequency social gamblers. Their theory was that the conditioning by association that they were testing for should have taken place for those who had developed a regular gambling habit albeit not to a point of experiencing a gambling problem. The fact that it was the problem-gambling group that stood out as being different in this respect suggests that the kind of gambling cue reactivity for which they found evidence may be more a feature of problem gambling than of regular gambling per se.

The role of cognition

Although operant learning, based on financial and complex emotional rewards from gambling, plus conditioning by association to a variety of stimuli or cues associated with gambling, might go a long way towards providing at least a partial explanation of problem gambling, the cognitive behavioural 'revolution' of the 1970s makes it almost obligatory now to consider the contribution of cognitive factors (Shewan and Brown, 1993). A complete cognitive-behavioural theory would include people's attitudes, beliefs, expectancies, illusions and biases.

Attitudes to risk taking

One line of study concerns attitudes towards taking risks. There have now been a number of studies that have taken an experimental approach to investigating the circumstances under which people take risks of the kind involved in gambling. Some of the findings suggest that preferences for risk or caution, displayed under one set of conditions, can be altered and even reversed under different conditions. One finding is that people tend to be risk-averse when playing for gains (e.g. preferring a 100 per cent chance of receiving £100 versus a 50 per cent chance of receiving £200) and risk-seeking when faced with potential losses (e.g. tending to prefer a 50 per cent chance of losing £200 to a certain loss of £100) (Tversky and Kahneman, 1981; Breslin et al, 1999).

Another hypothesis, supported in studies by Nygren (1998), is that under low-risk conditions, positive mood or set is associated with a tendency to take more risks, whereas under high-risk conditions the opposite is the case, with those who are more positive being more likely to play safe. This is consistent with other work on risky decision-making showing that people in a positive mood tend to be more conservative or self-protective in situations where there is a focus on meaningful loss or where loss is very likely. It is as if a loss for such people carries an enhanced 'disutility', or as if greater 'regret' is anticipated because loss would represent a greater departure from a current 'reference point' that is positive in value.

A study reported by Petry and Casarella (1999) is another that involved participants making choices, this time between smaller immediate and larger delayed monetary rewards. The methodology of such 'delay discounting' studies involved working out, from participants' choices, how much a delayed reward is 'worth' to the participant in terms of its equivalent immediate reward. It is known that the worth of monetary rewards drops with increasing delay, according to a hyperbolic function. The interest to Petry and Casarella was whether 'substance abusers' and especially problem gamblers, showed more rapid discounting of delayed rewards than controls. The results clearly supported this hypothesis, with the fall-off in value of rewards with increasing delay being greatest for problem gamblers with substance problems, intermediate for substance misusers without gambling problems, and least for the controls. For example, US$1000 delayed for a year was on average worth the equivalent of an immediate $500 to control participants, around $350 for substance misusers without gambling problems, and only around $100 for problem gambling substance misusers. Petry and Casarella suggested that such rapid discounting and delayed rewards may be one index of impulsivity.

Expectancies

Another line of work that has been very popular in the study of alcohol concerns the 'expectancies' that people hold regarding the effects that the activity is likely to have for them. There is much evidence in that field that positive expectancies are correlated with the extent of the activity and with problems connected with it (drinking and drinking-related problems in that case) (e.g. Cooper et al, 1992). One study that has examined 'outcome expectancies' for gambling is that reported by Walters and Contri (1998), carried out with medium security prisoners (all men) in the USA, a group that contained relatively high proportions of men who had wagered very large amounts of money and who scored as 'pathological gamblers' on SOGS. They developed their own measure of expectancies – the Gambling Expectancy Effects Questionnaire (GEEQ) – which required the participants to rate on seven-point scales (from 'never' to 'always') a number of adjectives or phrases following the sentence stem, "gambling for money makes me . . .". Four expectancy scores were calculated (positive, negative, arousing, sedating). Four groups were compared: non-gamblers, non-problem gamblers, 'possible problem gamblers' (SOGS scores between one and four), and 'probable pathological gamblers' (SOGS scores of five or more).

Apart from sedating expectancies which were equally low in all four groups, the 'probable pathological gamblers' scored significantly higher on all types of expectancy than other groups, with 'possible problem gamblers' also being higher than non-gamblers or non-problem gamblers. This was true, as Walters and Contri had expected, for positive expectancies (gambling for money makes me: 'important', 'expert', 'in control') and arousing expectancies (e.g. 'excited'). But the same was true also for negative expectancies (e.g. 'afraid', 'angry'). Figure 4.4 shows this effect, with the probable pathological gambling group demonstrating their heightened ambivalence towards gambling by scoring highest on both positive and negative expectancies.

The near miss

The phenomenon of the near miss (or as others have called it, perhaps more accurately, the 'near win'), which was discussed as a structural feature of gambling earlier in this chapter, might also be interpreted in cognitive terms. Griffiths (1995a) suggested that near misses might be motivating because they produced frustration or 'cognitive regret' (Kahneman and Tversky, 1982, cited by Griffiths, 1995a). Elster (1999) preferred the idea that near wins might serve to confirm beliefs about one's ability to predict outcomes. Rogers (1998) believed that near misses induced some players to believe that they were getting closer to winning. Maybe each of those ideas holds some truth, but what they have in common is the assumption that the gambler's thought processes are likely to enter into the picture.

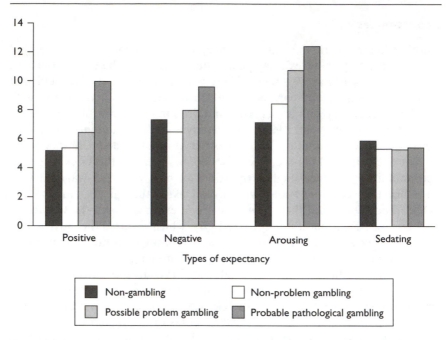

Figure 4.4 Expectancies for the emotional effects of gambling (reproduced with permission from Walters and Contri, 1998, Table 4)

Cognitive biases

The cognitive approach that has featured most strongly in relation to gambling has concerned itself with a variety of mental biases and illusions. The assumption behind that approach is that gambling can not be understood as a rational activity, as has been concluded in some of the historical, sociological or observational studies looked at in Chapter 1 and earlier in the present chapter, but can only be explained by supposing that gamblers think about the activity in an illogical or distorted way. That approach has some intuitive appeal to it since in commercial forms of gambling the odds are always stacked against the gambler and in some cases, such as the NL, the odds are heavily stacked in that direction. There is in fact a great deal of evidence now that gambling is associated with a number of different forms of cognitive bias and distortion, those for which there is strongest evidence being shown in Table 4.1.

The varieties of irrationality evident in gambling have been well described by a number of writers on the subject (e.g. Ladouceur and Walker, 1996; Rogers, 1998). The different biases that have been described can for convenience be placed into two broad groups: (1) those based upon a misunderstanding of chance and randomness which lead a gambler to believe

Table 4.1 Common cognitive biases and distortions that occur during gambling (based on Ladouceur and Walker, 1996, and Rogers, 1998)

Over-estimate of probability of large prizes
Belief that short runs of events should appear 'random'
The gamblers' fallacy
Entrapment
Belief in hot and cold numbers
Unrealistic optimism
Perceived luckiness
Superstitious thinking
Illusion of control
Erroneous beliefs
Biased evaluation of outcomes

that the outcome of a gamble is more predictable than in fact it is; and (2) beliefs held by gamblers that they can influence the outcome when in fact the outcome is unpredictable (or that they have more control over the outcome than is in fact the case) – an 'illusion of control'.

With regard to the first of these, Rogers (1998) started his review by making the general point that most people have a poor understanding of probability, tending to underestimate high-frequency events and over-estimate low-frequency ones, and generally show over-confidence in their judgements of probability. This may particularly be the case with something like the NL, since odds of several million to one lie well outside the range of most people's everyday experience of probabilities. Where accurate judgements are difficult to make people use a variety of 'heuristics' or cognitive 'rules of thumb' that provide quick and easy ways of coming to a decision (Tversky and Kahneman, 1982; Wagenaar, 1988, both cited by Rogers, 1998). One of these is the 'availability heuristic' whereby the probability of an event is over-estimated if it comes relatively easily to mind because, like lottery jackpots for example, it is distinctive, arousing or well-publicised.

A second heuristic, much studied, is the 'representativeness heuristic' whereby small samples of events (such as a short run of plays or bets) are assumed to be representative of the whole population of events or a much longer run of plays or bets. One effect of that rule of thumb is the assumption that a short run of gambling outcomes will have the appearance of being random. That is to misunderstand probabilities since it is in the nature of such things that short runs of events often have the appearance of being anything but random. Consistent with that idea is the finding that lottery numbers that do not look random, such as 11, 22 or 33 or strings of adjacent numbers, such as 11, 12, 13, are less popular than others. Some combinations of numbers are, erroneously, considered to be very unlikely (e.g. 1, 2, 3, 4, 5, 6) (Ladouceur and Walker, 1996).

Failure to grasp the essential point about a series of chance or random events, that each event is independent of all others and that the probabilities of the outcomes of an event remain the same whatever have been the outcomes of preceding events, underlies a form of irrationality that has been observed to be so common amongst gamblers that it has earned the title of the 'gambler's fallacy'. In roulette, for example, players believe that certain numbers are 'due' because they have not come up for a while (Ladouceur and Walker, 1996). The operation of the gambler's fallacy in play on the UK NL has been studied by Coups et al (1998) and by Rogers and Webley (1998). Coups et al asked members of their volunteer adult sample two questions designed to assess the gambler's fallacy: how likely the six numbers drawn in last week's lottery were to be drawn again compared to another set of six numbers; and how likely a particular number already drawn ten times in the last year was to be drawn again in the next year compared to a number only having been drawn once in the year. Fifty per cent of their participants showed some level of misunderstanding of probability; for example 39 per cent indicated that the six numbers drawn the previous week were not as likely as others to be drawn. Rogers and Webley (1998, cited by Rogers, 1998) found that regular lottery players, compared to occasional and non-players, were more likely to believe that a jackpot win (all six numbers matched) was less likely if the draw was preceded by one in which six numbers had been matched successfully.

'Entrapment' is the name that has been given to the "process whereby individuals escalate their commitment to a previously chosen, though failing course of action in order to justify or make good on prior investments" (Brockner and Roubin, 1985, cited by Rogers, 1998, p.120). It has been claimed, for example, that as many as 60 per cent of NL players choose the same numbers every week (Hill and Williamson, 1998, cited by Rogers, 1998) and that many players feel trapped into repeatedly betting on the same numbers through fear of missing a potential win on numbers in which much has already been 'invested'. Other false beliefs, also connected to misunderstanding about randomness, are superstitious thinking (e.g. ritualised selection of specific numbers like birthdays and anniversaries, gambling at specific locations, or use of special clothes, jewellery or lucky talismans), belief in 'hot' numbers (seen to be drawn with some regularity and hence thought to have a greater than average chance of being drawn again), and a belief in 'luck' (either as a stable characteristic of the gambler himself or herself, or as a temporary state as in a 'run of good luck') (Ladouceur and Walker, 1996; Rogers, 1998).

The illusion of control

But it is the 'illusion of control' that has been "Probably the most single influential contribution to the cognitive psychology of gambling . . ."

(Griffiths, 1995a, p.21). The idea was introduced by Langer (1975) who defined the illusion of control as being "an expectancy of a personal success inappropriately higher than the objective probability would warrant" (p.316, cited by Griffiths, 1995a, p.21). It had already been observed, for example, that dice players behaved in ways that suggested they thought they could control the outcome to some extent. For example players would throw the dice softly for low numbers and harder for high numbers, and were less confident if asked to bet after someone else had thrown a dice rather than throwing it themselves. Langer carried out a number of her own experiments on the subject, reporting for example that participants bet more when cutting cards against a 'nervous' competitor than against a 'confident' one, would sell previously bought lottery tickets for a higher price if they had picked them themselves, and that those given early experience of winning at a coin-tossing game (even though they won overall no more often than others) subsequently rated themselves as more skilful, remembered more wins, and thought that over future trials they would be more successful than did others (Langer, 1975; Langer and Roth, 1975, both cited by Griffiths, 1995a and by Coventry and Norman, 1998). According to Rogers (1998) many UK NL players prefer to choose their own numbers rather than use the official 'lucky dip' option of having numbers randomly generated by a computer, and have been found to be generally reluctant to exchange their own lottery tickets for replacement ones.

Ladouceur and colleagues conducted a further series of experiments to test the hypothesis that the illusion of control would be enhanced by anything that increased the apparent similarity of gambling to a game of skill. Anything that increased active participation or involvement, or increased familiarity with the game, might have this effect. For example, Ladouceur and Mayrand (1987) increased activity in playing a simulated game of roulette, by allowing some players to throw the ball themselves. Compared to those who had the ball thrown for them, as in casinos, active participants bet significantly more money. In another experiment Ladouceur et al (1986) found that money bet on a roulette game increased, as did level of confidence, as a session progressed, and from one session to the next. Ladouceur and Walker (1996, p.97) commented about that finding, "Since the outcomes in roulette are unpredictable, it is amazing to find that subjects report a feeling of mastering the game." In yet another experiment Ladouceur and Mayrand (1987) compared roulette players who bet as normally before the throw of the ball, with an artificial condition in which players bet after the ball had been thrown and had come to rest, the outcome being hidden by a large piece of cardboard. The results supported their hypothesis, derived from the idea of illusion of control, that bets placed before the throw would be significantly higher than those placed afterwards.

Another way in which the illusion of control can be enhanced is through 'biased evaluation of outcomes' otherwise known as 'hindsight bias'. This was first described by Gilovich (1983, cited by Griffiths, 1995a) who observed how sports betters who had backed a losing team spent more time discussing and trying to explain the result than did those who had backed the winner. He speculated that people were in effect transforming the win into a 'fluke' and the loss into a 'near miss'. In a subsequent experiment, Gilovich and Douglas (1986, cited by Ladouceur and Walker, 1996) arranged for some players on a bingo-like game to experience a 'fluke' win (one player had only one square left to fill in, when the other player won by having a run of luck and completed half the coupon in successive turns). Those who won on the game (whether clearly or by 'fluke') increased their bets on the next game, but so too did those who had experienced a 'fluke' loss. Only players who had experienced a clear loss decreased their bets.

The relevance of the illusion of control for understanding problem gambling amongst adolescents and young adults has been stressed by Carroll and Huxley (1994) and Griffith (1995a) who both found that young problem gamblers differed from non-problem gamblers by having a greater belief in the role of skill in machine gambling, and in giving over-estimates of the amounts of money they were likely to win. Moore and Ohtsuka (1999), too, in a study of over 1,000 older adolescents and young adults recruited from secondary schools and universities in Melbourne, Australia, found evidence for a "complex of irrational beliefs that are related to gambling . . ." (p.345). Young men in particular appeared to be "quite naïve about gambling in the sense of having overinflated views about their chances of winning and their role in making winning occur" (p.345). Three questionnaire factors were identified: 'illusion of control' (e.g. One day I'm going to strike it lucky at gambling; To win at gambling you need to think positively); 'need money' (e.g. I need to win some money to balance my budget; The only way I'll ever get ahead is if I win a decent prize gambling); and 'belief in systems' (You can win at the pokies [Australian slang for video-poker machines] if you adopt the right system; You can 'beat the system' at the casino if you know how). Scores on each of those three scales were significantly correlated with frequency of gambling, and even more strongly correlated with problem gambling (score on SOGS). Scores on the first two factors were significantly higher amongst males than females, and amongst school compared to university students.

Evidence for the importance of irrational thinking in gambling has been strengthened by use of the 'thinking-aloud' method introduced into the field by Gaboury and Ladouceur (1989). They asked ten participants (five men and five women), selected through advertisement, to play a gambling machine, thinking aloud as they did so. Everything the participants said was tape-recorded and subsequently categorised as either 'adequate' or 'inadequate' (i.e. erroneous). Examples are shown in Table 4.2. Inadequate verbalizations significantly outnumbered adequate by seven to three. A second study involved 20 new participants, recruited in the same way,

Table 4.2 Examples of adequate and inadequate verbalizations produced
during a thinking-aloud gambling experiment (reproduced with
permission from Gaboury and Ladouceur, 1989, Table 1)

Adequate verbalizations

A. Verbalize probabilities, discuss the odds of the game or the machine e.g. 'The odds aren't any better if I bet on three rows instead of one, it doesn't change anything'.

B. Verbalize the fact that there is no possible control over the game, that it is luck. Mention the impossibility of developing a strategy e.g. 'It's a machine, we have no control over it, it's all luck'.

C. Differentiate between irrationality and reality e.g. '. . . so I should have more luck the next trial (inadequate) . . . it doesn't necessarily mean that I will win'.

D. A conclusion concerning the general appreciation about the game in long-term context e.g. 'There's more chance of losing than winning at this game'.

E. An analysis of the game, from an objective point of view, and of the various behaviors of players e.g. 'I can't believe people play this game for a whole evening. There must be something that attracts them'.

Inadequate verbalizations

A. Mention cause and effect relationship e.g. 'I won on three rows, I'm going to bet on those rows again, this is a good game'.

B. Formulation of hypothesis concerning the game, a system for winning, predictions e.g. 'I played many times on one row. In about five trials, I'll play on three rows. It should be a better bet then'.

C. Confirmation of an hypothesis, a prediction or the opposite: surprise when a prediction is not confirmed e.g. 'I knew it. I told you so'. 'It wasn't this turn that I was supposed to win'.

D. Personification of the machine e.g. 'This machine is making me mad on purpose'.

E. Put the fault or merit on oneself, perception of personal skill and/or control. Reference to personal abilities e.g. 'I'm getting good at this game. I think I've mastered it'.

F. References to a personal state such as luck e.g. 'I'm lucky today, I should buy a lotto ticket'.

playing roulette. Again inadequate verbalizations outnumbered adequate, this time by about four to one. The ratio was higher for those who believed that roulette was not just a question of chance and that the use of strategies could enhance the probability of winning. But inadequate verbalizations much exceeded adequate ones even for those who believed that winning at roulette was only a question of chance, and almost all machine players in the first study believed that winning was a matter of chance alone. Ladouceur and Walker (1996) discussed the apparent anomaly. How was it that many players of machines and roulette correctly described these as games of chance whilst their verbal behaviour during play suggested irrational thinking? As they said, "It is as if there are two modes of thinking about the game: spontaneous, uncensored reactions to the events in the game while the game is in progress, and rational consideration of the realities of the game when not involved" (p.103).

The thinking-aloud method has now been used in a number of studies. Griffiths (1994) has used the method with young British gambling machine players, again finding evidence for irrational verbalizations, and furthermore finding a higher proportion of such verbalizations amongst regular compared to occasional players. Coventry and Norman (1998) used the method with students taking part in a computer-based simulated gambling task, finding again an excess of 'irrational' over 'rational' verbalizations even though they employed a tighter definition of what constituted an irrational utterance. They confined their definition to verbalizations that clearly demonstrated a lack of understanding of probability theory (e.g. I haven't won for a while, so I must be about to win) with rational verbalizations being confined to those that did reflect such an understanding (e.g. It doesn't matter whether I have just won or lost – the task is still chance). They excluded some other kinds of statement that Ladouceur and colleagues and Griffiths had, incorrectly in their view, included as irrational. These included a sub-category that Griffiths had found to be common amongst young machine players, namely 'personifications' of the machine such as 'This machine doesn't like me'. Interesting findings were reported by Coulombe et al (1992) when they simultaneously monitored arousal (increased heart rate) and verbalizations whilst regular and occasional video-poker players, recruited in bars and arcades in the Quebec city area, played a video-poker game. Not only did they find that regular players emitted more erroneous verbalizations than occasional players, but they also found a significant positive correlation between the number of erroneous verbalizations and degree of arousal.

Summarising work on the gambler's fallacy, Ladouceur and Walker (1996, pp.105–106) put it thus:

> Players elaborate strategies, develop confidence in their skills, and interpret both success and failure as significant in the process of predicting the outcome. This point is crucial for understanding the psychology of gambling. Despite the fact that the players concentrate and calculate with diligence, it is all futile . . . But the belief that these stratagems are effective is at the core of the desire to continue gambling.

Chasing losses

It has often been maintained that the phenomenon which gamblers themselves refer to as 'chasing one's losses' or simply 'chasing' is of central importance for explaining problem gambling (Lesieur, 1994; Dickerson, 1990; Orford et al, 1996). The relevant SOGS item defines chasing as 'go[ing] back another day to win back money you've lost'. Since the implication is that the likelihood of gambling on another day is increased because of losses experienced on a previous day, this would qualify as a form of 'entrapment', by all accounts a particularly important one. Detailed study of chasing has confirmed its likely importance in the development of problem gambling, but has also clarified and widened the concept. A particularly thorough study of chasing was carried out by O'Connor (2000) who held focus groups and conducted questionnaire studies with both sports betters and gambling-machine players in Australia. The importance of chasing was demonstrated by finding very significant correlations between chasing and such variables as degree of impaired control over gambling (as assessed by the Scale of Gambling Choices, SGC, Baron et al, 1995, cited by O'Connor, 2000), the amount of time and money spent on gambling per week, debts, and a relatively early age of starting regular gambling (especially starting as a teenager).

Chasing was not confined, as the SOGS item might suggest, to between-session chasing. Within-session chasing was more commonly found, although it might be less useful in discriminating problem gamblers from others. Nor was chasing solely a response to losses. In terms of behaviour the most important signs appeared to be increasing the size of bets or stakes after a loss, or after a win, plus continuing to bet instead of stopping after a loss. There were also important cognitive-emotional aspects to chasing, particularly anticipated relief at the prospect of winning, which was especially important for people with little to lose and much to win, for example following the experience of heavy losses or the existence of debts.

The core of the experience of chasing, as described by O'Connor's gamblers, appeared to be the use of inferior betting selections, or less sensible play, under the pressure created by losing or badly needing to win. As one sports better who took part in one of O'Connor's focus groups put it, chasing was "having a bet according to how much you are losing, not according to the chances of the horse winning, as you might do when you are dead-square or before the meeting/session began" (p.57). Although O'Connor's work has told us much in detail about the nature of chasing, it admittedly leaves unanswered the important question of the stage in the development of problem gambling at which chasing comes into the picture. Does it pre-date and perhaps predict later problem gambling? Is it part and parcel of the development of problem gambling? Or is it simply an important sign that problem gambling has already developed?

A number of other incidental but important findings were thrown up by O'Connor's work. One was the importance to the gamblers he spoke to of the experience of 'near misses' in encouraging chasing. O'Connor cited Delfabbro and Winefield (1999), who have pointed out that technical advances in gambling-machine design in Australia – for example facing players with nine lines of symbols with winning combinations on horizontal lines, in V-shapes, and in a variety of zig-zag combinations – may result in almost every outcome being a near miss.

The role of alcohol

If it is the case that factors such as mood influence a person's willingness to take risks on gambling-like games and tasks, as discussed earlier, then it might be supposed that the taking of substances and level of intoxication would also be of influence. Since alcohol is 'our favourite drug' and gambling often occurs in settings where alcohol is consumed, it is not surprising that the link between drinking and gambling has been explored in a number of studies. The repeated finding that comparatively large proportions of problem gamblers also have drinking problems or are heavy drinkers has already been referred to earlier. There are also reports that machine gamblers and off-course sports gamblers in Australia find difficulty in resisting starting gambling after drinking or are more likely to report 'chasing' behaviour (O'Connor et al, 1995; Baron and Dickerson, 1999, both cited by Kyngdon and Dickerson, 1999). A substantial minority of heavy-drinking men in an English study reported that after drinking they had spent more money on gambling than they otherwise would have done (Orford et al, 1998).

The question that arises is whether consuming alcohol increases the likelihood of people gambling heavily or excessively. There is certainly some evidence to support that view. Giacopassi et al (1998) reported the results from questionnaires completed by over 800 students in two universities in the USA (Reno and Memphis, both with casinos in the vicinity, of long-standing in the case of Reno). Slightly over half of the Memphis students and about two-thirds of those in Reno had gambled in a casino, often under the legal age of 21. Of those who had, approximately 25 per cent answered 'frequently' or 'always' to the question, Do you drink while you gamble? The frequently/always group was significantly more likely to have visited a casino four or more times in the previous year, to typically spend two or more hours gambling, to go to casinos with three or more friends, and to play table games as opposed to machines. The most interesting results were significant for men (who were twice as likely as women to be in the frequently/always drink group) but not for women. Compared to men in the never/rarely drinking group, the frequently/always drink group reported placing larger bets on average, on some occasions having had to get additional money while at the casino, and having ever lost more than they could afford. Whilst acknowledging that motivations and meanings associated with gambling may be different for women and men, Giacopassi et al speculated about the relationship between drinking and gambling as follows:

> It is reasonable to conclude, then, that drinking has a negative effect on gambling behaviour in two ways. First, by acting as a disinhibitor, the alcohol frees the individual from normal social and financial restraints

and allows the individual to wager more than is prudent. Second, alcohol's effect on cognitive abilities makes it more likely that the individual will not 'play smart', will not make the appropriate plays to optimize whatever chance there is of winning, and will make it more likely that the individual will lose the imprudent wager (p.147).

The results of experimental studies have been mixed. A number have found no significant effect of drinking on gambling-like risk-taking (e.g. Wilde et al, 1989; Meier et al, 1996, both cited by Breslin et al, 1999). As Breslin et al pointed out, however, it is possible that these studies have insufficient 'ecological validity'. They may, for example, have failed to use games or tasks that are sufficiently like gambling: Wilde et al (1989) used a general knowledge quiz with sizeable monetary prizes for example. The most important way in which they believed experiments may have failed to provide an adequate test of the link between drinking and gambling is in terms of their failure to arouse motivational conflict. Much work on the disinhibiting effects of alcohol has shown that drinking has such an effect only when participants are in a state of some conflict about action (e.g. to be aggressive or not, to show sexual behaviour or not, to gamble or not). If conflict is not aroused then drinking would not be expected to have an effect. A further limitation of most of these studies is that they did not involve as participants people who were regular gamblers: most commonly the participants were college students unselected for gambling.

   Some experiments have found evidence to support an effect of drinking on gambling. Sjöberg (1969, cited by Breslin et al, 1999) asked male college students to rate their willingness to gamble on a number of different lottery games varying in prize, payoff and probability of winning. A moderate dose of alcohol (0.5g/kg) significantly increased participants' willingness to gamble, although a higher dose (0.7g/kg) significantly decreased willingness. Kyngdon and Dickerson's (1999) study is the only one to have made sure that their participants (all men, mostly students) were regular gamblers (playing gaming machines more than once a month) as well as being regular drinkers. They also used a gambling-like game (designed to be a convincing analogue of machine gambling) which was carefully chosen to test the tendency to persist with gambling in the face of losses (the chances of winning were arranged to fall as the game went on) – which is arguably an aspect of gambling of particular relevance to the development of problems. Compared to a 'placebo' group who drank non-alcoholic beer or wine, the group who drank three drinks (equivalent to 31g of pure alcohol) over approximately 30 minutes played significantly more trials before giving up (39 versus 20 on average), and were significantly more likely to finish the experiment having lost all the A$10 they were given to play with (50 per cent versus 15 per cent lost all their credit). Those who had taken non-alcoholic drinks persisted on average until the chances of winning had fallen to 60 per cent, whilst those who had taken alcohol persisted on average until the probability of winning had fallen to 40 per cent. A further finding was that those who had drunk alcohol wagered a significantly greater amount of money immediately after experiencing a loss than after a win, whereas there was no such difference for the placebo group.

The role of alcohol in encouraging 'chasing' was prominent in O'Connor's (2000) research on chasing. For example: 60 per cent of sports betters reported taking alcohol before or during gambling sessions and 50 per cent reported that drinking increased the likelihood of chasing; 65 per cent of machine gamblers reported drinking before or during sessions and between a third and a half reported alcohol-related chasing. In both groups, chasing losses after consuming alcohol was correlated with impaired control scores. O'Connor concluded that, although setting variables associated with drinking might contribute in addition to the direct effect of alcohol on diminished judgement or disinhibition, these findings implicated the role of alcohol in decisions to chase, and added to the growing body of research suggesting an association between drinking and at-risk gambling.

Biological factors

Finally, there has been a small number of studies exploring the possibility that problem gamblers may have something special about them which can be detected at a biological level. Two approaches have been taken, one through examining brain functioning (by looking at either electrical or neurochemical measures), and the other via genetic studies.

Brain studies

A comparatively early suggestion was that the endogenous opioids (or 'endorphins'), a group of peptides found in the brain which mimic the biological properties of opiate drugs, might somehow be involved. The main study was that of Blaszczynski et al (1986) who found lower levels of one type of endorphin (beta-endorphin) in the blood plasma of horse-race 'pathological gamblers' (but not poker-machine players) prior to gambling, in comparison with controls. They speculated that horse-race gambling might serve to elevate deficient beta-endorphin levels, although they found no evidence for that in their own experiment (which admittedly might have failed to mimic real-life gambling sufficiently realistically).

Other studies of brain functioning have focused instead upon some of the main known neurotransmitter chemicals in the brain, such as serotonin, noradrenalin, and dopamine. A small number of studies have reported findings suggesting abnormality of serotonin response amongst 'pathological gamblers', but these have been inconsistent and even opposite, one finding evidence for hypersensitivity, another hyposensitivity (NRC, 1999).

Roy et al (1988) failed to support a role for serotonin but did find evidence for a greater than normal concentration of noradrenalin or a metabolite of it in the cerebrospinal fluid, blood and urine of 'pathological gamblers', and a more recent study has produced similar findings (Bergh et al, 1997, cited by NRC, 1999). Another line of enquiry into brain function has involved electroencephalographic (EEG) measurement to test the theory that 'pathological gambling' might be related to 'hemispheric dysregulation' or a failure to coordinate activity in the two sides of the brain. Goldstein and Carlton (1988), in a small study of eight 'pathological gamblers' and eight controls, found some evidence suggesting that electrical brain activity amongst the former group did not switch as quickly as it did in the latter group from activity on one side of the brain (when asked to perform a verbal task) to the other side (when asked to perform a visual task). They interpreted this result as support for the idea that pathological gambling was associated with repetitive engagement in an activity from which a person found it difficult to disengage.

The literature on brain functioning and problem gambling, as well as being fragmented and displaying a failure to follow up on individual findings, is weak in terms of specifying mechanisms and hypotheses. It is often unclear whether what is being proposed is a pre-existing abnormality that confers a specific vulnerability for problem gambling (probably rather unlikely); a pre-existing abnormality that confers vulnerability to a range of addictive or 'impulse control' disorders (more likely); a biological response which might explain the rewarding and potentially addictive properties of gambling (or certain types of gambling); an accumulated response to a history of heavy gambling; or an accumulated response to a history of heavy alcohol or other drug use with which problem gambling is often associated.

Brain functioning studies of problem gambling are in any case likely to take a different direction from now on, taking advantage of new technology by examining brain functioning at baseline and during and after gambling on different types of activity, using brain imaging techniques such as PET (positron emission tomography) or MRI (magnetic resonance imaging) as well as EEG (NRC, 1999).

Genetic studies

Meanwhile, genetic studies constitute another area of research activity. Two studies have suggested that some part of the vulnerability to problem gambling may be inherited genetically. These were both studies using the twin method which relies for its estimate of heritability on the difference in similarity between monozygotic (MZ) and dizygotic (DZ) twins. Because the former are identical genetically, and the latter no more similar genetically than non-twin brothers and sisters, greater similarity for gambling amongst

MZ than DZ twins would suggest a role for genetics. Unfortunately this is now thought to be a comparatively weak method since it depends crucially on the assumption that the two types of twin do not differ significantly in terms of similarity of their environments as children or adults, and also that genetics and environment (nature and nurture) are clearly separate and uncorrelated (Searles, 1988). The stronger method, the adoption method, so far absent in the field of gambling studies, would compare the offspring of problem gamblers brought up by them, those adopted at birth and brought up by non-biological parents without gambling problems, and controls.

Nevertheless the twin studies that have been carried out do suggest a role for genetic influence. The larger study, of over 3,000 male–male twin pairs in which both twins served in the US military during the Vietnam era (Eisen et al, 1998) suggested that inherited factors (plus shared environmental experiences) might explain between 46 per cent and 55 per cent of the variance in reports of pathological gambling symptoms (depending upon the exact criterion used). The much smaller study involved 155 young adult twin pairs identified from state birth records in Minnesota, USA (Winters and Rich, 1998). That study is interesting because of its suggestion that the role of genetics might be very different for men and women, for different types of gambling activity, and for different gambling criteria. For one thing, MZ and DZ twin pairs were equally similar in terms of having gambled at all in the last year, having gambled monthly in the last year on at least one activity, and having gambled at all prior to age 18. Where differences emerged were in terms of frequency of gambling in the last year. Even then significant differences in similarity between MZ and DZ twins were evident only for the more popular, readily available, high potential payout forms of gambling such as lottery gambling, scratchcards, gambling machines, and 'casino cards' (referred to collectively by Winters and Rich as 'high action' games). These differences emerged mostly for men and not for women (gambling machines being an exception), which is interesting since research on problem drinking has also found stronger evidence of genetic influence amongst men than women (Searles, 1988).

Modern methods of genotyping, using blood samples, has enabled an exploration of how genetic vulnerability might be carried, and here Comings and his associates have taken the lead. Since in the addictive behaviours field generally there has been a concentration of work focusing on the role of the brain dopamine system (e.g. Wise, 1994), their work has concentrated on the possibility that pathological gamblers might have inherited a variant of one of the five known dopamine receptor genes, in particular the second or D2 receptor gene. Amongst a sample of pathological gamblers recruited from in-patient and out-patient gambling treatment programmes and Gamblers Anonymous, in the USA, compared to several hundred controls, Comings et al (1996) found a very significantly higher rate of one particular variant known as the D_2A1 allele. In a later report based on the same sample Comings et al (1997) reported in addition a variant form of the D1 receptor gene, and others have reported significant findings in the case of the D4 gene (Perez de Castro et al, 1997, cited by NRC, 1999). Again, despite the promise of these studies, interpretation is hampered by a lack of specificity about the roles such variants might play in the development of problem gambling. In related fields it is now generally accepted that complex forms of human behaviour are likely to be influenced by genetic inheritance to some degree, but that many genes in combination are likely to be involved (polygenetic inheritance), and that different combinations may contribute to different outcomes (e.g. to alcohol dependence or alcohol-related crime, Murray and Stabenau, 1982; Schuckit, 1987). Furthermore what is being suggested is not a mechanism specific to gambling, but rather processes that may be shared by a variety of addictive or 'impulse control' disorders, including alcohol dependence, cocaine addiction, smoking, and even 'attention deficit disorder' and Tourette's syndrome (e.g. Comings et al, 1997).

Summarising the area of biological studies, it is clear that the picture remains fragmented and confused. There have been a number of interesting leads, mostly not followed up, and the beginning of an emergence of a few better established ideas which, however, are unlikely to be specific to gambling. It may be an exaggeration to say, as did the NRC report (1999, p.124), that "Currently evidence is accumulating for the role of biological factors in the etiology of pathological gambling."

The greatest weight of existing research on the causes of problem gambling falls, not in the areas of genetics and brain studies, but rather in the domains of familial and other social modelling and encouragements to gambling, the availability and attractiveness of forms of gambling themselves, financial and emotional rewards from gambling, broader personal and social functions served by gambling, and cognitive processes. Between them the studies that have been carried out begin to help create an understanding of how it is that gambling gets out of control for some people. In Chapter 7 we shall return to consider this emerging understanding and how the studies to be summarised in the next two chapters contribute to it.

Chapter 5

Gambling and problem gambling in Britain: summary of results of the British Gambling Prevalence Survey

Background to the survey

Britain was slow to carry out its first national survey of adult gambling. We saw in Chapter 3 that national or state-wide surveys had been carried out in a number of other countries, and that a national survey of young people, up to and including age 15, had been carried out in Britain by Fisher (1999). A start was made to fill in the gap in our knowledge about British adults and their gambling in 1999 when the first British Gambling Prevalence Survey, of people aged 16 years or over, was carried out by the National Centre for Social Research (NatCen).

A number of factors combined to produce sufficient motivation and funding for the survey. The study was coordinated by the non-statutory organisation GamCare. As part of its work in pursuit of the objectives of preventing problem gambling and promoting treatment services, GamCare campaigned in support of such a national study. It was successful in generating sufficient interest to financially support the project. Those who contributed funds included government departments (the Home Office; the Department for Culture, Media and Sport, DCMS), organisations that might be described as 'quasi-autonomous' non-government organisations (the National Lottery Commission, NLC; the Gaming Board for Great Britain; the British Horseracing Board; the Tote; and the Horse Race Betting Levy Board), organisations representing the gambling industry or the leisure industry more generally (the Bingo Association, BA; the British Casino Association, BCA; the Brewers' and Licensed Retail Association, BLRA; the British Amusement Catering Trades Association, BACTA; the Betting Office Licensees Association, BOLA; the National Bingo Game Association, NBGA) and individual gambling industry companies (Camelot; Rank Leisure Gaming Sector; Technical Casino Services; London Clubs International; Ladbrokes Gaming Division; William Hill; Corals; Stakis Casinos).

Undoubtedly a range of interests in the study were represented amongst such a diverse group. It can probably be said that they were collectively responding to a growing national interest in gambling. The inauguration of the National Lottery (NL) had raised questions about whether Britain was becoming a 'nation of gamblers' and how great or small was now the prevalence of problem gambling. As explained in Chapter 2, the NL had created some turmoil within the gambling industry, much of which was alarmed at the possible harmful effects on other sectors of the industry. At the same time there were prospects for further deregulation of gambling in the wake of the start of the NL. There was much interest in new forms and modes of gambling such as 'spread betting' and gambling via the internet, which were giving rise to both anticipation of new commercial prospects and alarm at the potential for creating problems. The British Government was about to announce the setting up of its Gambling Review Body (see Chapter 8). There was a shared interest in 'setting a benchmark' or 'establishing a baseline' by carrying out a first national survey against which results of future surveys could be compared: it was recognised that gambling was in a fluid state in Britain. The main aims of the survey were therefore to find out (1) how many people participate in a range of gambling activities, and (2) of those, how many might be problem gamblers.

A steering group was set up consisting of the Director of GamCare (who chaired the Group), the Chairman of GamCare, and representatives from the Home Office, DCMS, the Gaming Board, NLC, BA, BCA, BLRA, BACTA, BOLA, NBGA, and Camelot. The group met a number of times prior to awarding the research contract to NatCen, whilst detailed planning for the survey was taking place (KS and BE from NatCen, and JO as the 'academic link' were in attendance at these meetings), and again to consider results and drafts of final reports (also with KS, BE and JO in attendance). Further meetings of the whole group, and meetings of a sub-group were held to consider specifically the qualitative study, to be described in detail in Chapter 6 (CW, LM and JO were represented at those meetings). These meetings were perceived by the present authors as mostly lively, stimulating, challenging and constructive. The considerable involvement of the gambling industry in funding and steering the project will probably strike some readers as unusual and perhaps unfortunate. Others might see representation of the industry as being of positive value. It is in any case a reflection of the close association that exists between government and the gambling industry, discussed in Chapter 2, and the dearth of independent funding for gambling research. It does raise the question whether the research was truly independent and free of contamination from commercial interests. We believe that it was: the use of an independent survey organisation and the inclusion of the key researchers on the steering group ensured that expert opinion prevailed. But the question of the independence of research is an important one, and we shall return to consider the matter again in Chapter 8.

What questions to ask?

Space is always limited in devising a questionnaire for the general population. The longer the questionnaire the more costs rise and respondents' patience is stretched, and response rate put at risk. Some hard decisions had to be made. In the event the decision was taken to concentrate on straightforward questions about participation in a number of forms of gambling in the last 12 months, some more detailed questions about gambling in the previous week including frequency, location and amount of expenditure, standard screening questions to assess problem gambling, plus a small number of additional questions about internet gambling and spread betting in the previous week, attitudes towards gambling, parental gambling and help seeking and knowledge of sources of help for problem gambling. Also included were standard questions about sex, age, marital status, education, economic activity, occupation and income.

Sampling and procedure

A random survey of the population, aged 16 and over, living in private households in England, Wales and Scotland was carried out. Those living in institutions were not covered. The sampling frame was the small-user postcode address file (PAF); 280 postcode sectors were chosen as the primary sampling units (PSUs). Before selection the sectors were stratified by region (12 regions), population density (three bands) and the proportion of household heads in non-manual occupations. Within each postcode sector 25 addresses were randomly selected. In total 7,000 addresses were selected. Within each household, all members aged 16 and over were eligible for inclusion in the survey.

The first draft of the questionnaire was submitted to two stages of pre-testing, each of which consisted of two parts: 'cognitive testing' and a pilot. The first stage took place in February 1999. Ten cognitive interviews were carried out, five of which were with residents of a house for problem gamblers. The pilot involved interviews with another 44 people. Cognitive interviewing was done by a researcher, and involved asking respondents to 'think aloud' while completing the questionnaire – a useful way of finding out how questions are interpreted. It was the cognitive interviews which revealed that the questions on expenditure, using simply the word 'spend', were being interpreted in a number of different ways (see Blaszczynski et al, 1997 and Chapter 3). After considerable discussion with the steering group, it was decided to develop and test another draft of the questionnaire which found a solution to that problem by making a distinction between two types of gambling activity (types A and B, see the section on expenditure below). The questionnaire was shortened (as it was longer than anticipated) and a number of other, minor amendments were made.

Table 5.1 The British Gambling Prevalence Survey: response rate

		%	
Addresses issued	7,000		
Non-residential	639		
		%	
In-scope	6,361	100	
No contact at address	290	5	
Refused all information	1,283	20	
Other reason no interview	169	3	
Household questionnaire completed	4,619	73	
			%
Eligible adults	8,584		100
Personal refusal	242		3
Proxy refusal	179		2
Ill/away/incapacitated	75		1
Not returned	408		5
Self-completion questionnaire returned	7,680		89
Overall response			65

The second draft questionnaire was submitted to a second stage of pre-testing in June 1999. Cognitive interviews were carried out with nine people and pilot interviews with another 20. The redrafted expenditure section was much improved, and the majority of respondents were consistent in their interpretation of the questions. Thus, it was decided to proceed with this version, although it was recognised that it introduced the limitation of not allowing a calculation of 'total' spend (on all activities) for an individual.

Main fieldwork began in early September 1999. Interviewers were personally briefed by the researchers at 12 half-day briefings which took place around Britain. An advance letter was sent to each sampled address detailing the aims of the survey and explaining that an interviewer would shortly be visiting the address. At each household, interviewers attempted to obtain a face-to-face interview with the 'highest income householder', collecting socio-demographic information about the household. Once the household questionnaire had been completed, every person aged 16 and over in the household was asked to fill in a self-completion questionnaire, which collected information about their gambling behaviour. Interviewers were instructed either to wait while the questionnaire was completed, or to return at a later date to collect it. Fieldwork finished in January 2000.

Table 5.1 gives details of the response rate. In summary, interviews were achieved at 4,619 households (a response rate of 73 per cent after removing unoccupied and non-residential addresses) and self-completion questionnaires were returned by 7,680 out of 8,584 eligible individuals in those households (a response rate of 89 per cent). This represents an overall response rate of 65 per cent.

Compared to the whole British adult population, according to 1998 estimates published by the Office for National Statistics (1999), women were slightly over-represented amongst those completing a questionnaire (53.0 per cent compared to the population estimate of 51.4 per cent), as were both men and women in the age groups between 35 and 74 years. Men, and those under 35 and over 74 years of age, were slightly under-represented. When estimating prevalence figures in research of this kind it is customary to refine the estimates so that the sample providing the data matches the sex/age distribution of the general population. This is done by giving a lower 'weight' to data from those in over-represented sub-groups and a higher weight to those in under-represented sub-groups. Since the sample was a close representation of the general population in terms of sex and age, the adjustments that were made were small. The most extreme weights applied to women in the age group 35 to 44 years (who were the most over-represented and whose data were weighted 0.87) and men in the age group 20 to 24 years (who were most under-represented and whose data were weighted 1.34). Unless otherwise stated, it is the adjusted, weighted results that will be given in this chapter. The results that follow are largely a summary of the full report of the British Gambling Prevalence Survey provided in Sproston et al (2000).

PREVALENCE OF GAMBLING

Gambling last year and last week

The questionnaire listed 11 gambling activities and respondents were asked to indicate whether or not they had participated in each activity over the past 12 months. 'Participation' was defined as having *spent your own money* on the activity, so that it would include, for example, having a lottery ticket purchased on his or her behalf if the money used to buy the ticket was the respondent's own. The 11 activities included in the list were intended to cover all types of gambling available in Britain at the time of the survey (although some might have added premium bonds – see Chapter 1). Respondents were also given the opportunity to report taking part in any other gambling activity not listed amongst the 11 forms of gambling, and a very small number of people did so. The questionnaire then presented the same 11 types of activity in the form of a grid, asking respondents to state whether they had taken part in the activity within the last 7 days (as well as the number of days in the week, venue, and expenditure – see below).

In Table 5.2 are shown percentages of respondents who reported gambling on each of the 11 activities, firstly in the last 12 months (shown both as percentages of all respondents and as percentages of only those who reported any gambling in the last year), and secondly in the last 7 days (again with percentages shown both for all respondents and for only those who reported any gambling in the last week). Of all respondents 72 per cent

Table 5.2 Percentages of gamblers, and of all respondents, engaging in each of 11 forms of gambling in the last year and in the last week

Gambling activity	Gambling last 12 months		Gambling last 7 days	
	All	*Past-year gamblers*	*All*	*Past-week gamblers*
	Base* (wtd) = 7,700	Base (wtd) = 5,543	Base (wtd) = 7,700	Base (wtd) = 4,088
	%	%	%	%
National Lottery draw	65	90	47	89
Another lottery	8	11	4	7
Scratchcards	22	30	8	16
Football pools	9	12	6	11
Bingo	7	10	4	7
Fruit machines	14	19	6	11
Horse races	13	18	3	6
Dog races	4	5	1	2
Betting with a bookmaker (other than on horse or dog races)	3	4	1	2
Table games in a casino	3	4	<1	1
Private bets (e.g. with friends or colleagues)	11	16	4	7
Any gambling activity	72	100	53	100

* Bases shown in this and subsequent tables are the weighted (wtd) bases, on which percentages have been calculated, unless otherwise stated

reported taking part in any gambling activity in the last 12 months and 53 per cent in the last 7 days. Those figures suggest as best estimates that nearly 33 million adults in Britain were participating in one or more gambling activities in a period of a year, and about 24 million in any one week. Taking part in the National Lottery (NL) draw was by far the most popular activity in the last year or in the last week. The NL was followed by scratchcards, fruit machines, horse races and private betting (all more prominent in the figures for the last 12 months), and football pools, bingo and other lotteries (more prominent in the figures for the last 7 days). Spread betting, as a method of gambling, was as common in the last week as some of the less popular forms of gambling, but internet gambling in the last week was rare. With hindsight, it might have been useful to ask about both in relation to the whole of the last year.

From Figure 5.1 we can see that the largest number of 'last-year gamblers' reported gambling on only one of the 11 gambling activities; in 85 per cent of such cases that activity was the NL. A smaller but still substantial proportion of 'last-year gamblers' reported two activities; nearly always the NL plus one other of a range of different activities, the most common being scratchcards. Betting on dog races, betting with a bookmaker (other than on

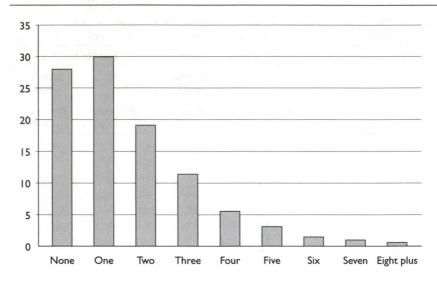

Figure 5.1 Number of gambling activities engaged in within the last year (percentage of the total sample)

horse or dog races), and betting on table games in a casino were all very rare amongst those who reported only one or two gambling activities in the last year. Decreasing proportions of people reported three, four, five and six or more gambling activities. As the number of reported activities rose, the likelihood of reporting each one of the separate gambling activities rose also, but the increase was particularly steep for fruit-machine gambling, betting on horse races, and private betting. Thus the different gambling activities occupy very different positions: the NL for example was an activity engaged in by the large majority of all gamblers, the most numerous of whom are those who engage in no other kinds of gambling. Horse-race betting, to take a contrasting example, was reported by only a small minority of those who gambled on only one or two activities, but by the majority of those who gambled on five or six or more. These different positions are shown more clearly in Table 5.3 which shows, for each gambling activity separately, the proportions of those who gambled exclusively on that activity in the last year, those who gambled on that activity plus one other, that activity plus two others, and so on. For example, of those who played the NL in the last year, 41 per cent engaged in that activity and no other. Of those who played casino table games, on the other hand, only 2 per cent confined themselves to that activity alone whilst 36 per cent had engaged in five or more other activities.

A statistical procedure known as hierarchical cluster analysis identified the nine groups of participants shown in Table 5.4. We have further amalgamated those groups into the four larger groupings shown in the table: non-

Table 5.3 Number of other gambling activities engaged in during the last
year by those reporting each type of activity

Type of gambling activity engaged in:	Number of other gambling activities engaged in within the last 12 months						Base (wtd)
	0	1	2	3	4	5 or more	
National Lottery draw	41	27	16	8	4	4	4,964
Another lottery	13	22	23	15	10	17	511
Scratchcards	3	33	28	16	10	10	1,608
Football pools	4	31	26	15	10	15	665
Bingo	8	27	24	19	11	11	550
Fruit machines	6	16	27	21	14	16	1,051
Horse races	6	18	25	17	15	18	1,006
Dog races	2	10	16	17	19	35	301
Betting with a bookmaker (other than on horse or dog races)	2	6	15	17	19	41	213
Table games in a casino	2	10	16	16	19	36	201
Private bets (e.g. with friends or colleagues)	6	18	25	18	15	18	860

Table 5.4 Groups of gamblers identified in the British Gambling Prevalence
Survey

Non-gamblers	1. Non-gamblers
NL and/or scratchcards only gamblers	2. NL Draw and/or scratchcards
Focused-interest gamblers	3. NL Draw or NL Draw and scratchcards, plus dog racing
	4. NL Draw or NL Draw and scratchcards, plus bingo
	5. NL Draw or NL Draw and scratchcards, plus football pools
	6. NL Draw or NL Draw and scratchcards, plus another lottery
	7. NL Draw or NL Draw and scratchcards, plus fruit machines
	8. NL Draw or NL Draw and scratchcards, plus horse races
Multiple-interest gamblers	9. NL Draw or NL Draw and scratchcards, plus several other gambling activities from: fruit machines, horse races, dog races, betting with a bookmaker on other events, table games in a casino, private betting

gamblers; NL-only and/or scratchcards-only gamblers; 'focused-interest'
gamblers (NL with or without scratchcards plus one other gambling activity); and 'multiple-interest' gamblers (NL with or without scratchcards plus
two or more other activities).

Participants provided more detail about their gambling in the last 7 days
and those results also revealed the different positions occupied by the
different activities. Figure 5.2 shows the numbers of days in the last week

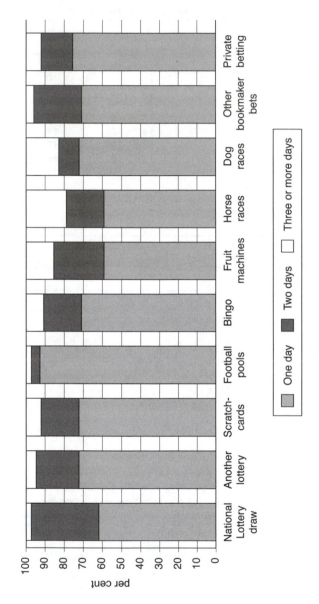

Figure 5.2 Numbers of days participated in each gambling activity in the past week (last-week gamblers only)

on which respondents had engaged in each of the separate activities. From this it can be seen, for example, that doing the football pools was a once-a-week activity for the large majority, the NL a once or twice a week activity, but that substantial minorities reported fruit-machine gambling, betting on dog races, and particularly horse-race betting on 3 or more days in the last week. For those who used spread betting as a method, the average frequency was just over 2 days in the previous week, a higher average than that obtained for any of the basic 11 forms of gambling.

A table was drawn up showing the frequency of betting on the different activities at or via different locations. The full table is a large one and can be found in Chapter 2 of the full report (Sproston et al, 2000). Some of the most notable findings were as follows: fruit-machine gambling takes place in a wide variety of locations but the majority of occasions of fruit-machine gambling in the last week (64 per cent) were reported to take place at a pub. Pubs were also significant for private betting, 25 per cent of which took place there. People's places of work provided opportunities for a number of forms of gambling (25 per cent of private betting, 9 per cent of both NL and football pools, 7 per cent for other lotteries, and 3 per cent for fruit machines). Local food shops were not insignificant as places to purchase NL draw tickets or scratchcards (8 per cent and 11 per cent respectively), and the same was true for petrol stations (5 per cent and 8 per cent respectively), and post offices (6 per cent and 9 per cent). Five per cent of horse-race betting, 6 per cent dog racing and 3 per cent other bookmaking betting took place over the telephone. A very small proportion of last-week gambling activity (0.2 per cent) was reported to have taken place via the internet.

Expenditure

During pre-testing of the questionnaire it emerged that at least four different interpretations of 'spend' were being employed by respondents:

- Amount 'staked', that is the amount bet on an *individual* event (e.g. a horse race, a lottery ticket).
- 'Outlay', that is the *sum* of multiple bets risked during a gambling session/episode.
- 'Turnover', that is the total amount gambled, *including* any re-invested winnings.
- 'Net expenditure', that is the amount gambled *minus* any winnings.

To minimise ambiguity, therefore, the gambling activities were separated into two groups with explicit instructions on how calculations should be made. The two groups were based on the results of the questionnaire pre-testing. It emerged that, for the majority of people, some activities (type A) were naturally calculated in terms of 'stake' (NL and other lottery tickets, football pools coupons, and bingo tickets), while the other gambling activities (type B) tended to be thought of more in terms of 'net expenditure' (for example, playing fruit machines or betting on horse races). In order to keep the questionnaire as simple as possible, no information was collected on the *amounts won*, even in the case of type-B activities. Therefore, while it was possible to calculate average *stake* (type A) or average *loss* (type B), it was not possible to calculate average *net* expenditure. In order to obtain a broad assessment of whether or not the data were representative of normal expenditure, respondents were asked whether the previous 7 days had represented a 'typical week' in terms of the amount of money they had spent on gambling. The majority of respondents (72 per cent) said that the 7 days in question *did* represent a 'typical week', 9 per cent said that they usually spent *more* and 11 per cent that they usually spent *less* in a 'typical week' (others could not answer, for example because they spent nothing the previous week or spent different amounts from week to week).

Table 5.5 shows the proportions of those gambling in the last week on the different activities who staked or lost (depending on the activity) amounts in different categories varying from less than £1 to more than £50. It can be seen that, for the large majority, total amounts staked or lost in the last week were small – £10 or less. The exceptions were: bingo (20 per cent staking more than £10, more often the case for women than for men); fruit-machine gambling (10 per cent losing £10 or more); betting on horse races (also 10 per cent, mostly men); dog racing (17 per cent, almost exclusively men); and playing table games in a casino (44 per cent, mostly men). As a method of gambling, spread betting was also quite often (15 per cent) associated with losses of £10 or more. In fact, for a small number of last-week gamblers, spread betting as a method, and casino table games as a form of gambling activity, had been associated with losses of more than £100: 7 per cent of occasions when spread betting was reported and 17 per cent of occasions of playing casino table games (note should be taken of the quite small numbers on which expenditure figures are based in the case of activities such as dog racing, casino games and spread betting). Table 5.5 also shows the proportions of last-week gamblers staking different amounts on all four type-A activities taken together, and losing different amounts on all seven type-B activities together (note that the latter sum ignores winnings: it is possible for example that a respondent might have won a substantial amount on one activity but show as a loss because of losing on one or more of the other type-B activities).

Respondents were also asked a single question about the largest amount of money they had ever lost through gambling in a single day. The large majority reported never losing money gambling (22 per cent) or never losing as much as £10 (62 per cent). The proportion of men reporting ever losing £10 or more (25 per cent) was three times as great as the proportion

Table 5.5 Amounts staked or lost on each form of gambling in the last week (past-week gamblers only)

Amount staked:	NL draw %	Other lottery %	Football pools %	Bingo tickets %	Total staked on all 4 activities %
<£1	5	16	23	11	12
£1–£5	84	73	68	42	74
£5.01–£10	9	9	5	27	9
£10.01–£20	2	1	3	16	3
£20.01–£50	<1	1	<1	4	1
>£50	<1	–	<1	<1	<1
Base (wtd)	3605	27	449	273	4088

Amount lost:	Scratchcards %	Fruit machines %	Horses %	Dogs %	Bookmaker Other %	Casino[a] games %	Private bets %	Sum of losses on all 7 activities[b] %	Spread betting %
Broke even or won	28	27	31	25	23	35	43	N/A	49
<£1	14	10	6	6	17		16	80[c]	
£1–£5	52	41	40	27	52	21[d]	26	13	37[d]
£5.01–£10	5	12	13	25	4	7	5	3	6
£10.01–£20	1	7	6	11	3	17	3	2	2
£20.01–£50	–	2	4	6	1	20	1	1	7
>£50	<1	1	–	–	–		1	<1	
Base (wtd)	648	427	219	64	71	29	300	4088	63

a Note that these percentages may be unreliable due to the low base figure for casino games
b Ignores winnings (see note in the text)
c Includes respondents who did not engage in any of these seven activities last week
d Lost less than £10

of women who reported such losses (8 per cent). The overall proportion reporting ever losing £100 or more in a day was 2 per cent, the proportion being much higher for men (3.5 per cent) than for women (0.3 per cent).

Who participates in gambling?

Table 5.6 shows the relationship between a number of demographic, social and economic variables and gambling group (non, NL/scratchcards only, focused interest, multiple interest), stake on all type-A activities taken together, and sum of losses on all type-B activities.

Men and women

Men were more likely than women to have gambled at all within the past year: 76 per cent of men compared with 68 per cent of women. On average, men participated in more activities in the past year than did women (with a mean number for men of 1.9, and for women of 1.3), and were over twice as likely to have gambled on four activities or more: 16 per cent of men compared with 7 per cent of women. Men were two to three times as likely as women to be in the group we have referred to as multiple-interest gamblers. On average they reported losing nearly four times as much money on type-B activities as women, and staking somewhat more on type-A activities.

Looking at each of the activities separately, men were more likely than women to have participated in 8 of the 11 activities. The biggest differences were found for fruit machines (20 per cent men, 8 per cent women), private betting (17 per cent men, 6 per cent women), horse races (18 per cent men, 9 per cent women) and the football pools (13 per cent men, 5 per cent women). For only one activity were women more likely to have played than men (which was bingo, played by 10 per cent of women and 5 per cent of men).

Age groups

By age group there were differences both in overall participation and in types of gambling. Most notably, participation rates and the average number of gambling activities were lowest in the two older age categories. At the other end of the age spectrum, the proportion of 16–24 year olds who reported any gambling in the last year (66 per cent) was lower than for most age groups, but amongst last-year gamblers the average number of gambling activities decreased linearly with age as Figure 5.3 shows. Hence the two youngest age groups contained the highest proportions of multiple-interest gamblers, and the two oldest groups the lowest proportions. Type-A staking was highest in the middle to older years, but type-B losses were highest amongst the youngest groups, declining steadily thereafter.

Table 5.6 The relationship between multiple-interest gambling, total staked and sum of losses, and demographic, social and economic variables

		Multiple-interest gamblers %	Mean total stake on type-A activities £	Mean sum of losses on type-B activities £
Sex				
	Men	10.4	2.11	1.51
	Women	3.9	1.66	0.40
Age group				
	16–24	10.5	0.93	1.45
	25–34	12.5	1.94	1.54
	35–44	7.9	2.20	0.91
	45–54	6.0	2.27	0.86
	55–64	4.3	2.27	0.50
	65+	1.3	1.47	0.37
Marital status				
	Married	6.1	1.98	0.75
	Separated or divorced	8.5	2.27	0.89
	Widowed	0.9	1.74	0.32
	Single	11.6	1.50	1.73
Economic activity				
	In paid work	9.9	2.17	1.14
	Looking after the home	2.7	1.55	0.40
	Unemployed	6.8	1.73	1.73
	Disabled or sick	6.0	1.86	0.88
	Retired	1.6	1.63	0.40
	Students	6.7	0.36	1.24
Social class of highest income householder	I, II	7.2	1.53	0.87
	III NM	7.9	1.72	0.63
	III M	7.3	2.25	0.92
	IV, V	6.0	2.27	1.09
Household income level	<£15,600	5.6	1.86	0.86
	£15,600 to £31,199	7.2	2.14	1.04
	£31,200 and over	9.8	1.56	0.79
Qualifications				
	Professional or above	8.0	1.47	0.86
	O/A levels	9.3	1.66	1.33
	Other, or no qualifications	5.3	2.31	0.76

There was also some variation in the types of gambling activity that people of different ages were attracted to. The lowest levels of participation in the NL draw were found among the oldest (75+) and youngest (16–24) respondents (45 per cent and 52 per cent respectively). The youngest age group was the most likely to purchase scratchcards (36 per cent), play fruit

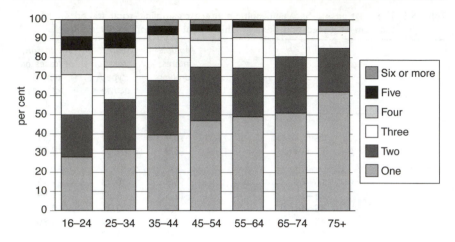

Figure 5.3 Number of gambling activities last year, by age (last-year gamblers only)

machines (32 per cent) and, along with the 25–34 age group, make private bets (21 per cent and 18 per cent respectively). In general, the oldest respondents (65–74 and 75+) were the least likely to participate in most types of gambling, except for bingo where they were the most likely to (9 per cent compared to 6–7 per cent amongst younger groups). The most marked variation by age was for fruit-machine gambling which fell progressively from 32 per cent for 16–24 year olds to 15 per cent for 35–44 year olds and 6 per cent of 55–64 year olds to a low of just 1 per cent amongst those aged 75 years or older.

Marital status

Participation in gambling activities was also related to marital status, although this is almost certainly a reflection of the age relationship described in the previous section. Widowed respondents (who were the oldest) were the least likely to have gambled over the past year. The pattern for single respondents was similar to that for 16–24 year olds: a relatively high proportion had not gambled at all, but those who had were more likely than average to be multiple-interest gamblers. They were also the highest losers on type-B forms of gambling but the lowest stakers on type-A forms. The married, separated and divorced were the higher stakers.

Economic activity

Compared to age and sex, differences by economic activity, socioeconomic status, household income, and educational qualifications were comparatively slight. Looked at by economic activity category, the lowest rate of participation in any gambling in the past year was reported by those in full-time education (32 per cent) and the highest by those in paid work (80 per cent). Amongst last-year gamblers only, however, the average number of gambling activities, as well as proportions in the focused-interest and multiple-interest gambling groups were highest amongst those in full-time education, the unemployed, and those in paid work, and were lowest amongst those who were retired or looking after the home (almost entirely women). Those in paid work were the highest stakers (type-A activities) and students the lowest, but in terms of sum of losses on type-B activities students and unemployed people had the highest averages.

Participation in the individual gambling activities also varied according to people's economic activity. Some of the significant differences, compared with the average, include: people in full-time education were much less likely than others to play the NL draw (only 37 per cent), but were much more likely to play fruit machines (22 per cent) and to make private bets (17 per cent). Retired people were less likely to purchase scratchcards (only 10 per cent), play fruit machines (3 per cent) or make private bets (4 per cent), but were more likely to play bingo (9 per cent). Respondents who could not work because of a long-term illness or disability were more likely than average to report playing bingo (12 per cent), but were less likely to make private bets (5 per cent). People in paid work were more likely to report participation in each of the following four activities: the National Lottery draw (73 per cent), scratchcards (27 per cent), horse races (17 per cent), and casino gambling (4 per cent).

Social class

In terms of the socioeconomic status of the 'householder' (the person in whose name the accommodation was owned or rented: where there was more than one householder, the one with the highest income) differences in participation were small although those in social class I (professional occupations) had the lowest rate of participating in any form of gambling in the last year (66 per cent compared to 71–75 per cent for each of the other groups). Social class I respondents were the least likely of all groups to report gambling on most of the individual activities. The social class gradient was particularly strong in the case of bingo for which participation rates varied progressively from a low of 3 per cent for social class I to 20 per cent for social class V. Interestingly enough there was a virtual absence of any relationship with social class for fruit-machine gambling, horse-race betting and betting on dog races. The class gradient was reversed in the case of casino table games (a low of 1 per cent participation in social class V varying to a high of 5 per cent in social class I). Neither average number of activities engaged in nor proportions of multiple-interest gamblers varied much by social class but both type-A staking and type-B losses were higher for those living in households where the highest earner had a manual occupation.

Household income

Respondents were shown a card which contained thirteen different levels of income, and they were asked to choose which of the bands represented their *household's* gross income from all sources (i.e. before any deductions for tax, etc.). The median category was £15,600 to £20,799, which means that the majority of individuals lived in households with a gross income level below £20,800. Ten per cent reported a household income less than £5,200 and a further 16 per cent said their household income was between £5,200 and £10,399. At the other extreme 6 per cent reported household income of £60,000 or more and a further 6 per cent between £46,800 and £59,999.

By household income, participation rate, number of gambling activities, and proportion of multiple-interest gamblers were all lowest in the group with the smallest incomes (less than £5,200 per annum), but otherwise showed little variation with income. What did vary by income, however, was engagement in different forms of gambling. The clearest positive correlations with income were casino table games (a low of 1 per cent participating in the lowest income group to a high of 7 per cent in the highest income group) and private betting (a low of 6 per cent in the lowest income group to a high of 20 per cent in the highest income group). Horse-race betting showed the same positive relationship but to a lesser degree (from 10 per cent to 20 per cent). The gradient was reversed in the case of bingo (12 per cent amongst those with incomes below £10,400 compared to 5 per cent or less amongst those with incomes of £26,000 or more).

Average total stake (type-A activities) and average sum of losses (type B) varied only slightly by income. When average stake and loss are calculated as percentages of income (based on median incomes of £8,500, £22,800 and £45,500 for the three groups shown in Figure 5.4) the picture is much clearer, with the highest averages in the low-income group and lowest averages in the high-income group.

Education

By highest educational or vocational qualification held at the time of the survey, differences in participation were comparatively slight, but groups at either end of the spectrum (either with a degree qualification or with no educational qualifications) were least likely to have engaged in any form of gambling in the last year, having the smallest number of gambling activities, and the lowest proportions of multiple-interest gamblers. The same slight curvilinear relationship pertained for participation in most of the individual gambling activities. The exceptions were table games in a casino and private

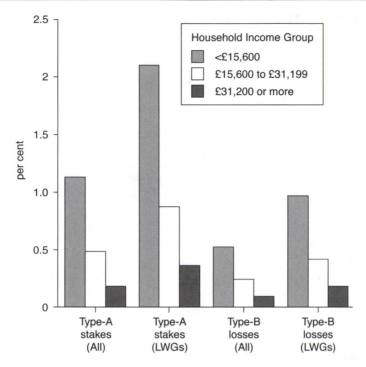

Figure 5.4 Total staked (type-A activities) and sum of losses (type-B activities) last
week, as a percentage of household income, by income group (all and last-
week gamblers)

betting, which showed a slight positive relationship with educational
attainment, and football pools and bingo which showed the reverse relationship. Those with least qualifications had the highest average type-A
stakes, but those with A levels the highest type-B losses.

Ethnic group

The proportion of the whole sample who said they belonged to an ethnic-
cultural group other than white was 5.0 per cent. Little can conclusively be
said about such a small number, containing people from a variety of
different groups. The proportion who reported no gambling at all in the last
year (46 per cent) was considerably higher than the proportion of the
majority white group (27 per cent) and was particularly high amongst the
150 South Asian respondents (58 per cent, but note that the South Asian
group is itself very diverse in terms of religion and ethnicity). The proportion of last-year gamblers who were multiple-interest gamblers (11.6 per
cent) was not very different from the proportion found in the white group
(9.2 per cent).

PREVALENCE OF PROBLEM GAMBLING

Introduction

The other main aim of the survey was to estimate the prevalence of problem gambling amongst British adults. This had never been done before. Arriving at a best estimate of the number of people who have such problems involves overcoming a number of technical difficulties. The first, already discussed earlier in this chapter, is how to draw a sample representative of the general population. The second concerns the choice of instrument or instruments for assessing problem gambling. For the British survey the two sets of questions shown in Table 5.7 were used: the South Oaks Gambling Screen (SOGS; Lesieur and Blume, 1987) and a slight modification of the set of ten questions developed by Fisher (1996, 2000) for her casino study, based on DSM-IV (American Psychiatric Association, 1994) (see Chapter 3). They were judged to have the widest currency internationally, but either one alone was open to the criticisms already discussed fully in Chapter 3. Use of both instruments allowed us to capitalise on the advantages of each, and to correlate and compare the results. All questions referred to 'the last 12 months'; it is therefore 1-year prevalence that is being reported not lifetime prevalence as has sometimes been reported in earlier studies from the USA and elsewhere (see Chapter 3).

While the original thresholds for classification on the SOGS are 3 to 4 to indicate a 'problem gambler' and 5 or more to indicate a 'probable pathological gambler', there has been recent consensus that these cut-offs are too low (see the Australian Productivity Commission report (APC, 1999) for a useful discussion of this issue). These arguments have fuelled criticism that the SOGS overestimates the prevalence of problem gambling by including too many false positives in its classification (see Chapter 3). Nevertheless, some studies continue to use a threshold of 3 or more to identify 'problem gamblers' (e.g. Rönnberg et al, 1999). In contrast, a number of Australian studies (e.g. Dickerson et al, 1996) have used 10 or more as the threshold for SOGS, but the more recent APC (1999) report concluded that 5 or more is the most appropriate cut-off, and that was the threshold used for the SOGS in the British Gambling Prevalence Survey.

The threshold for problem gambling as measured by the DSM-IV-based questions has been less contentious. The cut-off used in the British survey is the same as that advocated by the American Psychiatric Association (1994) and Lesieur and Rosenthal (1991), i.e. 3 or more represents a 'problem gambler'. However, the classification used here does not incorporate the additional threshold of 5 or more, used in some surveys to identify 'probable pathological gamblers', 'severe problem gamblers' or 'level 4 gamblers' (Dickerson and Hinchy, 1988; Lesieur and Rosenthal, 1991; Shaffer et al, 1997). That decision was made for the sake of clarity and simplicity.

Table 5.7 South Oaks Gambling Screen (SOGS) and DSM-IV questions used in the British Gambling Prevalence Survey (all 'in the last 12 months')

SOGS (all Yes or No, a Yes counting 1 to the total, except items 1 and 2)

1. When you gamble, how often do you go back another day to win back money you lost?[a]
2. Have you claimed to be winning money from gambling when in fact, you lost?[b]
3. Do you spend more time or money gambling than you intended?
4. Have people criticised your gambling?
5. Have you felt guilty about the way you gamble or what happens when you gamble?
6. Have you felt like you would like to stop gambling but didn't think you could?
7. Have you hidden betting slips, lottery tickets, gambling money or other signs of gambling from your spouse or partner, your children or other important people in your life?
8. Have you argued with people you live with over how you handle money? If Yes, have these arguments centred on your gambling?
9. Have you missed time from work, school or college due to gambling?
10. Have you borrowed from someone and not paid them back as a result of your gambling?
11. Have you borrowed from household money to finance gambling?
12. Have you borrowed money from your spouse or partner to finance gambling?
13. Have you borrowed money from other relatives or in-laws to finance gambling?
14. Have you borrowed money from banks, building societies, loan companies or credit companies for gambling or to pay gambling debts?
15. Have you made cash withdrawals on credit cards to get money for gambling or to pay gambling debts?
16. Have you received loans from 'loan sharks' to gamble or to pay gambling debts?
17. Have you cashed in stocks, bonds or other securities to finance gambling?
18. Have you sold personal or family property to gamble or to pay gambling debts?
19. Have you borrowed money from your bank or building society account by writing cheques that bounced to get money for gambling or to pay gambling debts?
20. Do you feel you have a problem with betting money or gambling?

a – 'every time I lost' or 'most of the time I lost' = 1
b – 'Yes, most of the time' or 'some of the time (less than half the time I lost)' = 1

DSM-IV ('very often' or 'fairly often' = 1, 'occasionally' or 'never' = 0 for all items except items 7–10)

1. How often have you found yourself thinking about gambling (that is reliving past gambling experiences, planning the next time you will play, or thinking of ways to get money to gamble)?
2. Have you needed to gamble with more and more money to get the excitement you are looking for?
3. Have you felt restless or irritable when trying to cut down gambling?
4. Have you gambled to escape from problems or when you are feeling depressed, anxious or bad about yourself?
5. Have you lied to family, or others, to hide the extent of your gambling?
6. Have you made unsuccessful attempts to control, cut back or stop gambling?
7. Have you committed a crime in order to finance gambling or to pay gambling debts?[c]

continues overleaf

Table 5.7 (cont.)

8. Have you risked or lost an important relationship, job, educational or work opportunity because of gambling?[c]
9. Have you asked others to provide money to help with a desperate financial situation caused by gambling?[c]
10. When you gamble, how often do you go back another day to win back money you lost?[d]

c – 'very often' or 'fairly often' or 'occasionally' = 1
d – 'every time I lost' or 'most of the time I lost' = 1

Furthermore, as Allcock (1994) stated, the term 'problem gambler' avoids many of the negative judgements and conceptual issues associated with the notion of 'pathological gambling'. Hence the term 'problem gambler' is used here in an inclusive sense to refer to anyone scoring above the designated thresholds of the screening instruments.

Prevalence

Table 5.8 shows the frequency distribution of SOGS scores, and Table 5.9 shows the same for DSM-IV scores. In each case the distributions are shown twice: first, for all respondents whether or not they reported any last-year gambling (those who reported no gambling in the last 12 months were not asked to complete the SOGS and DSM-IV questions, and hence are included amongst the zero scorers), and secondly for only those who

Table 5.8 SOGS scores: last-year gamblers and all respondents

	All respondents Base (wtd) = 7,770		Last-year gamblers Base (wtd) = 5,543	
	%	cumulative %	%	cumulative %
10 or more	0.1	0.1	0.1	0.1
9	<0.1	0.2	0.1	0.2
8	0.2	0.3	0.2	0.5
7	0.1	0.4	0.2	0.6
6	0.2	0.6	0.2	0.8
5	0.2	0.8	0.3	1.1
4	0.4	1.2	0.5	1.7
3	0.8	2.0	1.1	2.8
2	1.5	3.5	2.0	4.8
1	5.7	9.1	7.9	12.7
0	90.9	100.0	87.3	100.0

Note: the dashed line represents the threshold above which SOGS scores were taken to indicate problem gambling

Table 5.9 DSM-IV scores: last-year gamblers and all respondents

	All respondents Base (wtd) = 7,680		Last-year gamblers Base (wtd) = 5,550	
	%	cumulative %	%	cumulative %
6 or more	0.2	0.2	0.3	0.3
5	<0.1	0.3	<0.1	0.4
4	0.1	0.4	0.2	0.6
3	0.2	0.6	0.2	0.8
2	0.5	1.0	0.7	1.5
1	2.4	3.5	3.3	4.8
0	96.5	100.0	95.2	100.0

Note: the dashed line represents the threshold above which DSM scores were taken to indicate problem gambling

reported any gambling in the last 12 months. For each frequency distribution, the percentage of respondents obtaining each score is shown, as well as the cumulated percentage of respondents (i.e. the percentage obtaining the designated score or higher).

From the tables it can be seen that the best estimate of problem gambling prevalence was 0.8 per cent according to SOGS (or 1.1 per cent of last-year gamblers), and 0.6 per cent according to DSM-IV (or 0.8 per cent of last-year gamblers). Translated into an estimate of the number of British adults with gambling problems, the SOGS estimate is approximately 370,000 and the DSM-IV figure about 275,000. Since a survey estimate is subject to sampling error, it should always be considered with reference to confidence intervals. In this case we can state with 95 per cent confidence that the percentage of adults who are problem gamblers lies somewhere between 0.6 per cent and 1.0 per cent according to SOGS (that is between 275,000 and 460,000 people) and between 0.4 per cent and 0.8 per cent according to DSM-IV (that is between 185,000 and 370,000 people).

Prevalence by sex and age

Figures 5.5 and 5.6 show how estimated prevalence, according to SOGS and DSM-IV respectively, varied with sex and age. Estimated prevalence amongst men was two to three times that amongst women (1.3 per cent versus 0.5 per cent for SOGS; 0.9 per cent versus 0.3 per cent for DSM-IV). The figures also show that problem gambling prevalence was inversely correlated with age, although the relationship is much clearer for men than for women. Younger men (under 35 years of age according to SOGS, and under 25 years according to DSM-IV) are therefore the sex/age group with the highest prevalence.

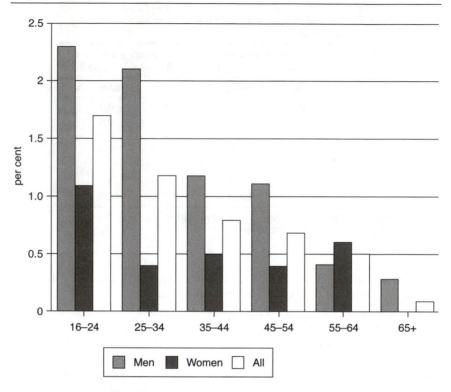

Figure 5.5 SOGS problem-gambling prevalence, by sex and age (whole sample)

Other demographic, social and economic characteristics that were examined for their relationship with prevalence of problem gambling are shown
in Table 5.10: type of economic activity (those in education or training,
unemployed, or unavailable for work because of illness or disability having
the highest rates); socio-economic status of the highest income householder
(the higher rate being associated with manual occupations); household
income level (highest rates for those with lowest incomes and lowest rates
for the highest income group); and qualification level (highest rates for the
intermediate group). Each of those results was similar according to SOGS
and DSM. Marital status was a factor that showed a different pattern
according to the two instruments (both showed single people with a higher
prevalence than those who were married or living as married, but in addition those who were separated or divorced had a particularly high prevalence according to SOGS but not according to DSM-IV).

In addition to those socio-demographic variables, respondents were also
asked the following question: Thinking about your parents/step-parents/
guardians, do or did either of them regularly bet money or gamble? If the
answer to that question was yes, respondents were also asked: Do you feel

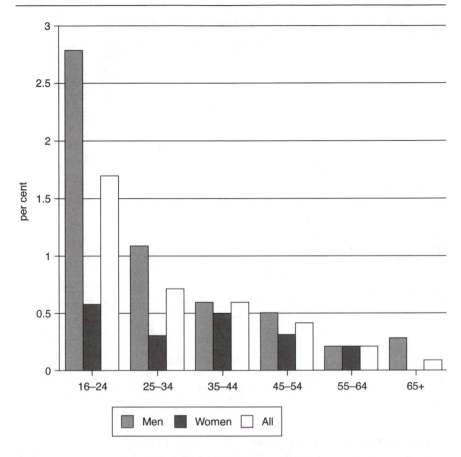

Figure 5.6 DSM-IV problem-gambling prevalence, by sex and age (whole sample)

that either of your parents/guardians/step-parents have or had a problem with betting or gambling? Of all respondents, 3 per cent said yes to the latter question, and this was several times more likely for those who scored as problem gamblers, whether on SOGS or DSM-IV.

Table 5.11 shows the results of combining all of the socio-demographic variables mentioned above, plus the question on parental problem gambling, into a single analysis. Such a multivariate analysis is necessary because the influences of those variables are not independent of one another (retired people are older, to give an obvious example) and the multivariate analysis takes account of this covariation by calculating the association of each variable with prevalence whilst holding the others constant. The analysis of choice here is logistic regression analysis which enables the calculation of 'odds ratios'. For example, the table shows for men an odds ratio of being classified as a problem gambler according to SOGS of 1.73. This can be

Table 5.10 Problem-gambling prevalence by demographic, social and economic variables

		SOGS problem gamblers %	DSM-IV problem gamblers %
Marital status			
	Married/living as married	0.5	0.3
	Separated/divorced	2.4	0.6
	Widowed	0.3	–
	Single	1.8	1.6
Economic activity status			
	In paid work	1.0	0.6
	Retired	0.3	0.1
	Other	1.3	1.0
Social class of highest income householder			
	Manual	1.1	0.7
	Non-manual	0.5	0.4
Household income level			
	Less than £15,600	1.5	1.0
	£15,600 to £31,199	1.0	0.5
	£31,200 and over	0.2	0.3
Qualification level			
	Professional qualification or above	0.4	0.5
	O/A levels	1.2	0.8
	Other or no qualifications	0.9	0.5

interpreted to mean that men were 1.73 times more likely than average to be classified as problem gamblers. These analyses show that parental problem gambling emerged as a highly significant correlate of problem gambling according to both criteria, and that lower income and male sex were also significant or highly significant according to both criteria. In addition marital status was of some independent significance but only in the case of the SOGS criterion.

Prevalence by type of gambling activity

Rates of problem gambling varied greatly by type of gambling activity and the number of activities that respondents had engaged in. Figure 5.7 shows prevalence by types of activity engaged in during the last 12 months. These results suggest that having played the NL is associated with only a fairly average prevalence of problem gambling, whilst other activities, particularly casino table games, betting with a bookmaker on activities other than horse or dog racing, and betting on dog races, are associated with higher rates. Note that these figures are about gambling on different activities whether or

Table 5.11 Summary of the results of logistic regression analyses (significant
variables only shown)

According to SOGS (cases = 7,366)		According to DSM-IV (cases = 7,480)	
Overall significance of the variable	Odds ratios	Overall significance of the variable	Odds ratios
Sex***		Sex**	
Male	1.73***	Male	1.67**
Female	0.58***	Female	0.60**
Whether either parent had a gambling problem***		Whether either parent had a gambling problem***	
Yes	2.44***	Yes	3.18***
No	0.41***	No	0.31***
Household income**		Household income**	
<£15,600	2.96***	<£15,600	2.71**
£15,600–£31,199	1.93*	£15,600–£31,199	1.33
£31,200+	0.42	£31,200+	0.78
Marital status*			
Married/living as married	0.54*		
Separated/divorced	2.14*		
Widowed	0.58		
Single	1.50		

* $p<0.05$ ** $p<0.01$ *** $p<0.001$

not respondents had gambled on other activities besides. Hence most of the
NL players, as we know from results presented earlier in this chapter, have
not taken part in more than one other gambling activity in the year,
whereas those who have bet on dog races, for example, are likely to have
taken part in a number of gambling activities besides dog racing.

The pattern of results is very similar if the analysis is based on engagement in different gambling activities in the past week, although for most
activities the estimated prevalence amongst past-week gamblers was higher
than amongst past-year gamblers, as might be expected. The estimated
prevalence of problem gambling amongst past-week dog-race betters,
according to SOGS, was as high as 18.3 per cent, and amongst those betting
with a bookmaker on events other than horse or dog races, 14.1 per cent.
The equivalent figures for past-week horse-race gamblers and fruit-machine
players were 8.6 per cent and 6.3 per cent respectively. All figures were
somewhat lower if the criterion was DSM-IV problem-gambling. Estimated
problem gambling rates for past-week players of casino table games were

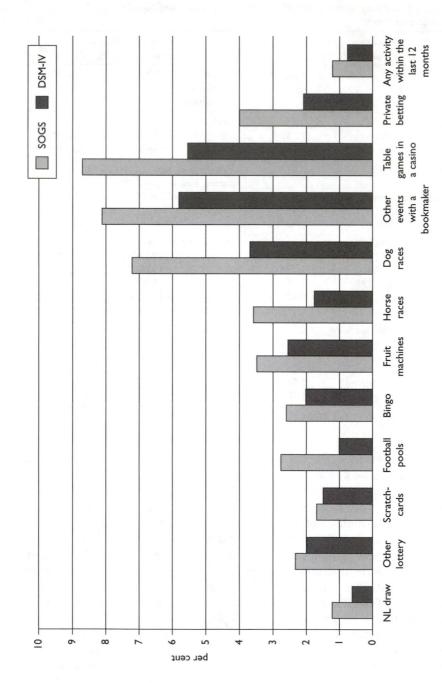

Figure 5.7 Problem-gambling prevalence by type of gambling activity in the last 12 months (last-year gamblers only)

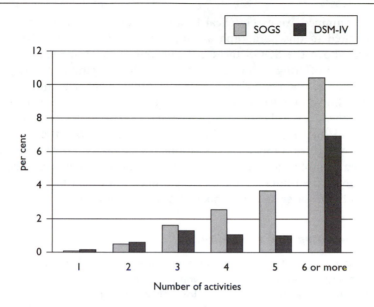

Figure 5.8 Problem-gambling prevalence by number of gambling activities in the last 12 months (last-year gamblers only)

particularly high (SOGS 34.5 per cent, DSM-IV 25.8 per cent), but those figures should be treated with caution because quite small numbers were involved and hence confidence intervals around those figures are high.

The more activities respondents had engaged in the more likely it was that they would score as problem gamblers, as Figure 5.8 shows. In terms of the gambling groups established earlier, rates of problem gambling were very low amongst NL and/or scratchcard-only gamblers (1 or 2 per 1000), somewhat above average for focused-interest gamblers, and considerably higher still amongst multiple-interest gamblers (5.5 per cent SOGS, 2.6 per cent DSM-IV). It should be noted, however, that because there are nearly five times as many focused-interest gamblers as there are multiple-interest gamblers, these two groups contribute roughly equal numbers to the group of those classified as having gambling problems.

A question then arises whether the risk of problem gambling is solely associated with gambling on a relatively large number of activities, or whether certain forms of gambling are in themselves risky even if a person's gambling is focused on or even exclusive to that form of gambling. Unfortunately the numbers of survey respondents whose gambling was focused upon forms of gambling other than the NL were too small to be able to reach any conclusions about rates of different kinds of focused-interest problem gambling. Confining attention to those who had gambled in the last year but on no more than two types of activity at most, the largest group that could be examined were scratchcard gamblers of whom there were 563 (numbers cited in this paragraph are unweighted). Of that number, only one scored above the SOGS threshold and only two above the DSM-IV threshold, thus offering no evidence that scratchcard gambling was particularly risky. The numbers of football-pools, bingo, fruit-machine, private-betting and horse-race gamblers who had gambled on no more than two activities in the last year lay in each case between 190 and 250. In each case a small handful (between one and three people) scored above the threshold which are low figures compared to all gamblers of those types. That suggests that problem gambling amongst, for example, focused-interest fruit-machine gamblers or focused-interest horse-race gamblers, does exist, but that the risk probably increases as the number of other activities increases.

Problem gambling and expenditure

Estimated prevalence was higher amongst those who staked or lost more than very small amounts of money, even in the case of those activities that were generally associated with very low prevalence rates. As Table 5.12 shows, this was the case for those who staked £5 or more on the NL in the last week or who spent more than £5 on bingo tickets. The same was true for those who reported losing more than £5 on fruit machines or horse-race betting in the last week. Numbers were too small to make these calculations in the case of some of the other individual activities. Sum of losses in the previous week on type-B activities was strongly associated with problem gambling (46 per cent of SOGS problem gamblers and 37 per cent of DSM-IV problem gamblers reporting losing more than £10 in total compared to 3 per cent for the whole sample). The relationship with total staked on type-A activities was weaker (15 per cent of SOGS and 10 per cent of DSM-IV problem gamblers staking more than £10 compared with 5 per cent for the whole sample). About half of those scoring in the problem-gambling range, whether according to SOGS or the DSM-IV questions, had at some time lost £50 or more in a single day's gambling, which was very unusual for other respondents (4 per cent).

Attitudes to gambling experience

Problem gamblers, whether classified by SOGS or DSM-IV, were more likely than others to answer 'always' or 'often' to attitude statements, whether they were positive towards gambling (making good friends through gambling, helping to relax, feeling excited, involving skill, giving pleasure and fun, or helping financially) or negative (lost more than won, and feeling extremely depressed after losing – the latter item showing a particularly strong relationship with problem gambling). (See Table 5.13 which shows results for SOGS; those for DSM were similar.)

Table 5.12 Problem-gambling prevalence by stake or loss on different gambling activities in the last 7 days (past-week gamblers)

		SOGS problem gamblers %	DSM-IV problem gamblers %
Stake on type-A activities			
National Lottery draw	£1 or less	0.5	0.3
	£1.01–£5	1.0	0.7
	£5.01–£10	2.5	1.8
	More than £10	7.9	3.9
Football pools	Less than £1	–	1.0
	£1 or more	3.0	0.9
Bingo tickets	£5 or less	0.7	2.9
	£5.01–£10	5.7	2.8
	More than £10	3.6	3.5
All type-A activities	£1 or less	0.9	0.6
	£1.01 to £10	1.1	0.9
	More than £10	5.3	2.1
Loss on type-B activities			
Scratchcards	Broke even or won	2.8	3.4
	Lost less than £1	1.1	–
	Lost £1 or more	3.0	3.2
Fruit machines	Broke even or won	7.1	5.3
	Lost £5 or less	1.5	0.9
	Lost more than £5	15.2	9.4
Private betting	Broke even or won	5.0	5.4
	Lost less than £1	4.1	2.0
	Lost £1 or more	8.7	2.8
Horse races	Broke even or won	12.5	8.8
	Lost £5 or less	3.2	2.0
	Lost more than £5	16.0	6.3
Sum of losses on all type-B activities	£1 or less	0.5	0.4
	£1.01 to £10	1.8	1.5
	£10.01 to £20	16.3	8.2
	More than £20	20.8	13.5

Seeking help

Just under half of all problem gamblers (either judged by SOGS or DSM-IV questions) thought that they had ever had a problem with betting or gambling (the figure for the whole sample was 4.7 per cent), and one in five or less reported ever seeking help for a gambling problem (12 per cent of SOGS problem gamblers and 18 per cent of DSM-IV problem gamblers). Of the handful who had sought help, six had sought help from friends, five each from Gamblers Anonymous and other relatives, four from a psychiatrist,

Table 5.13 Attitudes to gambling experience: SOGS problem gamblers (PG) and non-problem gamblers (NPG) compared (past-year gamblers only)

		Always or often %	Sometimes %	Rarely or never %
Winning at gambling has	PG	8.8	35.1	54.4
helped me financially	NPG	1.0	9.7	73.0
Gambling has given me	PG	42.9	39.3	17.9
pleasure and fun	NPG	15.9	38.8	32.9
After losing at gambling I	PG	35.7	32.1	30.4
have felt extremely depressed	NPG	2.5	4.7	73.7
I think gambling involves skill	PG	35.1	21.1	40.4
	NPG	7.1	29.5	46.7
I have lost more than I have	PG	71.9	15.8	12.3
won at gambling	NPG	49.8	18.7	17.2
When I gambled I felt excited	PG	49.1	33.3	15.8
	NPG	11.3	27.6	46.4
Gambling has helped me	PG	26.3	28.1	43.9
to relax	NPG	4.9	10.9	66.6
I have made good friends	PG	19.3	24.6	49.1
through gambling	NPG	3.0	4.2	68.3

Note: rows do not add to 100% since 'not applicable' answers have not been included in the table

psychologist, doctor or counsellor, one from a religious leader, and two from other people (unweighted numbers). Of the whole sample, over half had heard of GA, compared to which Gam-Anon, GamCare and any other services for problem gambling were virtually unknown.

SOGS and DSM-IV compared

In view of the controversy that has surrounded the use of different problem-gambling screening instruments, and in particular the criticism that has been levelled against SOGS that it over-estimates prevalence, it was of interest to compare directly the two instruments used in the survey. Table 5.14 shows a cross-tabulation of the SOGS and DSM-IV problem-gambler classifications (unweighted numbers). Since SOGS indicates a higher prevalence of problem gambling than the DSM-IV questions, it is perhaps not surprising that over half (31 out of 57) of people classified by SOGS as problem gamblers were *not* identified as problem gamblers according to the DSM-IV. Conversely, over a third (15 out of 41) of people who were classified as problem gamblers according to the DSM-IV, were *not* classified as problem gamblers by SOGS. This suggests that it is not simply the case that SOGS has a lower threshold for measuring problem gambling than the DSM-IV.

Table 5.14 SOGS and DSM-IV problem-gambler classifications
cross-tabulated (unweighted numbers)

| | | *SOGS problem gambler* | | |
		No	Yes	Total
DSM-IV	No	7,608	31	7,639
problem gambler	Yes	15	26	41
	Total	7,623	57	7,680

A weighted kappa statistic showed that the agreement between the two problem-gambling screens was only very moderate (0.52; no agreement would be expressed as a value of 0 and perfect agreement as a value of 1). Since both instruments should have been measuring the same construct, however intangible, such a moderate level of agreement is disappointing. There may be a number of explanations. The simplest is that neither set of questions is as reliable as might be hoped: if two unreliable scores are correlated, the size of the correlation between them can not be better than moderate. The internal reliability coefficient (Cronbach's alpha) was 0.78 for the 20 items constituting SOGS, and 0.76 for the 10 DSM-IV questions (based on past-year gamblers only). Although these figures are satisfactorily high, they do fall short of the level of reliability that might be expected of an established and much used scale such as SOGS, or a set of questions based upon such widely used criteria as DSM-IV. Since internal reliability increases, other things being equal, with the number of items, it might have been expected that SOGS would produce a particularly high level of reliability. As it is those figures set a limit on the size of the correlation that can be expected between the two instruments (a limit of $0.78 \times 0.76 = 0.59$).

Moderate reliability might itself be traced either to the inclusion of a number of items that correlated poorly with the rest (hence bringing down the overall level of reliability of the set of questions as a whole) or to the existence of a number of separate underlying factors (in that case the separate factors might be reliably assessed by sub-sets of items, but the set of questions as a whole would be no more than moderately reliable because they would be throwing together items that were measuring different constructs). This is a technical matter of psychometrics and has been more fully reported elsewhere (Orford et al, 2003). It was the case that some items had less than ideal characteristics. Six SOGS items received very low rates of endorsement (mostly items to do with obtaining money for gambling), as did one DSM-IV item (Have you committed a crime in order to finance gambling or to pay gambling debts?). Furthermore the item about chasing losses (When you gamble, how often do you go back another day to win back money you've lost?) had an unsatisfactorily low item-total correlation in both SOGS and DSM-IV (it was the only duplicated item).

Moderate reliability appeared to be due more, however, to the existence of separate underlying factors than to poor items. Factor analyses of both sets of items suggested the existence of at least two separate underlying factors. In each case, one factor appeared to represent degree of dependence on gambling (SOGS items about intentions unfulfilled, hiding extent of gambling from others, criticisms and arguments, and feelings of guilt and wishing to stop gambling; and in the case of DSM-IV questions, often thinking about gambling, needing to gamble with more and more money, feeling restless or irritable when not gambling, gambling to escape, and going back another day) although the respective SOGS and DSM-IV factors correlated only moderately (0.57) suggesting that they were not measuring precisely the same thing. The second factor in each case appeared to represent gambling-related problems (SOGS items to do with missing time from work or education, and items to do with borrowing or selling possessions to gamble or to pay gambling debts; and DSM items to do with crime, risking or losing a relationship, and asking others for money). In this case the two respective factors correlated only weakly (0.25) suggesting that the types of gambling-related problems that they were tapping were rather different.

A related possibility is that SOGS and DSM-IV questions were picking up different kinds of problem gambler. Analysis did indeed suggest that the profiles of problem gamblers classified according to the two instruments were in certain respects different. The group classified as problem gamblers according to SOGS contained a significantly higher proportion of respondents who were separated or divorced, who were multiple-interest gamblers, who took part in four or more gambling activities in the past year, who had bet on football pools in the last year, who had bet on horse racing in the last year, and who thought they had lost more than they had won gambling. The group of problem gamblers classified according to DSM-IV on the other hand contained a significantly high proportion of respondents aged between 16 and 24 years and a higher proportion of those with professional or higher educational qualifications.

Summary

It would be impossible to summarise neatly all the results presented in this chapter. Some will be discussed further in Chapter 7. For the moment let it suffice to highlight certain of the findings. Most people had gambled in the previous year although many had not. Many who had gambled had done so only on the NL draw and/or scratchcards. Most who had gambled in the last week had staked or lost quite small amounts. Extent of gambling varied markedly by age and sex and much less by social class or income. As a percentage of income, however, expenditure on gambling appeared to be inversely related to income. Small proportions, albeit large numbers in absolute terms when translated into estimates for the whole population (between a quarter and half a million), scored above the threshold on one or other of the two problem-gambling screening measures. Those who did so were more likely to be male, to have had parents with gambling problems, and to be of low income.

Chapter 6

Exploring problem-gambling behaviour in depth: summary of a qualitative study

The British Gambling Prevalence Survey was complemented by a qualitative interview study carried out by the Qualitative Research Unit at the National Centre for Social Research (NatCen). Adopting a qualitative approach affords an opportunity to explore respondents' views and behaviour in relation to gambling in much more depth than is possible during a survey. Additional money to carry out such a study was made available by the same consortium that funded the prevalence survey (see Chapter 5).

It is important to be clear at the outset what a piece of qualitative research of this kind can achieve, and equally what it can not be expected to do. The value of qualitative research, now widely recognised in the social and health sciences, lies in its ability to probe the nature of a problem or experience, to illuminate what was previously mysterious about it, and to develop theory and hypotheses on the basis of detailed examination of the phenomenon (Strauss and Corbin, 1998; Silverman, 2000). Research that needs the careful measurement of variables and sufficient numbers to be able to apply statistical tests to examine hypotheses, or which, like the British Gambling Prevalence Survey, requires very large numbers of participants in order to estimate the prevalence of a phenomenon with any degree of reliability, cannot provide the depth required. The opposite side of the same coin is that in the case of qualitative research, with the small numbers that are inevitably involved – large numbers are less important than diversity of coverage and sensitivity of analysis – there is no possibility, or intention, of drawing a representative sample or inferring anything about prevalence, associations between variables, or the validity of screening instruments. Thus in the present study there was no intention of checking the validity of SOGS or the DSM-IV set of questions for example, or determining whether any one form of gambling was more dangerous than another.

The purpose of the qualitative study was, rather, to enhance understanding of people who were identified as problem gamblers from the British Gambling Prevalence Survey (i.e. people who scored 3 or more on DSM-IV or 5 or more on SOGS). The specific objectives were to explore in detail:

- interviewees' perceptions about what constitutes problem gambling
- the context in which they gambled regularly and the activities they engaged with
- the process through which they embarked upon, and experienced, a gambling episode
- how they perceived their own gambling behaviour
- the factors which they believed caused gambling to become a problem.

Design of the study

The sample

Of those who participated in the British Gambling Prevalence Survey and scored above the threshold on SOGS and/or DSM-IV, 44 indicated that they would be willing to take part in a further interview. Letters were sent to all of that number, and attempts were then made to contact people directly by telephone or in person. Of those who were contactable (a number of telephone numbers had become unobtainable or addresses changed in the 10 months between the prevalence survey and the qualitative study) 17 agreed to take part (resources available would have allowed up to 20 interviews).

Table 6.1 displays the sample profile in terms of sex, age, gambling activities engaged in, and SOGS/DSM-IV scores. This shows that there was a good spread of ages and that both sexes were represented, although men predominated. It also shows that most participants at the time of the study were gamblers of the type we referred to in Chapter 5 as 'multiple-interest gamblers' with a number of 'focused-interest gamblers'. A number of different gambling activities were well represented, although some activities such as bingo and casino table game playing were engaged in by only very small numbers. In those respects the sample was reasonably diverse as we had hoped.

Special attention needs to be drawn to the range of SOGS and DSM-IV scores of the participants in the qualitative study. With a small number of exceptions, this was a sample of people who scored at or just above the threshold on one or other of the two screening instruments (and in only three cases on both). It would probably be wrong to conclude that this indicates that survey respondents with higher scores (and therefore probably more serious problems) were comparatively reluctant to take part in the qualitative study or that they were more difficult than others to trace. Because the distribution of SOGS and DSM-IV scores in the sample as a whole was very skewed, as was anticipated (see Tables 5.8 and 5.9, Chapter 5), scores at or above the threshold are more common than higher scores, and this is reflected in the sample of participants in the qualitative study. It was to be expected that the resulting sample would be mainly made up of those who are in the 'grey area' indicated by screening test scores that are,

Table 6.1 The qualitative study: sample profile

	Number of respondents
Sex	
Male	12
Female	5
Age	
16–24	3
25–34	4
35–44	5
45–54	3
55+	2
SOGS[a]/DSM-IV[b] scores	
On or above threshold on SOGS & DSM-IV	3
On or above threshold on SOGS only	11
On or above threshold on DSM-IV only	3
Gambling group	
Focused interest	3
Multiple interest	14
Forms of gambling	
National Lottery	14
Other lottery	3
Scratchcards	4
Football pools	6
Bingo	2
Fruit machines	9
Horse racing	13
Dog racing	4
Other betting with a bookmaker	2
Casino table games	2
Private betting	3

a – SOGS scores were: 1 (× 2), 4, 5 (× 4), 6, 7 (× 4), 8 (× 3), 10, 18
b – DSM-IV scores were: 0 (× 4), 1, 2 (× 6), 3 (× 2), 4, 6 (× 3)

at most, at, or only just above, the threshold. The result is therefore likely to be very different from a typical sample of people in treatment for gambling problems or who are attending Gamblers Anonymous. This is to our advantage since there have already been a number of detailed qualitative or clinical studies of people who have volunteered themselves as having gambling problems. Such studies (see Chapter 3) included participants who were clearly identified as problem gamblers either because they were in treatment or were GA members (Lesieur, 1984; Ladouceur et al, 1994) or had been specially recruited for studies on problem gambling (e.g. Custer and Milt, 1985). We know of no previous in-depth studies of adults whose responses to sets of questions such as SOGS and DSM-IV suggest that their gambling lies somewhere between the unproblematic gambling of the majority of the population and that of the minority, already well described, whose gambling clearly constitutes a serious problem. The study described in the present chapter thus afforded a unique opportunity to throw light on this middle ground which is occupied, according to the results of the British Gambling Prevalence Survey (see Chapter 5), by somewhere in the region of a quarter of a million adults in Britain.

The procedure followed

Interviewers followed a topic guide. The main headings in the guide were: images of gambling; first gambling activity; present gambling behaviour; recent gambling activity; and downsides to gambling. The full topic guide included detailed instructions about probing and exploring issues under each of the main headings. For example, under the *first gambling activity* heading, interviewers were instructed to ask participants to describe the circumstances of their first gambling experiences; which gambling activities were undertaken; reasons for gambling at that time; the factors that influenced starting to gamble, including the influence of other people and events; and the attractions of gambling at that stage. To give another example, under the *downsides to gambling* heading, interviewers were instructed to explore the nature of downsides experienced by the participants; the impact on themselves and others; whether participants thought gambling could become a problem and if so in what ways; whether they themselves had (or had had) a problem with gambling, and if so the details of it and factors which might have caused it; whether they had ever sought help over gambling; and whether in the participant's view anything could be done to treat or prevent gambling problems, and if so what. Although a topic guide of this kind helps to ensure systematic coverage of key points, it is used flexibly, to allow issues of relevance to individual respondents to be covered in greater detail.

Interviews were conducted, by members of the research team, in respondents' homes, each lasting about 1½ hours. In order to thank people for their time and help, each participant was given a £15 voucher. After securing permission all interviews were tape-recorded.

A full set of verbatim transcriptions was produced from the tape-recordings of the interviews. The analysis of the interview data was undertaken using Framework, a qualitative analytic method developed by the Qualitative Research Unit (Ritchie and Spencer, 1994) at NatCen. Framework involves a process in which each verbatim transcript is systematically analysed in a number of stages. In the first stage, the key topics and issues, which have emerged from the data, are identified through familiarisation with the transcripts. A series of thematic charts (tables or grids with rows for participants and columns for topics) is devised and data from each interview are then summarised and entered under each topic area. Using this method, the experiences and attitudes of all respondents are explored within a common analytical framework based on respondents' own accounts. Ordering and synthesising the data in this way helps to highlight the full set of views expressed by respondents and the factors which underpin or influence them. This process also has the benefit of enabling both 'within case' analysis (i.e. exploration of an individual's attitudes and experiences) and 'across case' analysis (i.e. a comparing and contrasting of the attitudes and experiences of different respondents).

The results will now be presented, topic by topic, starting with definitions and images of gambling, and proceeding to examine first experiences of gambling, participants' varied experiences of gambling and their stated motivations for gambling, life histories of gambling and factors believed to have influenced changes in gambling, and respondents' experiences of losing control over gambling. Each section will be illustrated with direct quotations which are always shown in italics. Results of the qualitative study are presented in greater detail in the full report by White et al (2001).

Definitions and images of gambling

Definitions of gambling

In general money and risk were the two key dimensions that respondents alluded to when defining gambling. Risking or laying out money to win, or to gain more money, or wanting to "*speculate to accumulate*", were common responses to the mention of the word 'gambling'.

> [Gambling] *is handing over of money to try and get money or the enticement of the fact that you could actually win money* (Male, 36 years).

> *Anything that involves the risk . . . of losing money, or of gaining money, that is, to me, is a gamble* (Female, 39 years).

Thus a bet which does not involve money, or scratchcards that come free with a newspaper, were not generally perceived as gambling. There were only two activities that were universally classed by respondents as gambling – formal betting (i.e. betting carried out in a bookmaker's office, at the races or dog track) and playing fruit machines. Apart from those, other commonly mentioned activities which were perceived as gambling included playing roulette, poker and other card games in a casino, the National Lottery (NL) and other foreign lotteries, scratchcards, bingo, pools and football coupons. These activities, however, were sometimes called into question and perceived to be outside the boundaries of gambling.

A few participants viewed gambling in a broader sense and indicated that any activity involving some level of risk (irrespective of whether money was involved or not) was gambling. For these respondents, crossing the road, starting a business, taking drugs, or even flipping a coin, could all be seen as gambling because they required the person to take a risk and engage in an activity where the outcome was unknown.

> *Anything you take a chance on is a gamble, so whether you put money on or not, you know, it could be the same with life, anything is a gamble* (Female, 26 years).

More commonly, however, the boundaries around 'gambling' were restricted, rather than expanded, according to the operation of one or more criteria. The first of these was the amount of money being risked. It was argued that the financial risk would have to be above a certain level before it could be considered gambling. It was therefore sometimes argued that a stake of 10p or 15p could not be classed as gambling.

It was also said that the amount of money was dependent on the financial circumstances of an individual. Consequently a person who used spare change might not be perceived as gambling but a person who spent money 'needed' for bills and other living expenses would be viewed as gambling. One young man, for example, referred to playing machines only with "*leftovers*" after paying for weekly essentials. Sometimes assessments about the amount of money were closely associated with the context in which the activity occurred.

> *If you knew that you needed that £5 to get a weekend's shopping or something like that, and you put it – in a fruit machine or the lottery, that to me is gambling because you need that money for another reason. Whereas if you've got a couple of quid just, you know, in your pocket or whatever, and you know, you've got your food in and you're out with your mates. . . you're gonna buy it on a drink anyway, so you know, it's not for any sort of like set purpose, it's just like a shot in the dark, it's a hope, a hope of a chance. So that I don't class, you know, in my eyes it's not gambling – that is just a bit of optimism* (Male, 34 years).

A different criterion was whether there would be any return from the money being risked. By this criterion an activity such as buying stocks and shares was not considered to be gambling by some because, it was argued, it would be certain to result in some level of financial return.

Context was mentioned as a defining feature of gambling with reference to a range of factors: the physical environment in which the activity was being undertaken, whether other people were involved, the nature of the relationship between these people, and the reason why they were engaging in an activity. Under different circumstances people included or excluded activities from their definition of gambling. For example, engaging in a social activity such as playing cards with family and friends at home, or playing bingo at a local club, might not be considered gambling. Similarly engaging in a bit of *"harmless fun"* such as a private bet with friends or colleagues at work might not be viewed as gambling. But these activities would be classed as gambling under any one of the following circumstances: if the motivation for gambling was to win as much money as possible, or if these activities were undertaken in a more formal environment such as in a 'bookie's shop', a casino or an amusement arcade.

> *Bingo – to me, is light relief . . . people . . . want somewhere to go, something to do, something – you know, socially, if you like – you, you get the OAPs who go together . . . that's something they get to do, once, twice, maybe three times a week . . . I don't think you can call a group of friends getting round to have a few hands of cards as real gambling . . . I think . . . it's a bit of light relief, you get five – four or five blokes sitting round a table playing cards, having a few beers, you know, telling a few jokes, whatever – [but] it becomes gambling when you can't leave it alone* (Male, 47 years).

The degree of control a person perceives he or she has over an activity was another positive defining feature of gambling. It was argued that gambling requires a level of skill that involves pitting the wits of the person gambling against the wits of someone else. There was, however, less agreement about which activities fell into this category and people varied in their views about whether they believed they were able to exercise skill or control over a particular activity. For example, in circumstances where an activity like the NL was felt to be a complete *"lottery"*, devoid of skill or control by the person, then buying a ticket was not seen as gambling.

> *It's not a gamble, it's a lottery . . . I know it's – it sounds just the same word, but to me to take a gamble is to risk say . . . eight horses running – you've got a chance of winning, a small chance, but in a lottery that means it's millions and millions to one, so it's not a gamble, it's just, just chucking away the money* (Male, 67 years).

In the same way other activities which were perceived as being games of chance, such as doing the pools or playing roulette, were not viewed as gambling by some.

Finally and more unusually it was acknowledged that the definition of gambling was dependent on whether there was perceived to be a stigma attached to an activity, or whether there were negative consequences arising from engaging in a particular activity. For example, if it was felt that there was a potential to become addicted, then the activity would be defined as gambling. By this criterion activities such as the NL which were perceived to be more socially acceptable activities might not be viewed as gambling.

Images of gamblers

Participants recognised the diversity of gambling activities and generally subscribed to familiar images associated with different forms of gambling: for example betting in a bookie's as a male activity, particularly carried out by older men who might spend considerable amounts of time there, bingo as an actively that appealed to women and retired people of both sexes, and casinos where one might find professional gamblers. Otherwise there was recognition by some that gambling might be class related, being attractive to people from the 'working class' who were keen to improve their circumstances; there was talk of the skills required in order to be good at gambling, for example a need to be good at maths in order to understand the chances of risks on a particular activity; and a perception that gamblers were optimists, continuing to believe they were going to win despite evidence pointing to their losses. Regularly recurring themes, however, were losing control over gambling and becoming addicted.

A wide range of terms were used to describe people who gamble. While these covered a variety of labels including "*dabbler*", "*sensible gambler*", "*social gambler*", "*compulsive gambler*", "*hard core gambler*", "*big gambler*", "*heavy gambler*", "*professional gambler*" and "*addict*", they can broadly be grouped into two different types of gambler. First, there were those who were said to be in control of their gambling, who engage with gambling on an occasional or part time, social or leisure basis, and vary as to whether they are motivated by the desire to win money. The remainder are people who are not perceived to be in control of their gambling: they have a passion or compulsion for gambling and are gambling large stakes, often beyond their means, and may be getting into debt or experiencing other problems relating to their gambling. In the case of the latter group, there were felt to be negative associations with the label 'gambler'.

> *It's certainly not a very good label, it's like being an alcoholic or a drug addict or anything else, it's just as bad, if not worse* (Female, 38 years).

> *To me social gambling is, you know, when there's like a group of you doing it, whereas a hard core gambler would probably sit there and, you know, blank out everything else that's going around them and just literally concentrate on trying to win as much money as possible* (Male, 34 years).

Interviewees spoke of an element of compulsion to gamble in the way it gets a *"hold"* of a person or people become *"hooked"* or *"addicted"* to it irrespective of whether they win or lose. Parallels were also drawn between gambling and other addictive behaviour like taking drugs and drinking alcohol.

> *You can get addicted to it . . . it gives you a thrill and – you just feel like you want to go down and put a bet on or go to a fruit machine and just waste money away* (Male, 19 years).

> *It's like a drug isn't it – it's like smoking really, it gets you, doesn't it,* [it] *catches you* (Male, 38 years).

In contrast with other addictions it was said that gambling was the most dangerous, because at some point the effects of alcohol and drugs will result in a person being unable to continue drinking or taking drugs, whereas a gambler's compulsion will intensify the longer gambling continues, irrespective of whether the gambler is winning or losing.

> *There's only one thing about gambling compared to any other addiction. It's far, far more dangerous than an alcoholic or drug abuser . . . a drug addict will take his drugs and pass out or an alcoholic will drink that much that he goes into a stupor* [but] *there's nothing to stop a compulsive gambler standing there with a bank vault open for him to gamble . . . he would empty the vault before he would fall asleep* (Male, 36 years).

Gambling was said to be a *"mug's game"* because it is bound up with losing and *"throwing money away"*. It was said that there is only ever one winner – and that is the bookie.

In summary of this first topic of definitions and images we can conclude, apart from the fact that these things differ widely amongst individuals, that the theme of gambling being under control and within a person's means was a central one. Participants in the qualitative study readily drew the distinction between gambling that was under control and that which was out of control, some even preferring to confine the use of the word 'gambling' to the latter. The possibility that gambling could be an addiction was widely recognised.

First experiences of gambling

Whether it was betting on dog racing with his father, accepting a 'red hot tip' on a horse from a friend, gambling on a fruit machine at her parents' social club, going to bingo with her mother, playing toss the coin with friends at school, or playing cards with friends for pennies, initial encounters with gambling tended to have occurred relatively early on in the lives of the interviewees. For some this was as young as 8 or 10 years old. In other cases gambling was first encountered slightly later during the teenage years, particularly between the ages of 13 to 18. There were also cases, however, where first experiences occurred in the early twenties.

Respondents emphasised the key role played by 'other people' in influencing their early experiences. Although the nature and extent of the influence of other people varied, key roles were attributed to family members and friends. Some reported being influenced by their own families' gambling behaviour and attitudes towards gambling. Parents in particular were considered to have played a key role. The exact nature of that role varied, however, as did the importance accorded to their influence.

First, some felt that growing up in an environment where parents or other family members gambled regularly had influenced them to try gambling, particularly where a positive image of gambling had been conveyed. Witnessing others take a keen interest in gambling was influential in two main ways. Initially it made gambling appear an 'attractive' activity. Seeing other family members gamble regularly and take a keen interest in gambling, was felt to have sparked interest in respondents themselves. Being exposed to parents' stories about exciting trips to the casino, or their big wins at the races, had made gambling sound particularly attractive and created the impression that gambling was both glamorous and financially lucrative.

My mum used to gamble a lot at the casino when I was a kid . . . it always seemed really interesting . . . somewhere I'd like to go when I grew up (Male, 33 years).

I remember my dad coming in on the odd time saying he'd won a £100 jackpot [on the fruit machines] *. . . I remember thinking ooh how great I wish I could play those* (Female, 35 years).

Second, seeing the interest of family members in gambling created the impression that gambling was an acceptable and 'natural' activity. In these circumstances respondents had been exposed to gambling through hearing parents discussing gambling or accompanying parents to the bookmaker's. As a consequence some recalled growing up with the belief that gambling was something they would inevitably engage in.

To me [accompanying my father to the bookie's] *was just an everyday thing . . . like with the shop*[ping], *or go*[ing] *up the cash and carry with him – it's just one of them things that's gotta be done. It was a part of our*

> *life like . . . You know, see him taking money off people . . .* [I] *just thought that's the way life goes on like* (Male, 39 years).

Parents were also sometimes reported as playing a more direct role in initiating gambling, particularly in circumstances where they gambled regularly themselves. Parents were said to have encouraged respondents to accompany them to the dogs, horse racing or bingo, introduced them to fruit machines, or placed bets on behalf of respondents if they were under the legal age.

In other more exceptional cases, growing up in an environment where parents were perceived to openly disapprove of gambling was also considered to have made an impact. One respondent, for example, felt with hindsight that she had been motivated to try gambling as a way of reacting against, rather than conforming to the beliefs of her parents.

Friends rather than parents were considered to have either played a more important or additional role in encouraging gambling in other cases. This was particularly true where parents had shown little interest in gambling themselves or where respondents had first experienced gambling after leaving the parental home. Again, the nature and extent of friends' influence varied. This partly depended upon the context in which gambling was first encountered. For those who first gambled at school or with friends at a young age, there was some recognition that the decision to do so had been partly driven by a desire to conform to their peer group.

> *My friends had a big influence on me* [my gambling] *at the time – I'm a follower not a leader and I always try and follow what they say . . . It's very hard to turn round and say no 'cos you don't want to lose friendships you know 'cos being young and that, you know, you're very conscious of . . . your friends* (Female, 26 years).

Others described being particularly influenced by individual friends or a group of friends who managed to convince them of the merits of gambling. Here, respondents recalled being tempted to try gambling by work colleagues or drinking partners who convinced them of the impossibility of losing, after receiving insider tips on the outcome of races.

Parents, friends and other people were therefore thought to have played key roles in conveying the appeal of gambling and in motivating participants to try gambling. Indeed in some cases respondents could not recall any other motivations or reasons why they had initially tried gambling. There were others, however, who recalled being motivated to try gambling from the outset, irrespective of, or in some cases in addition to, the role others had played in encouraging them to take that step. In these instances, respondents recalled being particularly motivated and attracted by the potential gambling seemed to offer for financial reward, fun and excitement, or emulating adult behaviour.

In addition to the above, some respondents also felt that the environment in which they had grown up had played an influential role in encouraging gambling. This was particularly true of those who grew up in seaside locations in close proximity to arcades and/or in locations where it was perceived that there was little else for teenagers to occupy their time with.

Salience of first experiences

It was clear, however, that the salience of first gambling experiences varied quite considerably. At one extreme were those who did not recall these first encounters as being particularly salient or as having much impact on them in terms of their later attitudes towards and interest in gambling. At the other extreme were those who considered their first experiences to have had much more of a lasting impact on them. The reasons for this difference were not always entirely apparent from respondents' accounts. However, the outcome of these initial gambling sessions seemed to play a role here.

In the main, first experiences had more of an impact where respondents experienced what they perceived to be a big win or, conversely, significant loss relative to their income at the time. Winning what was seen as a significant amount early on was felt to have had a big influence on attitudes towards gambling. The amount considered to be a 'big win' varied from £5 to £100. For example, respondents recalled being positively surprised at *"how easy it was to make money at gambling"* and how quickly they became convinced that they could do this again.

> *If you win something like that, then you tend to think there's more to come and you can keep winning* (Male, 47 years).

Losing on the first encounter had an equally significant impact, albeit in the opposite direction, particularly where the amount lost was considerable, relative to the participant's income at the time. One respondent, for example, ended up losing a quarter of his wage packet on his first bet. Here there were recollections of disillusionment, disappointment and frustration. Although these experiences did not seem to put respondents off gambling altogether, they sometimes led individuals to avoid particular activities or to take a more measured approach when undertaking that gambling activity in the future.

> *Because I were told it would be the winner . . . I'd built myself up for it to be winning, . . . and me mate came across and said, 'It lost.' I were gutted, totally gutted, cos I ended up losing a fiver . . . I've never bet on the horses since* (Male, 29 years).

In summary, then, we can conclude that the salience of the first gambling experiences varies and is not always high. What does emerge as central, on the other hand, is the key role played by other people, particularly parents, in actively encouraging or modelling an interest in gambling.

Varied experiences and motivations

The largest part of the interview was devoted to participants describing the forms their gambling had taken, why they thought they had gambled, and the details of gambling occasions, focusing at one point in the interview on a single, typical, recent occasion of gambling. What particularly struck us about the results was the great variation represented, in terms of the experiences themselves, the motivations for gambling articulated by the participants, and their descriptions of the emotions associated with gambling.

Variation in the preparations for gambling

One theme running through these descriptions of participants' gambling experiences has to do with the exercise of judgement, choice and skill. For one thing people described making judgements about the activities undertaken. The decision about whether to take part in a particular form of gambling, or whether to continue with it, was said to have been made on the basis of whether informed choice could be exercised, what degree of risk was involved, and generally whether the activity was perceived to offer good value for money. For those reasons one man who regularly bet on horse racing, avoided betting on fillies or on dog racing. For a woman participant, the Irish lottery, which gave attractive returns for three numbers correct, was much preferred to the NL. For one man it was question of choosing bets that he considered offered what he called, "*a viable gamble*".

The ways in which judgements and decisions were made before and during individual occasions of gambling also varied. For some, the decision about which horses or dogs to bet on, which machine to play, or which numbers to choose on the NL, was made quickly with little reference to other sources of information. These tended to be people who were more doubtful about the difference that taking a systematic approach made and were more convinced that success in gambling was as much to do with luck as skill. Others by comparison reported how they had developed systems or methods to aid their decision-making process. Although there were variations in effort individuals devoted to developing these systems and the emphasis they placed on them, underlying this behaviour was a belief that it was possible to exert some control over the outcome of gambling activities. Some lottery players simply chose their numbers according to family birthdays, or had set numbers which they placed on the lottery each week.

Others had developed more complex, in-depth systems to aid their choice of numbers. One, for example, had kept detailed records of the numbers that had emerged each week for the last three years in order to identify patterns from which he then chose his numbers.

> *I don't believe that it's all to do entirely with luck . . . I think there is a fair bit of knowledge to it as well . . . a lot of people just look at the numbers and say 'bom bom bom' but I keep a check of the numbers so I actually know what numbers have come out and I know how often what numbers are coming out and those are the numbers I go for . . . if you keep a check on them properly, you can see which numbers are coming out over a few months the most often* (Male, 46 years).

Others had, over the years, developed personal strategies for playing fruit machines, which they believed positively improved their chances of winning. Strategies mentioned included: observing how machines are paying out before choosing which machines to play (some for example will not play machines that have recently paid out jackpots or larger sums of money perceiving there to be a cycle which the machine follows in paying out); playing fruit machines with lower jackpots, believing these machines to pay out more frequently than higher jackpot machines; and using cancel and nudge buttons to manipulate the outcome of the machine. Some respondents who regularly bet on horses had similarly developed a range of systems and procedures to aid them in their decision-making process. These ranged from analysing the previous form of runners to undertaking a more in-depth analysis taking into account not only form, but also trainers and jockeys, and tips from the racing press. Even when systems were in operation, the amount of preparation prior to a gambling occasion also varied. Some followed an automatic routine without the need for much thought, for example gambling on fruit machines that were played regularly, or sticking to lottery numbers that were always used (even in one person's case maintaining numbers used by a close relative who had died).

Amongst those who reported some level of preparation, some planned their activities in advance of a session, while others waited until they were at the gambling establishment. For example, betting decisions were sometimes made some hours before racing commenced so that respondents could return home in time to watch the coverage on television; whereas others did not make their decision about what to bet on, or which numbers to choose for the NL, until they were at their chosen gambling venue. In the case of betting they then remained at the bookmakers for the duration of the races, or moved between the bookie's shop and the pub so they could spontaneously decide which races to bet on. In the same way, the decision about which fruit machine to gamble on was made once a person arrived at the amusement arcade.

Typically, betting at a bookie's and doing the football pools were the activities that seemed to require the most advance preparation. One respondent for example spent much of his time outside of the betting shop monitoring the progress of certain horses on teletext or reading tipsters' columns in the racing press to enable him to make more informed betting choices. Others similarly talked of routinely spending up to 3–4 hours preparing for their betting sessions by consulting the racing press or newspapers to assist them in choosing likely winners. One young respondent also toured a number of different bookmakers' offices to check the prices being offered before finally deciding where to make his bets.

Often respondents had bought a paper or watched a television programme immediately prior to their gambling sessions. In addition, they sometimes engaged in discussions with other gambling colleagues. The media, particularly the specialist coverage of gambling in the press and on television, was a source of knowledge and awareness about gambling, and hence had a big influence on gambling behaviour. In addition to the racing press, television was specifically mentioned by respondents who indicated that decisions about which races they wished to bet on were sometimes based on whether there would be TV coverage of the event. It was also said by one respondent that the decision to participate in the NL was dependent on it being broadcast on TV.

Varied motivations

What was said in reply to questions about reasons for gambling, or what people got out of their gambling, also varied. These are obviously complex questions which are not always easy to answer. Motivations evolved and developed, and particular ways of gambling often become habitual. It was not uncommon for interviewees to express difficulty explaining why they gambled. Nevertheless all respondents, albeit with a certain amount of probing, spoke of one or more of the following six types of motivation for gambling. The first was, simply, the anticipation of winning. This factor was acknowledged as a motivation across the spectrum of gambling forms and frequencies. People spoke of the *"chance of a good win"*, or *"the thought of actually winning money"*.

> *You go in to win that's basically why you go in . . . the desire to win* (Male, 34 years).

> *I think it's basically if you have 10 losing bets, that one winning bet just brings you back and makes you think, 'oh yeah, maybe I can* [win]' (Male, 44 years).

Sometimes people had a specific goal for their winnings, for example, to pay a bill or to take a partner or relative out socially, but others fantasised about a range of possible uses for their money. One woman, for example, talked about the prospect of doing her house up.

The second variety of motivation – fun, enjoyment, and something to do – was emphasised by respondents who viewed it as a hobby or pursuit for their spare time. The nature of the pleasure arose, not only from the act of gambling itself, but also from the studying, planning and choosing that was often involved.

> [I like to gamble for] *the fun and pleasure . . . I like to watch the numbers come up and see what's winning* (Male, 47 years).

Closely related was the motive of having something to do, wanting to relieve boredom, or occupy time. It was sometimes used as a replacement activity for working, when unemployed or retired.

> *If I'm bored and . . . pissed off . . . I'd be in there all day . . . it's just the thrill of the bet* (Male, 19 years).

Providing an opportunity for social engagement was the third type of motivation. Although some gambling was solitary, the pleasure of gambling was often recognised to have an important social dimension.

> *It's purely done for a bit of fun . . . it's just a laugh, and it's just a social thing . . . we could be playing for matchsticks and we'd get the same kind of fun . . . It's sort of a social place as well,* [you] *see all the people you know, and it's like a meeting place as well* (Male, 34 years).

The social motivation for gambling was specifically articulated in circumstances where respondents were, for example, living alone and lacking friends, or where they lacked an alternative means to socialise. The reason they gambled was therefore to provide a venue to go to and an opportunity to meet and talk with others.

> [I socialise with] *friends I met through gambling, because previously, as I say, I've lived here 12 years and I retired eight years ago . . . so I didn't have any friends as such* (Male, 67 years).

Distraction from emotional problems and difficulties was a motivation for some respondents. For them gambling was a way to "*blot*" or "*blank out*" difficult and traumatic moments in their lives. Being lonely, depressed, and having relationship problems were all mentioned as being factors which had precipitated a need to escape to gambling. It was also reported as providing a relief from burdens and responsibilities, or from the dull monotony of day-to-day life. In these circumstances people said gambling provided a sense of freedom from these situations – a place where nobody could touch or bother them.

> *It takes your mind off it* [something you can't cope with], *you know, you've got all these flashing machines and the noise and everything else and you totally blank everything else out, and you're purely concentrating on what you're doing . . . Yeah, it's a stress reliever, if you like, if I can't cope with something or if I don't know what to do, then I go and gamble* (Female, 36 years).

> *It's an escape . . . it's like your own world in a bookie's like and you're in charge and you'll decide what you're gonna spend your money on and you've nobody telling you what to do and you're not at work or owt like that so you can just . . . relax . . . You've got nobody to bother you, nobody moaning, shouting at you, do this or that, you're your own boss sort of thing, you're independent to do what you want with your money* (Male, 34 years).

People also talked about being motivated to gamble because it provided a boost to their confidence and a feeling of satisfaction and power. Being good at gambling, or by providing the chance to take charge of one aspect of life, or simply having the satisfaction of winning – getting one over the bookmaker or beating a machine – were all ways in which people felt self-esteem had been increased as a result of gambling.

> *I didn't have a very good self-esteem. I didn't think very highly of myself – I still don't at times. That's a lot of the problem . . . cos if you find something you think you are good at you'll stick to it and I thought I was good at gambling* (Male, 36 years).

Finally, some referred to their gambling being motivated by habit or compulsion. Participants who gave reasons that fell in this category ranged from those who could not go without buying a lottery ticket (out of superstition that they might miss buying the winning ticket) to those who described being almost obsessed with gambling. In the latter case people talked about spending long periods of time thinking about gambling, having a continuous urge to gamble, or being unable to stop gambling or refrain from spending all their money on gambling. There were then felt to be few attractions to gambling.

> *It's like a need, it eats away inside you it really does. It's there gnawing at you and you get depressed, you get moody and you know you get very, very snappy and very argumentative* [when you can't gamble] (Female, 26 years).

It's a compulsion now, because I feel that if I don't have a bet I'm not going to be able to pay this or able to pay that, as simple as that, I just don't have the money (Male, 47 years).

Varied emotions

The emotions that people might experience before, during and after a gambling episode were a particular focus of that part of the interview when participants were asked to describe a recent typical occasion of gambling. The ease with which respondents reported such emotions was variable. For some the activity was described as routine or habitual, and in other instances the experience of gambling was said not to evoke much in the way of emotions. Sometimes interviewers sensed that participants were not comfortable discussing their feelings.

Little emotional anticipation *before* a gambling episode was described, especially when activities were routine or habitual, although it was some-times said that a previous win had left respondents feeling quite buoyant and optimistic about their next gamble. There were, however, two types of circumstances where excitement and anticipation of a particular session was reported. The first was when people were looking forward to an activity that they periodically engaged with. The second was where people were using gambling as a release from emotional problems or to relieve boredom or the monotony of their daily lives. In these circumstances respondents indicated they had been looking forward to their gambling session with some eagerness and excitement. It was also sometimes said that a consider-able amount of time was spent when not gambling thinking about and anticipating the next session. One respondent was closely monitoring the clock at work to check when his shift was over and he would be free to begin his next gambling session.

I knew I was going to finish about 11.30, so I'm looking at the clock from 10 o'clock onwards, thinking 'well, after another hour and a half, then I can be in the bookie's' . . . the sooner the time goes the quicker you can get to the bookie's in order to have your first bet, its like a drug really (Male, 47 years).

Respondents varied in the way they described their emotions *during* the gambling experience. The routine nature of some respondents' gambling resulted in them simply going through the motions of buying lottery tickets, or placing bets without much consideration or thought about what would result. In contrast other respondents experienced a series of fluctuating highs and lows while gambling. These highs and lows were triggered by the anticipation and excitement of winning. Indeed some people talked about fantasising about what they would spend their winnings on. The closer a person came to winning the more intense were the emotions experienced. This was experienced by a few respondents as a *"horrible feeling"* or a *"knot in the pit of the stomach"*.

> *You go through all the emotion, jubilation cos you're winning and then you get to the panic because you want to win so badly . . . you don't care what you're spending, your stomach starts to churn and you're feeling sick because you know you shouldn't put any more in* (Female, 26 years).

The degree to which activities aroused such feelings depended on the extent to which a respondent could engage and interact with gambling. For example, activities such as playing bingo or fruit machines provided something to do while gambling. The opportunity to interact with a machine had sometimes resulted in respondents concentrating so hard on what they were doing that they had blanked out and switched off to everything around them. Indeed one woman said she had almost completely forgotten that her young child was in a pushchair beside her.

> *You're purely concentrating on what the machine is doing and not aware of other people around you, your mind just totally switches off . . . It doesn't matter what's going on outside . . . you don't know how much you're putting in, you only know when you need to go up and get some more change or when you open your wallet and think, 'well I had £30 in there, I've now got £10 in there'* (Female, 38 years).

The degree of effort and time that respondents invested in their preparations for gambling also inspired similar feelings whether or not there was an opportunity to interact directly with the gambling activity. Hence, people who were betting on horse or dog races or completing football coupons also reported having similar anxieties while they watched a race or listened to the football results. It also seemed that feelings were intensified in circumstances where there was an opportunity for respondents to draw out and prolong a gambling session by betting on more races, playing more games of bingo, or putting more money in a fruit machine.

It was also said that the atmosphere in which people gambled had heightened the degree of suspense and excitement experienced. Gambling on the fruit machines with a group of friends who were coaxing and encouraging each other, or soaking up the atmosphere in the bookie's where people were shouting and screaming for a particular horse or dog to win, were examples.

The part of the process which respondents found easiest to articulate was the *outcome* of the activity. Not surprisingly the experience of winning or losing offered a more tangible focus for discussing emotions. There were two ways in which respondents reacted to losing. The first was by being resigned and philosophical about financial loss. Indeed it was suggested that if people were willing to risk their money then they should also be prepared for the possibility of loss.

> *If you're having a gamble you should be prepared to lose, if you win you win, if you lose you lose. That to me is the way to see it. If you put on all the money you've saved for the holiday and you lose it, that's gambling* (Male, 67 years).

The second reaction was by feeling a bit down or despondent or even being '*gutted*' about losing. Underpinning these feelings was often a sense of guilt and irritation about having wasted money or at having spent money that should have been devoted to other constructive uses. These feelings seemed to have been further aggravated in circumstances where people had nearly won.

> *If I go* [to bingo] *when I've got no money I don't usually win and then I get on a downer. It depresses you and I say I'm not going again and you know . . . I start swearing and everything* [about] *wasting my money* (Female, 55 years).

> *The more you lose the more upset you get – I think then oh I could have spent that on a new jumper or tee shirt, a new football shirt or something and that's what makes you feel upset* (Male, 17 years).

Occasionally people described having been moody or having retreated within themselves as a result of losing. This was also sometimes felt to have made an impact on others around them, and people at home and at work had noticed and sometimes remarked upon the difference in an individual's behaviour. It was also said to have affected the way in which respondents interacted with others they were gambling with. In one case a participant had become quite angry and aggressive with her partner because he had won the game of bingo that she had lost.

The experience of winning was commonly experienced as a "*buzz*", a "*high*" or a feeling of "*jubilation*". It was also said that there was a degree of satisfaction as a result of having picked the winner or having beaten the bookie.

> *You get an exhilaration from it . . . you get a buzz, you think 'hello I've done something right, achieved something, got that bit more over someone else'. I've been in the bookmaker's before and they've said that's got no chance of winning and I've bet on it and won . . . when that happens winning makes me think I'm better than the bookie's* (Male, 47 years).

The emotional impact of winning and losing appeared to be moderated when respondents were regularly gambling or were engaging in a series of activities with a mix of wins and losses, when people could be more philosophical about losing because they were more measured or cautious about the amount of money being risked, when lost money was spare money, or when people were using gambling as a way to escape from emotional problems or difficulties or to relieve boredom.

The principal conclusion of this section on the experience of gambling episodes must be how varied is the experience of gambling and how difficult it is to generalise about it. First, the amount of preparation for gambling varied as did the importance of skill, choice and judgement, all of which were very important for some interviewees. Stated motivations for gambling varied also, including both financial gain and emotional change in the form of excitement or the relief of boredom. Social motivation was important for some, and escape from stress and a lift in self-esteem were also important for some. Emotionally some described gambling as a bland activity, but others described emotional ups and downs connected with their gambling including strong emotions associated with winning and losing.

Life pathways and influences

Gambling life pathways

Apart from the two teenage participants, all had a history of gambling to describe which had already lasted for ten years or more, and for some of the older participants a history that spanned as much as 30 or 40 years. On the basis of what they told interviewers about their gambling 'careers' a number of things were readily apparent. The first is that nearly all (but, significantly, not everyone) described a period in their lives when gambling had been out of control and/or had amounted to a problem, although a variety of different expressions were used to describe gambling at those times. Second, almost all believed that their gambling was now relatively controlled compared with how it had been at one time. Third, some life pathways were quite similar to others suggesting that these patterns might be grouped into a smaller number of 'ideal types'. No one way of creating a typology of pathways is entirely satisfactory since each pattern is individual and unique. Nevertheless we believe that three broad types of life history pattern were discernible: one *fluctuating*, a second *stable*, and the third *declining*.

In some cases gambling histories were characterised by fluctuations in activity over time. In these cases the pattern of activity took the form of peaks and troughs or a cycle of escalations and depressions. Individuals with this history of gambling had reported experiencing at least two periods in their lives when gambling had reached its peak, each lasting between six months and two years. For all of these individuals peaks in gambling behaviour were combined with troughs in activity. The level of activity maintained during these trough periods varied, but was generally markedly less than during peak periods. What was typical of all these cases was that the shift in activity had often been quite sudden and dramatic. One respondent reported changing from spending £10–15 on betting every day to betting £5 once a week on the horses. Another described how he suddenly changed the amount he was spending on the horses from £100 a day to £10 a day. Fluctuations in behaviour had sometimes been even more dramatic with respondents describing periods of their life when they had changed from gambling very regularly to not gambling at all. The duration of these trough periods was generally between six months and one year, but in one exceptional case gambling had stopped completely for 30 years before escalating once more.

Others by comparison reported that their gambling behaviour had been much more stable over time, although all those with this history of behaviour reported that they had experienced escalations in gambling activity at some point in their lives. These peaks in gambling activity tended to have occurred soon after respondents first started gambling on a regular basis, but were generally short-lived before gambling behaviour stabilised at relatively lower levels. Others had very similar stories, although in some cases gambling activity had increased more gradually prior to reaching a peak and had then stabilised at lower levels. Gambling at lower levels tended to mean both less frequent gambling and a lower proportion of income spent on gambling activities. In some cases, this shift in pattern was also accompanied by a change in gambling activities, for example from machine gambling in arcades to betting on the NL and occasionally horse races.

Finally, there were others in the study who reported a gradual decline in their gambling activity over time, although again respondents with this pattern of behaviour reported a period early on in their lives when gambling had escalated.

Life influences on gambling behaviour

A number of factors were identified by participants as having been influential in determining how and why they gambled at any point in their gambling careers. Clearly these different factors were intertwined and the impact they had depended on the way in which they combined and interacted in different formations. The ways in which they operated together determined the motivations for gambling, the judgements and decisions which were made about the range of gambling activities undertaken, and the amount of money and duration of time spent. They also explained the different peaks and troughs which people experienced as they travelled along their different gambling pathways. Table 6.2 shows factors to which increases in gambling behaviour were attributed and those to which a decline and sometimes abstention from gambling were attributed.

Factors affecting level of disposable income played a pivotal role. It is interesting to note, however, that having a limited amount of money available to spend on gambling influenced respondents in different ways. Sometimes it had motivated people to spend more money in order to boost or supplement a low income. Others, however, were more measured and controlled in their behaviour, setting aside for gambling a particular sum of money that was within their means.

Just as other people, particularly family, had been of influence in taking up gambling in the first place, so were the influences of other people thought to be important throughout a lifetime of gambling. Those influences clearly reflected age and the changing nature of a person's roles and responsibilities.

> [I stopped gambling immediately I got married] *I was working, I was buying a house and . . . I had to get furniture together and everything like that, and everything in them days was on hire purchase, and I think about half my income went out on hire purchase so I couldn't afford to gamble . . . If you are married then you either make a success of it or you don't. Now . . . if you gamble and your wife doesn't gamble, and the money's short in the house, then your marriage is gonna go on the rocks, straightaway. And . . . I'd no inclination to gamble any more, I just finished* (Male, 67 years).

The nature of the influence that other people exerted can be broadly categorised into encouragements and discouragements. Where gambling had been encouraged it was the frequency of gambling and/or the judgements and decisions about what and how much to gamble that had been influenced by other people. Active influences which encouraged gambling took the form of other people exposing respondents to gambling activities, discussing and sharing information about gambling which had enabled participants to decide how to gamble and the amount to spend, splitting bets, and sometimes even asking the respondent to gamble on their behalf. Engaging socially with family and friends had also encouraged respondents to gamble.

In contrast, active influences which discouraged gambling took the form of discussions with parents and partners who were disapproving of the gambling behaviour.

> *If I spend loads my mum moans a bit . . . They don't like* [me] *to waste* [my] *money really. They always say 'oh I wish you'd cut down' . . . I listen to them but then after about a week I go and spend more then* (Male, 17 years).

Table 6.2 Factors to which increases and decreases in gambling were attributed

Factors to which increased gambling was attributed	Factors to which decreased gambling was attributed
Increased levels of disposable income as a result of: – a new job – wage rise – pension settlement – changing spending priorities	Limited or reduced levels of disposable income as a result of: – changing jobs, unemployment – other demands on resources (children, partner, mortgage, bills)
Limited or reduced levels of disposable income as a result of: – unemployment – other demands on resources (bills, debts, etc.)	
Exposure to new gambling activities as a result of: – work colleagues – social circumstances – moving home, easier access – the media	Exposure to gambling activities restricted or prevented as a result of: – legal restrictions because of age – becoming house bound – being based at army base when joined forces – losing a job which had exposed respondent to gambling – moving home, reduced access
Changing personal circumstances – leaving home and feeling isolated – breakdown of personal relationships (with partner, child, parent) – death of a partner – having a child	Changing personal circumstances – starting college/training course/or job – working hours changing – assuming marital/family responsibilities (e.g. having children) – new social acquaintances (meeting partner/friends not connected with gambling) – prospect of relationship breakdown (e.g. ultimatum from partner)
Experience of gambling – chasing losses/wins	Experience of gambling – financial debts from gambling – personal problems resulting from gambling – observed others getting into problems with gambling
Under influence of alcohol – reduced self-control – alcohol integral part of setting	Giving up alcohol or smoking, so avoiding situations where will encounter either
	Professional help – visit a psychiatrist/GA

. . . it was her [girl-friend's] *birthday and . . . she was coming back down to meet us whatever, I think 9 o'clock she was coming back down. I was at home in bed like and she wasn't too impressed and I woke, like she came up to my house and like woke up Sunday morning. She goes 'oh shall we go away for the day'. I said 'I've got no money', she said 'what you done with it?' I says 'I spent it all yesterday on drink and horses' and like she went, like she was concerned, she like went for me like a dose of salts like and I just like, gradually cut down like* (Male, 22 years).

In some cases these conversations had a perceptible impact and respondents said they had reduced or even stopped gambling for a period of time. For example, an ultimatum from a partner resulted in the reduction of gambling behaviour or sometimes even abstention for a period of time. Otherwise there were reports of how partners and other family members controlled the frequency with which a person could gamble by limiting the amount spent on gambling. It was also said to have resulted in respondents tempering their own behaviour for fear of igniting a perceived attraction to gambling on the part of another family member.

Passive influences took the form of respondents observing the behaviour of others and this had both encouraged and discouraged gambling behaviour. For example, observing others winning money had conveyed the idea that gambling was financially lucrative. One example was a woman who had a close relative who had won more than £50,000 on the NL draw and a work colleague who had won over £100,000 at bingo. On the other hand observing a parent with a gambling problem, or people losing and wasting their money, or getting into problems with gambling was said to have had a sobering and controlling influence on respondents' gambling.

There were, however, some participants who maintained that no one influenced their gambling behaviour. People who were gambling in a solitary manner were unlikely to be exposed to others. It was even sometimes said that respondents concealed their gambling behaviour and therefore consciously avoided social contact. Others reported that while they might have discussed and sometimes even jointly engaged in activities with others, that had no impact on their gambling. Typically the content of such discussions was more concerned with comparing notes about the outcome of a particular gamble rather than sharing strategies about what to do.

When you talk to people like that, it's more of a – sort of bravado thing, isn't it, it's a big laugh, you know, 'oh, I just lost all me wages on the horses' (Male, 44 years).

The universal availability and accessibility of gambling was identified as another factor which had been influential. In the main this was described as having lured and encouraged people to gamble. As evidence of this respondents reported being tempted to gamble because the local bookie was situated just around the corner, or as a result of their socialising in a pub where there was a fruit machine. Being encouraged to gamble because they were exposed to gambling activities through their work environment or being employed by the gambling industry or a public house were also cited as examples here. It was also said that people had been tempted to enter the draw for the NL or to buy a scratchcard because they were exposed to them in the shops they visited.

> *They're staring at you . . . all these scratchcards and the lottery, win this it could be you . . . So you think, well I'll try £1, I'll get a lucky dip . . . and, I've been doing it since it started, that's five years, six years* (Male, 34 years).

Respondents also noted the way in which they were encouraged to gamble as a result of living by the seaside and within easy reach of amusement arcades.

> *If you've never lived by the sea, if you don't live where there are places like that then nine times out of ten you know you come down here, you think oh well it's just a game so you go in, do it and when you go home it's forgotten about but* [when you live] *here it's always around you. It's non-stop and especially when the nice summer comes. I mean you're out on the beach and you think oh I'll just pop in here you know* [and] *it's like every day you go you know* (Female, 26 years).

The susceptibility to engage in more than one activity was also noted when people found themselves in a gambling establishment like their local bookie's. In these circumstances people said they had ended up placing a bet on the dogs in addition to the horses, or they had succumbed to a promotional campaign being offered at their local bookie's which had resulted in them gambling more frequently than intended. For example, a promotional campaign offering a William Hill telephone account had resulted in more time and money being spent on gambling.

Where the role of alcohol was noted as having been a factor it was reported as reducing self control where gambling was concerned. It was said to have had an impact when participants played fruit machines in the pub, when periods of time were spent moving between the local bookie and the local pub, and when people engaged in games of cards with their friends or family. In these circumstances alcohol was perceived to be an integral part of gambling activities. It was felt to have prolonged the amount of time people spent gambling as well as the amount of money being staked. It was said that the reason for this was that under the influence of alcohol people are apt to delude themselves for longer about the prospect of winning.

> *It* [alcohol] *made a lot* [of difference] *because you got more relaxed and more blasé so you know if you weren't drinking and you lost you know you'd think I'm not going again you know that's enough now. You have a point where you say no but when you're drinking you're very blasé about it and you're . . . so much more relaxed, you're thinking oh well maybe next time, so in it goes again, we'll have another go* [and you], *still don't* [win but you think] *oh well it's got to be* [and so] *you know you just carry on* (Female, 26 years).

There were, however, some people who maintained that drinking alcohol did not have any impact on their gambling behaviour. In an exceptional case it was said that gambling had provided a replacement activity for a drinking problem.

In summary, respondents told us of peaks in their gambling careers, often occurring early on, some continuing to experience ups and downs in their gambling but others describing their gambling as relatively controlled since then. The factors thought to be responsible for increases and decreases in gambling during the lifetime were multiple, including disposable income, family and other social influences, the availability of gambling opportunities, and the consumption of alcohol.

When gambling becomes a problem

Variation in control over gambling

The sample was divided into those who described their current gambling as controlled, and others who acknowledged it to be uncontrolled. What characterised the former was the control they described exercising over their gambling, in terms of the amount of money devoted to gambling, the frequency with which gambling activities were undertaken, and the decisions and judgements made about money during gambling sessions. These respondents referred, for example, to gambling *"within my means"*, never gambling *"unless I had the money in me pocket . . . if I could afford to lose it"*, or *"I get me gas and electric and me food and then I decide what I've got to spend"*. Respondents describing this more controlled pattern of behaviour typically gambled on a regular basis, in the main between one and three times a week, but in one exceptional case every day. The proportion of money that respondents were willing to set aside for gambling did vary, however. There were those who set aside a small proportion of their income for gambling (less than 5 per cent). For example one man explained that he was currently spending about £10 a week on gambling activities which constituted less than 5 per cent of his income. He was careful to set himself a financial limit and normally spent about £5 on fruit machines when he was in the pub, and £2 a week on the National Lottery. Every month he got together with his friends to play cards for money, although they limited the stakes to under £10. He normally ended up spending £10 during those evenings.

Others by comparison devoted a higher proportion of their income, but were equally careful not to exceed this amount. For example another man currently played the fruit machines about three to four times a week and usually spent £20, which was about 30 per cent of his weekly wage. He regarded the money he set aside for gambling as money he could afford to lose and might vary this amount if he had other financial commitments to meet. He believed that he could control the amount he gambled and, rather than chase his losses, he tended to give up once he had lost all the money set aside for gambling.

For those who described their current gambling as uncontrolled, the pattern of current gambling behaviour was more irregular and undisciplined and respondents did not appear to exert as much control over their gambling activity, particularly in terms of the amount spent. Those currently displaying a more uncontrolled pattern of behaviour tended to be individuals whose gambling history had taken a fluctuating path. Respondents in this group reported engaging in gambling activities more often than controlled gamblers (at least 3–4 times a week). However, the frequency with which gambling was undertaken could vary from week to week, with gambling becoming more intense and frequent when chasing losses. Those currently displaying this pattern of behaviour reported spending a higher proportion of their weekly income on gambling (over 10 per cent and in some cases 40-50 per cent of their weekly income), and often exceeding any limit they set themselves out of both compulsion to continue gambling and/or a desire to chase losses. Although gamblers in this group sometimes tried to adopt the same process of setting aside a set amount of money for gambling, they found these limits difficult to keep to.

An example was one man who described how he always went straight to the bookie's on a Friday night after collecting his wages. He usually ended up spending a couple of hours betting before going home. He then returned on a Saturday. Whilst at the bookie's he normally placed bets on the dogs and the horses and played the fruit machines and usually got through at least £50 during the weekend, which was about 40 per cent of his weekly income. He acknowledged that he could not afford to spend this much, but found it difficult to resist the compulsion to gamble more in order to chase his losses or build on winnings. He admitted that he often found himself dipping into money he had put aside for rent or bills and often fell behind with his payments.

How much I spend depends on how much money I've got and who I can afford not to pay, you know, the bills – it's no good, you know, I'll pay the rent but then I get behind with the water rates, the gas bill's due, the TV, the telephone's been disconnected (Male, in his forties).

A sub-group of currently uncontrolled gamblers described a pattern of behaviour which might be categorised as 'binge' gambling. These respondents reported adopting a pattern of behaviour during gambling sessions which resembled that of other uncontrolled gamblers. They talked of spending a considerable amount of both money (in these instances over 40 per cent of their weekly income) and time during these sessions. The difference, however, was that gambling was undertaken on a more sporadic basis. Those displaying this pattern of behaviour were often in the process of trying to control their gambling behaviour, or were in a situation where someone else had taken control of their finances. As in the example above, respondents reported difficulties in keeping spending under control as they became so absorbed by their overriding concern to chase losses and/or continue gambling, that they paid little regard to the amount they were actually spending.

An example was a woman who had found it difficult to gamble very often over the previous year, since a family member had taken control of her finances. At certain times she had managed to get enough money together to spend an afternoon playing the fruit machines at the local arcade. She only ever gambled if she had at least £30 to spend. Once she started playing, she found it difficult to stop and got so absorbed that she did not realise how much money she was spending. She always continued gambling until she had lost all of her money including any winnings and might end up going to the bank to draw out more money to prolong the session in the arcade.

There was one person within the sample who had stopped gambling. This respondent was also in the process of trying to control his gambling and was currently receiving support from Gamblers Anonymous.

The experience of gambling being out of control

Whether or not respondents described their current gambling as uncontrolled, nearly all could describe periods earlier in life when they had had difficulty controlling their gambling. At the peak of their gambling, participants were generally gambling between 4 to 7 days a week and spending over 50 per cent of their weekly income on gambling. One man, for example, recalled a period early in his life where he found it, *"impossible to stay out of the bookie's"*, and found himself gambling everyday, spending increasing amounts of money on horse racing, finishing up at the end of a typical week having lost 60 per cent of his weekly income. Another respondent described a period in her life when she was gambling on slot machines every day, sometimes spending all day in the arcades using any m~~~~~~~~~ could lay her hands on. For others peaks in gambling activity ~~~~~~~~~ en they found themselves spending a considerable amount of ~~~~~~~~~ either at the bookie's shop or in the arcades, sacrificing their ~~~~~~~~~ families for gambling, and spending up to 70 per cent of their income on gambling.

Another respondent, for example, started gambling on fruit machines in the arcades when she was 16 years old. She recalled that her gambling soon "*snowballed*", and at 18 she was gambling every day, spending nearly all the benefits she received (£50) and as a result encountering financial difficulties. Her gambling behaviour changed very soon after this experience and she stopped playing fruit machines altogether. Since that time she had mainly been spending up to £5 a week on the lottery and had the occasional £2 bet on the horses.

Another participant started gambling on a regular basis as a boy. He regularly went to dog races accompanied by his father, who used to place bets (between 60p and £1) on his behalf, and also played toss-the-coin against the wall with his friends at school, spending most of his pocket money (about £2 a week). On starting work his levels of gambling activity began to increase and gambling began to "*get a hold of me*". At that time, he was betting on both horse racing and dogs, and playing cards for money with friends, sometimes spending his whole wage packet (£200) on gambling. Soon after he was forced to cut back on his gambling after his wife issued an ultimatum and took control of his finances. Since that time, he had restricted the amount he spent on gambling to £20 a week (about 5 per cent of his income) and over time had established a pattern of gambling mainly on horses or dogs throughout the week and doing the pools at weekends.

One respondent, now aged 45 years, began gambling at 18 when she started to accompany her mother on her regular trips to bingo. Her gambling "*built up quite quickly*" over the next two years and she soon began playing every day, spending over £50 a week (about 90 per cent of her income at the time) and as a result found herself in debt. Since that time, she had gradually cut down on her bingo playing and now just went about once or twice a week spending about 10 per cent of her weekly income.

The downsides of gambling

Amongst the downsides to their gambling, the one that was universally mentioned by respondents was their inability to control their gambling. The way in which this was reported varied from people who occasionally felt they lost control and spent more time and money gambling than intended, to those who were losing control on a much more regular basis. At its extreme it was said that there was a potential to become "*hooked*" or "*addicted*" to gambling and as a consequence other aspects of life had taken second place.

Some respondents described the experience of being uncontrolled about their gambling as one of *"compulsion"*. It was said that the compulsion stemmed from the *"buzz"* or *"drug"* that compelled a person to continue gambling almost irrespective of the outcome. In these circumstances people said the compulsion to gamble activated them into a cycle of gambling which resulted either in chasing financial losses or repeating wins, sometimes without much concern for the actual financial reward.

If I win . . . £200, then the next day I probably would put £50 on, you know, so the more I win the heavier I will gamble (Male, 44 years).

You put £1 on and it gets beat, if you've got another one you'll put another one on and try and get that £1 back that you've lost and you're constantly chasing your money. Even if you do win you probably increase your stake and put a bit more on 'cos you think you're gonna win more (Male, 34 years).

Along with feeling that gambling was out of control, another negative feature of gambling for some was when it ceased to be enjoyable or was no longer motivated by pleasure. While the pleasure of the activity had dominated early attractions and motivations, these were often replaced by factors that were connected with the need to gamble. At the point where people felt they had become more hooked or addicted to gambling, it seemed to have ceased to have any positive appeal. Feeling miserable or being on a *"downer"* after gambling, or no longer experiencing the highs after winning, were among the experiences reported.

The other negative sides to gambling were closely linked to the experience of gambling being out of control. There were three principal such downsides: financial, personal-emotional, and social.

The financial debts resulting from gambling were not surprisingly a key issue mentioned and had a number of implications. The inability to pay household bills, rent or mortgage, the need to lie and fend off creditors or legal action, or to raise money from friends or family members, were all alluded to as facets of this negative side to gambling. Amongst those who were able to arrive at a figure for the actual extent of their financial debt this varied from around £200 to over £1,000. The criterion by which this was assessed was the amount of disposable income a person had rather than the total amount actually spent. In this way one participant who had lost a sum of £25,000 in a period of around five years justified the view that he did not have a problem on the grounds that he did not actually need this money.

As a consequence of the debt, people had ended up borrowing from others, or taking loans out which they were subsequently unable to repay. It was also said, more exceptionally, that respondents had ended up stealing and resorting to criminal activities in order to raise the necessary funds to gamble.

> *When you start spending every spare penny you've got, when you start deceiving, cheating and lying that's when it becomes a problem . . . I had bank loans, credit cards debts . . . any credit I could get hold of and built up £1,000 in debt. They started chasing me and there was no way I could pay all the arrears as I was only on £60 a week* (Female, 39 years).

There were also felt to be significant emotional and psychological disadvantages of gambling getting out of control. Among the examples given were anxiety states, depression and mood swings, and difficulties eating and sleeping, sometimes underpinned by financial worries and relationship problems, but at other times brought on by the highs and lows of losing and winning while gambling. The way in which gambling could become like a *"drug"* or *"disease"* and result in people surrendering to it, risking every aspect of their lives in order to gamble, was also perceived as symptomatic of its emotionally and psychologically damaging qualities. Respondents also talked about the way gambling could result in people engaging in solitary activities resulting in them becoming more isolated and lonely. Otherwise the destructive qualities of gambling were mentioned in relation to the way it could result in self-loathing and harm and even suicidal tendencies.

Related to the above two downsides was the impact that gambling could have on relations with others with whom gamblers live and work. Respondents talked primarily about arguments and rows with family members and partners about the time and money they had spent while gambling. The way in which gambling could disrupt and result in the breakdown of relationships was also noted within this context. The experience of mood swings and depression resulting from losing at gambling were also noted as having affected relations at home and, less typically, at work. It was also exceptionally said to have resulted in violent behaviour towards other family members.

> *Well, if you're losing money you get depressed, sometimes you get a bout of depression that you've lost money and that and there's friction between you and your girlfriend because you've lost money and you won't elaborate on why you're depressed and you think oh well I'm just fed up and you don't like to because you know you're gonna get a load of verbal abuse . . . because you've just been stupid* (Male, 39 years).

Respondents also referred to the way they had deceived others around them by lying and cheating in order to conceal the extent to which they were gambling and the debts that had resulted from it. The deterioration of their relationships was a marker for the progression of the problem, and a catalyst for addressing a gambling problem was sometimes an ultimatum from a partner. But sometimes problems had progressed beyond this point and had resulted in an irretrievable breakdown of a relationship.

At that point I was just constantly chasing my tail and feeling low . . . I was coming home after gambling and creating arguments with my wife, upsetting my boys . . . it was because of the torment that I was lashing out on my wife and the boys because I knew I didn't have any money to give my wife, to pay for bills that came in (Male, 36 years).

The downside of it is that I'm nearly 40 years old and I've got nothing . . . it's ruined relationships, because rather than go out with friends I go gambling. It's just ruined friendships . . . I started lying as to where I was going . . . purely so nobody would find out what I was doing (Female, 39 years).

Overcoming problem gambling

There were two cases where people had sought help from specialist services. Others had preferred to overcome their problems themselves. Sometimes they had resolved these with the aid and encouragement of a supportive partner or significant other. Partners had sometimes played a crucial role in providing emotional support, or a distraction from gambling. It was also reported that partners or other family members had actually taken charge of the gambler's finances and, as a result, limited the amount of money they had access to. Otherwise family members were said to have helped to control the amount that was being spent on gambling. One young respondent said his nan worked at the amusement arcade changing money for the fruit machines. By holding back some of the money he changed, she was able to curb the amount he spent on gambling. A number of strategies had been used to overcome problems with gambling. In some cases people resorted to self-control and made a conscious decision to gamble within their means and reduce the amount spent. Others, however, limited the amount they took out or avoided going past the amusement arcade in order to curb their gambling.

The point at which people decided to take their gambling in hand varied. For some people it was a gradual realisation of the amount lost, or the extent of debts, or the futility of their gambling. But for others there were specific catalysts which had induced a personal turning point. These included: an ultimatum from a partner who was threatening to leave unless gambling was controlled; changing personal and financial circumstances, for example following the birth of a child and the reduction in income which resulted; forming a close relationship with someone who either did not gamble or disapproved of gambling; and the threat of legal action and the prospect of going to court for debts.

Of those who were currently controlling their gambling, some were optimistic about the future and others more uncertain. Those who reported currently experiencing problems with their gambling indicated that, although they were trying to exercise control, they were unlikely to reduce or give up gambling since it played such an important role in their lives.

Awareness about specialist support or treatment services was confined to Gamblers Anonymous, and more exceptionally a psychiatrist or hospital treatment centre. Of the two participants who had sought specialist help, one had visited his GP who had then referred him to a psychiatrist whom he had visited on three or four occasions. A second respondent had been going to GA for a very long time. Although both reported anxieties about initially seeking help, they both spoke positively about the service they received and the resulting effects. Some other respondents were not aware that there was anywhere they could go for help with the gambling problem. Others would not have wanted to seek help either because they did not consider they had problems that needed help, or through feelings of shame and embarrassment, not being good at articulating thoughts and feelings to another person, or not wishing to allow another person to comment on what was going wrong. Some doubted that GA or professionals could help, or that anyone else's advice would stop a person from gambling. It was also said that GA existed for 'big time' gamblers only.

There was much support, however, for the idea that professional support services offering help for people with gambling problems should be more widely available. There was variation in the nature of the help that was thought to be required. Some people talked about the need for practical financial advice to sort out debts or to obtain loans. Others wanted emotional support or a listening ear and a chance to off-load anxieties and concerns. It was also thought that counselling would be effective, particularly in enabling people to understand why they gambled, which it was felt would help in overcoming problems. It was also sometimes said that the people providing the help would only be effective if they had experienced gambling problems themselves. The government and the gambling industry were thought to have a responsibility for financing such professional services.

There were mixed views about whether it was possible to prevent problem gambling. Some thought that gambling was so accessible that it would be impossible to do anything to prevent it. Others, however, indicated that the availability of gambling should be controlled or regulated, so that people would be steered away from temptation. Particular recommendations cited were removing machines from pubs and cutting down the advertising of scratchcards or raising the age of legal sale.

They've not just got it in shops and things, they've got it in papers, magazines, it's everywhere you're turning now, it's all gambling oriented isn't it . . . I think to be honest to advertise any kind of scratch card never ought to be allowed because of the odds, it never ought to be allowed because more people chase money on scratch cards than anything, if they get addicted to them that's worse than getting addicted to a fruit machine, to me (male, 43 years).

. . . it's another way of companies earning money, businesses earning money, you know – they've all got bright flashing lights and some people are lulled into it . . . The slot machines should be banned from the pubs – you know, there should be dedicated amusement arcades for that kind of thing. I certainly think it's to the detriment of some kind of social interaction because . . . pubs are a public house where people go to talk, and chat, and gather, and stuff like that – not to sit there and . . . (Male, 35 years).

I wish it [machine gambling] *wasn't so accessible, it wasn't right there in front of you . . . You know they ought to put it away somewhere else where it's not going to attract a load of young kids because you know you go down there and it's just there, you go to the beach and it's there and you can't help it so I mean I try not to go too near the beach because I know I would want to go in there . . . I think it should be down a road where people would have to go . . . If they want to do that they would have to go down that road, it's not a road you would normally go down unless you wanted to go there . . .* (Female, 26 years).

Such recommendations come from a group of people with a special, personal knowledge of the dangers of gambling. Something of their experiences has been explored in this chapter. They have an important message for us as we grapple with issues surrounding the future of gambling in Britain, and we shall return to consider some of the lessons we can learn from them in the concluding chapter. The participants in the qualitative study were also experts on the subject of problem gambling, and in Chapter 7 we draw together what they told us with the results of the prevalence survey summarised in Chapter 5 and with what is known from other research and expert literature.

What we now know about problem gambling and its treatment

What can we conclude, having reviewed previous work on the subject and having summarised the results of the British Gambling Prevalence Survey and the qualitative study, about the existence, nature and causes of what we have been calling 'problem gambling'? Although, as was stated at the beginning of Chapter 4, there has been a great deal of speculation on the topic and much remains to be established, nevertheless there are a number of conclusions about which we can now be quite confident.

Gambling can get out of control

Our first confident conclusion is that gambling does have the capacity to get out of control. That may sound like a statement of the obvious, but it is an important statement and something to be clear about. It means that gambling is a potentially dangerous activity. It means, too, that public debate on the position of gambling in Britain, as in other countries, should feature the capacity of gambling to become out of control as one of the threads of the argument. Public discourse on gambling should make reference to out-of-control gambling.

We know that gambling carries that risk from a number of sources, several of which were referred to in Chapter 3. They include notable studies of Gamblers Anonymous members and other gamblers from the 1980s and 1990s (e.g. Lesieur, 1984; Custer and Milt, 1985; Ladouceur et al, 1994) and reports by clinicians from the 1960s onwards (e.g. Barker and Miller, 1968). But we can go back further to individual accounts, testimonies and auto-biographies from the early 20th century cited by writers like Chinn (1991) and Clapson (1992) and to the recognition of gambling 'mania' including that of the writer Dostoevsky (Stekel, 1924; Squires, 1937). In fact we can go even further back, as far as the 17th century to find descriptions of individual out-of-control gambling (France, 1902). The 17 people inter-viewed in the year 2000 for the qualitative study reported here (Chapter 6) were experts on this dangerous downside to gambling. Although most of them thought their gambling had been more out of control in the past than it had been recently, and many of them felt that they now had their gambling under control, all recognised the potential for out-of-control gambling and nearly all were able to speak of it from their own experience.

When asked to describe gamblers, a major distinction drawn by that group of problem gamblers (remember that all had, some months previously, scored above the threshold on one or other of our two problem-gambling screening instruments) was that between controlled and uncontrolled gambling. The former was likely to be described as occasional, social, within one's means, whilst the latter was passionate, compulsive, for large stakes, beyond one's means and leading to debts and other problems. Someone who engaged in the former might be described as a 'sensible gambler', 'social gambler', or a 'dabbler', the latter as a 'big gambler', 'heavy gambler', 'hard core gambler', or 'addict'. Parallels with alcohol or drug addiction were drawn.

These were not merely theoretical distinctions and descriptions that might be applied to other people. Most of the participants in the qualitative study described their own gambling, now or in the past, as uncontrolled. Typically that would involve gambling at least several days each week, feeling 'hooked' or that gambling had 'a hold' on one, experiencing a compulsion to gamble, exceeding any spending limit that might have been set, and spending a significant part of the weekly income on gambling (more than 10 per cent, in some cases as much as 40 or 50 per cent, and occasionally all the week's wages). What several said about these experiences added to what we already know about the importance of cycles of gambling involving 'chasing' losses or attempting to repeat wins, forms of 'entrapment' that have been thought to play a crucial role in explaining problem gambling (Dickerson, 1990; Lesieur, 1994; Orford et al, 1996).

These accounts also added to the picture, familiar from much previous work, of the destruction that such out-of-control gambling can wreak on a person's personal life. They included examples that made it clear how being addicted to gambling could lead to debts, stealing, deceiving and lying, arguments, even violence, and the breakdown of relationships, as well as personal depression and even suicidal feelings (lending support to the link between gambling and depression which evidence reviewed in Chapter 3 suggested was likely to be a cause and effect relationship). Although that is not new information, these accounts are amongst the clearest we have in explaining how out-of-control gambling and its effects can compound each other in a destructive downward spiral involving amongst other things the emotional ups and downs of winning and losing while gambling, borrowing money that one is unable to pay back, having family rows, being chased by creditors, experiencing anxiety or depression and difficulties eating and sleeping, and experiencing feelings of desperation and self-deprecation. Whilst it is important to acknowledge that not all of the 17 interviewees reported all those experiences, it is also important to note the unique nature of that sample. Unlike other studies of problem or 'pathological' gambling that have recruited members of Gamblers Anonymous or people who acknowledged that they had gambling problems, the sample of gamblers whose accounts were given in Chapter 6 were personally approached by the research team because they were known to have scored above the threshold on a screening questionnaire. They are thus likely to be typical of that very large number of British adults – we estimate in the region of a third of a million – who fall into that group, most of whom would not label themselves as having a 'gambling problem'.

Prevalence

To be exact, our best estimates of the number of British adults, 16 years of age or over, who had experienced a gambling problem in the 12 months prior to the British Gambling Prevalence Survey reported in Chapter 5, were 370,000 according to the South Oaks Gambling Screen (SOGS) or 275,000 according to a set of questions based on the DSM-IV criteria. Those estimates correspond to 0.8 per cent and 0.6 per cent of the adult population. Although it will be argued by some that those are low percentages, it can hardly be denied that they translate into very large numbers. To put those numbers into perspective, it is worth comparing our estimate of just over 300,000 adults (the mid point between our two estimates) with estimates of the size of the drug problem in Britain. Frischer et al (2001), using a variety of respected methods for reaching such estimates, produced a figure of 165,000 for people who have ever injected drugs, 200,000 as the best estimate of the number of problem opiate users and 270,000 for problem drug users of all types. The OPCS survey of psychiatric disorders amongst 16–64 year olds carried out in 1993 (Meltzer et al, 1994) reported a higher rate for last-year 'drug dependence' of 2.2 per cent, roughly corresponding to one million people. Whichever estimate is taken, it can be concluded that problem gambling should be taken almost as seriously, if not equally as seriously, as problem drug use. Yet drug misuse, unlike problem gambling, is firmly established as a major form of mental health problem, for the treatment of which all health authorities are very properly held accountable.

We should not be sanguine, however, about existing methods for assessing the prevalence of gambling problems. Criticisms of SOGS and other techniques were reviewed in Chapter 3. Particularly noted was the view that SOGS might over-estimate prevalence in the general population because it had been developed and validated in a clinical population where the rate of false positives was likely to be low. On the other hand, we noted that it had also been suggested that the rate of false negatives might be high in general population surveys. We were also rather surprised to find a number of people who scored in the problem-gambling range on the DSM-IV questions but *not* on SOGS, as well as those whom we had anticipated who showed the opposite pattern. The force of the argument that there is a tendency for screening instruments to over-estimate the problem, is counteracted by the fact that such surveys are likely to completely miss certain sections of the population for whom we think prevalence is likely to be unusually high. The latter include people who are homeless or who are resident in hospital or prison, as well as those who live alone and with whom contact could not be established (and whose 'household' could not therefore be included), and individuals who declined to complete a questionnaire. In further defence of the methods used in the British Gambling Prevalence Survey, we can point out that ours was one of the few such studies to follow the advice to include two screening measures rather than to rely on one alone (e.g. Abbott and Volberg, 1999): the fact that the two estimates are not greatly discrepant adds strength to the findings. Furthermore, the estimates for Britain are not greatly out of line with those from other countries using SOGS. The British estimate is a little more than a third that for Australia (not surprising in view of the reputation of that country for heavy gambling), about two-thirds the size of estimates for New Zealand and the USA, and about a third higher than the Swedish estimate (again not surprising in view of the greater controls on gambling that have pertained in that country).

Where the greatest risks lie

The British Gambling Prevalence Survey asked respondents about 11 different forms of gambling activity. One of the recurring themes in the research literature on gambling as well as in historical accounts of British gambling in the twentieth century and earlier is the need to recognise the very different places that different forms of gambling occupy in people's social and personal lives. The prevalence survey produced results to support that idea. The different gambling activities included those with very distinct 'profiles' in terms of such parameters as percentage of the population who had engaged in the activity in the last year, the frequency in the last week, average stake or amount lost, the number of other gambling activities that had also been engaged in, and the rate of problem gambling amongst those who had engaged in the activity. The National Lottery (NL) was engaged in by the majority, a large proportion of whom took part in no other form of gambling; the rate of problem gambling among the latter group was lower than average. Horse-race gambling, on the other hand, was engaged in by a much smaller proportion of the population, but proportionately more often three or more times a week and by people who were much more likely to engage in a number of other gambling activities as well. Average expenditure was higher on horse-race gambling than on the NL, and the rate of problem gambling was higher.

In fact rates of problem gambling were substantially higher for those who engaged in certain forms of gambling, notably playing casino table games, betting with a bookmaker on events other than racing, and betting on dog races. That may partly reflect the potential of those particular forms to create out-of-control gambling but may also partly be attributable to the fact that people engaging in those activities are very likely to be engaging in a number of different forms of gambling activity. Such 'multiple-interest gamblers', as we called them in Chapter 5, have a higher prevalence of problem gambling than others. At the other end of the spectrum are the NL draw and scratchcards, much more likely to be played by people who do not take part in other gambling activities, and associated with comparatively low rates of problem gambling. Occupying an intermediate position are private betting, fruit-machine gambling, betting on horse races, playing bingo, betting on other lotteries, and doing the football pools. The small numbers of survey respondents who were engaging exclusively in what appeared to be the highest-risk gambling activities makes it difficult to answer the question whether such activities are in themselves particularly dangerous. It should also be recalled that the one previous British study of the prevalence of problem gambling amongst casino patrons reported a very high rate (Fisher, 1996, 2000). Nor should it be too hastily concluded that the apparently low-risk activities, such as lotteries, are completely safe. Even amongst those exclusively playing the NL the rate of problem gambling was one in a thousand, a not negligible figure, and more than one participant in the qualitative study described the problems they had been having in specifically controlling spending on the NL and foreign lotteries. Furthermore, when interpreting prevalence rates account should always be taken of the base rate in the population. If the rate of problems connected with activity A is one tenth that associated with activity B, but ten times as many people engage in activity A than in B, then each activity contributes equal numbers of problems even though activity B is, for any one person, by far the more dangerous activity. A form of gambling like the NL, with apparently low addiction potential in its present form (its potential to create addiction may rise if draws were more frequent or means of betting on the result more varied, accessible, or interactive) may cause a sizeable number of problems simply because it is so widely engaged in.

Note should be taken of the fact that scratchcard gambling, which was very often engaged in by those who played the NL but took part in no other form of gambling, was associated with a prevalence rate of problem gambling that was somewhat raised compared to those who only played the NL. But it was not as high as might have been predicted by those who feared that scratchcards, because of the rapid feedback of results and the opportunity for rapid restaking and continued play, might constitute a particularly risky form of gambling.

Because of the controversy surrounding machine gambling, and the suggestions that had been widely made that machines may have particular 'addiction potential', it is worth noting the results for that activity specifically. The rate of problem gambling amongst last-year machine gamblers was 3.4 per cent according to SOGS which puts it above lotteries, football pools and bingo and almost on a level with horse-race betting. Gambling on machines was more likely than other activities (except for the NL draw, scratchcards and doing the football pools) to be at least a weekly activity. It is important to note, therefore, that the prevalence of problem gambling amongst those who had played machines in the last week was 6.3 per cent according to SOGS. Also of interest is the fact that prevalence estimates for machine gamblers were comparatively high according to the DSM-IV questions. When that was the criteria, the rate amongst those who reported playing machines in the last year (2.6 per cent) was higher than the estimates for horse racing and for private betting.

Much more research needs to be carried out in order to understand exactly where the risks lie, and why some forms of gambling might be more dangerous than others. What is very clear from the survey results, however, is that the risk of problem gambling is not at all evenly distributed across the population. For that reason the overall adult 12-month prevalence rate of 0.6 or 0.8 per cent may give a misleading impression, since that includes people who are at zero or negligible risk such as those who engage in no gambling at all, or who stake very small sums on the NL once a week, or who are 65 years of age or over. Prevalence rates immediately look higher if they are based upon only those who gambled at all in the last 12 months, and are larger again if we look at those age, sex and social groups who appear to be at highest risk, or if we concentrate on those who gamble more frequently (last-week gamblers), those who gamble on what appeared to be the higher-risk activities or who had engaged in relatively many gambling activities in the last year. For example the estimated rate of problem gambling amongst those who on a weekly basis bet with a bookmaker on events other than racing is between 10 and 15 per cent according to both SOGS and the DSM-IV questions.

There was also confirmation of much previous evidence from Britain and other countries that gambling and problem gambling are not evenly distributed according to age and sex. Older people and women were less likely than younger people and men to gamble on most of the activities, and they had lower rates of problem gambling. The relationship between machine gambling and age was particularly strong. There were some exceptions to those general trends, however. The sex and age differences were small or non-existent in the case of the NL and other lotteries. Women were just as likely to engage in scratchcard gambling as were men, and doing the football pools was most common amongst middle-aged to older men. The general trends were in fact reversed in the case of bingo which was more commonly engaged in by women than men and slightly more commonly by older people than younger.

The relationship of age to problem gambling is worth considering carefully because of the weight of evidence, reviewed in Chapter 3, that young people are most at risk. The lower age limit for the prevalence survey was 16 years, so nothing can be said about gambling of younger teenagers, but it does nicely complement the prevalence survey carried out by Fisher (1999) of 12–15 year olds in England and Wales. What was interesting in the adult survey results was that problem-gambling prevalence was strongly inversely correlated with age, with the highest rates amongst 16–24 year olds and the lowest rates amongst those aged 65 years or more. Indeed the rate for 16–24 year olds was twice the average for the whole sample according to SOGS, and around three times the average according to the DSM-IV questions.

Because of the importance of social class in the history of British gambling (see Chapter 1), and the often-repeated assertion that those on lower incomes run the greatest risks from gambling, results of the British Gambling Prevalence Survey on those topics are particularly interesting. First, it was still the case that different forms of gambling were preferred by members of different social classes (defined by occupation), notably casino gambling being preferred by those in higher status groups and bingo by those in lower SES groups. Otherwise, forms of gambling by and large showed little relationship with social class: betting on horse races and gambling on machines were virtually 'classless' for example. Those in full-time education, the 16–24 year old age group, and those on the very smallest incomes were more likely than other groups to be non-gamblers (although when they did gamble, students and young adults were more likely to be multiple-interest gamblers). Casino gambling, private betting, and to a lesser extent horse-race betting were positively related to income, and bingo (again an exception) was negatively related to income. Overall, however, engagement in gambling activities bore little relationship to income group, and when we looked at average stake (on type-A activities) and average losses (on type-B activities) in the week before the survey, nor did they have much relation to income either.

What that suggests, of course, is that those on the relatively lower incomes were spending more on gambling, as a proportion of income, compared to those on higher incomes. We were able to show this effect clearly in Chapter 5, and it is probably the explanation for the associations found between the social and economic variables and *problem* gambling. Those who were not in paid work (nor retired), those in households where the highest income earner was in a manual occupation, and those on lower incomes had significantly higher rates of problem gambling. It was the last of these, income grouping, that emerged from the statistical analysis as being one of the main correlates of problem gambling, whether according to SOGS or the DSM-IV questions. This is the clearest demonstration yet of a link between income, spending on gambling as a proportion of income, and problem gambling. In the USA, the NRC (1999) report also concluded that those on lower incomes spent a higher proportion of their incomes on gambling and tended to have a higher prevalence of problem gambling, and there was previous evidence that household expenditure on gambling as a proportion of income had risen most in low-income groups after the introduction of the UK NL (Grun and McKeigue, 2000) (see Chapter 4). The economics of gambling are probably of immense importance, on a personal and household level as well as a commercial level, as Gamblers Anonymous is only too well aware (see the later section on treatment on page 226). Economic aspects have perhaps not been given the attention they deserve in models of problem gambling as an addiction, dependence or impulse-control disorder. Interviewees in the qualitative study (Chapter 6) made repeated references to the importance of people's financial resources. Not only were the latter of importance in judging whether gambling constituted a problem or not (whether it was beyond a person's means, done with spare money, etc.), but sometimes even 'gambling' itself was confined as a term to circumstances in which people were gambling more than they could easily afford.

How problem gambling can be explained

There is no simple explanation for problem gambling, as the review in Chapter 4 makes clear, but a number of writers have attempted to integrate pieces of the jigsaw into a coherent picture of the psychology of problem gambling. They include Brown (1986), Walker (1992), Sharpe and Tarrier (1993), Griffiths (1995a), the Australian Productivity Commission report (1999), Dickerson and Baron (2000), and Orford (2001). Although there is not complete consensus, a number of general points do emerge. There is agreement, first, on the point made at the beginning of Chapter 4: the origins of problem gambling are multiple; it can only be understood in terms of the combined influence of a number of different factors, no doubt weighted differently for different people. Figure 7.1, which illustrates that complexity well, reproduces the diagrammatic representation of the causal pathways for problem gambling suggested by the Australian Productivity Commission (1999).

Cognition, in the form of biases and illusions of various kinds, plays a central role in all these models of gambling and problem gambling, and heightened arousal is never far from the centre of the picture for most of them. Both were topics we found had been emphasized in research on the possible causes of problem gambling (see Chapter 4). Walker (1992) referred to his model as a sociocognitive one, placing rather more emphasis on social factors than did the other psychological theories. Dickerson's

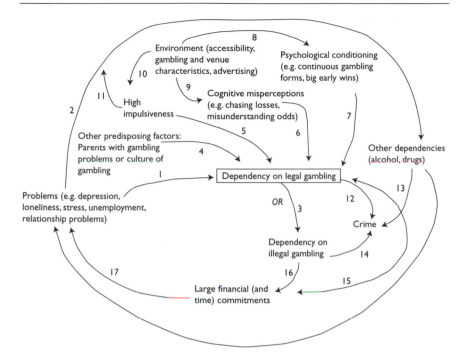

Figure 7.1 Causal pathways and problem gambling (reproduced with permission from the Australian Productivity Commission, 1999, figure 7.5, copyright Commonwealth of Australia)

detailed work on gambling has developed over a number of years but has tended to emphasis arousal, mood state (particularly depression), and factors that affect mood such as alcohol consumption (e.g. Dickerson and Baron, 2000). Sharpe and Tarrier's (1993) model highlighted gambling-related cognitions and elevated autonomic arousal, as well as poor coping skills which may confer vulnerability but also be adversely affected as a consequence of continued gambling losses.

An important general point made by these authors is the idea that people's gambling changes and develops over time. This introduction of a time dimension emphasizes the need for a longitudinal or developmental component to any complete theory of problem gambling. For example, Brown (1986) wrote of four stages: *induction* when social and cultural conditions were likely to be most important; *adoption* when behavioural reinforcement schedules plus many other factors would be of importance; the *promotion* of gambling to be a significant or even the central and dominant leisure activity in a person's life; and *addiction*. Walker's (1992) way of illustrating the developmental aspect is shown in Figure 7.2. An important point to note here is that development is not thought to be solely

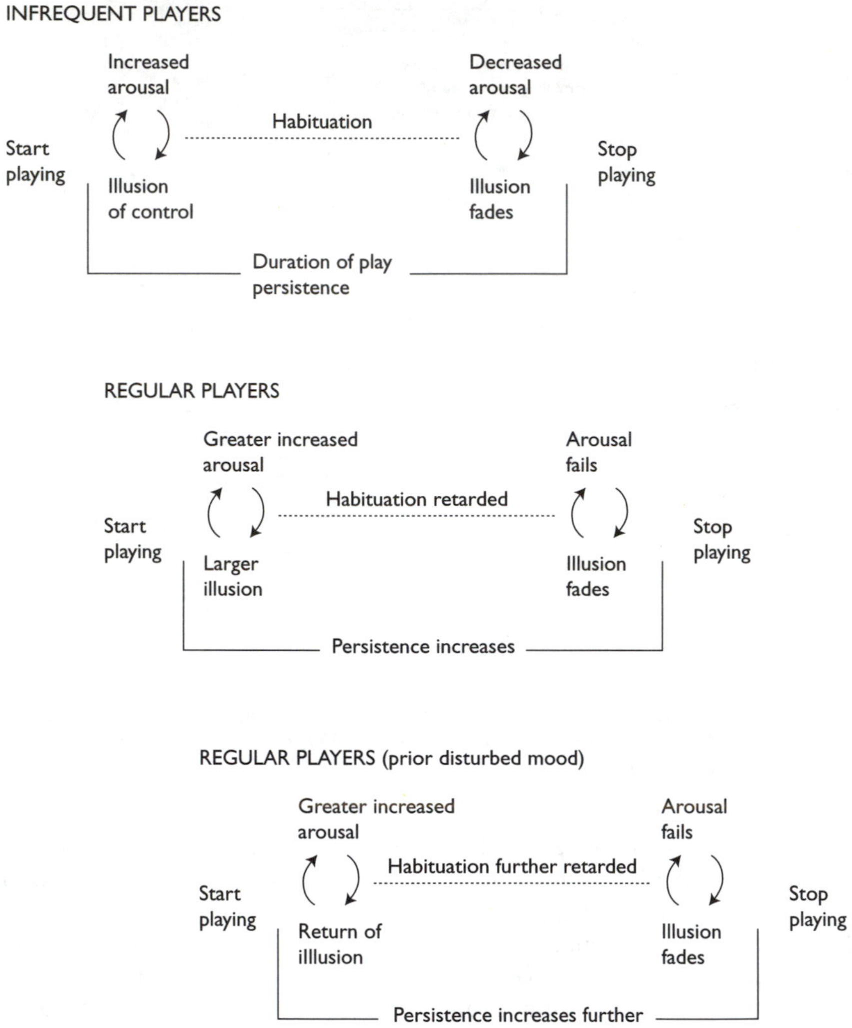

INFREQUENT PLAYERS

Increased
arousal

Decreased
arousal

Start
playing

Habituation

Stop
playing

Illusion
of control

Illusion
fades

Duration of play
persistence

REGULAR PLAYERS

Greater increased
arousal

Arousal
fails

Start
playing

Habituation retarded

Stop
playing

Larger
illusion

Illusion
fades

Persistence increases

REGULAR PLAYERS (prior disturbed mood)

Greater increased
arousal

Arousal
fails

Start
playing

Habituation further retarded

Stop
playing

Return of
illlusion

Illusion
fades

Persistence increases further

Figure 7.2 The development of persistent gambling according to Walker (1992, figure 4.2)

in one direction; heavy gambling may progress to the point at which crippling losses are being experienced, but equally heavy gambling may revert to lower level gambling. Orford's (2001) model of problem gambling as an 'excessive appetite' is another that includes a developmental component: that model refers to the development of *attachment* to gambling, the further development of *strong attachment*, and the yet further development of gambling to the point at which it is incurring *costs and conflict*. At a relatively early stage, conditioning, cognitive, and coping factors (referred to as primary processes) are particularly important; at a later stage negative reinforcement cycles including chasing (secondary processes) enter the picture, and yet later tertiary processes take place, including demoralisation, poor information processing, compulsive behaviour, and dissocialisation.

Two additional points, both of which we have met before, should be made in relation to these integrative models. One is that there is very little in the detail of these models which is not also relevant to other forms of addiction (Brown, 1986; Griffiths, 1995a), behaviour over which control is impaired (Dickerson and Baron, 2000), or excessive appetitive behaviour (Orford, 2001), unless it be the focus that all these models place upon the cognitive aspects peculiar to gambling (e.g. the 'gambler's fallacy', and the 'illusion of control'), and the considerable emphasis that most of them place upon arousal associated with gambling. The second point to note is the warning that different forms of gambling are very different and that we might need somewhat different theories to account for problem gambling of different kinds. Walker (1992, p.130) put it particularly strongly: "Piling the different games together and believing that involvement in any one is just like involvement in any other is analogous to piling chalk and cheese together and believing that the rat will eat it all."

Results of the prevalence and qualitative studies threw additional light on some of the details of the multi-factorial, developmental model of problem gambling which appears to be evolving from research and attempts at integrating the findings. One such aspect is the circumstances of the early gambling 'careers' of those who later go on to experience difficulty controlling their gambling. It has often been claimed that later problem gamblers start gambling at an earlier age than other people, are more likely to have a parent who gambles heavily, and are particularly likely to experience a big win early on. We concluded in Chapter 4 that strong evidence existed, from a number of different countries, on the positive influence of parental gambling. There was relatively little evidence on the early start theory, although several British studies found support for it (Fisher, 1993a). Although the early big win hypothesis was in line with an operant learning theory approach to gambling, there was only anecdotal support for it.

We can say with some confidence that the two studies reported in Chapters 5 and 6 provide support for parental influence. Indeed it was a good example of the way in which a large-scale survey and a smaller but much more in-depth qualitative study can provide complementary evidence which strengthens their common conclusion. In this case believing that one had a parent with a gambling problem was one of the main correlates of scoring above the threshold oneself on a problem-gambling screening measure (lower income and male sex were the only other factors which were so important). It should be remembered, however, that we are talking here of a statistical association. Only a minority of respondents, even of those who scored in the problem-gambling range themselves, reported a parent with a gambling problem. In any case we should be careful not to assume that a correlation necessarily implies that we have found a cause. Confidence that we might be looking at a genuine causative factor is strengthened, however, by what interviewers were told in the course of the qualitative study. Respondents in the latter study emphasised the key role played by other people, particularly parents, who had influenced their early gambling experiences. How this influence was exercised was clearly and convincingly explained. Families not only set a norm for gambling, creating the impression that it was an acceptable and natural activity, often demonstrating and coaching youngsters in how to gamble, but parents and others also conveyed a positive image of gambling, taking a keen interest in it and making it appear an attractive activity.

It is sometimes suggested that non-gambling parents, or parents who are anti-gambling, are likely to have problem-gambling offspring because the latter rebel against their parents' position. That possibility cannot be denied, and in fact that was exceptionally stated to have occurred for respondents in the qualitative study. But there is no evidence in the gambling field to suggest that that occurs at all often. Indeed all the evidence, plus everything that we know about the relationship between parental and offspring behaviour more generally, leads to the conclusion that positive rather than reverse influence is the norm.

Information about early wins was not collected in the survey, but the findings of the qualitative study help to put that hypothesis into perspective. A number of respondents could remember early wins, but the salience of the earliest youthful experiences varied, and it seems likely that the 'early big win' hypothesis has been too precisely stated. What seems more likely is that future problem gamblers experience early circumstances (or in some cases such circumstances later in life) that create the ground for the establishment of a cognitive-emotional-behavioural attraction or attachment to gambling which may, for some, later grow into a particularly strong attachment which gets out of hand. A big early win may be part of that fertile ground out of which problem gambling might grow, but so too may observing a family member winning or becoming excited about gambling. If an early win is remembered it need not be a particularly large one. What seems to be more important is the positive emotion associated with the activity and the generation of a cognitive set towards gambling and the prospect of winning. Winning is, after all, part of the experience for anyone who gambles other than very occasionally.

Nor did the survey ask about the age at which gambling had started, although most of the participants in the qualitative study had started gambling in their teens and some at very young ages. The early-start hypothesis therefore remains to be further tested, but there are reasons for predicting that it would be supported. For one thing, if it is the case that the 'ground' for a strong attachment to gambling first needs to be laid for problem gambling to develop, then the earlier in life that is done the more effective and long lasting it is likely to be. Further support comes from evidence in related fields that early initiation is correlated with the extent of later engagement and the risk of associated problems: that applies to smoking, alcohol consumption, drug taking and sexual behaviour (e.g. McGee and Newcomb, 1992). It would be surprising if it were otherwise for gambling.

The idea that problem gambling requires a fertile ground in which to grow, and that family members and others often, probably unwittingly, assist in laying that ground through their own positive attachment to gambling and their encouragement of others, is in keeping with a broader public health perspective. That perspective, which, as we shall see in Chapter 8, was largely missing from the report of the Gambling Review Body (2001), highlights the importance of the availability and accessibility of opportunities to gamble. A key component of that model, reviewed in Chapter 4, is the 'single distribution' theory which supposes that changes in opportunity affect the total population across the whole distribution from those who engage in a health-related behaviour regularly and heavily to those who engage in it only lightly and infrequently. Hence as opportunities to gamble increase so would an increase in gambling be expected across the board with a consequent increase in the incidence and prevalence of problem gambling. Such a model is widely accepted in the case of alcohol consumption and in the case of gambling the evidence reviewed in Chapter 4 was strongly in support of a link between availability and problems. The view that increased opportunities to gamble lead to rises in problem gambling has been accepted by authoritative review bodies in Australia (APC, 1999), the USA (NRC, 1999) and in the UK (GRB, 2001). The 'early fertile ground' theory is consistent with that public health model since households and families, as well as friendship, work and other social networks would be expected to be amongst the strongest means by which increased opportunities would work their way through to raised levels of problems.

Also consistent with that way of understanding gambling and problem gambling were survey and qualitative study findings regarding the continued influence of other people throughout lifetimes of gambling, and the role of gambling locations. There was evidence from the survey, for example, that the public house and people's places of work continued to be sites for gambling as they were in the early 20th century when the legal framework regulating gambling was totally different in Britain (see Chapter 1). Respondents in the qualitative study also referred to the availability of machine gambling in seaside arcades, as well as the ubiquity of the NL, as factors that encouraged problem gambling. Each of these points touches on matters of social policy that are highly controversial in Britain at the beginning of the 21st century, and more research is needed. The question of machines in seaside 'family entertainment centres' as the GRB report (2001) called them is particularly so. The GRB was clearly uncomfortable about it, and recommended leaving seaside arcades as they were for five years pending further research.

By comparison, theories that suppose some pre-existing and pre-disposing individual abnormality, whether of the genes, brain functioning, personality or mental health, have either not stood up to scrutiny or are at a very early stage of examination. The evidence is not consistently in support of personality traits such as sensation-seeking and there is insufficient evidence for theories that give the brain endorphins a central role. A variant dopamine receptor gene, an impulsive personality, a certain attitude towards risk taking and the discounting of delayed rewards, and depression, are all current contenders, but there is as yet no very convincing evidence for any of them. Conceptualisation in this area is weak in any case, with much confusion about whether any abnormalities that were confirmed could really be said to be predisposing and causative or, on the other hand, the consequences of problem gambling. Any predispositions that were discovered might be specific to problem gambling but would more likely be non-specific vulnerability factors for a range of difficulties.

The existing literature, reviewed in Chapter 4, was more favourable to a consideration of problem gambling as a developmental process. Memories and expectancies of financial and emotional reward from gambling, plus social norms and encouragements, a set of cues associated with favourite forms of gambling as secondary reinforcers, and a range of mental biases and illusions about the nature of randomness and the role of control and skill, are the factors that have attracted most attention as the likely key elements in such a process. Although there is no way that the survey or qualitative study could be used to test such a general theory, the latter was at least consistent with the view that gambling can serve a variety of functions, and can be associated with a variety of strong emotions. Amongst the motivations for gambling that were mentioned by participants were: the anticipation of winning money, fun and enjoyment, socialising, something to do, distraction from problems and difficulties, and to lift self-esteem. Although not everyone found it easy to talk about emotions, the ups and downs of feelings experienced during gambling were described, and the most readily mentioned were feelings of buzz or excitement associated with winning and a variety of negative emotions associated with losing, varying from the resigned and philosophical to the despondent and dispirited.

The cognitive element in this cognitive-social-behavioural process model of problem gambling is a particularly important one. A great deal of modern psychological research has focused on cognitive biases and illusions which constitute one of the few topic areas unique to the gambling field: there is nothing quite like it in the literature on drinking for example. It is also a source of debate and friction within the wider realm of discourses about gambling. Historians such as Chinn (1991) and Reith (1999) have regretted the tendency to 'pathologise' gamblers and to assume that gambling is always irrational. In their accounts they have stressed the rational, socially consonant side to gambling, and the positive mental abilities and personal characteristics associated with gambling. Social scientists and close observers of gambling, such as Goffman (1967) and Rosecrance (1988) also emphasised admirable qualities associated with gambling such as rational decision-making, play, skill, and courage. It is perhaps foolish to think that research could help us choose between these two opposing facets to gambling. It might be better to think of them as two competing sets of experiences, attributions or constructions, constantly in dialectical relationship one to the other, always with the possibility that one side of gambling will gain ascendancy at the expense of the other. Certainly both were in evidence in the accounts given by the participants in the qualitative study. Whilst acknowledging the out-of-control nature of their gambling, some respondents spoke at length about the careful preparation they engaged in before betting, the judgements required, the choice exercised or skill displayed. Orientation towards skill and choice varied considerably, however, and not everyone put much preparation or planning into betting selections. Equally, there was evidence of illusory planning based on a misunderstanding of randomness; for example detailed study of previous winning numbers on the NL.

What kind of addiction is problem gambling?

Where do we now stand on the question, raised in Chapter 3, whether problem gambling can be said to be an addiction? One answer, which really side-steps the question, is that it depends what is meant by 'addiction'. If by the latter term is meant a form of consumption or activity that is so out of control that it is difficult to resist despite the harm that it is causing, then the answer is probably 'yes'. If, on the other hand, what is meant is a dependence on a substance or the equivalent to a substance, that induces changes in the brain such that tolerance occurs and withdrawal symptoms are experienced, then the answer is probably 'no' (Gray, 2001). The first author of the present volume has argued elsewhere (Orford, 2001) that the former definition of 'addiction' is much more useful, closer to the commonly understood usage of the term, and in fact more apt for describing a range of 'excessive appetites', even including those involving drugs such as alcohol, cocaine or heroin. Hence gambling, far from being an interloper, is in fact a core member of the addiction set.

This is not to say, however, that current ways of conceptualising problem gambling, embodied in definitions of 'pathological gambling' or 'problem gambling' in the DSM or ICD systems of classification, and in sets of screening questions such as the SOGS and the questions based on DSM-IV used in the British Gambling Prevalence Survey, are above criticism. Far from it. The historians whose work was reviewed in Chapter 1 have helped us see how the dominant public discourse about problem gambling changed from one, at the beginning of the 20th century, that depicted all working-class gambling (and sometimes all gambling) as problematic, to another, by the close of the century, which made a distinction between the gambling of the majority which was enjoyable and harmless and that of a minority (sometimes incorrectly said to be a 'tiny minority') whose gambling was problematic, 'compulsive' or 'pathological'. That distinction was probably always there to be drawn, but it was earlier submerged under the dominant view about the dangers of gambling generally to society or to a whole class. Certainly Dickens recognised the distinction in an essay on *Betting Shops*:

> Some fools who are under no control, will always be found wandering away to ruin; but the greatest part of that extensive deportment of the commonality are under some control, and the great need is that it be better organised (Charles Dickens, 1852, p.336, cited by Clapson, 1992, p.207).

As Castellani (2000) convincingly argued at length, an illness model of addiction was the one most readily available to help conceptualise what was problematic about the gambling of the minority whilst allowing the gambling of the majority to be recognised as acceptable and non-problematic. Recognising that a minority of people have serious problems with their gambling, calling it 'pathological' by analogy with illness, defining it and listing its symptoms, and developing screening measures with agreed thresholds, and establishing prevalence rates using approved epidemiological methods as was done in the British Gambling Prevalence Survey and other similar surveys in other parts of the world, may have great advantages. Thereby, the cause of considerable suffering for many individuals and families is recognised, the approximate scale of the problem is assessed, and treatments are developed, to name just three advantages.

But that way of looking at the problem does not provide an easy fit in a number of ways and it has had a number of opponents. In Chapter 3 we cited a number of critics of the idea of drawing a line that would separate the pathological from the normal (Dickerson and Hinchy, 1988; McConaghy, 1991; Walker, 1992; Becoña, 1993; Fisher, 1996). Dickerson (e.g. Dickerson and Baron, 2000) is one who has consistently argued for viewing gambling-related harms and costs as lying on a continuum, degree of control over gambling being a central concept. Brown (1986, p.1013) put it thus: "The crossing over from 'normal' into 'addictive' gambling behaviour is impossible to define with any degree of satisfactory generality or likelihood of consensus." Rosecrance (1988), who eloquently described the rise of the medical model in this field, also favoured a non-illness model based on the idea of control versus losing control over gambling. His distinctive view contrasted what he called 'successful gambling' with gambling in which a person lost composure and abandoned sensible gambling strategies. Castellani's (2000) view was also that the 'medical model' now needed to be rewritten. Another critic, Brown (1993), would build a concept of addiction around the notion that an activity such as gambling could, for some individuals, become 'monopolistic', inappropriately dominating their lives.

A number of observations might be made based on the prevalence survey and qualitative study. First, as described in Chapter 5, we faced a problem of where exactly to place the SOGS and DSM-IV thresholds, above which respondents would be said to have a gambling problem. This is a problem that others have had to face and it led to much discussion in the survey Steering Group which, it will be recalled, contained a number of representatives of the gambling industry. We believe we set the thresholds in line with the majority consensus in the international gambling research community, but the charge of arbitrariness is difficult to defend against. It is a reflection of the arbitrariness of the lists of symptoms according to the DSM definition of pathological gambling which, it was noted in Chapter 3, have changed considerably over the course of only a few years.

A second observation is that key gambling variables, derived from prevalence survey data, were continuous but markedly skewed towards the upper end of the distribution. This was the case for the number of gambling activities engaged in in the last year or in the last week, amount staked on type-A activities in the last week and amount lost on type-B activities, as well as scores on the SOGS questions and the DSM-IV questions. Such a state of affairs is hardly surprising since the same is true of the distribution of alcohol consumption in the population as well as distributions of a host of behavioural, social and economic variables (Orford, 2001). It implies two important things, however. One is that in the long tails to such distributions there stand ever-decreasing minorities of people who are more and more deviant from the population norm. Some people do engage in many more gambling activities than is the norm, or spend markedly more than others on gambling, or have extremely high scores on screening measures compared to most. They are statistically quite abnormal, and are likely to be those whose gambling is most costly, most out of control, most unsuccessful, most monopolistic, or most illness-like. At the same time, these continuous but skewed distributions imply that any cut-off that is imposed is certain to be arbitrary. It could not be otherwise.

The results of the interviews with 17 gamblers in the qualitative study are also difficult to fit into an illness model. They were mostly people who were 'just above threshold'. As was likely statistically, they were mostly in the tail of the distribution curve but not right at the end of it. They recognised the potential for gambling to get out of control, and had mostly experienced this themselves. They had nearly all at some time moved from gambling being out of control to having it under a greater degree of control. Most thought that their gambling was now better controlled than it had been in the past. Most did not believe they currently had a gambling problem even though a few months previously they had scored above the threshold on a screening measure. It was as if they were using a continuum of control discourse rather than one of illness.

Treatment for problem gambling

Can problem gamblers change? Is problem gambling treatable? If so, what treatments work? Is there a best treatment? Can Gamblers Anonymous be recommended? What about adolescents, women gamblers, and family members affected by and concerned about the problem gambling of a relative? Most of those questions have been at least considered by experts in Britain (Bellringer, 1999; Griffiths and MacDonald, 1999) and to a greater extent in the USA (e.g. López-Viets and Miller, 1997; National Research Council, 1999; Petry and Armentano, 1999; McCown and Chamberlain, 2000), although all of these authors make the point that very little controlled research has yet been carried out, and what can currently be said about treatment is mostly based upon clinical experience, trial and error, and borrowing ideas and methods from related fields, particularly the treatment of alcohol and drug problems. In fact almost all the issues that are debated in the context of the treatment of problem gambling, as well as the forms of treatment that are developing, have their parallels in the field of treatment for substance misuse and dependence. The main difference is that the problem-gambling treatment field is lagging 20 or 30 years or more behind. The forms of treatment and help that are being developed include: Gamblers Anonymous (GA) and GamAnon; residential forms of treatment; a variety of forms of counselling and psychotherapy; multi-modal treatment approaches; varieties of cognitive behavioural therapy (CBT); pharmacological treatments; treatments involving partners and other family members; and telephone hotlines.

GA is the longest established, originating, as noted in Chapter 3, in 1957. Lesieur (1990) reported that GA had grown in the USA from 16 chapters in 1960 to 130 in 1979 and approximately 600 by 1988. By the latter date there were groups in Argentina, Australia, Brazil, English and French Canada, England, Germany, Holland, Ireland, Israel, Japan, Kenya, Korea, New Zealand, Panama, Puerto Rica, Scotland, and Uganda as well as in nearly all states in the USA. By the late 1990s Bellringer (1999) estimated that there were around 200 meetings of GA each week in Britain and Ireland together. Meetings of GamAnon, for partners, parents, and family and friends of problem gamblers, often take place at the same time and at the same venue, but in a separate room. Most of those who have written from their experience of treating problem gambling have been very positive about GA, writing of it as an important component of the help that is available (e.g. Bellringer, 1999; McCown and Chamberlain, 2000).

The treatment evaluation literature, on the other hand, has been more cautious about GA, pointing to a very small number of studies (e.g. Brown, 1985; and Stewart and Brown, 1988, based on a study in Scotland) suggesting that drop-out rates are high and follow-up gambling abstinence rates low. It would be inappropriate to conclude much from such a small number of studies, and in any case it is not agreed that a self-help organisation like GA can or should be evaluated in the same way as a professional treatment. It can be argued that GA, like AA on which it was modelled, is a voluntary association of people who provide mutual help for one another. Hence drop-outs might more appropriately be interpreted as people deciding not to become members. Unlike treatment, membership is often continued for months or years or even a lifetime, often opening up a support network extending far beyond an individual chapter or location. These same issues arise in relation to AA, which has also grown impressively as an organisation despite professional ambivalence. Indeed scientific scepticism about AA has given way in recent years to a more humble acceptance of the limitations of professional treatment and a greater awareness of the positive role that mutual-help can play for large numbers of people (e.g. Emrick et al, 1993; Miller and Kurtz, 1994; Tonigan et al, 1996; Orford, 2001).

Those who have got to know GA well, and have been in a position to compare it with AA, have made interesting comments about the differences between the two organisations (Browne, 1991; McCown and Chamberlain, 2000). On the basis of his observational study of 100 AA and 70 GA meetings in California in 1989 and 1990 and a number of interviews with members, Browne (1991) concluded that the two were very different despite the common 12-step idea. The main differences were the down-playing of the explicitly spiritual aspects (e.g. the word 'God' had been removed from the 12 GA steps), a de-emphasising of the 12 steps themselves and of 'working the steps' which is so important to AA, a far greater emphasis upon members' financial circumstances in GA (e.g. Step 3 required GA members to make a searching and fearless moral *and financial* inventory of themselves), but most particularly the GA conception of the central problem being excessive gambling. Unlike in AA, where the dominant position, according to Browne's observations, was that alcohol is important but the main problem is to do with character and spirituality, in GA the dominant view was that gambling is the problem. In any event, with awareness and knowledge of gambling problems being so sparse, and treatment facilities so limited, there can be no doubt that GA has grown in response to a need and currently represents one of the largest concentrations of experience and knowledge of problem gambling in Britain.

Turning to professional treatment, meta-analyses of outcome evaluation studies have been carried out by Blaszczynski and Silov (1995), López-Viets and Miller (1997) and by the US National Research Council (1999). All found that this field was at a very early stage of development. A number of uncontrolled single case studies had been reported and a number of case series, but the latter often included very small numbers, there was often no follow up or the follow-up interval was not stated, and when there was a follow up, high proportions of those treated had been lost. This is not a criticism of the treatments, but simply a reflection of what always happens in a relatively new and developing field of treatment. Although those studies lacked the necessary controls for conclusions to be confidently drawn about the effectiveness of treatment, the reviewers have drawn encouraging conclusions about the possibility of change for people with gambling problems who enter treatment. López-Viets and Miller (1997), for example, concluded that it was not uncommon for two-thirds of problem gamblers to be abstinent or to be controlling their gambler at 6- or 12-months follow up. The best of those studies was a follow up of 274 people treated in Minnesota, USA (Stinchfield and Winters, 1996, cited by NRC, 1999). The treatment in that study used a multi-modal approach, combining individual and group psychotherapy, lectures, participation in self-help groups, and family counselling. Abstinence rates of 43 per cent at 6-months follow up and 42 per cent at 12 months were reported, with an additional 20 per cent (at 6 months) and 24 per cent (at 12 months) gambling in a controlled way.

Studies including control groups had been very few. A series of studies, using behaviour therapy techniques, was reported by McConaghy et al (1983, 1988, 1991). Their particular interest was in a treatment they developed for problem gamblers, which they termed imaginal desensitisation (ID), a form of behaviour therapy in which a person visualises, in a relaxed state, situations leading to gambling, and then imagines *not* completing the gambling behaviour. Control groups received other forms of behaviour therapy. ID fared well in those studies, but the numbers of participants and/ or the proportion followed up were small, and the differences between groups in terms of outcome slight. A Spanish study reported by Echeburúa et al (1996) found a significantly higher success rate at 6-months follow up for those randomly assigned to a behavioural treatment (either individual stimulus control and in-vivo exposure with response prevention, or group cognitive restructuring) compared to results for a waiting-list control group. Finally, Sylvain et al (1997) reported a small trial in which 29 problem gamblers were randomly assigned to treatment or a waiting-list control group. The central element of treatment was the cognitive correction of erroneous perceptions about gambling, theoretically based upon the idea of cognitive distortions maintaining gambling, especially Langer's (1975) idea of the 'illusion of control' (see Chapter 4). Other elements of the treatment were problem-solving training, social-skills training, and relapse prevention. Post-treatment results were significantly better for those in the treatment group. These good results were maintained at 6-months follow up, although by that time no comparison with controls was possible.

Two types of rationale exist for the use of medication in the treatment of problem gambling. The first is based on the limited evidence (see Chapter 4) that brain systems involving neurotransmitters such as serotonin, norepinephrine and dopamine may in some way be involved in problem gambling, plus a certain amount of clinical intuition and trial and error. Under that rationale, drugs affecting such systems have been tried, including lithium carbonate, carbamazepine, fluvoxamine, naltrexone and clomipramine. The second reason for the use of medication, such as anti-depressants, is the high rate of psychological problems, particularly depression and suicidal thoughts, to be found amongst people with gambling problems (NRC, 1999; Petry and Armentano, 1999).

All in all, a wide variety of types of treatment have been tried, and although evidence for the efficacy of treatment is as yet limited, reviewers find grounds for optimism. Currently it is behavioural, and particularly cognitive-behavioural, forms of treatment that have started to receive closer attention and about which reviewers tend to be most positive. There is a certain logic to that since, if gambling itself is the central problem for a person, then a reduction in that behaviour must be a main goal of treatment, and in the case of gambling there is good evidence that unhelpful ways of thinking (faulty cognitions) are an important part of the picture (see Chapter 4).

Rather than focus on treatment type, others have focused on the treatment setting or modality, such as residential versus non-residential treatment, or telephone or brief treatment versus lengthier treatment. In the USA the first specialised treatment programmes for people with gambling problems were in-patient hospital treatment programmes. Although their number is tiny compared to such programmes for people with alcohol or drug problems, there are now a number of such in-patient facilities across the USA, and for some authors hospitalisation is the treatment modality of choice (e.g. McCown and Chamberlain, 2000). On the other hand, it is admitted that health insurance in the USA does not cover such treatment for gambling problems (although treatment entry can be 'laundered' as treatment for depression or some other condition), paying for such treatment is beyond most people, and in reality problems as prevalent as problem gambling will have to be treated, if at all, by professionals in primary health care or mental health or probation services, and not always by those who specialise in the treatment of problem gambling (NRC, 1999).

In Britain there is only one specialised residential facility for problem gamblers, namely the Gordon House Association (named after its founder Gordon Moody, who figured in Chapter 1). Rather than a hospital,

Gordon House (now two houses in fact) is a house in an ordinary street, run in conjunction with a voluntary sector housing association, including a therapeutic programme described in detail by Bellringer (1999).

Another feature of the recent British approach to helping people with gambling problems is the setting up by the national organisation GamCare of a telephone helpline staffed 12 hours a day by trained volunteers (GA also operates its own helpline) (Bellringer, 1999). Griffiths et al (1999) have provided some figures about the operation of the GamCare helpline during its first 12 months. In that period a total of 1,729 calls were received, of which 51 per cent were from problem gamblers themselves and a further 26 per cent from relatives (others being from professionals, the media, others requesting information, or simply people calling and then putting the telephone down). The largest proportion of all those calls directly related to a gambling problem were concerned with fruit-machine gambling (45 per cent), with 37 per cent concerning off-course betting and 11 per cent casino gambling (scratchcards only 2 per cent, and the National Lottery 1 per cent). Twelve per cent of callers who gave their ages were under 18 years old, and the large majority of those calls concerned problems with machines (82 per cent). Griffiths et al also noted that a significant minority of callers volunteered information about health-related consequences, including depression, anxiety, stomach problems, other stress-related disorders, and suicidal ideas. Such helplines were operating in 35 of the states in the USA according to NRC (1999).

Brief treatments have received much attention in the treatment of alcohol problems (e.g. Bien et al, 1993), and there have been two reports of using such treatments for problem gambling. Dickerson et al (1990) reported the positive results of two variations of a brief treatment which used a self-help manual adapted from one developed by Robertson and Heather (1987) for excessive drinkers. Gamblers were recruited by advertising publicly and were randomly assigned either to receive the manual through the post or in the course of an interview lasting between half an hour and two hours. The number of gambling sessions, and money spent on gambling per week, decreased for both groups, and these changes were maintained six months after initial contact, although money spent per gambling session had gone up again by 6-months follow up. Hodgins et al (2001) found a 20–45 minute 'motivational enhancement' interview carried out on the telephone, plus a mailed self-help workbook, to be effective (compared to the work-book alone or being on a waiting list) for Canadians who responded to media announcements asking for people who were concerned about their gambling and wanted to cut down or to stop on their own.

There are many other treatment questions that resonate with those dis-cussed in the alcohol and drug treatment fields. Just two of these are: Can people with gambling problems make positive changes without treatment? Can someone who has had a gambling problem ever return to gambling but in a controlled, trouble-free fashion? It would be surprising if the answers to these two questions were other than 'yes' and 'yes', since there is much evidence that people who have had serious drinking problems, for example, can sometimes overcome these without treatment (e.g. Sobell et al, 1991) and can sometimes return to 'normal' or 'controlled' drinking (e.g. Heather and Robertson, 1983). In the case of gambling problems, there is now some evidence for the phenomenon of 'unaided quitting'. Hodgins and el-Guebaly (2000) advertised for former problem gamblers who had received no treatment in Canada and studied 43 who responded, and Marotta (1999, cited by Klingemann et al, 2001) studied 29 untreated ex-problem gamblers in the USA.

Whether people who have had gambling problems can ever safely return to gambling remains controversial. GA, like AA, is based on the idea that its members are suffering from a disease that is incurable and can be controlled only by abstaining totally. McCown and Chamberlain (2000) are probably typical of most professional specialists in the USA in acknowledging that return to controlled gambling might occasionally be possible but believing that it is rare and much safer to opt for total abstinence. Working in Australia, the McConaghy group have been much more positive about the possibility and in each of their outcome evaluation studies they reported a number of their participants who had apparently successfully controlled their gambling.

Most writers on the subject of treatment for gambling problems have noted the under-representation of women, and of members of ethnic minority groups (e.g. NRC, 1999). Particularly surprising, in view of the evidence for the high prevalence of gambling problems amongst adolescents (see Chapter 3) is the almost complete absence of reference in the professional and scientific literature to the treatment of adolescent problem gambling. It may be that some of the types of treatment that have been most prominent in the USA, such as hospital in-patient programmes and GA, are not suitable for adolescents, and that other ways of responding need to be developed. In Britain this lack has at least been discussed and more appropriate ways of meeting the treatment needs of adolescents suggested (Bellringer, 1999; Griffiths and MacDonald, 1999).

Finally, mention should be made of the involvement of family members in treatment for problem gambling, since it is widely recognised that family members are often so closely involved in the problem, and so much affected by it, that their involvement in treatment is likely to be helpful to them as family members and to the treatment of the person with the gambling problem (e.g. Bellringer, 1999; Griffiths and MacDonald, 1999; NRC, 1999; Petry and Armentano, 1999; McCown and Chamberlain, 2000). Detailed suggestions have been made about the ways in which family members might be involved (e.g. Bellringer, 1999), but no systematic studies of family-based treatments have been conducted to date. One way in which family members have become involved is through GamAnon, and through a procedure known in GA as the 'pressure-relief' group – another way in which GA differs from AA (Lesieur, 1990). In those groups, a GA member meets with family members or close friends and one or two long-standing members of GA, and is expected to reveal all his or her debts and to start making plans to pay them off.

A final issue regarding treatment, to which we shall return in the concluding chapter, is the source of funding for treatment. People with gambling problems, and their families, are in many respects 'marginal' people whose problems are little recognised, poorly understood, and not always greeted with much sympathy. Like people with alcohol and drug problems in the past (and often still), their treatment is not something for which public authorities take full responsibility. In the USA, NRC (1999) noted that many of the individual councils on problem gambling at the state level received some funding from the state or gambling industry organisations to support treatment for problem gambling, revenue generated by gambling in the state often being used to pay for these services. Most of the councils viewed the level of funding they received as insufficient: even in the more generous states, the amounts involved were small in comparison to revenues from legalised gambling. For example, in the state of New York a mere one tenth of one per cent of the state's income from legalised gambling went to its council on problem gambling, and in Minnesota the proportion was one half of one per cent. The same issue has had to be faced in Britain. The Gordon House Association, and GamCare, including its telephone helpline, have been directly supported by gambling industry organisations, although the sums involved are tiny in relation to need, and continuity of funding cannot be relied upon.

What we still need to know

Much still remains to be understood about problem gambling, both universally around the world and specifically in Britain. The need for future study falls into four areas: prevalence; the addiction potential of different forms of gambling; vulnerability and risk groups; and treatment.

As the accessibility of gambling in Britain rises, as seems likely to go on happening in the early years of the present century, the prevalence of problem gambling should be monitored regularly. The first British Gambling Prevalence Survey (BGPS) was planned in part to establish a baseline against which the results of further surveys might be compared. The BGPS should be repeated every five years and questions about gambling included more regularly in other exercises such as the General Household Survey. Future surveys will need to include more questions about spread betting and about gambling which uses advanced technology, such as internet gambling and use of interactive TV and mobile telephones for gambling.

It has been assumed that certain forms of gambling have a greater potential than others to create addiction, but that is still not clearly established. There is much support for the hypothesis that those types of gambling that allow for rapid cycles of play have greater capacity to entrap players into continuous play, particularly through the process of 'chasing losses', but there are alternative hypotheses. One, suggested by the results of the BGPS, is that the scope of a person's gambling is the important variable, with problem gambling being associated with the *number* of forms of gambling the person engages in rather than with the addiction potential of particular forms. Another hypothesis is that forms of gambling are more risky the more they give rise in the mind of the player to the view that skill is involved and control can be exercised. A different kind of hypothesis altogether is that the risk of addiction is correlated with the size of the prizes on offer. The possible role of alcohol consumption in increasing risky gambling also requires clarifying through further study.

Whether there are groups of people who are specially vulnerable for problem gambling, and if so who they are and what makes them vulnerable, needs much more investigation. Research in a number of countries, including the BGPS, has found raised prevalence rates amongst men, teenagers and young adults, those who live comparatively near to gambling facilities, those on comparatively low incomes, and those who have had parents with gambling problems. That work needs replicating, extending and deepening. In multi-cultural Britain there is a particular need to find out whether there are any special vulnerabilities and treatment needs amongst British South Asian, African and African-Caribbean, Chinese and other minority communities.

In view of how little research has been carried out on treatment for problem gambling, and the paucity of any treatment for problem gamblers in Britain, treatment research is of the highest priority. What is needed is the setting up of flexible systems of treatment, drawing on the best experience to date of different forms of treatment that have started to show promise, including brief treatments delivered by telephone or internet, and treatments that have been established as effective in closely related fields such as in the treatment of alcohol or other drug problems. These treatments and systems then need to be subjected to proper evaluation using research designs and methods that are of the highest standard. When setting up and evaluating treatments for problem gambling, the positive role that can be played by the large numbers of people who are concerned about and affected by the problem gambling of a family member or friend, and the needs that those people have in their own right, should not be neglected.

Chapter 8

A nation of gamblers? The 2001 Gambling Review Report and beyond

Reports of the British Gambling Prevalence Survey and the complementary qualitative study, summarised here in Chapters 5 and 6, came out in mid-2000 and early 2001 respectively. They were rapidly followed in mid-2001 by the much-anticipated report of the government's Gambling Review Body (GRB, 2001). In this chapter we summarise the recommendations of the GRB report and the immediate response in the British press, and consider its likely implications for the future of gambling in Britain.

The Gambling Review Report and its recommendations

Terms of reference

The GRB's terms of reference were as follows:

- Consider the current state of the gambling industry and the ways in which it might change over the next ten years in the light of economic pressures, the growth of e-commerce, technological developments and wider leisure industry and international trends.
- Consider the social impact of gambling and the costs and benefits.
- Consider, and make recommendations for, the kind and extent of regulation appropriate for gambling activities in Great Britain, having regard to:
  - their wider social impact;
  - the need to protect the young and vulnerable from exploitation and to protect all gamblers from unfair practices;
  - the importance of preventing gambling from being carried out in a way which allows crime, disorder or public nuisance;
  - the need to keep the industry free from infiltration by organised and other serious crime, and from money laundering risks;
  - the desirability of creating an environment in which the commercial opportunities for gambling, including its international competitiveness, maximise the UK's economic welfare; and

- the implication for the current system of taxation, and the scope for its further development.
- Consider the need for, and, if necessary, recommend new machinery appropriate for carrying out that regulation which achieves a more consistent and streamlined approach than is now possible and which is financed by the gambling industry itself.
- Consider the availability and effectiveness of treatment programmes for problem gamblers and make recommendations for their future provision, potential costings, and funding.
- In conducting this review, the GRB should not consider changes to the National Lottery. But it will need to look at the impact on the Lottery of any proposed changes, including an assessment of the potential effect on the income to good causes.

Move to the Department for Culture, Media and Sport

The setting up of the GRB was widely welcomed, particularly but not only by the gambling industry. Its recommendations promised to set the scene for gambling in Britain well into the 21st century, and were keenly awaited. Its report was published in July 2001. It constituted a very thorough review of the regulation of different forms of gambling in Britain, as the regulation then stood, and it contained 176 recommendations. Throughout, the report touched on controversies small and large. One of the most significant was referred to by the GRB's chairman, Sir Alan Budd, in the opening paragraph of his introduction, and again towards the end of the report. Whilst the GRB was deliberating, and following a general election which returned the Labour government to power with a renewed large majority, the government switched lead responsibility for gambling from the Home Office, which had commissioned the report, to the Department for Culture, Media and Sport (DCMS), to whom the report was therefore submitted. This highly significant move was not entirely welcome to the GRB, who drew a distinction between sponsorship of gambling and its regulation:

> We can readily accept that gambling is part of the leisure industry and that it would be appropriate for DCMS to sponsor it. However our concern has been with the regulation of gambling and, among other things, with the prevention of crime and harm to the vulnerable. That would appear to fall squarely with the responsibilities of the Home Office (para 34.4).

Although the issue of which government department is most appropriate to supervise gambling was not otherwise mentioned in the report, it does relate closely to what the report identified as the GRB's central dilemma – the need to reconcile the freedom of 'punters' to play whatever, whenever and wherever they choose and to be treated as consumers of leisure products, with Britain's good reputation (at least since the 1968 Act) for sensible regulation of gambling so that it be honest, crime-free, and non-exploitative, particularly where children are concerned. In general the report recommended moving British gambling towards greater freedom whilst recognising that gambling held dangers. The report considered the risk of problem gambling to be the greatest such danger and accepted the evidence that young people were most at risk.

General principles

More specifically a number of general principles were repeatedly referred to in the report of the GRB. One was the desire to minimise what it referred to as 'ambient gambling', that is gambling incidental to the main activities conducted on the premises in question. The strong preference was to provide players with good, safe opportunities to gamble on licensed, closely regulated premises where the principal function is gambling. A second principle was to restrict gambling to those of 18 years of age or over, with two important exceptions: lotteries and 'low stake/low prize' gambling machines. A third principle was not to extend opportunities to mix gambling and the consumption of alcohol on the same premises. A fourth principle was to allow local authorities discretion over whether to allow gambling premises, or particular types of gambling premise, in their areas, as well as over such matters as opening hours. A fifth principle, of central importance, was the need to extend and strengthen the effective system of regulation then exercised by the Gaming Board. The specific recommendation was that a new regulatory authority be set up, the Gambling Commission, which would license gambling operators and key workers of all kinds (thus extending the remit of the Gaming Board), with widespread powers including the detection and prosecution of illegal gambling (it was recognised that gambling remained vulnerable to crime whether in the form of money laundering, cheating of punters, fixing of sporting events, or coercing competitors).

New freedoms in the provision of gambling

Having so carefully considered the issues and dilemmas around the regulation of gambling (and showing ample evidence of having sought widely for opinions and facts, including citing frequently from our own research summarised in Chapter 5 of the present book, and commissioning their own Office for National Statistics survey of over 1500 British adults), how did the GRB translate its aims and principles into specific recommendations about different forms of gambling? Generally speaking the freedom principle won the day, and the large majority of the report's specific recommendations run in the direction of deregulation as many would have predicted (e.g. Reith, 1999). Of particular significance is the report's recommendation that the principle of 'unstimulated demand' and the consequent 'demand test' for new betting offices, bingo clubs and casinos, and the restriction of casinos to 'permitted areas' only, should be abolished. This would be a final break, foreseen by Dixon (1991), with the long tradition in Britain of allowing certain forms of gambling but at the same time not encouraging them. The Rothschild Commission, in its report in 1978, had struggled with the issue, even recognising that the British tradition might be thought paternalistic, but it had maintained the principle of unstimulated demand. The Home Office was recommending its retention in a consultation paper as late as 1996. The GRB of 2000–2001 also struggled with the issue, but came down in a different place.

The list of new freedoms that the report recommended extending to bingo halls, betting offices, and particularly casinos, is a long one. It included recommending removing the requirement of membership for casinos and bingo clubs, abolishing the 24-hour rule for casinos (requiring 24-hours' notice to be given before a potential punter could gamble), allowing larger numbers of new-style gaming machines with unlimited stakes and prizes in casinos only (the only limit being that there should be no more than eight such machines for every casino 'table'), allowing jackpot gambling machines in betting offices and 'all-cash' machines in bingo halls, and a greater variety of games in casinos and bingo halls (subject to Gambling Commission approval), permitting live entertainment in casinos, alcohol on the gaming floor and tipping of gaming staff, permitting unlimited stakes and prizes, multiple games and rollovers in bingo halls, and allowing betting on the National Lottery in betting shops (which would be able to offer better odds than the NL on the smaller 'wins' e.g. three correct numbers). The report recognised that these recommendations, if put into effect, would likely increase the number of casinos in Britain from the then 123 to perhaps around 450, that the prevalence of problem gambling would be likely to rise, and there would be a danger that the nature of the bingo game might change in the direction of 'harder' gambling. The report recognised also that the new freedoms suggested for casinos opened the way for 'resort casinos' on the Las Vegas model. Indeed the report referred specifically to a proposal to develop such a resort in Blackpool. The counterweights to all those recommendations were slight. Casinos would need to be of at least a certain size (a table gaming area of at least 2,000 square feet and at least eight tables) to prevent any night-club simply adding one or two gaming tables in a backroom. No betting would be allowed in bingo halls, and no alcohol in betting offices.

Applying more generally to gambling, advertising would be permitted subject to a Gambling Commission code (at the time advertising was permitted for some forms of gambling and not for others), on-line gambling would be permitted, and credit cards could be used for gambling with the single exception that it should not be possible to play gambling machines by directly inserting a credit card (the GRB noticed an increase in the siting of automated teller machines on gambling premises, and recommended that they should be located in such a way that players were required to have a break in gambling in order to take more money).

The GRB found the question of on-line gambling particularly challenging. Their general view was that it, ". . . should be seen as just another way of delivering a service" (para 30.13). They drew a distinction between on-line betting (using the internet or interactive television simply as a means of placing bets on real-time events), and on-line gambling when the stake is made on-line and the gambling itself is generated on-line by a random number generator of some kind. They rejected the idea that on-line gambling could be prohibited (as they believed was coming to be realised in the USA also), but recommended that it be licensed, regulated and tested by the Gambling Commission. Specific recommendations included careful identification of players (to prevent money laundering and under-age playing), that prizes should be paid out by the same method that the punter had used to stake (e.g. adding to a credit card account if such an account had been used to stake), that the operator should set up clocks and counting systems that would be regularly displayed on the screen (to keep players informed of how long they had been playing and how much they had won and lost), that facilities should be available to enable players to set maximum stakes and limits, and to self-ban, that prizes won by minors should be forfeited, that no premises should be used primarily for accessing on-line gambling, and that operators to be licensed by the Gambling Commission should be registered as British companies with servers in Great Britain and using UK web addresses for their gambling sites.

The lifting of certain restrictions on pools and society lotteries was also recommended. Pools competitions would be allowed to offer unlimited rollovers, and retail outlets could be used for pool competitions on any sport (not just football) and should be allowed to pay out small pools winnings as they already did for the NL. Restrictions on the size of stakes, prizes and maximum annual proceeds should be removed for societies' lotteries, and also allowed would be rollovers, on-line draws (but restricted to one a day in any particular premises to avoid the 'hard gambling' of repetitive, frequent on-line lottery games such as Pronto which had been withdrawn after government objection), interactive lottery games and lottery gaming machines (but only in premises where gaming machines may be sited, and only instead of, not in addition to, any entitlement to such machines).

Machine gambling

But it was gambling machines that the GRB found to be one of their most difficult issues and they devoted one of the longest chapters in their report to them. The problems were the varieties of types of machine that needed to be considered, the wide variety of locations in which they were then sited, many of them on premises where machine gambling was incidental, the different degrees of regulatory control (or none) that applied, the limited degree of control that the Gaming Board was permitted to exercise on this sector of gambling, the fact that machines were often sited illegally, the fact that maximum prizes had risen, even allowing for inflation, well beyond the limits set by the 1968 Act, and particularly the question of machine gambling by under-18 year olds. All in all:

> In Great Britain, the policy has been to avoid stimulating demand and to prevent excessive gambling by imposing controls on the numbers of, and stakes and prizes for, machines in particular locations. It is arguable that this objective has been defeated in view of the sheer number of locations with machines (para 23.5).

Being persuaded that machine gambling could be particularly addictive, and especially for young people, the GRB's inclination was clearly to prohibit all kinds of machine for under-18 year olds. Indeed their preference would have been to confine all forms of gambling to those aged 18 or over. That is what the majority of those who made submissions to them would have liked, including many representatives of the gambling industry who, by and large, saw gambling as an adult activity. The GRB drew short, however, of prohibiting children (of any age it seems) from gambling in what have traditionally been called 'seaside arcades' on the lowest category of machine (the so-called 'amusement with prizes' or AWP machines). The report preferred to call such premises 'family entertainment centres' and such machines 'low stake/low prize' machines. They were doubtful about the argument put forward by the British Amusement Catering Trades Association (BACTA) that banning under-18s from playing arcade machines would have a devastating effect on the seaside resort business, nor did they accept the argument of BACTA and others that low stake/low prize machines were trivial and should not be regarded as gambling at all. Nevertheless the GRB was persuaded that it would be too extreme to change the nature of the seaside experience by preventing children from playing such machines. Their uncertainty about this was palpable:

> Although we have concluded that children should be at liberty to enter, what we have termed, family entertainment centres, we remain uneasy about encouraging children to gamble. Most will come to no harm, but some will . . . if we were creating the regulations for the first time, we would certainly recommend that no gaming machines should be played by under 18s (paras 23.21 and 23.23).

Further research was recommended to examine the impact of machine gambling by children and it was suggested that government should formally review the position in five years time to determine whether such gambling by under-18s should continue to be permitted or whether Britain should come into line with other countries and ban children's gambling altogether. Part of the problem was the difficulty of distinguishing a 'seaside arcade' or 'family entertainment centre' from an 'inland arcade' which often contained a 'restricted area' where all-cash machines were located and under-18s not admitted. Some arcade operators were voluntarily restricting the whole of their arcades to 18s and over. Although the report was not able to satisfactorily define an 'inland arcade', it did recommend tightening up in a number of ways. The main recommendation was a ban on all types of gambling except in specified permitted places. Thereby machines in places such as cafes, takeaways or taxi-cab offices would no longer be permitted. There would be a maximum stake of 10p (down from 30p), a freeze on a maximum £5 prize, and prizes confined to cash (not tokens up to £8 as at present). Supervision of arcades would be tightened up.

The GRB was on the whole much more relaxed about adult machine gambling, and as already mentioned recommended the creation of a super class of machine for casinos and some easing of restriction on machines in bingo halls and betting offices. The report also recommended approval of a range of suggestions about the further development of all-cash, jackpot and casino machines. These include: use of banknotes and 'smart cards'; allowing winnings to be stored in the machine to be used for further play; machines to be able to pay out in coins, notes, cheques, credit added to a smart card, credit note, or redeemable tokens; 'multiple staking' (multiple stakes on a single line or staking on multiple lines); and multi-player machines.

The one exception to the report's liberal approach to adult machine gambling was all-cash machines in pubs. In line with their principles that ambient gambling should be avoided, and that the mixing of gambling and drinking should not be encouraged, the report admitted that, had they been starting from scratch, they would ban all gambling machines in pubs. To do so now they thought would be harsh, but the report did recommend a limit of two machines in total (at that time two were allowed in each bar), unless more were already in operation, and tighter controls on under-age playing.

Implications for the National Lottery

What would be the implication of these recommendations for Britain's National Lottery? The GRB was instructed not to consider changes to the NL which, since its inception, had been dealt with quite separately. The GRB report implied some criticism of this exceptional treatment for the NL, particularly in so far as the case for treating it differently rested on the mistaken idea that the NL was not really gambling at all. The GRB was quite clear that it was gambling, that there was evidence that it competed with other forms of gambling, particularly football pools, and that there was the possibility of the NL developing other sorts of game which would resemble other forms of gambling more closely. Should the time come when the regulatory and sponsoring/commercial functions of the National Lottery Commission were separated, they argued, then regulation of the NL should be taken over by the proposed Gambling Commission. Meanwhile the GRB thought it possible that NL takings might be reduced by some of the proposals they were making, especially by the unlimited prizes and rollovers on casino machines, pools and bingo. Larger bingo prizes might have a particular effect they thought.

The GRB report, possibly crucial for British gambling in the 21st century, appeared to have struggled with a large number of complex and controversial issues surrounding the subject, notably the future of casinos, gambling machines, and bingo, the dangers of problem gambling, and how to deal with gambling by young people. At the end of the day, however, the argument that gambling is a legitimate form of leisure consumption to which people are freely entitled, and which therefore should be facilitated, won the day. There was very little in the report which took a broader public health view of gambling, or which considered its wider 'social impact', even though the latter was specifically mentioned in its brief. There was nothing in the report, for example, that compared with the careful attempt by the Australian Productivity Commission report (1999) to examine in the round the costs and benefits of gambling to Australian society (see Chapter 2).

Press response to the Gambling Review Report

The GRB report was released to the press on 17 July 2001. For the following week the main national newspapers were searched for references to the report. That involved a thorough search of ten national daily newspapers and twelve national Sunday newspapers[1]. Thirty-five relevant reports, feature articles or letters were found and the following main themes were identified.

A huge shake-up proposed

The report was widely recognised in the press as recommending a major relaxation of regulations governing gambling. This was referred to as a "radical overhaul" and a "sweeping aside of restrictions" in the *Daily*

---

1 Work carried out by Mya Krishnan at the University of Birmingham

Express[2], a "liberalisation" and "relaxation", involving "sweeping changes" in the *Daily Telegraph*, a "huge shake-up" (*Sun*), the "biggest shake-up of gambling laws for 30 years . . . scrapping a series of restrictions" (*Daily Sport*), "dramatic plans to relax Britain's gambling laws" (*Daily Star*), a "massive shake-up" (*Daily Mail*) and the "first big shake-up since 1968, lifting many restrictions" (*The Guardian*). Two items made specific reference to the influence that the National Lottery had had in paving the way for such changes. One of them, in the *Independent*, referred to the gaming industry citing the NL, "as evidence that Britain has come of age as a gambling nation and that . . . laws are outdated". An article in the *Daily Express* stated, "There's no doubt that we have a funny attitude to gambling in this country . . . Why shouldn't we be allowed to gamble and have a drink and watch a show while we're doing so?" Whatever the GRB may have intended, the press clearly recognised their report as one that recommended the liberalisation of gambling on a large scale.

Welcomed by the gambling industry

The very favourable response of the gambling industry was picked up by most of the papers. According to *The Times* the report was "widely backed" by the gaming industry. In the *Daily Mail* the Chief Executive of Gala Leisure was quoted as saying that the report provided a "terrific opportunity" which would end "ludicrous anomalies", and the Managing Director of Leisure Parcs was reported as saying, "This is about unlimited stakes and prizes. You could walk in off the street and £1 could make you millions", and that it was essential that gaming laws were relaxed. The large headline to that press report was "Law shake-up gives casinos a winning hand". The GRB report was said to have been met by bosses of the gaming and betting industries with "delight". The *Mirror* also started its report by stating "Gambling firms hit the jackpot yesterday", and four named betting companies were said to be "thrilled at the proposals, which mean that they will be able to compete with the National Lottery's massive prizes". A representative of the casino and gambling group Gala Leisure was reported in the *Daily Telegraph* as saying that the report "went further than I thought it would". A report in the *Independent* offered the view that the report read like a "bookie's wish list".

The *Times* reported that the recommendations were a "boon to bookies", and that share prices of the Hilton Group (the owners of Ladbrokes) and of firms manufacturing gambling machines had risen. Prices of shares in some existing casino operating companies had gone down on the other hand, presumably anticipating new competition. The *Independent* saw the report

2 The majority of relevant press items appeared on 18 July; dates will only be mentioned when an item appeared on another day

as providing an opportunity especially for the "better capitalised" firms such as the 'hotels-to-gaming' group Hilton and for other companies catering for the "larger players". A few days later (23 July) both *The Times* and the *Independent* reported Ladbrokes' plans to create 1,000 new jobs, to open betting 'superstores', and their expectations of a 30 per cent increase in turnover. The company was expecting to benefit from changes proposed in the GRB report as well as from the opportunity provided by 'tax-free betting' (which had previously been announced by the government and which came into force in October 2001). The report in the *Independent* picked out the report's emphasis on the need to provide gambling customers with a "better level of service".

A vision of the future

Many papers tried to paint a picture of what gambling in Britain would look like in the future if the GRB's recommendations were acted upon. Two items referred to alcoholic drinks being allowed on the gaming floor in casinos, picking out 'alcohol' or 'booze' in bold headlines (*Daily Sport* and *Daily Star*). Two warned of the possible depressing effect on NL takings (*Daily Mail* and *Daily Express*). Two referred to the proposed Gambling Commission and the way it might offer protection to 'punters' (*The Guardian* and *Daily Sport*). Several referred to the recommendation that betting offices should be able to provide meals (e.g. the *Independent*), the *Daily Telegraph* having a vision of "curry betting shops".

But the vision that excited most press attention was that of Las Vegas-style casino gaming resorts, particularly the prospect that Blackpool on the north-west coast would be the first such resort in Britain. Almost all the papers referred to Blackpool, some at great length, and often accompanied by photographs, drawings or cartoons depicting Blackpool Tower and the seafront and proposed casino developments such as Pharaoh's Palace. Blackpool was said to have been in economic decline for some time, with a high rate of unemployment, a reduction in the number of hotels, having become a magnet for "drunken, drugged stag and hen nights" (*The Times*) and with an increase in crime generally (*Sunday Express*, 22 July). A local council spokesperson was quoted in the *Independent* as saying that it was, "the only solution to hauling Blackpool out of its downturn". Blackpool was said to be "poised", "all set to go", with development plans by Leisure Parcs already on the table. The *Sunday Express* (22 July) referred to the GRB report as being the "first milestone in the project . . . to kick-start Blackpool".

Compared to the casino leisure resort vision, the press in the week following release of the GRB report gave little attention to other potential developments which might be permitted if recommendations were followed. A report in the *Independent* mentioned large-prize fruit machines in casinos, and better odds on the NL in betting offices, and the likelihood that recommendations would lead to more betting offices. A report by the city correspondent for the *Daily Telegraph* quoted the Chief Executive of Gala as saying that the report had paved the way for the development of 'gambling sheds', combining casino, bingo hall, betting shop and other gaming activities, set around a food court: "We've been working on destination gambling venues for a long time and if they become permissible, we'd certainly be interested," he said. An article in *The Times* quoted the Director of the Centre for the Study of Gambling and Commercial Gaming at Salford University who said that as a conservative estimate he would expect to see the gambling industry's profits double, and "a huge growth in slot machine gambing in much larger international-style casinos with mega-jackpots and lots of different forms of gambling and other entertainment under one roof".

A probable increase in problem gambling

Several papers referred to an estimate of 400,000 problem gamblers in Britain, based, rather inexactly, on the findings of the Prevalence Survey summarised in Chapter 5, and the GRB report's expectation that its recommendations would lead to an increase in the prevalence of problem gambling was also referred to by several (*The Times, The Guardian*, the *Daily Mail* and the *Daily Express* on 18 July, and the *Mail on Sunday* on 22 July). *The Times* quoted Sir Alan Budd, Chairman of the GRB, as follows: "I don't think it is inevitable that it will go up, but I believe that it is probable that if the amount of gambling increases then the amount of problem gambling goes up . . . This was one of the very difficult judgements we had to reach, perhaps one of the hardest parts of our discussion." A report in the *Daily Mail* was one of the few to mention the recommendation that the gambling industry should fund research into the problem and that staff should be "trained to spot addicts". Several papers made mention of the fact that proposals for liberalisation were balanced by the recommendation to restrict access to gambling machines for under-18 year olds (*The Times, The Guardian, Mirror, Daily Sport*).

Warnings against the recommendations

In amongst the majority of press items that highlighted the good news brought by the report to the gambling industry and new plans for developments of gambling facilities, particularly in Blackpool, plus the occasional short paragraph mentioning the probable rise in problem gambling, a number of articles also appeared in the week following the report which struck a different note. To be expected were warnings by the Methodist church of a gambling "free-for-all" (*The Times, Daily Mail, Daily Express*), and a view from Gamblers Anonymous that the number of problem gamblers would increase and that what was needed was more treatment (*The Times, Daily Express*). Both the Methodists and GA thought that the report should have gone further and banned gambling machines from public places altogether. A number of articles, however, raised broader questions, warning that making gambling more accessible might not be good for society or for individual communities like Blackpool.

Two articles were particularly notable because they used as a starting point the writer's experience of problem gambling in his family. One was written by Roy Hattersley, former Deputy Leader of the British Labour party. He described his maternal grandfather's gambling problem, going on to argue that the libertarian philosophy on which the GRB's report was based had its limits:

> My grandfather was hugely intelligent, brave and handsome. Gambling ruined his life and the life of his family. But it is not only the stories of bills unpaid and bailiffs at the door – told to me by my Mother, that make me regret the prospect of Britain's gambling laws being modified . . . It seems possible that Britain . . . will become the gambling capital of Europe . . . The problem now is . . . a gradual and corrosive destruction of the values on which our society is based. Nobody can be sure the casinos will not become easy territory for drug pushers, but we can be certain that, once the international gamblers move in, they will be fertile ground for men who want to take money from people who cannot afford it . . . We have to ask, is it worth it? Will the sort of society which allows unrestricted gambling encourage the standards and values we want to inculcate into our children and grandchildren? . . . Respect for the individual requires us to allow men and women to make their own mistakes. But, in a civilised society, there is no freedom to exploit others and no liberty to destroy families. Unrestricted gambling risks exactly that (*Daily Mail*, 18 July 2001).

Although Michael Winner writing in the *Sun* (22 July), referring to his mother as a "sick, congenital gambler" who, through her gambling, lost at least £25 million of a large family fortune, did not draw the same conclusions as Roy Hattersley, he did draw a picture of current restrictions being ". . . swept away. Great slot machine monoliths will appear, blackjack, roulette, chemin de fer and other games for gamblers will be everywhere."

Four other reports that appeared in the national Sunday newspapers on 22 July also warned against the dangers of less restricted gambling for individuals and for society as a whole. In the *Independent on Sunday* the reporter described a visit to a casino, finishing with him going home broke in the early hours of the morning. The report concluded, "When the laws are changed it will be much easier to stroll in on a whim, hand over your cash and end up feeling as lousy as this. Good luck." A *Sunday Times* report, referring to the out-of-control casino industry in Britain in the 1960s, and the way that petty crime became associated with gambling machines in Dublin in the 1980s ("'It was worse than hard drugs or drink,' said an Irish friend who lived through that era"), described the GRB report as "a disaster . . . So why, you might ask, should the Budd Body want us to have more of it? The short answer is that Britain wants to become a nastier place. The long answer is that Budd had no choice. The deep answer is that freedom is seldom what it appears to be." That article picked out fruit machines as being particularly dangerous, and cited the Secretary of the Gaming Board who pointed out that removal of restrictions on the number of fruit machines allowed in casinos might prove to be the report's most radical innovation. "What we will get in Blackpool and elsewhere", the article went on, "are those vast Las Vegas-style gambling complexes filled with thousands of fruit machines being played day and night . . . It's not pretty, but that's where we're going."

In a guest feature by the Deputy Editor of the *New Statesman* which appeared in the *Observer*, the question was raised whether, even at the beginning of the 21st century, gambling might be considered as an immoral activity.

> . . . the libertarians' live-and-let-live attitude which underpins their current call for the liberalisation of the gaming laws, is simply the reckless selfishness of the haves with regards to the have-nots – let me play even at the cost of others' suffering. But a vote for gambling is also a vote for the collective abdication of responsibility. Gambling allows you to duck the consequences of your actions: you do not rely on your will or your moral compass to act as the agent of your fortune. Your fate is down to the roll of a dice rather than to you . . . Television is complicit in the creation of this grubby greed. Through its agency, the National Lottery has slowly legitimised gambling . . . It would seem that our public institutions – the Government, the media – are all in on the act: they think they've found the perfect way to milk our greed while simultaneously promoting it. And so, when it comes to dropping the restrictions on gambling, they're game. Are you? (*Observer*, 22 July 2001).

Another article that day, which appeared in the *Mail on Sunday* carried a large headline running across two pages, "Don't ruin our heritage with Las Vegas on sea", arguing that casinos at British holiday reorts would spoil the traditional family seaside holiday. Other reports that appeared in the press that week were less than totally enthusiastic about Blackpool becoming a casino resort. A report in the *Independent* thought that trying to be like Las Vegas was a "sign of defeat" for Blackpool. The *Independent* picked up on mixed views reported in the local *Gazette*. A fear on the part of some smaller businesses was reported. Others feared loss of the "old Blackpool". Atlantic City in the USA was cited as a community that had been economically regenerated as a result of such a development. Altogether there was thought to be a 50/50 split in Blackpool on the subject. In the *Daily Telegraph* both the Head of Development of Blackpool Borough Council, and the Secretary of the Blackpool Hotel and Guest House Association were cited as being favourable but with reservations. The former preferred to talk about, "architecturally stunning multi-purpose entertainment centres that happen to include gambling", and the latter thought, "This idea would help keep us ahead, but it would be only one of the eggs in the basket."

Government welcomes the report

Although a number of press reports made it clear that the GRB was making recommendations which would need to be considered by government, and that they would be subject to a public consultation process (e.g. the *Independent*), many of the reports and articles were phrased as if the recommendations were already government policy which the report had simply "unveiled" (e.g. the *Daily Sport*). *The Times* referred to Tessa Jowell, the Culture, Media and Sport Secretary, giving details of "plans to overhaul gaming laws". She was said to have indicated that she backed many of the proposals although they would go out to widespread consultation. She was reported to have stated:

> Our present gambling laws are badly in need of reform and updating but reform must go hand in hand with tough practical measures to protect young and vulnerable people. There is no doubt that our current laws, as well as being too complex and out of date, fail to reflect the extent to which gambling has become an everyday part of the way millions of people spend their leisure. But parents have a right to expect their children will be protected by the law (*The Times*, 18 July 2001).

The Guardian reported that the Culture Secretary had given "an encouraging welcome" to the proposal. The *Daily Sport* also said that she had "welcomed" the report, as did the *Daily Express*.

If the coverage the GRB report received in the press the week after it was released was a reflection of how the report would be received more widely then there could be little doubting in what mould it would be seen to have been cast. It was seen by the press as a derestricting, liberalising policy document, favourable to the gambling industry and likely to be well received by a deregulating government. At the same time the press allowed other voices to be heard, as one hopes the press would in a democratic country, which had not been reflected in the GRB report itself. A number of writers of feature articles dared to suggest, not only that there might be mixed views regarding Blackpool as a casino resort, but even that an increase in gambling might not be what the nation wanted or needed. Views may be more mixed on the subject of the future of gambling than some have assumed.

Negative views survive alongside the new liberal view

One view of gambling in modern-day Britain depicts it as a harmless, unproblematic, but large and important part of the leisure and entertainment industry. It is part of modern life to which the consumer has a right. Government regulation and restriction should be minimal. Anything else constitutes unfair and inefficient interference with the operation of a free market, infringes consumer freedom, and smacks of the nanny state. That tends to be the view, not surprisingly, of the gambling industry, and it was the view that most influenced the Gambling Review Report of 2001. That view is, however, a very partial perspective on a very complex subject. There are many facets to the study of gambling and problem gambling, and a number of parties with an interest in the subject whose positions are very different. Part of the 'harmless form of leisure' view of gambling is that morality does not come into it. The total sidelining of a moral discourse about gambling is comparatively new as we saw in Chapter 1. Indeed it appears only to be in the very last years of the 20th century that a moral view of gambling in Britain could be almost universally dismissed.

Yet the view that gambling was itself undignified, appealing to the irrational and irresponsible parts of human mentality, offering 'something for nothing', involving unnecessary risk, offering gain at the expense of others' loss, and being contrary to the principle of reward for effort, survived into the second half of the 20th century (Cornish, 1978; Herman, 1976). Such views were well represented in the report of the Royal Commission on Betting, Lotteries and Gaming in 1951, and in publications of the Churches' Council on Gambling (e.g. 1960-1968). They surfaced again in the British press immediately after the publication of the Gambling Review Report. Pockets of outright resistance to gambling have remained. For example, the Methodist church was vociferous in its objections to a national lottery, although since then it has given its approval for church groups to apply for National Lottery funds (Collins, 1996; Bellringer, 1999).

Although it is tempting to consign to the wastebin of history the view that gambling represents a national evil, it may be important to be reminded how recently our forebears have taken a very different view to the one that now prevails. Furthermore, it might be foolish to assume that such views are no longer in existence, submerged though they might be under the weight of current thinking. Certain ethnic and religious groups for example, minorities but large in number, are likely to continue to be much more ambivalent about gambling than the secular white British majority.

Families as a neglected constituency

The group in society who has probably always been the most conscious of the dangers of gambling consists of family members of problem gamblers. We have already met that group a few times in this book: in Chapter 2 when considering the divergent views of different groups regarding the setting up of casinos in the USA (Giacopassi et al, 1999), in Chapter 3 when describing some of the accounts of problem gambling provided by historians, clinicians and researchers such as Barker and Miller (1968), Custer and Milt (1985), Clapson (1992) and Griffiths (1993b), and in some responses to the Gambling Review Report in the British press earlier in this chapter. The report of the Australian Productivity Commission (APC, 1999) attempted to estimate the impact of problem gambling on family members. In the National Gambling Survey carried out for the Productivity Commission those identified as problem gamblers reported at a far higher rate than others that arguments over money had occurred in their families and that they had not had enough time for their families. In the complementary survey of clients at Australian counselling agencies, 69 per cent believed there had been an adverse effect of their gambling on partners, 54 per cent on children, 63 per cent on parents, 59 per cent on friends and 30 per cent on colleagues. Effects on partners were rated the most serious, 43 per cent of clients believing their gambling had had a 'major adverse effect' on partners. Krishnan and Orford (2002) reported an English study of 16 close family members, mainly parents and partners, of problem gamblers. They concluded that, very much like close relatives of people with drinking or drug problems, these family members were experiencing considerable stress, were searching for ways to try to control the excessive gambling and its effects on the family, very often feeling isolated and unsupported in the process. Lesieur and Rothchild (1989, cited by Abbott et al, 1995) specifically considered the impact on children, concluding that the latter often felt abandoned, depressed and angry, and suffered a raised risk of emotional and physical deprivation and abuse.

APC (1999) attempted to make an estimate of the numbers of family members so affected. They cited several suggested figures for the numbers of people adversely affected by a single problem gambler. Some had put that figure at 10 or more, including extended family, employer or employees or colleagues, friends and even creditors. APC on the basis of its survey of counselling clients put the figure at 7.4. Even if we take a more cautious approach, and estimate an average of two other people living under the same roof with a problem gambler, or otherwise very closely affected by and concerned about the problem gambling (people one might term 'concerned and affected others' or CAOs), then the estimate of the numbers so affected in any one year by problem gambling amongst British adults (based on the findings summarised in Chapter 5) is in the region of 600,000.

Castellani (2000) referred to the family of a problem gambler as, "A group with no discursive voice" (p.177). He pointed out that effects on his family had at no time been referred to in the Torniero trial around which Castellani's book was constructed (see Chapter 3). In general, family members, despite the large numbers affected by problem gambling, had been marginalised and neglected, a state of affairs that Castellani put down to the dominance of the medical model with its assumption that 'pathological gambling' could be described purely in individual terms with no reference to family, social or wider context:

> The girlfriends, the boyfriends, the parents, and the children all pay a price for their relationships with the pathological gambler. Their time, their money, their desires, and their lives are all sacrificed . . . What about the damage they've incurred? When do they get a break? When will someone understand their pain? . . . It will be interesting to see what happens once families start suing casinos and horse tracks on a more regular basis for the debts incurred by their loved ones. Only then will the gambling industry start to take notice of this problem (Castellani, 2000, pp.178–181).

It has to be noted that we ourselves have been guilty of this neglect. With hindsight it can be seen that it was a mistake omitting from the British Gambling Prevalence Survey any questions about the possible impact of other people's gambling on respondents, and the same was largely true in the qualitative study. The only exception was questions about parental gambling, but there the focus of interest was specifically on family influence on early experiences of gambling.

But negative views of gambling may continue to be even more widespread. Part of the KPMG (2000) report, commissioned by the gambling industry, was based on a telephone survey of 997 randomly selected individuals of 18 years of age or over, the sample being designed 'to reflect the structure of the general population'. Participants were asked to rate on a scale from 1 to 10 where they thought each of a number of different gambling activities lay from *perfectly acceptable* to *not at all acceptable*, and on a similar, second scale from *fun* to *serious*. Although the authors of the report make much of the fact that all but two of the activities (fruit machines in cafes or takeaways, and fruit machines in inland arcades) were on average rated on the acceptable side of the mid-point of the acceptability scale, the results can be looked at in a quite different light. If anti-gambling sentiment were completely dead, it would be expected that the large majority of the population would rate most gambling activities as utter fun and perfectly acceptable. In fact no single activity was rated by the majority in that way. The nearest any activity came to achieving that position was small lotteries (an average rating of just under 3 out of 10 for unacceptability, and between 3 and 4 out of 10 for seriousness), with bingo, the National Lottery and pools not far behind. The majority of activities were the wrong side of the mid-line for seriousness and approaching the mid-line for unacceptability (e.g. on-course betting on events, fruit machines in licensed betting offices, spread betting, off-course betting on events, off-course betting on greyhounds). Not surprisingly, anti-gambling views were even more evident amongst the minority (11 per cent) of the survey respondents who were classified as non-gamblers who saw the majority of all gambling activities as both serious and unacceptable. In the Office for National Statistics (ONS) survey commissioned by the GRB and conducted early in 2001, the large majority said their attitudes to gambling had remained unchanged in the last 10 years. Those who said their attitudes had become more negative (15 per cent) were more numerous than those reporting that their attitudes had become more positive (6 per cent). These results seem to belie the often proffered opinion in industry and government circles that attitudes have become much more accepting.

A national Dutch survey in 1986 found 62 per cent of the adult sample agreeing that gambling was ". . . wrong, and could lead to problems" (Hermkens and Kok, 1991). Even in Australia where ". . . unusually liberal laws have made a variety of gambling forms relatively respectable. . ." (McMillen, 1996, p.14), opinions about gambling remain much more negative than might be expected. In the course of the national survey carried out for APC (1999) two questions were asked about the respondents' attitudes. When asked whether they agreed or disagreed with the statement *gambling does more good than harm*, only 15 per cent indicated that they agreed (only 4 per cent *strongly*) and 71 per cent disagreed (47 per cent *strongly*). In response to the statement *gambling has provided more opportunities for recreational enjoyment*, 32 per cent agreed (7 per cent *strongly*) and 55 per cent disagreed (34 per cent *strongly*).

According to McMillen's (1996) analysis, the view of gambling in the USA in the 20th century was, at least until the later years of the century, more moralistic than that in the UK and Australia, partly as a legacy of the prohibition years prior to World War II, and partly as a consequence of the link between crime and gambling, particularly casino gambling. Most forms of gambling had been illegal in the USA until quite recently. As Castellani (2000) put it, "To the mainstream middle-class of the 1950s and 1960s . . . gambling was a morally and legally illegitimate activity" (p.27). Whilst widespread anti-gambling attitudes in countries such as the UK and Australia now only come to light when surveyed participants are directly asked relevant questions in the privacy of a confidential interview or questionnaire, such views are still evident in public debate in the USA, at least if Whyte's (1999) analysis of the setting up of the US National Gambling Impact Study Commission is anything to go by.

Controversy appears to have raged in the House of Representatives and Senate and in the US media. The American Gaming Association claimed that the list of matters to be studied by the Commission reflected "only the views of the anti-gaming moralists who introduced it" (cited by Whyte, p.310), and the President of the AGA stated, "While it sounds good at first blush, a close examination of the real intent of the proponents, as manifested in their own rhetoric, shows that their intent is the complete abolition, on moral grounds, of the gaming-entertainment industry" (cited by Whyte, p.311). The anti-gambling faction were equally vitriolic. One representative stated: "This is a sham and a disgrace and an insult to the American people who are being suckered in by an industry which thrives when it operates in the shadows . . .", and a senator gave his view that: "Many of the insidious tactics used by the gambling industry to bilk people out of their money must be considered by the Commission in order to understand fully the modern business of gambling" (cited by Whyte, pp. 315, 317). As Whyte put it in conclusion to his paper, ". . . the legislative history of this bill shows that gaming is still a very controversial topic" (p.318). That statement would well do as a summary, not just of present-day attitudes to gaming in the USA, but to sentiments about gambling of almost all forms in the UK and throughout the world.

Nevertheless there can be no doubt that there has been a significant shift in attitudes to gambling throughout the Western world in the last years of the 20th century. In the USA, for example, McMillen (1996) observed a shift since the 1970s from a predominant focus on the ". . . dysfunctional and immoral aspects of gambling . . ." (p.8) towards a greater emphasis on ". . . economic and legal-administrative factors associated with the smooth operation of a newly legal industry" (p.8). This was reflected, for example, in the writings of Eadington (e.g. Eadington and Cornelius, 1991, cited by McMillen, 1996) on casino policy in North America, built, as McMillen saw it, on a stand in favour of commercialisation, a *laissez-faire* approach to casino development, and a limited conception of the role of the state in controlling people's opportunities to gamble or in coercing them to forms of lifestyle behaviour thought to be healthy or moral. McMillen's (1996) analysis led him to the view that the days in which gambling was seen, unlike other leisure activities, in moral or ethical terms, and an assumption that the state had a responsibility to intervene to restrict gambling in the interests of the common good, had given way in recent times to a much greater emphasis on gambling as an acceptable leisure activity, to which people have a right, contributing positively to the leisure and tourist industries, and increasingly under the commercial control of transnational companies. As he put it, ". . . traditional gambling cultures are being colonised by global gambling culture . . ." (p.23).

Dombrink (1996), too, commented on the remarkable increase in the scale of legal gambling in the USA in the 1980s (a growth rate in double figures each year during that decade), the diversification of gambling activities during the same time, and the way in which gambling had avoided both much moral censure, and being the object of much public health concern. Dombrink considered this to require explanation, in view of the ambivalence with which gambling had been viewed in the USA historically, and in view of the moral 'backlash' of the 1980s in the USA which led to various moral 'wars' on other 'vices' such as abortion, prostitution, porno-graphy, homosexuality, and drugs. Much careful public relations work on the part of legal gambling operators had contributed to a view of gambling as a comparatively harmless, leisure activity which, in the process, made a very positive contribution to state funds.

There have been a number of sources of support for this new, more liberal attitude. One was the influence of social science in the 1960s and later. The former, negative view of gambling was challenged by sociologists such as Goffman (1967), who argued for the positive characteristics of gambling, such as the opportunity provided to demonstrate strength of character and commitment to values such as risk-taking and courage, the enjoyment of 'play' or 'free time', serving as a 'safety valve', an integral element of working-class culture, or as an escape or opportunity for self-realisation and creativity lacking in the workplace (Rosecrance, 1988, and see Chapter 4). Social scientists and others have claimed that the positive view of gambling has been most clearly developed in Australia where gambling has been legalised to an extent unknown in most other countries, and where it has even been ". . . celebrated as an important part of the national culture . . . seen as a positive force, reflecting the egalitarianism and hope of Australian society" (McMillen, 1996, p.17).

The role of government

But the gambling industry's biggest ally in fostering a changed climate has undoubtedly been governments. Castellani (2000) asked why gambling became legalised again in the USA, and why so fast. He concluded that it was not because the general public particularly wanted it, but because the interests of the gambling industry coincided with the needs of cities and states, particularly the more economically depressed, to raise extra revenue. McMillen (1996) also referred to the high level of government involvement in legalising and expanding gambling in countries such as the USA and Australia. As Castellani (2000) put it, the industry and governments have generated a campaign to persuade people of the benefits and harmlessness of gambling. The first step of the campaign had been to construct pro-gambling discourses of the following kind:

> If you legalise gambling, jobs will be created, money will be given to the schools, your town's economic recession will be lifted, the standard of living will increase, people from out of state will come in to gamble, the restaurants, hotels, malls, bars, and stores in your area will make money, and everyone will be happy (Castellani, 2000, pp.30–31).

Another essential component of the modern pro-gambling discourse is the idea that gambling is 'harmless', 'neighbourly' and even 'tasteful'. In Britain this is best illustrated by references to bingo and the NL, two forms of gambling which have come to occupy important positions in the sense of national identity. Of all the forms of gambling available in the UK, bingo is the one most commonly perceived to be associated with women. In fact Dixey's (1996) analysis of bingo suggested that it was associated both with gender and with social class (as we found in the prevalence survey, Chapter 5). For many working-class women, from the 1960s onwards, wrote Dixey, bingo halls provided a safe and congenial place to socialise. Indeed so ordinary a feature of life did going to bingo become, that 42 per cent of women surveyed in the early 1980s, when asked whether bingo was regarded as a form of gambling, said that it was not (Dixey, 1996). The Gaming Act of 1968 which established the Gaming Board and reintroduced a number of restrictions, recognised that bingo had become a very popular game, especially amongst housewives, and that provided players were not exposed to the temptations of 'hard gaming', it was appropriate to take "a benevolent view of bingo provided it remained a neighbourly form of gaming played for modest stakes . . ." (Gaming Board Report, 1969, cited by Dixey, p.138).

As was noted in Chapter 2, the British government's view was that the NL represented a harmless form of leisure pursuit:

> The Lottery should be seen as a tasteful and acceptable way to win money, whilst generating money for the National Lottery Distribution Fund (NLDF). It must be run in a fair and trustworthy manner that is beyond reproach (OFLOT, 1994, cited by Miers, 1996, p.344).

An important point was made by Castellani (2000), and one that is of great relevance to the present book, when he gave his opinion that a danger exists in this climate, with the gambling industry and governments as allies, that an objective appraisal of the balance between the benefits and costs of gambling to a community or country will be difficult to achieve. Because of governments' ". . . varied and contradictory role . . ." (McMillen, 1996, p.22), even state-sponsored research may be less than truly independent.

Industry-commissioned research, such as the KPMG (2000) report, should certainly not be expected to be unbiased. That report made a detailed assessment of the economic benefits of gambling, in the form of contributions to the national economy through taxes, national insurance and duties, income to charitable causes, amenity benefits such as racecourses, and the provision of employment within the gambling industry which then provides further, indirect economic benefit through personal expenditure and income tax. By contrast, the report made little attempt to estimate the costs of gambling to the nation. Not surprisingly, therefore, the report came to the following, unconvincing conclusion:

> . . . although we are unable to quantify the economic and social costs associated with criminal activity and problem gambling, we believe that on balance, the benefits derived greatly exceed these costs (KPMG, 2000, p.69).

Such is the nature of gambling, with its undoubted benefits and costs, and such is the ambivalence that has always surrounded it, that it seems very unlikely that the history of changing attitudes to gambling will ever come to an end. In fact historians have pointed to the tendency for ". . . the nature, extent and intensity of gambling in any society [to] fluctuate, with cyclical alternation between waves of extended gambling and phases of repression or social reform" (McMillen, 1996, p.23).

Will there be a backlash?

Several writers from the USA have suggested that attitudes to gambling in that country, and legislation reflecting those attitudes, have been cyclical in nature. Movement towards pro-gambling opinions and permissive legislation inevitably sow the seeds for a backlash and a movement in the opposite direction, and the same is true in reverse. If that is the case then the move towards liberalisation of gambling in the USA, which by the end of the 20th century had been happening for some time, should be due for a reverse (Rose, 1991; Goodman, 1995; Preston et al, 1998). Goodman (1995) described the proliferation of casinos in the USA in the 1990s, a change in public policy away from keeping casinos out of urban areas, and the growth and increasing automation of machine gambling. "The widespread use of casinos and gambling machines", he wrote, "represents a further breaking down of long-standing governmental attitudes against encouraging low-income people to gamble" (p.130). He saw signs of a growing backlash with evidence of a rise in problem gambling and signs that some jurisdictions would start to remove machines from certain locations. The latter had already happened in Nova Scotia in Canada where over 70 per cent of the province's machines had been removed.

Rose (1991) also predicted a backlash in a chapter sub-titled, *Gambling Will Be Outlawed in Forty Years*:

> The morality argument is dead. It is no longer considered acceptable to oppose gambling on the ground it is immoral . . . Government no longer enforces morals . . . with no one to say what is right or wrong, everything has become a cost/benefit analysis . . . The corporate and government executives and accountants who run the games have convinced themselves that everyone has accepted gambling as merely another form of entertainment. They forget that for hundreds of years gambling was viewed as a vice, or worse, as a sin. You cannot erase a life-time of learning through even the best television ads. . . No one realizes that people will eventually rebel against the image of the state as bookie . . . The 1990s and the first decade of the 21st century will be the final boom. By 2029 it will all be outlawed, again, for a while (pp.67–83).

Preston et al's (1998) contribution was to describe what they saw as some of the 'techniques of stigma neutralization' being used by proponents of gambling liberalisation in order to dismiss counter arguments. These techniques included exceptionalising (e.g. an activity is not really gambling because it is family entertainment or harmless fun), excusing (e.g. gambling can be excused because it promises to revitalise a community economically), normalising (e.g. gambling should not be stigmatised since it is entertainment, business, a right) and attacking the credibility of opponents (e.g. as moralists or killjoys).

These comments have come largely from the USA which perhaps has had a particular difficulty in achieving a balanced position in modern times when it comes to such activities as consuming alcohol, taking drugs or gambling (Rose, 1991), but it is unlikely that those arguments have no resonance at all in Britain. The 1960s was a decade in very recent memory in which overly permissive legislation had to be quickly corrected, and more recently some other European countries have found it necessary to put the expansion of gambling machines into reverse (e.g. Spain, Becoña et al, 1995, and Germany, Meyer, 1992; Fabian, 1995). The techniques of stigma neutralisation identified by Preston et al (1998) have certainly been on display: the arguments that the NL is not really gambling and is economically beneficial for public good causes, and that casino resorts will be good for communities economically, have been much in evidence; gambling machine playing by children at the seaside has been excused on the grounds that arcades are 'family entertainment centres'; and the moral argument against gambling has been effectively outlawed in official debate (e.g. Gambling Review Body, 2001) although not totally silenced, as we saw amongst the responses to the GRB report that appeared in the press.

What the British Gambling Review report failed to do

As might have been expected from a review body set up by a government committed to deregulation, chaired by a former chief economic adviser to the Treasury, referred to by Roy Hattersley in the *Daily Mail* (18 July 2001) as a "notable free marketeer", deliberating at a time when the tide of change nationally and internationally was towards liberalisation and expansion of gambling, the Budd Report's recommendations were almost all in a liberalising direction. That was well recognised in the British press. The winners would be the gambling industry, the government in its capacity as a collector of taxes, and those citizens who want more gambling facilities. Indeed *The Times* of 18 July 2001 contained a significant comment from Sir Alan Budd who said that the GRB had "bowed to industry demands" to allow slot machines with £5 payouts to continue in amusement arcades but with a review of the issue after five years.

The GRB report and remarks attributed to Sir Alan Budd in the press revealed an expectation that the rate of problem gambling in Britain would rise if the report's recommendations were put into effect. It was accepted that increased availability of gambling would lead to more problems. It might reasonably be asked how it is that a responsible body could make recommendations that they expected would lead to an increase in a problem so serious and so prevalent as problem gambling. The report could make no estimate of the likely increase in problems. Presumably such an increase was thought to be a price worth paying: that the suffering of a minority of unspecified size was an acceptable trade-off for increased profits for the gambling industry, increased taxes for the government and increased access to gambling for all.

A number of facts are worth remembering. The evidence supports the view that availability and problems are associated. The best estimate is that there are around one third of a million adults who have a gambling problem in Britain in any one year plus an even higher proportion of younger teenagers experiencing gambling problems, plus perhaps twice that number of people whose lives are adversely affected by the problem gambling of others. There are good grounds for believing that serious problem gambling is a causative factor for depression and suicide. Casino gambling appears to be associated with a particularly high rate of problem gambling. There is evidence from a number of different sources that gambling machines are dangerous, particularly for adolescents and young adults, and Britain is alone in allowing machine gambling by under-16s in certain arcades. Consuming alcohol and gambling tends to lead to gambling more than a person would otherwise have done.

Even on pragmatic grounds, therefore, the GRB report can be criticised for suggesting changes that would create more problems. It can particularly be accused of weakness in the face of much evidence on the vulnerability of young people to the risks associated with machine gambling. The recommendation that machines should continue to be available, at least for the time being, to children and adolescents in locations that the report euphemistically described as "family entertainment centres" is particularly strange in the light of the findings of two surveys referred to in the GRB report. One carried out by the Office for National Statistics (ONS) early in 2000, commissioned by the Home Office, found that the large majority (96 per cent) of those (a minority) who thought they knew what current controls on gambling were in Britain, did not want those controls to be relaxed. The second, an ONS survey commissioned by GRB and carried out early in 2001 found that 42 per cent of respondents disapproved of children playing on machines commonly found at the seaside and only 4 per cent approved. A further 41 per cent approved so long as an adult accompanied the child (a factor which our research suggests is as likely to encourage problem gambling as it is to discourage it) and 13 per cent neither approved or disapproved. GRB appeared to have taken more account of a survey in 2000 of visitors to seaside towns and amusement arcades commissioned by BACTA and BALPPA (the British Amusement Catering Trades Association and the British Association of Leisure Parks, Piers and Attractions) which reported 62 per cent of visitors considering amusement arcades to be either quite important or very important to seaside towns.

The word 'vulnerable' appears many times in the GRB report and was used again by the Culture, Media and Sport Secretary immediately after the report appeared. Nowhere in the report, however, is the word defined, other than in association with the word 'children' (as in 'children and the vulnerable' or simply collectively as the 'vulnerable') or with reference to problem gamblers themselves (a tautologous usage of the word). The report gave no serious consideration to the question of who, apart from the under-18s, might be particularly vulnerable for problem gambling. The report might have considered, for example, young adults over 18, single people, poor people, unemployed people, disabled people, or those living close to casinos, arcades or bingo clubs or at the seaside. Nor did the report make use of any model of risk or vulnerability that might have been expected if the topic was looked at from a public health perspective. There was no awareness, for example, of the single distribution model (Grun and McKeigue, 2000) (see Chapter 4).

There had been many previous suggestions that both research and treatment in the field of gambling and problem gambling should be increased and that at least some of that increase should be funded out of the proceeds of gambling itself (e.g. Royal Commission – the Rothschild Report, 1978; Brenner and Brenner, 1990; Lesieur, 1998) and GRB (2001) repeated that message. Their specific suggestion was that the gambling industry should set up a voluntarily funded Gambling Trust that would allocate funding for research and treatment. The report was of the opinion that the gambling industry could afford around £3 million a year (approximately £10 per problem gambler) particularly since the report's proposals would provide the gambling industry ". . . with the opportunity to expand its operations, and consequently the potential to increase its turnover and profit" (para 32.28). If the industry proved unable to provide funding at that level, then GRB recommended the government should impose a statutory levy.

There are several problems with that proposal. The first is the size of the proposed allocation: £3 million a year to cover both treatment and research is simply not enough in relation to the size of the problem. Secondly, it could well be argued that making the gambling industry responsible is an abdication of government responsibility. The industry already contributes greatly to government revenue, and government stands to gain further if gambling increases. As important and prevalent a matter as problem gambling should be directly funded by government, not by the gambling industry, and certainly not voluntarily.

Thirdly, and possibly most importantly, the proper independence of research is threatened if the funding body is operated by an industry that is profiting from the activities being researched. It is now well established in parallel fields where the same state of affairs might apply – such as research on pharmaceuticals and alcohol and tobacco products – that the independence of the academic and research community is vital. Research ethics in this area are quite properly governed by agreements such as the Farmington Consensus. Results are published in academic journals that increasingly require a declaration of funding sources and evidence that research has been carried out and reported totally independently without interference.

The authors of the present report had some experience of working with representatives of the gambling industry on the steering committee for the research summarised in Chapters 5 and 6. The industry was well represented on that committee and lively discussions were held during which some industry representatives argued strongly, for example, for setting tighter rather than looser definitions of what constituted 'problem gambling'. That was just one obvious example of how industry pressure might be brought to bear on researchers, but in any such discussions there are likely to be many such points of influence, explicit and implicit, overt and covert, deliberate and inadvertent. At the time of writing there were already indications that the gambling industry was questioning whether it should be responsible for research and treatment, whether £3 million was too much, and whether any research other than research on effectiveness of treatment was really necessary at all. If the field of gambling studies in Britain is to advance and develop it must be independent of the gambling industry.

Finally, despite the explicit reference to it in GRB's remit, the report failed to consider the wider social impact of the increased availability of gambling which their recommendations would be likely to lead to. The kinds of issues considered in the report of the Australian Productivity Commission (1999) and raised by a number of commentators writing in the British press in July 2001 were either not considered at all, or were quickly dismissed. In its failure to address those issues the GRB report was a disappointment, falling short of the standard of the report of the Australian Productivity Commission (1999) which considered the full impact of gambling on Australian society in great detail and with much care. The British GRB appeared to have taken a much more limited view of its remit: accepting that the deregulation of gambling in Britain should carry on apace, it considered in detail how that should happen, warning that its proposals would likely bring increased problems, and making some sensible suggestions about simplifying regulation and some comparatively minor suggestions for protecting the young and vulnerable (removing machines from cafes and takeaways, tightening up on existing regulations about under-age gambling in inland arcades, and proposing a review of access for children to machines in seaside arcades after five years). It should have asked a number of bigger questions.

Do the benefits of gambling accrue disproportionally to the well off and the harm disproportionally to the poor? How is an increase in the rate of problem gambling for some to be weighed in the balance against profits, taxes and increased access for the many? Does an increase in gambling facilities in a community really improve that community's fortunes economically? And if it does, are there any downsides for a community in having more gambling facilities? Is an increase in gambling consistent with our society's values? Do we wish to become a nation of gamblers?

Postscript

Plans to change the British gambling landscape continued apace in the months immediately following the submission to the publishers of the manuscript for the present book. The most significant events were: the publication in March 2002 of *A Safe Bet for Success*, the Department for Culture, Media and Sport's (DCMS) response to the Gambling Review Report of July 2001; the appearance in July 2002 of the report of the House of Commons Culture, Media and Sport Select Committee, entitled *The Government's Proposals for Gambling: Nothing to Lose?*; and the government's response to the Select Committee report in October of the same year. Results of ongoing consultations on the future licensing and regulation of internet gambling and the National Lottery (NL) were still awaited. In all other respects the matter of government policy on the regulatory framework for British gambling in the early 21st century was more or less wrapped up by the autumn of 2002, 15 months after the publication of the complex and controversial Gambling Review Report. Some proposals, such as permission for the serving of alcohol and the showing of live entertainment in casinos, had already been implemented without the need for fresh legislation, but other proposals would require a new Gambling Bill for which the government proposed to make parliamentary time no later than the 2003/04 session.

In view of the overwhelmingly liberalising and deregulating thrust of the Gambling Review Report's 176 recommendations, it might have been expected that the consultation undertaken by DCMS and the attention given by the Select Committee to the evidence it received from many quarters would have resulted in a certain toning down of the proposals. Exactly the opposite appears to have occurred. The large bulk of the Review Report's recommendations were accepted by the government in *A Safe Bet for Success*. Where recommendations were rejected or modified, these were all, with one notable exception, in the direction of even greater derestriction than the Review Report had recommended. The one exception concerned the National Lottery. The Review Report had suggested that betting offices might offer bets on the outcome of the NL. The government disagreed.

Otherwise the government proposed less restriction. In doing so it rejected two of the basic principles underlying the Gambling Review Report's recommendations. One was the principle of allowing local authorities the power to impose a ban on all, or particular types of, gambling premises in specified areas. Local authorities will be heavily involved in the licensing of gambling premises, but the interesting idea that there might be a substantial degree of local option appears to be dead and buried.

Most controversial is the government's rejection of one of the Review Report's most basic principles, that 'ambient gambling' should not be encouraged. It was in accordance with that principle that it was recommended that gaming machines should be restricted in premises other than those where gambling was the main activity. For example jackpot machines (formerly the 'top' category of machine, but now to be termed category B since machines with unlimited stakes and prizes, category A, would be allowed in casinos) should be removed from private clubs. The government disagreed and the Select Committee did not question that judgement.

More significant still were government intentions regarding low stake/low prize or category D machines, which the government persisted in calling 'amusement with prizes' machines. The Review Report was clear in its recommendation that such machines should not be permitted in places such as cafes, fish and chip shops and taxi-cab offices to which children have access and which might be difficult to supervise. DCMS was explicit in admitting that it was responding to concerns from the gambling industry over the ambient gambling principle, and it rejected the proposal that category D machines should be prohibited in that way. This was one of the very few instances in which the Select Committee tried to stand up to the government, encouraging the government to reconsider its rejections of these clear recommendations.

The controversy about children and category D gaming machines goes far beyond the question of whether or not they should be permitted in fish and chip shops. The Gambling Review Body had agonised over the question of whether Britain should continue to be the only known jurisdiction that allowed children to play on such machines (see Chapter 8) but, responding to industry pressure, had uneasily recommended that that state of affairs be allowed to continue in seaside arcades (now to be called 'family entertainment centres'). The Select Committee also found that it was on this question that the opinions they received varied most widely. Nevertheless they agreed with the government that there was insufficient evidence that access to such machines produced any harm for children, and in its subsequent response the government welcomed the Committee's endorsement of its approach. That conclusion was reached despite all the evidence of the kind presented earlier in this book (see Chapter 3) that children and young people are particularly vulnerable to problem gambling. Several pieces of evidence given to the Select Committee suggested that the distinction between higher and lower value machines was an artificial and disingenuous one: what might seem like a small prize to an adult might constitute an inducement to gamble to a child receiving a modest amount of pocket money, and gambling on a category D machine was ideal 'training' for later gambling on higher category machines. None of that evidence or points of view carried weight in the end. All were agreed, however, that this question of children and machine gambling constituted a high priority for future research.

Whilst not disagreeing with government proposals, the Select Committee also expressed some concern about the need to work out an effective Code of Practice for keeping children away from adult gaming machines (category C) which would be allowed in places to which children had access, such as family entertainment centres and pubs (to which other intended government legislation would make it easier for parents to bring children). The perpetuation of fine distinctions between venues such as 'family entertainment centres' (in parts of which children are not permitted – to be found not only at seaside arcades but also in bowling alleys, motorway service stations and theme parks), and 'adult gaming centres' (in which children are not allowed), and between the now to be enlarged number of separate types of gaming machine (categories A, B, C and D), will almost certainly increase public confusion and difficulties in control.

No one is in any doubt that gambling in Britain is set to change. As the Select Committee report put it, "There can be no doubt that once the Government's proposals are all implemented, there will be greater awareness by the public of a significantly larger range of gambling products" (para 92). The Committee also pointed out that there was no estimate of the social cost of the deregulation of gambling to be found in *A Safe Bet for Success*. It likened the decision facing the government about gambling to a decision whether to put a new drug on the market. Should the government, in the absence of evidence of safety, be cautious, or, in the absence of evidence that the product is unsafe, go ahead with further deregulation: "The key issue is that at present there is insufficient evidence on which to make judgements about safety" (p.42).

The Committee cited a report by National Economics Research Associates that estimated, on the basis of Australian experience of having liberalised its gambling laws, that the introduction of unlimited prize gaming machines itself could result in an increase in the number of problem gamblers in the UK to one million (para 45). It was of the opinion that the introduction of category A machines ". . . will create a radical change in the look of casinos" (para 77), and urged the government to strike a balance between table games and machines in casinos in order to prevent the spread of unsavoury 'gaming sheds', containing huge banks of casino slot machines, as are to be found in some other countries. In its response the government agreed that the introduction of such machines ". . . could radically change the product mix and appearance of the typical British casino (Section q) and agreed that it wished to avoid casinos becoming wholly dominated by gambling machines.

One welcome feature of the modern policy debate is the recognition on all sides that problem gambling is a reality and that an increased prevalence due to liberalisation and greater access to gambling does represent a real threat. That contrasts with the 1970s when the Rothschild Commission on gambling last considered British policy, dismissing compulsive gambling as a significant factor (see Chapter 1). The authors of the present book are naturally pleased to see that the government, supported by the Select Committee, have stated that the British Gambling Prevalence Survey, reported by Sproston et al (2000) and summarised here in Chapter 5, should be a benchmark for future surveys, at regular intervals, of gambling and problem gambling in Britain.

How the treatment of problem gambling and research on the subject is to be funded remains controversial. The government has followed the Gambling Review Report's recommendation that a gambling trust, voluntarily funded by the gambling industry at a present level of £3 million a year, should be set up for that purpose. Whilst agreeing with the general idea of such a trust, the Select Committee were attracted to the simple principle of 'polluter pays' and recommended that instead of the industry contributing voluntarily the government should impose a statutory levy. The government responded by acknowledging that such a levy might be necessary: the proposed Gambling Bill would include reserve powers to impose a levy if necessary. Meanwhile plans to set up a Gambling Industry Charitable Trust (GICT) moved forward. Consultants were appointed to draw up the options, and they reported at a workshop of interested parties in December 2002. The consultants expected to submit their final report at the end of March 2003 in anticipation of legislation in the first half of 2004 and beginning work by calling for proposals in the second half of that year. The consultants accepted the model of an industry trust in preference to a model of funding treatment and research more directly from government which is favoured in most other countries especially those in Europe. An independent chairperson and a constitution that would prevent domination by industry representatives is thought to guarantee the independence of the GICT, but is hardly likely to satisfy increasingly rigorous standards of independence in research. The dedication of trust funds for gambling-related treatment and research certainly ensures that there will be resources for which gambling does not have to compete with the many other calls on government funds, but that could work both ways. As was pointed out in Chapter 8, the amount of money the trust is expected to have at its disposal is small when judged against all national treatment and research needs in the gambling field, and the very existence of the GICT may encourage National Health Service (NHS) Trusts, government-funded Research

Councils, and other government-funded services in the belief that they need take no responsibility for funding such work. The Select Committee pointed out that it would be necessary for the government to undertake its own research and, through the NHS, the treatment of problem gambling. The government's response was a vague one: it would keep open the option of sponsoring additional research, was already making additional money available for the treatment of mental health problems, and would look to the newly established Primary Care Trusts to decide on treatment priorities.

References

Abbott, D.A., Cramer, S.L. and Sherrets, S.D. (1995) 'Pathological gambling and the family: practice implications', *Families in Society*, 76: 213–219.

Abbott, M.W. and Volberg, R.A. (1992) *Frequent Gamblers and Problem Gamblers in New Zealand: Report on Phase 2 of the National Survey*, Auckland, National Research Bureau.

Abbott, M.W. and Volberg, R.A. (1996) 'The New Zealand national survey of problem and pathological gambling', *Journal of Gambling Studies*, 12: 143–159.

Abbott, M.W. and Volberg, R.A. (1999) 'A reply to Gambino's "An epidemiologic note on verification bias: implications for estimation of rates"', *Journal of Gambling Studies*, 15: 233–242.

Allcock, C. (1986) 'Pathological gambling (review)', *Australian and New Zealand Journal of Psychiatry*, 20: 259–265.

Allcock, C. (1994) 'Cognitions in problem gambling', paper presented at the 9th international conference on gambling and risk taking, Las Vegas, May-June.

American Psychiatric Association (1994) *Diagnostic and Statistical Manual of Mental Disorders*, 4th edn. Washington DC: APA.

Anderson, G. and Brown, R.I.F. (1984) 'Real and laboratory gambling, sensation seeking and arousal', *British Journal of Psychology*, 75: 401–410.

Arlen, M. (1924) *The Green Hat*. London: Collins (cited by Clapson, 1992).

Australian Productivity Commission (APC) (1999) *Australia's Gambling Industries*. Report No. 10, Canberra: Ausinfo.

Barbeyrac, J. (1737) *Traite du Jeu*, 3 vols, Amsterdam (cited by France, 1902).

Barker, J. and Miller, M. (1968) 'Aversion therapy for compulsive gambling', *Journal of Nervous and Mental Disease*, 146: 285–302.

Barnes, G.M., Welte, J.W., Hoffman, J.H. and Dintcheff, B.A. (1999) 'Gambling and alcohol use among youth: influences of demographic, socialization, and individual factors', *Addictive Behaviors*, 24: 749–767.

Baron, E. and Dickerson, M.G. (1999) 'Alcohol consumption and self-control of gambling behaviour', *Journal of Gambling Studies*, 15: 3–15.

Baron, E., Dickerson, M.G. and Blaszczynski, A. (1995) 'The scale of gambling choices: preliminary development of an instrument to measure impaired control of gambling behaviour', in J. O'Connor (ed.) *High Stakes in the Nineties*, 2nd edn, Perth: Curtin University, 153–168.

Barratt, E.S., Patton, J., Olsson, N.G. and Zuker, G. (1981) 'Impulsivity and paced tapping', *Journal of Motor Behavior*, 13: 286–300.

Becoña, E. (1993) 'The prevalence of pathological gambling in Galicia (Spain)', *Journal of Gambling Studies*, 9: 353–369.

Becoña, E., Labrador, F., Echeburúa, E., Ochoa, E. and Vallejo, M.A. (1995) 'Slot machine gambling in Spain: an important and new social problem', *Journal of Gambling Studies*, 11: 265–286.

Bellringer, P. (1999) *Understanding Problem Gamblers: A Practitioner's Guide to Effective Intervention*, London: Free Association Books.

Bergler, E. (1936) 'On the psychology of the gambler', *Am Imago*, 22: 409–441.

Bergler, E. (1958) *The Psychology of Gambling*, London: Harrison.

Bergh, C., Eklund, T., Soedersten, P. and Nordin, C. (1997) 'Altered dopamine function in pathological gambling', *Psychological Medicine*, 27: 473–475.

Bien, T.H., Miller, W.R. and Tonigan, S. (1993) 'Brief intervention for alcohol problems: a review', *Addiction*, 88: 315–336.

Blaszczynski, A. and Farrell, E. (1998) 'A case series of 44 completed gambling-related suicides', *Journal of Gambling Studies*, 14: 93–109.

Blaszczynski, A. and Silov, D. (1995) 'Cognitive and behavioral therapies for pathological gambling', *Journal of Gambling Studies*, 11: 195–220.

Blaszczynski, A. and Steel, Z. (1998) 'Personality disorders among pathological gamblers', *Journal of Gambling Studies*, 14: 51–71.

Blaszczynski, A., Winter, A.S. and McConaghy, N. (1986) 'Plasma endorphin levels in pathological gamblers', *Journal of Gambling Behavior*, 2: 3–15.

Blaszczynski, A., Dumlao, V. and Lange, M. (1997) 'How much do you spend gambling? Ambiguities in survey questionnaire items', *Journal of Gambling Studies*, 13: 237–252.

Bloch, H. (1951) 'The sociology of gambling', *American Journal of Sociology*, 57: 216.

Bolen, D.W. and Boyd, W.H. (1968) 'Gambling and the gambler: a review and preliminary findings', *Archives of General Psychiatry*, 18: 617–630.

Brecksville Program for the Treatment of Compulsive Gambling, program brochure (cited by Castellani 2000).

Breen, R.B. and Zuckerman, M. (1999) '"Chasing" in gambling behavior: personality and cognitive determinants', *Personality and Individual Differences*, 27: 1097–1111.

Brenner, R. and Brenner, G.A. (1990) *Gambling and Speculation: A Theory, a History, and a Future of Some Human Decisions*, Cambridge: Cambridge University Press.

Breslin, F.C., Sobell, M.B., Cappell, H. and Vakili, S. (1999) 'The effects of alcohol, gender, and sensation seeking on the gambling choices of social drinkers', *Psychology of Addictive Behaviors*, 13: 243–252.

British Columbia, Ministry of Government Services (1994) *Report of the Gaming Policy Review*, Victoria: Queen's Printer.

Brockner, J. and Rubin, J.Z. (1985) *Entrapment in Escalating Conflicts: A Social Psychological Analysis*. New York: Springer.

Brown, R.I.F. (1985) 'The effectiveness of Gamblers Anonymous', in W.R. Eadington (ed.) *The Gambling Studies: Proceedings of the Sixth National Conference on Gambling and Risk Taking*, 5: 258–284.

Brown, R.I.F. (1986) 'Dropouts and continuers in Gamblers Anonymous: life-context and other factors', *Journal of Gambling Behavior*, 2: 130–140.

Brown, R.I.F. (1993) 'Some contributions of the study of gambling to the study of other addictions', in W.R. Eadington and J.A. Cornelius (eds.) *Gambling Behavior and Problem Gambling*, Reno: University of Nevada.

Brown, S. and Coventry, L. (1997) *Queen of Hearts: The Needs of Women with Gambling Problems*, Melbourne: Financial and Consumer Rights Council.

Browne, B.R. (1991) 'The selective adaptation of the Alcoholics Anonymous program by Gamblers Anonymous', *Journal of Gambling Studies*, 7, 187–206.

Burns, J. (1902) 'Brains rather than bets or beer: the straight tip to the workers', *Clarion Pamphlet*, No. 36 (cited by Dixon, 1991).

Bybee, S. (1988) 'Problem gambling: one view from the industry side', *Journal of Gambling Behavior*, 4 (cited by Castellani, 2000).

Carroll, D. and Huxley, J.A.A. (1994) 'Cognitive, dispositional, and psychophysiological correlates of dependent slot machine gambling in young people', *Journal of Applied Social Psychology*, 24: 1070–1083.

Castellani, B. (2000) *Pathological Gambling: The Making of a Medical Problem*, New York: State University of New York Press.

Castellani, B. and Rugle, L. (1995) 'A comparison of pathological gamblers to alcoholics and cocaine misusers on impulsivity, sensation seeking, and craving', *The International Journal of the Addictions*, 30: 275–289.

Cayuela, R. and Guirao, J.L. (1991) 'Characteristics and situation of gambling addiction in Spain', in W.R. Eadington and J.A. Cornelius (eds.) *Gambling and Public Policy: International Perspectives*, Reno, Nevada: University of Nevada.

Chinn, C. (1991) *Better Betting With a Decent Feller: Bookmaking, Betting and the British Working Class, 1750–1990*, Hemel Hempstead: Harvester Wheatsheaf.

Christiansen, E.M. (1998) 'Gambling and the American economy', *Annals of the American Academy of Political and Social Science*, 556: 36–52.

Churches' Council on Gambling (1960–1968) Annual Reports of the Churches' Council on Gambling, London: CCG (cited by Cornish, 1978).

Churchill, S. (1894) *Betting and Gambling*, London: James Nisbet, first edition 1893 (cited by Dixon, 1991).

Clapson, M. (1992) *A Bit of a Flutter: Popular Gambling and English Society, c.1823–1961*, Manchester: Manchester University Press.

Cocco, N., Sharpe, L. and Blaszczynski, A.P. (1995) 'Differences in preferred level of arousal in two sub-groups of problem gamblers: a preliminary report', *Journal of Gambling Studies*, 11: 221–229.

Colhoun, H., Ben-Shlomo, Y., Dong, W., Bost, L. and Marmot, M. (1997) 'Ecological analysis of collectivity of alcohol consumption in England: importance of average drinker', *British Medical Journal*, 314: 1164–1168.

Collins, A.F. (1996) 'The pathological gambler and the government of gambling', *History of the Human Sciences*, 9: 69–100.

Comings, D.E., Rosenthal, R.J., Lesieur, H.R., Rugle, L.J., Muhleman, D., Chiu, C., Dietz, G. and Gade, R. (1996) 'A study of the dopamine D_2 receptor gene in pathological gambling', *Pharmacogenetics*, 6: 223–234.

Comings, D.E., Gade, R., Wu, S., Chiu, C., Dietz, G., Muhleman, D., Saucier, G., Ferry, L., Rosenthal, R.J., Lesieur, H.R., Rugle, L.J. and MacMurray, P. (1997)

'Studies of the potential role of the dopamine D_1 receptor gene in addictive behaviors', *Molecular Psychiatry*, 2: 44–56.

Cooper, M.L., Russell, M., Skinner, J.B., Frone, M.R. and Mudar, P. (1992) 'Stress and alcohol use: moderating effects of gender, coping, and alcohol expectancies', *Journal of Abnormal Psychology*, 101: 139–152.

Cornish, D. (1978) *Gambling: A Review of the Literature and its Implications for Policy and Research* (Home Office Research Study, 42), London: HMSO.

Cotton (1674) *Compleat Gamester* (cited by France, 1902).

Coulombe, A., Ladouceur, B., Desharnais, R. and Jobin, J. (1992) 'Erroneous perceptions and arousal among regular occasional video poker players', *Journal of Gambling Studies*, 8: 235–244.

Coups, E., Haddock, G. and Webley, P. (1998) 'Correlates and predictors of lottery play in the United Kingdom', *Journal of Gambling Studies*, 14: 285–303.

Coventry, K.R. and Brown, R.I.F. (1993) 'Sensation seeking, gambling and gambling addictions', *Addiction*, 88: 541–554.

Coventry, K.R. and Norman, A.C. (1997) 'Arousal, sensation seeking and frequency of gambling in off-course horse racing bettors', *British Journal of Psychology*, 88: 671–681.

Coventry, K.R. and Norman, A.C. (1998) 'Arousal, erroneous verbalizations and the illusion of control during a computer-generated gambling task', *British Journal of Psychology*, 89: 629–645.

Coventry, K.R. and Hudson, J. (2001) 'Gender differences, physiological arousal and the role of winning in fruit machine gamblers', *Addiction*, 96: 871–879.

Creigh-Tyte, S. (1997) 'Building a National Lottery: reviewing British experience', *Journal of Gambling Studies*, 13: 321–341.

Crisp, B.R., Thomas, S.A., Jackson, A.C., Thomason, N., Smith, S., Borrell, J., Ho, W. and Holt, T.A. (2000) 'Sex differences in the treatment needs and outcomes of problem gamblers', *Research on Social Work Practice*, 10: 229–242.

Crockford, D.N. and el-Guebaly, N. (1998) 'Psychiatric comorbidity in pathological gambling: a critical review', *Canadian Journal of Psychiatry*, 43: 43–50.

Cunningham-Williams, R.M., Cottler, L.B., Compton, W.M. and Spitznagel, E.L. (1998) 'Taking chances: problem gamblers and mental health disorders: results from the St Louis epidemiological catchment area study', *American Journal of Public Health*, 88: 1093–1096.

Custer, R. (1982) 'An overview of compulsive gambling', in P.A. Carone, S.F. Yolles, S.N. Kieffer, and L.W. Krinsky (eds.) *Alcoholism, Drug Abuse, Gambling*, New York: Human Sciences Press.

Custer, R. and Milt, H. (1985) *When Luck Runs Out; Help for Compulsive Gamblers and their Families*, New York: Facts on File.

Delfabbro, P.H. and Winefield, A.H. (1999) 'Poker-machine gambling: an analysis of within session characteristics', *British Journal of Psychology*, 90: 425–439.

Dement, J.W. (1999) *Going for Broke: The Depiction of Compulsive Gambling in Film*, Lanham, Maryland: Scarecrow Press.

Devereux, E.C. (1949) 'Gambling and the social structure: a sociological study of lotteries and horse racing in contemporary America', unpublished thesis, Harvard University (cited by Rosecrance, 1988).

Dickens, C. (1852) 'Betting shops', *Household Words*, No. 18, 26 June, pp. 333–336 (cited by Clapson, 1992).

Dickerson, M. (1974) 'The effect of betting shop experience on gambling behaviour', unpublished thesis, University of Birmingham.

Dickerson, M. (1979) 'FI schedules and persistence at gambling in the UK betting office', *Journal of Applied Behavioral Analysis*, 12: 315–323.

Dickerson, M. (1990) 'Gambling: the psychology of a non-drug compulsion', *Drug and Alcohol Review*, 9: 187–199.

Dickerson, M. and Baron, E. (2000) 'Contemporary issues and future directions for research into pathological gambling', *Addiction*, 95: 1145–1160.

Dickerson, M. and Hinchy, J. (1988) 'The prevalence of excessive and pathological gambling in Australia', *Journal of Gambling Behavior*, 4: 135–151.

Dickerson, M., Hinchy, J. and Legg England, S. (1990) 'An evaluation of a minimal intervention for media-recruited problem gamblers', *Journal of Gambling Studies*, 6: 87–102.

Dickerson, M., Allcock, C., Blaszczynski, A., Nicholls, B., Williams, J. and Maddern, R. (1995) *An Examination of the Socio-economic Effects of Gambling on Individuals, Families and the Community, Including Research into the Costs of Problem Gambling in New South Wales: A Report Prepared for the Casino Community Fund Trustees*, Campbelltown: Australian Institute for Gambling Research.

Dickerson, M., Baron, E., Hong, S.M. and Cottrell, D. (1996) 'Estimating the extent and degree of gambling related problems in the Australian population: a national survey', *Journal of Gambling Studies*, 12: 161–178.

Diskin, K.M. and Hodgins, D.C. (1999) 'Narrowing of attention and dissociation in pathological video lottery gamblers', *Journal of Gambling Studies*, 15: 17–28.

Dixey, R. (1996) 'Bingo in Britain: an analysis of gender and class', in J. McMillen (ed.) *Gambling Cultures*, London: Routledge, 136–151.

Dixon, D. (1991) *From Prohibition to Regulation: Bookmaking, Anti-Gambling, and the Law*, Oxford: Clarendon Press.

Dombrink, J. (1996) 'Gambling and the legislation of vice: social movements, public health and public policy in the United States', in J. McMillen (ed.) *Gambling Cultures*, London: Routledge, 43–64.

Dostoevsky, F. (1866) *The Gambler* (cited in Reith, 1999).

Duffy, J.C. (1986) 'The distribution of alcohol consumption: 30 years on', *British Journal of Addiction*, 81: 735–748.

Eadington, W.R. and Cornelius, J.A. (eds.) (1991) *Gambling and Commercial Gaming. Essays in Business, Economics, Philosophy and Science*, Reno, Nevada: Institute for the Study of Gambling and Commercial Gaming, University of Nevada.

Echeburúa, E., Báez, C. and Fernández-Montalvo, J. (1996) 'Comparative effectiveness of three therapeutic modalities in the psychological treatment of pathological gambling: long-term outcome', *Behavioural and Cognitive Psychotherapy*, 24: 51–72.

Eisen, S.A., Lin, N., Lyons, M.J., Scherrer, J.F., Griffith, K., True, W.R., Goldberg, J. and Tsuang, M.T. (1998) 'Familial influences on gambling behavior: an analysis of 3359 twin pairs', *Addiction*, 93: 1375–1384.

Elster, J. (1999) 'Gambling and addiction', in J. Elster and O. Skog (eds.) *Getting Hooked: Rationality and Addiction*, Cambridge: Cambridge University Press.

Emrick, C.D., Tonigan, J.S., Montgomery, H. and Little, L. (1993) 'Alcoholics

Anonymous: what is currently known?', in B.S. McCrady and W.R. Miller (eds.) *Research on Alcoholics Anonymous: Opportunities and Alternatives*, New Brunswick, New Jersey: Rutgers Center of Alcohol Studies, 41–76.

Ernst and Young (1994) *Assessment of Casino Windsor: final report, November 1994*, Toronto, Ernst and Young (cited by Room et al, 1999).

Eysenck, H.J. (1967) *The Biological Basis of Personality*, Springfield, Illinois: Charles C. Thomas.

Fabian, T. (1995) 'Pathological gambling: a comparison of gambling at German-style slot machines and 'classical' gambling', *Journal of Gambling Studies*, 11: 249–263.

Farrell, A.D., Danish, S.J. and Howard, C.W. (1992) 'Risk factors for drug use in urban adolescents: identification and cross-validation', *American Journal of Community Psychology*, 20: 263–285.

Fenichel, O. (1945) *The Psychoanalytic Theory of Neuroses*, New York: Norton.

Fisher, S. (1992) 'Measuring pathological gambling in children: the case of fruit machines in the UK', *Journal of Gambling Studies*, 8: 263–285.

Fisher, S. (1993a) 'Gambling and pathological gambling in adolescents', *Journal of Gambling Studies*, 9: 277–288.

Fisher, S. (1993b) 'The pull of the fruit machine: a sociological typology of young players', *Sociological Review*, 41: 447–474.

Fisher, S. (1996) 'Gambling and problem gambling among casino patrons', a report to a consortium of the British casino industry, University of Plymouth.

Fisher, S. (1999) 'A prevalence study of gambling and problem gambling in British adolescents', *Addiction Research*, 7: 509–538.

Fisher, S. (2000) 'Measuring the prevalence of sector specific problem gambling: a study of casino patrons', *Journal of Gambling Studies*, 16: 25–52.

Fisher, S. and Balding, J. (1996) 'Under-16s find the lottery a good gamble', *Education and Health*, 13: 65–68.

Fisher, S. and Griffiths, M. (1995) 'Current trends in slot machine gambling: research and policy issues', *Journal of Gambling Studies*, 11: 239–247.

Forrest, D. (1999) 'The past and future of the British football pools', *Journal of Gambling Studies*, 15: 161–176.

France, C. (1902) 'The gambling impulsive', *American Journal of Psychology*, 13: 364–407.

Frank, M.L., Lester, D. and Wexler, A. (1991) 'Suicidal behavior among members of Gamblers Anonymous', *Journal of Gambling Studies*, 7: 249–254.

Freud, S. (1961) 'Dostoevsky and parricide (1928)' in J. Strachey (ed.) *The Complete Psychological Works of Sigmund Freud*, London: Hogarth, vol XXI, pp. 175–196.

Frey, J. (1986) 'Gambling: America's national pastime?', *Sports Illustrated* (cited by Rosecrance, 1988).

Frey, J. (1998) 'Federal involvement in US gaming regulation', *The Annals of the American Academy of Political and Social Science*, 556:138–152.

Frischer, M., Hickman, M., Kraus, L., Mariani, F. and Wiessing, L. (2001). 'A comparison of different methods for estimating the prevalence of problematic drug misuse in Great Britain', *Addiction*, 96: 1465–1476.

Gaboury, A. and Ladouceur, R. (1989) 'Erroneous perceptions and gambling', *Journal of Social Behavior and Personality*, 4: 411–420.

Gambino, B. (1999) 'Estimating confidence intervals and sampling proportions in two-stage prevalence designs', *Journal of Gambling Studies*, 15: 243–245.

Gambino, B., Fitzgerald, R., Shaffer, H., Renner, J. and Courtnage, P. (1993) 'Perceived family history of problem gambling and scores on SOGS', *Journal of Gambling Studies*, 9: 169–184.

Gambling Review Body, Department for Culture, Media and Sport (2001) *Gambling Review Report*, Norwich: HMSO.

Gaming Board (1969) *Report of the Gaming Board for Great Britain*, London: HMSO.

Gaming Board (1994) *Report of the Gaming Board for Great Britain 1993/94*, London: HMSO.

Gaming Board (1995) *Report of the Gaming Board for Great Britain 1994/95*, London: HMSO.

Gaming Board (2000) *Report of the Gaming Board for Great Britain 1999/2000*, London: HMSO.

Garratt, V.W. (1939) *A Man in the Street*, London: J.M. Dent (cited by Chinn, 1991).

Giacopassi, D., Stitt, B.G. and Vandiver, M. (1998) 'An analysis of the relationship of alcohol to casino gambling among college students', *Journal of Gambling Studies*, 14: 135–149.

Giacopassi, D., Nichols, M. and Stitt, B.G. (1999) 'Attitudes of community leaders in new casino jurisdictions regarding casino gambling's effects on crime and quality of life', *Journal of Gambling Studies*, 15: 123–147.

Gilovich, T. (1983) 'Biased evaluation and persistence in gambling', *Journal of Personality and Social Psychology*, 44: 1110–1126.

Gilovich, T. and Douglas, C. (1986) 'Biased evaluations of randomly determined gambling outcomes', *Journal of Experimental Social Psychology*, 22: 228–241.

Glautier, S. (1994) 'Classical conditioning, drug cues and drug addiction', in C.R. Legg and D. Booth (eds.) *Appetite, Neural and Behavioural Bases*, Oxford: Oxford University Press, 165–192.

Goffman, E. (1961) *Asylums: Essays on the Social Situation of Mental Patients and Other Inmates*, Garden City, New York: Anchor Books, Doubleday.

Goffman, E. (1967) *Interaction Ritual*, Garden City, New York: Anchor Books, Doubleday.

Goffman, E. (1969) *Where the Action Is: Three Essays*, London: Allen Lane/The Penguin Press.

Goldstein, L. and Carlton, P.L. (1988) 'Hemispheric EEG correlates of compulsive behavior: the case of pathological gamblers', *Research Communications in Psychology, Psychiatry and Behavior*, 13: 103–111.

Goodman, R. (1995) *The Luck Business: The Devastating Consequences and Broken Promises of America's Gambling Explosion*, New York: The Free Press.

Graham, J. (1988) *Amusement Machines: Dependency and Delinquency*, Home Office Research Study No. 101, London: HMSO.

Gray, J. (2001) 'The concept of addiction', in Gambling Review Report, annex G, 231–233.

Greene, G. (1938) *Brighton Rock*, London: Heinemann (cited by Clapson, 1992).

Greenson, R. (1947) 'On gambling', *Am Imago*, 4: 61–77.

Greenwood, W. (1933) *Love on the Dole*, London: Jonathan Cape.

Griffiths, M. (1990) 'Addiction to fruit machines: a preliminary study among young males', *Journal of Gambling Studies*, 6: 113–126.

Griffiths, M. (1993a) 'Factors in problem adolescent fruit machine gambling: results of a small postal survey', *Journal of Gambling Studies*, 9: 31–45.

Griffiths, M. (1993b) 'Fruit machine addiction in adolescents: a case study', *Journal of Gambling Studies*, 9: 387–399.

Griffiths, M. (1993c) 'Tolerance in gambling: an objective measure using the psychophysiological analysis of male fruit machine gamblers', *Addictive Behaviors*, 18: 365–372.

Griffiths, M. (1994) 'The role of cognitive bias and skill in fruit machine gambling', *British Journal of Psychology*, 85: 351–369.

Griffiths, M. (1995a) *Adolescent Gambling*, London: Routledge.

Griffiths, M. (1995b) 'The role of subjective mood states in the maintenance of fruit machine gambling behaviour', *Journal of Gambling Studies*, 11: 123–135.

Griffiths, M. (1996) 'Behavioral addiction: an issue for everybody'? *Employee Counseling Today: The Journal of Workplace Learning*, 8: 19–25.

Griffiths, M. and MacDonald, H.F. (1999) 'Counselling in the treatment of pathological gambling: an overview,' *British Journal of Guidance & Counselling*, 27: 179–189.

Griffiths, M. and Sutherland, I. (1998) 'Adolescent gambling and drug use', *Journal of Community and Applied Social Psychology*, 8: 423–427.

Griffiths, M., Scarfe, A. and Bellringer, P. (1999) 'The UK national telephone gambling helpline – results on the first year of operation', *Journal of Gambling Studies*, 15: 83–90.

Grun, L. and McKeigue, P. (2000) 'Prevalence of excessive gambling before and after introduction of a national lottery in the United Kingdom: another example of the single distribution theory', *Addiction*, 95: 959–966.

Gupta, R. and Derevensky, J.L. (1997) 'Familial and social influences on juvenile gambling behaviour', *Journal of Gambling Studies*, 13: 179–192.

Gupta, R. and Derevensky, J.L. (1998) 'Adolescent gambling behavior: a prevalence study and examination of the correlates associated with problem gambling', *Journal of Gambling Studies*, 14: 319–345.

Hammersley, R., Forsyth, A., Morrison, V. and Davies, J.B. (1989) 'The relationship between crime and opioid use', *British Journal of Addiction*, 84: 1029–1043.

Hawkins, J.D., Catalano, R.F. and Miller, J.Y. (1992) 'Risk and protective factors for alcohol and other drug problems in adolescence and early adulthood: implications for substance abuse prevention', *Psychological Bulletin*, 112: 64–105.

Heather, N. and Robertson, I. (1983) *Controlled Drinking*, London: Methuen.

Herman, R. (1976) *Gamblers and Gambling: Motives, Institutions and Controls*, Lexington, Massachusetts: Lexington Books.

Hermkens, P. and Kok, I. (1991) 'Gambling in the Netherlands developments, participation and compulsive gambling', in W.R. Eadington and J.A. Cornelius (eds.) *Gambling Behavior and Problem Gambling*, Reno, Nevada: University of Nevada.

Hickey, J.E., Haertzen, C.A. and Henningfield, J.E. (1986) 'Simulation of gambling responses on the addiction research center inventory', *Addictive Behaviors*, 11: 345–349.

Hill, E. and Williamson, J. (1998) 'Choose six numbers, any numbers', *The Psychologist, Bulletin of the British Psychological Society*, 11, 17–21.

Hodgins, D.C. and el-Guebaly, N. (2000) 'Natural and treatment-assisted recovery from gambling problems: a comparison of resolved and active gamblers', *Addiction*, 95: 777–789.

Hodgins, D.C., Currie, S.R. and el-Guebaly, N. (2001) 'Motivational enhancement and self-help treatments for problem gambling', *Journal of Consulting and Clinical Psychology*, 69: 50–57.

Hraba, J. and Lee, G. (1996) 'Gender, gambling and problem gambling', *Journal of Gambling Studies*, 12: 83–101.

Huxley, J. (1993) 'Fruit machine use in adolescents and adult women', unpublished thesis, University of Birmingham.

Huxley, J. and Carroll, D. (1992) 'A survey of fruit machine gambling in adolescents', *Journal of Gambling Studies*, 8: 167–179.

Jacobs, D.F. (1989) 'Illegal and undocumented: a review of teenage gambling and the plight of children of problem gamblers in America', in H.J. Shaffer, S. Stein, B. Gambino and T. Cummings (eds.) *Compulsive Gambling: Theory, Research and Practice*, Lexington, Massachusetts: Lexington Books.

Jacobs, D.F. (1993) 'Evidence supporting a general theory of addiction', in W.R. Eadington and J.A. Cornelius (eds.) *Gambling Behavior and Problem Gambling*, Reno, Nevada: University of Nevada.

Jaffe, J.H. (1992) 'Current concepts of addiction', in C.P. O'Brien and J.H. Jaffe (eds.) *Addictive States*, New York: Raven Press.

Jessor, R. and Jessor, S. (1977) *Problem Behavior and Psychosocial Development: a Longitudinal Study of Youth*, New York: Academic Press.

Johnson, E.E., Hamer, R., Nora, R.M., Tan, B., Eisenstein, N. and Engelhart, C. (1997) 'The lie/bet questionnaire for screening pathological gamblers', *Psychological Reports*, 80: 83–88.

Johnson, S. (1755) *A Dictionary of the English Language*, 1983 edition (cited by Clapson, 1992).

Kahneman, D. and Tversky, A. (1982) 'The psychology of preferences', *Scientific American*, January, 136–142.

Kallick, M., Suits, D., Dielman, T. and Hybels, J. (1979) *A Survey of American Gambling Attitudes and Behavior*, University of Michigan, Survey Research Center, Institute for Social Research.

Kassinove, J.I., Tsytsarev, S.V. and Davidson, I. (1998) 'Russian attitudes toward gambling', *Personality and Individual Differences*, 24: 41–46.

Klingemann, H., Sobell, L., Barker, J., Blomqvist, J., Cloud, W., Ellistand, T., Finfgeld, D., Granfield, R., Hodgins, D., Hunt, G., Junker, B., Moggi, F., Peele, S., Smart, R., Sobell, M. and Tucker, J. (2001) *Promoting Self-Change from Problem Substance Use: Practical Implications for Policy, Prevention and Treatment*, Dordrecht: Kluwer Academic Publishers.

Knapp, B.L. (2000) *Gambling, Game, and Psyche*, New York: State University of New York Press.

Knapp, T.J. (1997) 'Behaviorism and public policy: B.F. Skinner's views on gambling', *Behavior and Social Issues*, 7: 129–139.

Krishnan, M. and Orford, J. (2002) 'Gambling and the family from the stress-coping-support perspective', *International Gambling Studies*, 2: 61–83.

KPMG (2000) *The Economic Value and Public Perceptions of Gambling in the UK*. Report for Business In Sport and Leisure.

Kroeber, H. (1992) 'Roulette gamblers and gamblers at electronic game machines: where are the differences', *Journal of Gambling Studies*, 8: 79–92.

Kyngdon, A. and Dickerson, M. (1999) 'An experimental study of the effect of prior alcohol consumption on a simulated gambling activity', *Addiction*, 94: 697–707.

Ladouceur, R. and Mayrand, M. (1987) 'The level of involvement and the timing of betting in gambling', *Journal of Psychology*, 121: 169–175.

Ladouceur, R. and Walker, M. (1996) 'A cognitive perspective on gambling', in P.M. Salkovskis (ed.) *Trends in Cognitive and Behavioural Therapies*, 89–120, Chichester: Wiley.

Ladouceur, R., Tourigny, M. and Mayrand, M. (1986) 'Familiarity, group exposure, and risk-taking behaviour in gambling', *Journal of Psychology*, 120: 45–49.

Ladouceur, R., Boisvert, J.M., Pepin, M., Lorangere, M. and Sylvain, C. (1994) 'Social cost of pathological gambling', *Journal of Gambling Studies*, 10: 399–409.

Ladouceur, R., Boudreault, N., Jacques, C. and Vitaro, F. (1999a) 'Pathological gambling and related problems amongst adolescents', *Journal of Child & Adolescent Substance Abuse*, 8: 55–68.

Ladouceur, R., Jacques, C., Ferland, F. and Giroux, I. (1999b) 'Prevalence of problem gambling: a replication study 7 years later', *Canadian Journal of Psychiatry*, 44: 802–804.

Ladouceur, R., Bouchard, C., Rhéaume, N., Jacques, C., Ferland, F., Leblond, J. and Walker, M. (2000) 'Is the SOGS an accurate measure of pathological gambling among children, adolescents and adults?', *Journal of Gambling Studies*, 16: 1–21.

Langewish, M.W.J. and Frisch, G. (1998) 'Gambling behavior and pathology in relation to impulsivity, sensation seeking, and risky behavior in male college students', *Journal of Gambling Studies*, 14: 245–262.

Langer, E.J. (1975) 'The illusion of control', *Journal of Personality and Social Psychology*, 32, 311–328 (cited by Carroll and Huxley, 1994).

Langer, E.J. and Roth, J. (1975) 'Heads I win, tails it's chance: the illusion of control as a function of the sequence of outcomes in a purely chance task', *Journal of Personality and Social Psychology*, 32: 951–955.

Lea, S.E.G., Tarpy, R.M. and Webley, P. (1987) *The Individual in the Economy: A Textbook of Economic Psychology*, Cambridge: Cambridge University Press.

Leary, K. and Dickerson, M.G. (1985) 'Levels of arousal in high and low frequency gamblers' *Behavior Research and Therapy*, 23: 635–640.

Lee, J. (1989) *It's Good Fun Pressing Buttons: Young People and Fruit and Video Machine Use*, Leeds: Leeds City Council.

LeGrande, J. (1995) *The Observer*, 29 October 1995 (cited by Miers, 1996).

Lesieur, H.R. (1984) *The Chase: The Career of the Compulsive Gambler*, Rochester, Vermont: Schenkman.

Lesieur, H.R. (1988) 'The female pathological gambler', in W.R. Eadington (ed.) *Gambling Studies: Proceedings of the 7th International Conference on Gambling and Risk Taking*, 230–258, Reno: University of Nevada.

Lesieur, H.R. (1990) 'Working with and understanding Gamblers Anonymous', in T.J. Powell (ed.) *Working with Self-Help*, Silver Spring, Maryland: National Association of Social Workers Press.

Lesieur, H.R. (1994) 'Epidemiological surveys of pathological gambling: critique and suggestions for modification', *Journal of Gambling Studies*, 10: 385–397.

Lesieur, H.R. (1998) 'Costs and treatment of pathological gambling', *Annals of the American Academy of Political and Social Science*, 556: 153–171.

Lesieur, H.R. and Blume, S.B. (1987) 'The South Oaks Gambling Screen (SOGS): a new instrument for the identification of pathological gamblers', *American Journal of Psychiatry*, 144: 1184–1188.

Lesieur, H.R. and Rothschild, J. (1989) 'Children of Gamblers Anonymous members', *Journal of Gambling Behavior*, 5: 269–278.

Lesieur, H.R. and Rosenthal, R.J. (1991) 'Pathological gambling: a review of the literature (prepared for the American Psychiatric Association Task Force on DSM-IV committee on disorders of impulse control)', *Journal of Gambling Studies*, 7: 5–39.

Lesieur, H.R., Blume, S.B. and Zoppa, R.M. (1986) 'Alcoholism, drug abuse, and gambling', *Alcoholism: Clinical & Experimental Research*, 10: 33–38.

Leslie, E. (1890) *A Dangerous Friend, or Tom's Three Months in London*, London: George Cauldwell (cited by Dixon, 1991).

Lester, D. (1994) 'Access to gambling opportunities and compulsive gambling', *International Journal of the Addictions*, 29: 1611–1616.

López-Viets, V.C. and Miller, W.R. (1997) 'Treatment approaches for pathological gamblers', *Clinical Psychology Review*, 17: 689–702.

Lorenz, V.C. and Yaffee, R.A. (1984) 'Pathological gambling: medical, emotional and interpersonal aspects', paper presented at 6th national conference on gambling and risk taking, Atlantic City, New Jersey, December.

McConaghy, N. (1991) 'Case studies: a pathological or a compulsive gambler?' *Journal of Gambling Studies*, 7: 55–63.

McConaghy, N., Armstrong, M.S., Blaszczynski, A. and Allcock, C. (1983) 'Controlled comparison of aversive therapy and imaginal desensitization in compulsive gambling', *British Journal of Psychiatry*, 142: 366–372.

McConaghy, N., Armstrong, M.S., Blaszczynski, A. and Allcock, C. (1988) 'Behavior completion versus stimulus control in compulsive gambling', *Behavior Modification*, 12: 371–384.

McCormick, R.A. (1993) 'Disinhibition and negative affectivity in substance abusers with and without a gambling problem', *Addictive Behaviors*, 18: 331–336.

McCown, W.G. and Chamberlain, L.L. (2000) *Best Possible Odds: Contemporary Treatment Strategies for Gambling Disorders*, New York: Wiley.

MacDonald, J.R. (1905) 'Gambling and citizenship', in B.S. Rowntree (ed.) *Betting and Gambling: A National Evil*, London: Longmans, Green, 127–128 (cited by Chinn, 1991 and Dixon, 1991).

McGee, L. and Newcomb, M.D. (1992) 'General deviance syndrome: expanded hierarchical evaluations at four ages from early adolescence to adulthood', *Journal of Consulting and Clinical Psychology*, 60: 766–776.

McKibbin, R. (1979) 'Working class gambling in Britain, 1880–1939', *Past and Present*, 82: 147–178.

McMillen, J. (ed.) (1996) *Gambling Cultures: Studies in History and Interpretation*, London: Routledge.

McNeilly, D.P. and Burke, W.J. (2000) 'Late life gambling: the attitudes and behaviors of older adults', *Journal of Gambling Studies*, 16: 393–415.

Marotta, J.J. (1999) 'Recovery from gambling with and without treatment', unpublished thesis, University of Nevada.

Marshall, M., Balfour, R. and Kenner, A. (1998) 'Pathological gambling: prevalence, type of offence, co-morbid psychopathology and demographic characteristics in a prison population', unpublished submission to the Australian Productivity Commission.

Martínez-Pina, A., De Parga, J.L.G., Vallverdu, R.F., Planas, X.S., Mateo, M.M. and Aguado, V.M. (1991) 'The Catalonia survey: personality and intelligence structure in a sample of compulsive gamblers', *Journal of Gambling Studies*, 7: 275–299.

Masterman, C.F.G. (1905) 'Gambling and social reform', *Daily News*, 13 May 1905 (cited by Dixon, 1991).

Meier, S., Brigham, T.A., Ward, D.A., Myers, F. and Warren, L. (1996) 'Effects of blood alcohol concentrations on negative punishment: implications for decision making', *Journal of Studies on Alcohol*, 57: 85–96.

Meltzer, H., Gill, B. and Petticrew, M. (1994) *The Prevalence of Psychiatric Morbidity Among Adults Aged 16–61, Living in Private Households, in Great Britain*, OPCS Surveys of Psychiatric Morbidity in Great Britain, London: HMSO.

Meyer, G. (1989) *Glücksspieler in Selbsthilfegruppen: erste Ergebnisse einer empirischen Untersuchung*, Hamburg: Neuland (cited by Rosenthal and Lesieur, 1992).

Meyer, G. (1992) 'The gambling market in the Federal Republic of Germany and the helpseeking of pathological gamblers', *Journal of Gambling Studies*, 8: 11–20.

Meyer, G. and Stadler, M.A. (1999) 'Criminal behavior associated with pathological gambling', *Journal of Gambling Studies*, 15: 29–43.

Miers, D. (1996) 'The implementation and effects of Great Britain's National Lottery', *Journal of Gambling Studies*, 12: 343–373.

Miller, W.R. and Kurtz, E. (1994) 'Models of alcoholism used in treatment: contrasting AA and other perspectives with which it is often confused', *Journal of Studies on Alcohol*, 55: 159–166.

Minihan, M. (1967) *Dostoevsky: His Life and Work by Konstantin Mochulsky*, Princeton, New Jersey: Princeton University Press.

Mintel (1995) *Gambling*, London: Mintel (cited by Shepherd et al, 1998).

Moore, G. (1895) *Esther Waters*, Oxford, 1983 edition (cited by Clapson, 1992).

Moore, S.M. and Ohtsuka, K. (1997) 'Gambling activities of young Australians: developing a model of behaviour, *Journal of Gambling Studies*, 13: 207–236.

Moore, S.M. and Ohtsuka, K. (1999) 'Beliefs about control over gambling among young people, and their relations to problem gambling', *Psychology of Addictive Behaviors*, 13: 339–347.

Moran, E. (1970) 'Gambling as a form of dependence', *British Journal of Addiction*, 64: 419–428.

Moran, E. (1975) 'Pathological gambling', in *Contemporary Psychiatry, British Journal of Psychiatry*, Special Publication No. 9, Royal College of Psychiatrists, London.

Moran, E. (1987) *Gambling Among Schoolchildren: The Impact of the Fruit Machine*, London: The National Council on Gambling.

Moran, E. (1995) 'Majority of secondary school children buy tickets', *British Medical Journal*, 311: 1225–1226.

Moran, J. (1969) 'Taking the final risk', *Mental Health*, 21–22.

Mott, J. (1973) 'Miners, weavers and pigeon racing', in M. Smith et al, *Leisure and Society in Britain* (cited by Clapson, 1992).

Murray, R. and Stabenau, J. (1982) 'Genetic factors in alcoholism predisposition', in E. Pattison and E. Kaufman (eds.) *Encyclopedic Handbook of Alcoholism*, New York: Gardner Press.

NAGL (1893) *Bulletin of the National Anti-Gambling League*, 1(7):1 (cited by Reith, 1999).

NAGL (1918) *The War . . . and Gambling*, 28th Annual Report, London (cited by Dixon, 1991).

National Council on Welfare (1996) *Gambling in Canada*, no. H68–40/1996E, Ottawa: Minister of Supply and Services Canada.

National Heritage Committee (1993) *Third Report: National Lottery etc. Bill*, House of Commons Session 1992–93, London: HMSO (cited by Miers, 1996).

National Housing and Town Planning Council (1988) *The Use of the Fruit Machine*, London: The National Council on Gambling (cited by Griffiths, 1990).

National Research Council, National Academy of Sciences, Committee on the Social and Economic Impact of Pathological Gambling (1999) *Pathological Gambling: A Critical Review*, Washington DC: National Academy Press.

Newman, O. (1972) *Gambling: Hazard and Reward*, London: Athlone Press.

NORC (1999) 'Gambling impact and behavior study'. Report to the National Gambling Impact Study Commission, National Opinion Research Center at the University of Chicago, Gemini Research, the Lewin Group, and Christiansen/ Cummings Associates.

Nygren, T.E. (1998) 'Reacting to perceived high- and low-risk win-lose opportunities in a risky decision-making task: is it framing or affect or both?', *Motivation and Emotion*, 22: 73–98.

Ocean, G. and Smith, G.J. (1993) 'Social reward, conflict, and commitment: a theoretical model of gambling behavior', *Journal of Gambling Studies*, 9: 321–339.

O'Connor, J. (2000) 'An investigation of chasing behaviour', unpublished PhD thesis, University of Western Sydney, Macarthur.

O'Connor, J., Dickerson, M. and Philps, M. (1995) 'Chasing and its relationship to impaired-control over gambling', in *High Stakes in the Nineties*, 2nd edn, Curtin University, sixth National Conference of the Association for Gambling Studies, 169–183.

OFLOT (1994) *Director General of the National Lottery Annual Report*, London: HMSO (cited by Miers, 1996).

OFLOT (1996) *Social Research Programme* (cited by Miers, 1996).

Orford J. (2001) *Excessive Appetites: A Psychological View of Addictions* (2nd edition), Chichester: Wiley.

Orford, J., Waller, S. and Peto, J. (1974) 'Drinking behaviour and attitudes and their correlates amongst English university students, *Quarterly Journal of Studies on Alcohol*, 35: 1333–1353.

Orford, J., Morison, V. and Somers, M. (1996) 'Drinking and gambling: a comparison with implications for theories of addiction', *Drug and Alcohol Review*, 15: 47–56.

Orford, J., Dalton, S., Hartney, E., Ferrins-Brown, M., Kerr, C., and Maslin, J. (1998) The Birmingham Untreated Heavy Drinkers Project: final report on Wave 1 to the Department of Health, School of Psychology, The University of Birmingham.

Orford, J., Sproston, K. and Erens, B. (2003) 'SOG5 and DSMIV in the British Gambling Prevalence Survey: reliability and factor structure', *International Gambling Studies* (in press).

Peck, C.P. (1986) 'Risk-taking behavior and compulsive gambling', *American Psychologist*, 41: 461–465.

Pepys, S. (1976) *Diaries*, vol. 9 in R.C. Latham and W. Mathews (eds.), London: G Bell and Sons (cited by Reith, 1999).

Perez de Castro, L.A., Ibanez, A., Torres, P., Saiz-Ruiz, J. and Fernandez-Piqueras, J. (1997) 'Genetic association study between pathological gambling and a functional DNA polymorphism at the D4 receptor gene', *Pharmacogenetics*, 7: 345–348.

Petry, N.M. and Armentano, C. (1999) 'Prevalence, assessment, and treatment of pathological gambling: a review', *Psychiatric Services*, 50: 1021–1027.

Petry, N.M. and Casarella, T. (1999) 'Excessive discounting of delayed rewards in substance abusers with gambling problems' *Drug and Alcohol Dependence*, 56: 25–32.

Phillips, D.P., Welty, W.R. and Smith, M.M. (1997) 'Elevated suicide levels associated with legalized gambling', *Suicide and Life-Threatening Behavior*, 27: 373–378.

Pilgrim Trust (1938/1985) *Men Without Work*, New York: Garland (cited by Chinn, 1991).

Poe, E.A. (1839) *William Wilson*, short story (cited by B.L. Knapp, 2000).

Preston, F.W., Bernhard, B.J., Hunter, R.E. and Bybee, S.L. (1998) 'Gambling as stigmatized behavior: regional relabeling and the law', *Annals of the American Academy of Political and Social Science*, 556: 186–196.

Pugh, P. and Webley, P. (2000) 'Adolescent participation in the UK National Lottery games', *Journal of Adolescence*, 23: 1–11.

Rands, J. and Hooper, M. (1990) 'Survey of young people's use of slot machines within the Sedgemoor District in conjunction with Somerset Youth Association', unpublished manuscript (cited by Griffiths, 1995a).

Reid, R.L. (1986) 'The psychology of the near miss', *Journal of Gambling Behavior*, 2: 32–39.

Reith, G. (1999) *The Age of Chance: Gambling in Western Culture*, London: Routledge.

Ritchie, J. and Spencer, L. (1994) 'Qualitative data analysis for applied policy research', in A. Bryman and R.G. Burgess (eds.) *Analyzing Qualitative Data*, London: Routledge, 173–194.

Robertson, I. and Heather, N. (1987) *Let's Drink to Your Health! A Self-Help Guide to Sensible Drinking*, Hertford: British Psychological Society.

Rogers, P. (1998) 'The cognitive psychology of lottery gambling: a theoretical review', *Journal of Gambling Studies*, 14: 111–134.

Rogers, P. and Webley, P. (1998) 'It could be us! A cognitive and social psychological analysis of individual and syndicate based national lottery play in the UK', unpublished manuscript, University of Exeter.

Rönnberg, S., Volberg, R.A., Abbott, M.W., Moore, W.L., Andrén, A., Munck, I., Jonsson, J., Nilsson, T. and Svensson, O. (1999) 'Gambling and problem gambling in Sweden', report no 2 of the National Institute of Public Health Series on Gambling.

Room, R., Turner, N.E. and Ialomiteanu, A. (1999) 'Community effects of the opening of the Niagara Casino', *Addiction*, 94: 1449–1466.

Rose, I.N. (1991) 'The rise and fall of the third wave: gambling will be outlawed in forty years', in W.R. Eadington and J.A. Cornelius (eds.) *Gambling and Public Policy: International Perspectives*, Reno, Nevada: University of Nevada.

Rosecrance, J. (1988) *Gambling Without Guilt: The Legitimation of an American Pastime*, Pacific Grove, California: Brooks/Cole.

Rosenthal, R. (1987) 'The psychodynamics of pathological gambling: a review of the literature' in T. Galsk (ed.) *The Handbook of Pathological Gambling*, Springfield, Illinois: Charles C. Thomas.

Rosenthal, R. (1989) 'Pathological gambling and problem gambling', in H.J. Shaffer, S. Stein and B. Gambino (eds.) *Compulsive Gambling*, Lexington, Massachusetts: Lexington Books, 101–125.

Rosenthal, R. and Lesieur, H.R. (1992) 'Self-reported withdrawal symptoms and pathological gambling', *The American Journal on Addictions*, 1: 151–154.

Rosenthal, R. and Lorenz, V. (1992) 'The pathological gambler as criminal offender', *Clinical Forensic Psychiatry*, 15: 647–660.

Rotter, J.B. (1966) 'Generalized expectancies for internal versus external control of reinforcement', *Psychological Monographs*, 80 (whole number 609).

Rowntree, B.S. (1905) *Betting and Gambling: A National Evil*, London: Longmans, Green (cited by Dixon, 1991).

Roy, A., Adinoff, B., Roehrich, L., Lamparski, D., Custer, R., Lorenz, V., Barbaccia, M., Guidotti, A., Costa, E. and Linnoila, M. (1988) 'Pathological gambling: a psychobiological study', *Archives of General Psychiatry*, 45: 369–373.

Royal Commission on Betting, Lotteries and Gaming (the Willink Commission) (1951) *Final Report*, London: HMSO.

Royal Commission on Gambling (the Rothschild Commission) (1978) *Final Report*, London: HMSO.

Schuckit, M.A. (1987) 'Biological vulnerability to alcoholism', *Journal of Consulting and Clinical Psychology*, 55: 301–309.

Scott, M.B. (1968) *The Racing Game*, Chicago: Aldine (cited by Rosecrance, 1988).

Searles, J. (1988) 'The role of genetics in the pathogenesis of alcoholism', *Journal of Abnormal Psychology*, 97: 153–167.

Shaffer, H.J. and Hall, M.N. (1996) 'Estimating the prevalence of adolescent gambling disorders: a quantitative synthesis and guide toward standard gambling nomenclature', *Journal of Gambling Studies*, 12: 193–214.

Shaffer, H.J., LaBrie, R., Scanlan, K.M. and Cummings, T.N. (1994) 'Pathological gambling among adolescents: Massachusetts Gambling Screen (MAGS)', *Journal of Gambling Studies*, 10: 339–362.

Shaffer, H.J., Hall, M.N. and Vander Bilt, J. (1997) *Estimating the Prevalence of Disordered Gambling Behavior in the United States and Canada: A Meta-analysis*, Boston, Massachusetts: Harvard Medical School, Division on Addictions.

Sharpe, L. and Tarrier, N. (1993) 'Towards a cognitive-behavioural theory of problem gambling', *British Journal of Psychiatry*, 162: 407–412.

Sharpe, L., Tarrier, N., Schotte, D. and Spence, S.H. (1995) 'The role of autonomic arousal in problem gambling', *Addiction*, 90: 1529–1540.

Shepherd, R., Ghodse, H. and London, M. (1998) 'A pilot study examining gambling behaviour before and after the launch of the National Lottery and scratch cards in the UK', *Addiction Research*, 6: 5–12.

Shewan, D. and Brown, R.I.F. (1993) 'The role of fixed interval conditioning in promoting involvement in off-course betting', in W.R. Eadington and J.A. Cornelius (eds.) *Gambling Behavior and Problem Gambling*, Reno, Nevada: University of Nevada.

Silverman, D. (2000) *Doing Qualitative Research: A Practical Handbook*, London: Sage.

Simmel, E. (1920) 'Psychoanalysis of the gambler', *International Journal of Psychoanalysis*, 1: 352–353.

Sjoberg, L. (1969) 'Alcohol and gambling', *Psychopharmacologia*, 14: 284–298.

Skinner, B.F. (1953) *Science and Human Behavior*, New York: Macmillan.

Sobell, L.C., Sobell, M.B. and Toneatto, T. (1991) 'Recovery from alcohol problems without treatment', in N. Heather, W.R. Miller and J. Greeley (eds.) *Self-control and Addictive Behaviors*, Botany, NSW, Australia: Maxwell Macmillan, 198–242.

Social and Industrial Commission of the Church Assembly (SICCA) (1950) *Gambling: An Ethical Discussion*, London: Church Information Board (cited by Dixon, 1991).

Specker, S.M., Carlson, G.A., Edmondson, K.M., Johnson, P.E. and Marcotte, M. (1996) 'Psychopathology in pathological gamblers seeking treatment', *Journal of Gambling Studies*, 12: 67–82.

Spectrum Children's Trust (1988) *Slot Machine Playing by Children: Results of a Survey in Taunton and Minehead*, London (cited by Griffith, 1995a).

Spring, H. (1934) *Shabby Tiger*, London: Collins (cited by Clapson, 1992).

Sproston, K., Erens, B. and Orford, J. (2000) *Gambling Behaviour in Britain: Results from the British Gambling Prevalence Survey*, London: The National Centre for Social Research.

Squires, P. (1937) 'Fyodor Dostoevsky: a psychopathographical sketch', *Psychoanalytical Review*, 24: 365–388.

Stekel, W. (1924). *Peculiarities of Behaviour: Wandering Mania, Dipsomania, Cleptomania, Pyromania and Allied Impulsive Acts*, English publication 1938, London: Bodley Head (trans. J. van Teslaar).

Stewart, R.M. and Brown, R.I.F. (1988) 'An outcome study of Gamblers Anonymous', *British Journal of Psychiatry*, 152, 284–288.

Stinchfield, R. and Winters, K.C. (1998) 'Gambling and problem gambling among youths', *Annals of the American Academy of Political and Social Science*, 556: 172–185.

Strauss, A. and Corbin, J. (1998) *Basics of Qualitative Research: Grounded Theory Procedures and Techniques*, 2nd ed., Newbury Park, California: Sage.

Strickland, L. and Grote, F. (1967) 'Temporal presentation of winning symbols and slot-machine playing', *Journal of Experimental Psychology*, 74: 10–13.

Sullivan, S. (1994) 'Why compulsive gamblers are a high suicide risk', *Community Mental Health in New Zealand*, 8: 40–47.

Sylvain, C., Ladouceur, R. and Boisvert, J.M. (1997) 'Cognitive and behavioral treatment of pathological gambling: a controlled study', *Journal of Consulting and Clinical Psychology*, 65: 727–732.

Taber, J.I. (1982) 'Group psychotherapy with pathological gamblers', in W.R. Eadington (ed.) *The Gambling Papers: Proceedings of the Fifth National Conference on Gambling and Risk-Taking*, Reno: University of Nevada.

Tonigan, J.S., Toscova, R. and Miller, W.R. (1996) 'Meta-analysis of the literature on Alcoholics Anonymous: sample and study characteristics moderate findings', *Journal of Studies on Alcohol*, 57: 65–72.

Trevorrow, K. and Moore, S. (1998) 'The association between loneliness, social isolation and women's electronic gaming machine gambling', *Journal of Gambling Studies*, 14: 263–284.

Turner, N.E., Ialomiteanu, A. and Room, R. (1999) 'Checkered expectations: predictors of approval of opening a casino in the Niagara community', *Journal of Gambling Studies*, 15: 45–70.

Tversky, A. and Kahneman, D. (1981) 'The framing of decisions and the psychology of choice', *Science*, 211: 453–458.

Tversky, A. and Kahneman, D. (1982) 'Judgment under uncertainty: heuristics and biases', in D. Kahneman, P. Slovic and A. Tversky (eds.) *Judgment Under Uncertainty: Heuristics and Biases*, Cambridge: Cambridge University Press.

Vitaro, F., Ferland, F., Jacques, C. and Ladouceur, R. (1998) 'Gambling, substance use, and impulsivity during adolescence', *Psychology of Addictive Behaviors*, 12: 185–194.

Volberg, R. (1994) 'The prevalence and demographics of pathological gamblers: implications for public health', *American Journal of Public Health*, 84: 237–241.

Volberg, R. (1997) 'Replication studies of problem gambling', paper presented at the 10th International Conference on Gambling and Risk-Taking, Montreal.

Wagenaar, W.A. (1988) *Paradoxes of Gambling Behaviour*, Hove: Lawrence Erlbaum Associates.

Walker, M.B. (1989) 'Some problems with the concept of 'gambling addiction': should theories of addiction be generalised to include excessive gambling?', *Journal of Gambling Behavior*, 5, 179–200.

Walker, M.B. (1992) *The Psychology of Gambling*, Oxford: Butterworth-Heinemann.

Walker, M.B. and Dickerson, M.G. (1996) 'The prevalence of problem and pathological gambling: a critical analysis', *Journal of Gambling Studies*, 12: 233–249.

Walters, G.D. and Contri, D. (1998) 'Outcome expectancies for gambling: empirical modeling of a memory network in federal prison inmates', *Journal of Gambling Studies*, 14: 173–191.

Walton, F. (1990) *A Research Study on Young People and Gambling in Blackpool*, Blackpool (cited by Griffiths, 1995a).

Weinstein, D. and Deitch, L. (1974) *The Impact of Legalized Gambling: the Socio-economic Consequences of Lotteries and Off-Track Betting*, New York: Praeger.

Welte, J., Barnes, G., Wieczorek, W., Tidwell, M. and Parker, J. (2001) 'Alcohol and gambling pathology among US adults: prevalence, demographic patterns and comorbidity', *Journal of Studies on Alcohol*, 62: 706–712.

Westphal, J.R., Rush, J.A., Stevens, L. and Johnson, L.J. (2000) 'Gambling behavior of Louisiana students in grades 6 through 12', *Psychiatric Services*, 51: 96–99.

White, C., Mitchell, L. and Orford, J. (2001) *Exploring Gambling Behaviour In-Depth: A Qualitative Study*, London: National Centre for Social Research.

White, N.M. (1996) 'Addictive drugs as reinforcers: multiple partial actions on memory systems', *Addiction*, 91: 921–949.

Whyte, K.S. (1999) 'Analysis of the National Gambling Impact Study Commission act', *Journal of Gambling Studies*, 15: 309–318.

Wilde, G.J.S., Trimpop, R.M. and Joly, R. (1989) 'The effects of various amounts of ethanol upon risktaking tendency and confidence in task performance', *Proceedings of the 11th International Conference on Alcohol, Drugs, and Traffic Safety*, 494–499.

Winters, K.C. and Rich, T. (1998) 'A twin study of adult gambling behavior', *Journal of Gambling Studies*, 14: 213–225.

Winters, K.C., Stinchfield, R. and Fulkerson, J. (1993) 'Toward the development of an adolescent gambling problem severity scale', *Journal of Gambling Studies*, 9: 371–386.

Wise, R.A. (1994) 'A brief history of the anhedonia hypothesis', in C.R. Legg and D. Booth (eds.) *Appetite, Neural and Behavioural Bases*, Oxford: Oxford University Press, 243–263.

Wood, T.A. and Griffiths, M.D. (1998) 'The acquisition, development and maintenance of lottery and scratchcard gambling in adolescence', *Journal of Adolescence*, 21, 265–273.

Wray, I. and Dickerson, M. (1981) 'Cessation of high frequency gambling and withdrawal symptoms', *British Journal of Addiction*, 76: 401–405.

Yeoman, T. and Griffiths, M.D. (1996) 'Adolescent machine gambling and crime', *Journal of Adolescence*, 19, 183–188.

Zola, I.K. (1963) 'Observations on gambling in a lower-class setting', *Social Problems*, 10: 360.

Zuckerman, M. (1979) *Sensation Seeking: Beyond the Optimal Level of Arousal*, Hillsdale, New Jersey: Lawrence Erlbaum Associates.

Zurcher, L.A. (1970) 'The friendly poker game: a study of an ephemeral role', *Social Forces*, 49: 173–186.

Zweig, F. (1948) *Labour, Life and Poverty*, London: Gollancz (cited by Clapson, 1992).

Author index

Abbott, D.A. 249
Abbott, M.W. 23, 75–6, 77–8, 79, 80, 81, 96, 99, 102, 104, 105, 158, 212
Adinoff, B. 137
Aguado, V.M. 102
Allcock, C. 116, 160, 228
American Psychiatric Association 62, 64, 113, 158
Anderson, G. 120
Andrén, A. 23, 75–6, 80, 81, 96, 99, 104, 105, 158
Arlen, M. 52
Armentano, C. 226, 229, 231
Armstrong, M.S. 228
Australian Productivity Commission (APC) 21, 42, 43, 44, 45–6, 74, 79, 90, 93, 94–5, 98, 99, 105, 158, 216, 221, 241, 249, 251, 260

Baéz, C. 228
Balding, J. 84
Balfour, R. 99
Barbaccia, M. 137
Barbeyrac, J. 51
Barker, J. 54, 209, 231, 249
Barnes, G. 74, 102, 105
Barnes, G.M. 101, 105, 116
Baron, E. 64, 71, 133, 134, 158, 216–17, 219, 224
Barratt, E.S. 115
Becoña, E.B. 22, 72, 224, 256
Bell, F. 13
Bellringer, P. xi, 23, 28, 54, 98–9, 226, 227, 230, 231, 248
Ben-Shlomo, Y. 93
Bergh, C. 137
Bergler, E. 53, 63–4, 112–13
Bernhard, B.J. 255, 256

Bien, T.H. 230
Blaszczynski, A. 56, 57–8, 80, 114, 133, 136, 142, 228
Blaszczynski, A.P. 106, 122
Bleuler, E. 63
Bloch, H. 107
Blomqvist, J. 231
Blume, S.B. 73, 99, 158
Boisvert, J.M. 55, 56, 176, 209, 228
Bolen, D.W. 113
Booth, W. 13
Borrell, J. 81, 82
Bost, L. 93
Bouchard, C. 87
Boudreault, N. 87, 102
Boyd, W.H. 113
Brecksville Program for the Treatment of Compulsive Gambling 71
Breen, R.B. 116
Brenner, G.A. 1, 12, 13, 258
Brenner, R. 1, 12, 13, 258
Breslin, F.C. 135
Brigham, T.A. 135
British Columbia Gaming Policy Review 42
Brockner, J. 128
Brooks 53
Brown, R.I.F. 115, 120, 123, 216, 217, 219, 224, 225, 227
Brown, S. 81
Browne, B.R. 227
Burke, W.J. 82
Burns, J. 8
Bybee, S. 70, 71
Bybee, S.L. 255, 256

Cappell, H. 135
Carlson, G.A. 114

Carlton, P.L. 137
Carroll, D. 82, 111, 116, 119, 120, 130
Casarella, T. 124
Castellani, B. 21, 54, 62, 63, 64, 65, 70, 71, 116, 224, 225, 250, 253–4
Catalano, R.F. 89
Cayuela, R. 22, 96
Chamberlain, L.L. 226, 227, 229, 231
Chinn, C. 1, 2, 7, 8, 9, 10, 12, 13, 14–15, 50, 51, 52–3, 107, 111, 209, 223
Chiu, C. 138, 139
Christiansen, E.M. 21
Churches' Committee on Gambling (later Churches' Council on Gambling) 10
Churches' Council on Gambling 248
Churchill, S. 8
Clapson, M. 1, 2–4, 5, 6, 11, 12, 13, 14, 15, 17, 50, 51, 52, 53, 107, 209, 249
Cloud, W. 231
Cocco, N. 106, 122
Colhoun, H. 93
Collins, A.F. 10, 62, 63, 64, 248
Comings, D.E. 130, 138
Compton, W.M. 56, 114
Contri, D. 125
Cooper, M.L. 125
Corbin, J. 174
Cornelius, J.A. 252
Cornish, D. 69, 76, 90, 95–6, 97, 117, 119, 248
Costa, E. 137
Cottler, L.B. 56, 114
Cotton (1674) 51
Cottrell, D. 158
Coulombe, A. 120, 132
Coups, E. 101, 104, 128
Courtnage, P. 99, 106
Coventry, K.R. 115, 120, 122, 129, 132
Coventry, L. 81
Cramer, S.L. 249
Creigh-Tyte, S. 25, 27, 28–9, 30, 32, 42, 93
Crisp, B.R. 81, 82
Crockford, D.N. 102
Cummings, T.N. 21–2
Cunningham-Williams, R.M. 56, 114
Currie, S.R. 230
Custer, R. 53, 56, 64, 70, 105, 119, 121–2, 137, 176, 209, 249

Dalton, S. 134
Danish, S.J. 101
Davidson, I. 23
Davies, J.B. 58
De Parga, J.L.G. 102
Deitch, L. 96
Delfabbro, P.H. 133
Dement, J.W. 53
Derevensky, J.L. 84, 86–7, 99–100, 102
Desharnais, R. 120, 132
Devereux, E.C. 106
Dickens, C. 224
Dickerson, M. 56, 64, 67, 71, 76, 77, 79, 90, 102, 119, 120, 132, 133, 134, 135–6, 158, 210, 216–17, 219, 224, 230
Dickerson, M.G. 77, 80, 120, 134, 158
Dielman, T. 73
Dietz, G. 138, 139
Dintcheff, B.A. 101, 105, 116
Diskin, K.M. 121
Dixey, R. 254
Dixon, D. 1, 2, 4, 6, 7, 8, 9, 10–11, 12, 13, 14, 15, 16–18, 19–20, 52, 107, 237
Dombrink, J. 253
Dong, W. 93
Dostoevsky, F. 51, 53, 112, 122, 209
Douglas, C. 130
Duffy, J.C. 93
Dumlao, V. 80, 142

Eadington, W.R. 252
Echeburúa, E. 22, 228, 256
Edmondson, K.M. 114
Eisen, S.A. 138
Eisenstein, N. 79
Eklund, T. 137
el-Guebaly, N. 102, 230, 231
Ellistand, T. 231
Elster, J. 68–9, 117, 121, 125
Emrick, C.D. 227
Engelhart, C. 79
Erens, B. x, 36, 49, 79, 144, 149, 171
Ernst and Young (1994) 41
Evans, P. xi
Eysenck, H.J. 115

Fabian, T. 256
Farrell, A.D. 56, 57–8, 101
Fenichel, O. 63
Ferland, F. 87, 91–2, 116

Fernández-Montalvo, J. 228
Fernandez-Piqueras, J. 139
Ferrins-Brown, M. 134
Ferry, L. 139
Finfgeld, D. 231
Fisher, S. 21, 22, 23, 76–7, 79, 82, 83–4,
    88, 96, 99, 100, 101–2, 105, 108–11,
    140, 158, 213, 215, 219, 224
Fitzgerald, R. 99, 106
Forrest, D. 29, 30
Forsyth, A. 58
France, C. 51, 209
Frank, M.L. 56
Freud, S. 63, 112
Frey, J. 22, 107
Frisch, G. 116
Frishcher, M. 211
Frone, M.R. 125
Fulkerson, J. 85

Gaboury, A. 130–1
Gade, R. 138, 139
Gambino, B. 77–8, 79, 99, 106
Gambling Review Body (GRB) x–xi,
    30, 33, 35, 38, 39, 48–9, 141, 221, 222,
    234–6, 237, 238–9, 240–1, 242, 243,
    244, 246, 247–8, 251, 256, 257–60
Gaming Board 18, 19, 25–6, 28, 30,
    32–4, 35, 36, 37–8, 46, 47, 48, 49, 140,
    141, 236, 239, 246, 254
Garratt, V.W. 50–1
Ghodse, H. 92, 93, 103–4
Giacopassi, D. 42, 102, 134–5, 249
Gill, B. 211
Gilovich, T. 130
Giroux, I. 91–2
Glautier, S. 122
Goffman, E. 107, 111, 223, 253
Goldberg, J. 138
Goldstein, L. 137
Goodman, R. 21, 32, 255
Graham, J. 82
Granfield, R. 231
Gray, J. 223
Greene, G. 52
Greenson, R. 113
Greenwood, W. 52–3
Griffith, K. 138
Griffiths, M. 21, 22, 23, 60–1, 70, 82,
    96–7, 98, 100, 101, 105, 107, 108, 111,
    116, 117, 119, 120, 122, 125, 129, 130,
    132, 216, 219, 226, 230, 231, 249

Griffiths, M.D. 100, 101
Grote, F. 97
Grun, L. 92–3, 104, 216, 258
Guidotti, A. 137
Guirao, J.L. 22, 96
Gupta, R. 84, 86–7, 99–100, 102

Haddock, G. 101, 104, 128
Haertzen, C.A. 119
Hall, M.N. 72–3, 85, 87–8, 158
Hamer, R. 79
Hammersley, R. 58
Hartney, E. 134
Hawkins, J.D. 89
Heather, N. 230, 231
Henningfield, J.E. 119
Herman, R. 107, 248
Hermkens, P. 22–3, 251
Hickey, J.E. 119
Hickman, M. 211
Hill, E. 128
Hinchy, J. 77, 79, 158, 224, 230
Ho, W. 81, 82
Hodgins, D. 231
Hodgins, D.C. 121, 230, 231
Hoffman, J.H. 101, 105, 116
Holt, T.A. 81, 82
Hong, S.M. 158
Hopper, M. 82
Howard, C.W. 101
Hraba, J. 81
Hudson, J. 120
Hunt, G. 231
Hunter, R.E. 255, 256
Huxley, J. 82, 111, 120
Huxley, J.A.A. 116, 119, 120, 130
Hybels, J. 73

Ialomiteanu, A. 21, 39, 41, 42
Ibanez, A. 139

Jackson, A.C. 81, 82
Jacobs, D.F. 62, 85, 86, 87, 121
Jacques, C. 87, 91–2, 102, 116
Jaffe, J.H. 69
Jessor, R. 89, 101
Jessor, S. 89, 101
Jobin, J. 120, 132
Johnson, E.E. 79
Johnson, L.J. 86, 102, 105
Johnson, P.E. 114
Johnson, S. 6

Joly, R. 135
Jonsson, J. 23, 75–6, 80, 81, 96, 99, 104, 105, 158
Junker, B. 231

Kahneman, D. 124, 125, 127
Kallick, M. 73
Kassinove, J.I. 23
Kenner, A. 99
Kerr, C. 134
Klingemann, H. 231
Knapp, B.L. 52
Knapp, T.J. 117, 118, 119
Kok, I. 22–3, 251
KPMG (2000) 22, 25, 26–7, 29, 30, 34, 36, 37, 42, 43, 46, 47–8, 250–1, 255
Kraepelin, E. 63
Kraus, L. 211
Krishnan, M. 249
Kroeber, H. 106, 115
Kurtz, E. 227
Kyngdon, A. 102, 134, 135–6

Labrador, F. 22, 256
LaBrie, R. 21–2
Ladoucer, B. 120, 132
Ladouceur, R. 55, 56, 87, 91–2, 102, 116, 126, 127, 128, 129, 130–1, 132, 176, 209, 228
Lamparski, D. 137
Lange, M. 80, 142
Langer, E.J. 129, 228
Langewish, M.W.J. 116
Lea, S.E.G. 69
Leary, K. 120
Leblond, J. 87
Lee, G. 81
Lee, J. 82
Legg England, S. 230
LeGrande, J. 103
Lesieur, H.R. 54–5, 65, 66, 67, 68, 69, 73, 74, 79, 83, 99, 119–20, 121, 132, 138, 139, 158, 176, 209, 210, 226, 232, 249, 258
Leslie, E. 52
Lester, D. 56, 93, 94
Lin, N. 138
Linnoila, M. 137
Little, L. 227
London, M. 92, 93, 103–4
López-Viets, V.C. 226, 228
Lorangere, M. 55, 56, 176, 209

Lorenz, V. 102, 137
Lorenz, V.C. 56
Lyons, M.J. 138

McConaghy, N. 71–2, 136, 224, 228
McCormick, R.A. 116
McCown, W.G. 226, 227, 229, 231
MacDonald, H.F. 226, 231
McGee, L. 221
McKeigue, P. 92–3, 104, 216, 258
McKibbin, R. 13
McMillen, J. 251, 252, 253, 254, 255
MacMurray, P. 139
McNeilly, D.P. 82
Marcotte, M. 114
Mariani, F. 211
Marmot, M. 93
Marotta, J.J. 231
Marshall, M. 99
Martínez-Pina, A. 102
Maslin, J. 134
Masterman, C.F.G. 4
Mateo, M.M. 102
Maudsley, H. (1868) 63
Mayrand, M. 55, 56, 59, 87, 129
Meier, S. 135
Meltzer, H. 211
Meyer, G. 22, 58, 59, 67, 256
Miers, D. 1, 6, 27–8, 29, 30, 32, 33, 97, 103, 254
Miller, J.Y. 89
Miller, M. 54, 209, 249
Miller, W.R. 226, 227, 228, 230
Milt, H. 53, 56, 64, 70, 119, 121–2, 176, 209, 249
Minihan, M. 122
Mintel 93
Mitchell, L. x, 49, 178
Moggi, F. 231
Montgomery, H. 227
Moore, G. 52
Moore, S. 81–2
Moore, S.M. 87, 130
Moore, W.L. 23, 75–6, 80, 81, 96, 99, 104, 105, 158
Moran, E. 97, 119
Moran, J. 56
Moran, R. 53–4, 60, 82
Morison, V. 67–8, 132, 210
Morrison, V. 58
Mott, J. 13
Mudar, P. 125

Muhleman, D. 138, 139
Munck, I. 23, 75–6, 80, 81, 96, 99, 104, 105, 158
Murray, R. 139
Myers, F. 135

National Anti-Gambling League (NAGL) 7, 8–9, 10
National Heritage Committee 28
National Housing and Town Planning Council 82–3
National Opinion Research Center (NORC) 74, 79, 81
National Research Council (NRC) 72, 73, 74–5, 81, 85, 86, 91, 101, 102, 104–5, 113, 114, 136, 137, 139, 216, 221, 226, 228, 229, 230, 231, 232
Newcomb, M.D. 221
Newman, O. 107
Nichols, M. 42, 102, 134–5
Nilsson, T. 23, 75–6, 80, 81, 96, 99, 104, 105, 158
Nora, R.M. 79
Nordin, C. 137
Norman, A.C. 115, 120, 122, 129, 132
Nygren, T.E. 124

Ocean, G. 107–8
Ochoa, E. 22, 256
O'Connor, J. 133, 134, 136
Office of the National Lottery (OFLOT) 28, 103, 254
Ohtsuka, K. 87, 130
Olsson, N.G. 115
Orford, J. x, 36, 49, 65, 66, 67–8, 69, 70, 79, 89, 101, 117, 132, 134, 144, 149, 171, 178, 210, 216, 217, 218–19, 223, 225, 227, 249

Parker, J. 74, 102, 105
Patton, J. 115
Peck, C.P. 68
Peele, S. 231
Pepin, M. 55, 56, 176, 209
Pepys, S. 2
Perez de Castro, L.A. 139
Peto, J. 101
Petry, N.M. 124, 226, 229, 231
Petticrew, M. 211
Phillips, D.P. 56
Philps, M. 134

Planas, X.S. 102
Poe, E.A. 52
Preston, F.W. 255, 256
Pugh, P. 84, 104

Rands, J. 82
Reid, R.L. 97
Reisz 53
Reith, G. 1, 2, 6, 7, 12, 50, 121, 223
Renner, J. 99, 106
Rhéaume, N. 59, 87
Rich, T. 138
Ritchie, J. 177
Robertson, I. 230, 231
Roehrich, L. 137
Rogers, P. 125, 126, 127, 128, 129
Rönnberg, S. 23, 75–6, 80, 81, 96, 99, 104, 105, 158
Room, R. 21, 39, 41, 42
Rose, I.N. 21, 255, 256
Rosecrance, J. 106, 107, 111, 223, 224–5, 253
Rosenthal, R. 65, 66, 67, 68–9, 83, 102, 112, 113
Rosenthal, R.J. 121, 138, 139, 158
Roth, J. 129
Rothschild, J. 249
Rotter, J.B. 116
Roubin, J.Z. 128
Rowntree, B.S. 13
Roy, A. 137
Royal Commission on Betting, Lotteries and Gaming (Willink Commission) (1949–51) 5, 15, 18, 96, 248
Royal Commission on Gambling (the Rothschild Commission Report) (1978) 19, 19–20, 27, 63, 237, 258
Rugle, L. 116
Rugle, L.J. 138, 139
Rush, J.A. 86, 102, 105
Russell, M. 125

Saiz-Ruiz, J. 139
Saucier, G. 139
Scanlan, K.M. 21–2
Scarfe, A. 230
Scherrer, J.F. 138
Schotte, D. 122, 123
Schuckit, M.A. 139
Scott, M.B. 107
Searles, J. 138
Shaffer, H. 99, 106

Shaffer, H.J. 21–2, 72–3, 85, 87–8, 158
Sharpe, L. 106, 122, 123, 216, 217
Shepherd, R. 92, 93, 103–4
Sherrets, S.D. 249
Shewan, D. 123
Silov, D. 228
Silverman, D. 174
Simmel, E. 112
Sjöberg, L. 135
Skinner, B.F. 118
Skinner, J.B. 125
Smart, R. 231
Smith, G.J. 107–8
Smith, M.M. 56
Smith, S. 81, 82
Sobell, L. 231
Sobell, L.C. 231
Sobell, M. 231
Sobell, M.B. 135, 231
Social and Industrial Commission of the Church Assembly 7
Soedersten, P. 137
Somers, M. 67–8, 132, 210
Specker, S.M. 114
Spectrum Children's Trust 82
Spence, S.H. 122, 123
Spencer, L. 177
Spitznagel, E.L. 56, 114
Spring, H. 52
Sproston, K. x, 36, 49, 79, 144, 149, 171
Squires, P. 51, 209
Stabenau, J. 139
Stadler, M.A. 58, 59
Steel, Z. 114
Stekel, W. 53, 209
Stevens, L. 86, 102, 105
Stewart, R.M. 227
Stinchfield, R. 85, 87, 228
Stitt, B.G. 42, 102, 134–5, 249
Strauss, A. 174
Strickland, L. 97
Suits, D. 73
Sullivan, S. 56
Sutherland, I. 101
Svensson, O. 23, 75–6, 80, 81, 96, 99, 104, 105, 158
Sylvain, C. 55, 56, 176, 209, 228

Taber, J.I. 113
Tan, B. 79
Tarpy, R.M. 69

Tarrier, N. 122, 123, 216, 217
Thomas, S.A. 81, 82
Thomason, N. 81, 82
Tidwell, M. 74, 102, 105
Toneatto, T. 231
Tonigan, J.S. 227
Tonigan, S. 230
Torres, P. 139
Toscova, R. 227
Tourigny, M. 55, 56, 59, 87, 129
Trevorrow, K. 81–2
Trimpop, R.M. 135
True, W.R. 138
Tsuang, M.T. 138
Tsytsarev, S.V. 23
Tucker, J. 231
Turner, N.E. 21, 39, 41, 42
Tversky, A. 124, 125, 127

Vakili, S. 135
Vallejo, M.A. 22, 256
Vallverdu, R.F. 102
Vander Bilt, J. 72–3, 158
Vandiver, M. 249
Vitaro, F. 87, 102, 116
Volberg, R. 81, 90
Volberg, R.A. 23, 75–6, 77–8, 79, 80, 81, 96, 99, 102, 104, 105, 158, 212

Wagenaar, W.A. 127
Walker, M. 87, 126, 127, 128, 129, 130, 131, 132
Walker, M.B. 70, 74, 77, 79, 80, 90, 115–16, 117, 216–17, 219, 224
Waller, S. 101
Walters, G.D. 125
Walton, F. 82
Ward, D.A. 135
Warren, L. 135
Webley, P. 69, 84, 101, 104, 128
Weinstein, D. 96
Weissing, L. 211
Welte, J. 74, 102, 105
Welte, J.W. 101, 105, 116
Welty, W.R. 56
Westphal, J.R. 86, 102, 105
Wexler, A. 56
White, C. x, 49, 178
White, N.M. 122
Whyte, K.S. 252
Wieczorek, W. 74, 102, 105
Wilde, G.J.S. 135

Williamson, J. 128
Winefield, A.H. 133
Winter, A.S. 136
Winters, K.C. 85, 87, 138, 228
Wise, R.A. 122, 138
Wood, T.A. 100, 101
Wray, I. 67
Wu, S. 139

Yaffee, R.A. 56
Yeoman, T. 61

Zola, I.K. 107
Zoppa, R.M. 99
Zuckerman, M. 115, 116
Zurcher, L.A. 107
Zweig, F. 51

Subject index

accessibility of gambling *see* availability/ accessibility of gambling
across case analysis 178
action-seeking behaviour 109–10, 121
addiction 219; unreliable definition/ understanding of 65, 69; *see also* addiction to gambling; alcohol consumption/dependence; drug use/ dependence
addiction to gambling 41, 62–72; addiction potential 213–14, 232, 233; classification of 64–7, **66**, 71–2; confusion regarding the validity of 69–70; diagnosis 65; as disorder of dependence 65, 66–7; as disorder of impulse control 64, 66–7; future research into 232, 233; modelled on addiction to alcohol/drugs 65, 66, 70; and the need for industry regulation 46; as pure addiction 70; qualitative study of 181, 182, 203–5; as stage of gambling 217; type of addiction 223–6; in young people 60–1
Addiction Research Center Inventory 119
adoption method 138
advertising 48, 207–8, 237
African Americans 105
age 152–4, *154*, 161–4, *162*, *163*; age limits on gambling 236, 239, 244; of gambling onset (early start hypothesis) 105–6, 219, 220–1; and problem gambling 214–15; *see also* children; young people
alcohol consumption/dependence 67, 68; and availability of alcohol 90, 93; and disinhibition 134–5; and expectancy 125; and gambling on the same

premises 236, 237, 240, 243, 257; link with problem gambling 101–3, 134–6; modelling of addiction to gambling on 65, 66, 70; parallels with problem gambling 182, 210; prevalence 75; and the reduction of self control 199–200; role in chasing 136; single distribution theory of 93; treatment of and the treatment of problem gambling 226, 227, 230–1
Alcoholics Anonymous (AA) 227, 231, 232
ambient gambling 236
ambivalent attitudes to gambling 4, 6–7, 125, *125*, 249, 253, 255
American Gaming Association (AGA) 252
American Indians 22, 91
American Journal of Psychology 51
amusement arcades 22, 23, 221–2; availability of 199; as cultural spaces 111; expenditure/spend on 202–3, 206; first gambling experience in 185; and the Gambling Review Report 2001 239–40, 257, 258, 260; illegal 46; liberal attitudes to 256; and the qualitative interview study of problem gambling 180, 185, 187, 199, 202–3, 206; seaside 185, 199, 221–2, 239–40, 256, 258, 260; and the social functions of gambling 108–11
amusement-with-prizes (AWP) machines 34, 35, 36, 239
anti-depressants 229
anti-gambling organisations 7–11
anti-gambling sentiment 2, 6–11, 16, 248–53

Anti-Puritan League 9
antisocial personality disorder (ASPD) 114
anxiety 56, 58, 67, 68, 205
'Apprentices' 109
arousal 119–20, *120*, 121, 123, 125, *126*, 132, 216, 217, 219
atmosphere 192
attachment 218
attitudes to gambling 1, 168, *170*; 20th century 13–20; ambivalent 4, 6–7, 125, *125*, 249, 253, 255; class divisions in 12; effects of the National Lottery on 32, 251; liberalisation of 252–3, 256; negative 2, 6–11, 16, 248–53; positive 253–4, 255, 260; regarding risk taking 124
Australia 21, 27, 28–9, 57, 106, 241; attitudes to gambling 251–2, 253; availability of gambling 90, 93, 94, 221; chasing losses 133; classical conditioning of gambling 123; cost-benefit analysis of gambling 39, 42, 44–6; help seeking in 93, 94; internet gambling 36; machine gambling 44–5; prevalence of problem gambling 75, 79, 81–2, 87, 90, 212; social groups at risk 99; substance abuse and gambling 102; treatment of problem gambling 231
Australian Casino Association 43
Austria 29
availability heuristic 127
availability/accessibility of gambling 89–98, 221–2; and the British Gambling Prevalence Survey 1999 257, 259–60; and help-seeking behaviour 93–4; limiting 207–8; multifaceted nature of 95, *95*; and prevalence of problem gambling 90–3, 198–9; and the structural characteristics of gambling activities 95–8

bans, self-requested 59
bear-bating 2
'beating the system' 107, 190
beginner's luck 119, 185
benefits of gambling 39–49, 222, 253–4, 255, 260
Betting Act 1853 2, 9, 13

Betting and Gaming Act 1960 14, 18–19, 46
Betting, Gaming and Lotteries (Amendment) Act 1984 19–20
Betting and Loans (Infants) Act 1892 15
Betting and Lotteries Act 1934 17
Betting Office Licensees Association (BOLA) 140, 141
betting offices: gambling machines in 36; and the Gambling Review Report 2001 237, 243, 244; regulation 18, 19–20; and sex differences 82; spread of 23; *see also* bookmakers; dog racing; horse racing; off-course betting
biases: cognitive 126–8, **127**; hindsight (biased evaluation of outcomes) 129–30; research 254–5
big six (card game) 34
binge gambling 202
bingo 23; age factors 214–15; attitudes to 251, 254; and the British Gambling Prevalence Survey 1999 145, 150, 152, 154, 155, 156, 157, 168; commercialisation of 22; deregulation 35; effects of the National Lottery on 30; emotional responses to 192, 193; expenditure/spend on 150, 203; as first gambling experience 182, 184; and gambling machines 34; and the Gambling Review Report 2001 237, 241, 244; image 181; and income 215; and internet gambling 37; participants 152, 154, 155, 156, 157; and problem gambling 81, 82, 168, 213, 214; and the qualitative interview study of problem gambling 175, 178, 180, 181, 182, 184, 192, 193, 198, 203; regulation of 25; and sex differences 81, 82, 214–15, 254; and social class 215, 254; turnover 25, 30
Bingo Association (BA) 30, 140, 141
biological theories of problem gambling 136–9, 222; brain studies 136–7; genetic studies 137–9
Birmingham University x
births, marriages, deaths, gambling on 2
blackjack (card game) 34
Blackpool 237, 243, 244, 245, 246–7, 248

bookmakers 2, 12, 13; availability of
199; and the British Gambling
Prevalence Survey 1999 145–6, 149;
emotional responses to 193;
expenditure/spend on 201, 203; as first
gambling experience 183–4; illegal 14,
15–16, 46; image 181; and internet
gambling 37; National Anti-
Gambling League's attack on 9; not
dogs/horses 145–6, 149, 164, 213;
preparation for 187, 188; and problem
gambling 164, 214; and the qualitative
interview study of problem gambling
178, 180, 181, 183–4, 187, 188, 193,
199, 201, 203; regulation of 17, 18;
rise of 1; and telephone betting 23; use
of runners/dummies 14, 15; *see also*
betting offices; dog racing; horse
racing; off-course betting
boredom relief, gambling as 189, 191,
194
Bottomley, Horatio 14
bowls 4, 5
brain studies 136–7, 229
Brewers' and Licensed Retail
Association (BLRA) 140, 141
British Amusement Catering Trades
Association (BACTA) 25, 35, 140,
141, 239, 258
British Association of Leisure Parks,
Piers and Attractions (BALPPA) 258
British Broadcasting Corporation
(BBC) 28, 48
British Casino Association (BCA) 34,
140, 141
British Gambling Prevalence Survey
1999 x, 26, 49, 76, 80, 83, 140–73,
208–9, 211–16, 222, 224–5, 233–4,
244; aims 141; background 140–1; on
expenditure/spend 149–52, **151**; and
future research 232; gambling
groupings 146–7, **147**; on gambling
last year and last week 144–9, **145**,
146, **147**, *148*, 214; instruments for
assessing problem gambling 158–61,
159–60, **161**, 162–72, *162*, *163*, **165**,
166, *167*, **170**; and marginalisation of
the family 250; participants 152–7,
153; and the prevalence of gambling
144–57; and the prevalence of
problem gambling 158–70; and the
qualitative interview study of problem

gambling 174–5, 177; questions asked
142; response rate 143, **143**; sampling
and procedure 142–4; sampling
problems 143–4, 158
British Horseracing Board 48, 140
Budd, Sir Alan 235, 244, 246, 257
Business in Sport and Leisure (BISL)
23–5
Butler, Home Secretary 18

Cadburys 10
Camelot 28, 140, 141
Canada 21, 28–9, 255; availability-
prevalence link 90, 92; cost-benefit
analysis of gambling 39–42, **40**, 43;
emotional rewards of gambling 121;
problem gambling 55, 56, 72–3, 75,
85, 86–7, 230, 231; social functions of
gambling 107–8; social groups at risk
99–100; treatment of problem
gambling 230, 231
capitalism 7
carbamazepine 229
card games 5, 51; casino-type 34;
expenditure/spend on 201; as first
gambling experience 183; and the
illusion of control 129; and player sex
differences 82; and the qualitative
interview study of problem gambling
178, 180, 183, 201; *see also specific
card games*
'career', gambling 194–5, 217–19, *218*
Caribbean 36
casino brag (card game) 34
casino stud poker (card game) 34
casinos/casino table games: and age at
which gambling started 105; and
alcohol consumption 237, 243; and
arousal level 120; backlash against the
liberalisation of 255; and the British
Gambling Prevalence Survey 1999
146, 150, 155, 156–7, 164, 165–7; and
classical conditioning 122; cost-benefit
analysis of 39–43, **40**; deregulation of
34–5; diversification of games 34; the
drop 25; expenditure/spend on 150; as
first gambling experience 183; and the
gambler's fallacy 128; gambling
machines in 34–5, 237, 240, 246;
gambling prevalence estimates 76–7,
81; and the Gambling Review Report
2001 237, 240, 241, 243, 244, 245–7,

248; image 181; and income 215; and
internet gambling 37; *laissez-faire*
attitude to 252; legalisation, 1960s 5,
18; participants 155, 156–7; and
player sex differences 81; and problem
gambling 57, 59, 62, 76–7, 81, 164,
165–7, 213, 257; and the qualitative
interview study of problem gambling
175, 178, 180, 181, 183; regulation of
25, 35, 48; resort casinos 237, 243,
246–7, 248, 256; riverboat casinos 32,
91; and self-banning 59; and social
class 215; and the social functions of
gambling 107–8; spread of 21–2, 23;
and telephone helplines 230; turnover
25; US attitudes to 251; and young
people 62
causes of problem gambling 89–139;
role of alcohol 134–6; availability/
accessibility 89–98; biological factors
136–9, 222; cautions regarding 105–6;
chasing losses 132–3; role of
cognition 123–32; ecology 89–98;
multifaceted nature of 89, 216–23,
217; person-centred theories 90;
positive personal-social functions of
gambling 106–11; psychodynamic/
personality theories 112–17; social
groups at risk 98–106; theories based
on reward/reinforcement 117–23
chance 7
character strength 107, 108–9, 111
charity sweepstakes 17, 18
chasing losses 132–3, 136, 171, 210, 233
children: effects of problem gambling on
249, 250; and street betting 15; *see
also* young people
choice 186–7, 194, 223
Churchill, Winston 16, 17
classical/Pavlovian conditioning 122–3
clomipramine 229
cock fighting 2
cognition 123–32, 216–19, 222–3, 228;
attitudes to risk taking 124; cognitive
biases 126–8, **127**; expectancies 125;
illusion of control 127, 128–32; near
misses 125
cognitive behavioural therapy (CBT)
226, 228–9
coin games 2–4, 129
commercialisation of gambling 19–20,
22

competitive advantage 30
compulsive gambling 181, 182, 190–1,
204
Connoisseur, The 2
Conservative Party 27, 33
consumer surplus 43–4
context 179–80
control 1, 107, 109, 111, 210; belief in
exerting 186; degree of 180, 182;
illusion of 127, 128–32, 228; locus of
115–16; loss of 181, 182, 194, 201–5,
209–12, 223, 224–5, 226; reduction
through drinking alcohol 199–200;
variation in 200–2
Corals 140
cost-benefit analysis 39–46, **40**
counselling 207, 226, 228
Court of Appeal 9
credit card gambling 237–8
crime associated with gambling 44,
204–5; amongst young gamblers 60,
61–2, 83, 85, 110; due to problem
gambling 55, 57, 58–9, 60, 61–2, 83,
85; and the Gambling Review Report
2001 236, 246; nature of offences 59;
and the need for regulation 46, 47; in
the USA 251
criminal justice system 64
crown bowling 5
Customs and Excise 17
cycles of gambling 204, 210

D1 receptor gene 139
D2 receptor gene 138
D4 receptor gene 139
Daily Express 60, 241–2, 243, 244, 245,
247
Daily Mail 242, 243, 244, 245, 257
Daily Sport 242, 243, 244, 247
Daily Star 242, 243
Daily Telegraph 242, 243, 244, 247
debt *see* financial problems
deception 205–6
decision making 186–7, 194
decriminalisation of gambling 16–17
delay discounting studies 124
demand: elasticity of 43–4; unstimulated
237
demarcation of offering 48
Denmark 29
Department for Culture, Media and
Sport (DCMS) xi, 140, 141, 235–6

dependence *see* addiction; addiction to gambling; alcohol consumption/dependence; drug use/dependence
depression 56, 58, 205, 210, 229, 230, 257
deregulation *see* liberalisation of gambling
Deregulation and Contracting Out Act 1994 33–4
destructive aspects of gambling 203–6, 210–11; *see also* financial problems/debt
developmental aspect of gambling 217–19, *218*, 222
Diagnostic and Statistical Manual of Mental Disorders (DSM) 62, 64, 69, 70, 71, 72, 73, 86, 113, 223
Diagnostic and Statistical Manual of Mental Disorders, Third Edition (DSM-III) 64–5, 70, 85
Diagnostic and Statistical Manual of Mental Disorders, Third Edition-Revised (DSM-III-R) 65, 71, 73, 74, 77, 123
Diagnostic and Statistical Manual of Mental Disorders, Fourth Edition (DSM-IV) 65–7, **66**, 74, 76, 79, 81, 87, 92, 211–12, 214–16, 224; comparison with the South Oaks Gambling Screen 170–2, **170**; DSM-IV-J 83, 84, 86–7, 100; DSM-IV-MR-J 83–4; and the qualitative interview study of problem gambling 174, 175, 176–7; reliability 171–2; thresholds 225; use in the British Gambling Prevalence Survey 1999 158, **159–60**, 160–1, **161**, 162–3, *163*, 165–72, **165**
dice 34, 129
disabled people 155
disordered gambling 73
disposable income 2, 103, 196, 204, 206–7
dissociative states 121
distributions, skewed 225
dog fighting 2
dog racing 1, 4, 18, 23; availability of 199; and the British Gambling Prevalence Survey 1999 145–6, 149, 150, 155, 164, 165; emotional responses to 192; expenditure/spend on 150, 201, 203; as first gambling experience 182, 184; participants 155;

and problem gambling 164, 165, 213; and the qualitative interview study of problem gambling 178, 182, 184, 186, 192, 199, 201, 203; and social class 12
dopamine/dopamine receptors 138–9, 229
"downers" 204
drug use/dependence 67, 71, 223; genetic aspects of 139; link with problem gambling 101–3; modelling of addiction to gambling on 65, 66, 70; parallels with problem gambling 182, 210; prevalence 75, 211; and substance availability/accessibility 90; tolerance/withdrawal 69; treatment of and the treatment of problem gambling 226, 230–1
duties on gambling 16, 17, 19; *see also* taxation

e-commerce 37; *see also* internet gambling
early fertile ground theory 221
early start hypothesis 105–6, 219, 220–1
early win hypothesis 119, 219, 220
East Germany 23
Eastern Europe 23
Easy Play 29
ecology 89–98
economic activity of gamblers 154–5, 162, **164**
economic benefits of gambling 39, 40, **40**, 41–3, 254, 255
Economist, The 15
education 104, 108, 155, 156–7, 162, **164**, 215
Edward VII, King of England 8
elasticity of demand 43–4
electroencephalograph (EEG) 137
electromyography (EMG) 123
emotional responses to gambling 222; emotional release/distraction 189–90, 191, 194; emotional rewards of gambling 119–22, *120*; in uncontrolled gambling 205; varied 191–4
employment 15; *see also* unemployment
endorphins 222
Enlightenment 6
entrapment 128, 133, 210, 233

environmental problems of gambling 39, 40, **40**
ephemeral role of gambling 107
'Escape Artists' 110–11
escapism 106–7, 109–11, 121, 189–90, 191, 194
ethnicity 104–5, 108, 157, 233
event frequency 96
excitement 119–20, *120*, 121, 191, 222
expectancies: negative 125, *126*; positive 125, *126*
expenditure/spend 212; and the availability-prevalence link 92–3, *94*; controlling 200–1, 206; cost-benefit analysis of 43–4; and criminal activity 204–5; as definition of gambling 178, 179; differing interpretations of 149–50; estimating 80, **80**; family/household 92–3, *94*, 216; and fluctuating life pathways 195; international increases in 21, 22; on lotteries 29, 30, **31**, 103–4, 201, 203, 212, 216; of lower income groups 103, 215–16; net 149, 150; on normal gambling according to the British Gambling Prevalence Survey 1999 149–52, **151**, 156, *157*; per capita 26–7, 29, 90; as percentage of total consumer spend 30, **31**; on problem gambling according to the British Gambling Prevalence Survey 1999 168, **169**; as a proportion of income 103–4, 156, *157*, 215–16; uncontrolled 201–3, 204–5; of young gamblers 110; *see also* financial problems/debt
extraversion 115, 117

false negatives 78, 79, 211
false positives 77, 78–9, 158, 211
families, effects of gambling on 51, 54–7, 59, 72, 205, 245; neglect by the Gambling Review Report 2001 249–53; overcoming problem gambling 206–7; treatment of problem gambling 226, 231–2; young person's gambling 60, 61–2, 85; *see also* parental gambling; partners
Family Expenditure Survey (FES) 92–3
fantasies: of grandeur 112, 113; of winning 188–9, 191

Farmington Consensus 259
feminisation of gambling 81–2
fiction, gambling in 52–3
films, gambling in 53
financial problems/debt: amongst young gamblers 60–1, 110; and criminal activity 55, 58–9; due to problem gambling 54, 55, 57, 58, 201–3, 204–5, 206–7; secondary poverty 50; and suicide 57, 58, 60
Financial Services Authority (FSA) 38
financial support 207
fines 15, 16
first gambling experiences 177, 182–6; influences 182–5, 186; salience 185–6
fixed-ratio (FR) schedules 118
fluvoxamine 229
focused-interest gamblers 147, 155, 167, 168, 175
Football Association (FA) 11
Football League 11
football pools 4–5, 10–11, 18; age factors 214; and the British Gambling Prevalence Survey 1999 145, 149, 150, 152, 157, 168, 172; deregulation 33; effect of the National Lottery on 29–30, 33; emotional responses to 192; expenditure/spend on 150; and the Gambling Review Report 2001 238, 241; and internet gambling 37; jackpots 5; participants 152, 157; preparation for 188; and problem gambling 168, 172, 213, 214; public attitudes to 251; and the qualitative interview study of problem gambling 178, 188, 192, 203; spread of 23; 'treble chance' 5, 29; turnover 29–30
forms of gambling 1, 212–13; diversity of 2–6; form-specific theories of gambling 219; and social class 12; *see also specific forms of gambling*
Framework 177–8
France 23, 35
frequency distribution curves 93
friends' gambling 100–1, 184

Gala Leisure 242, 244
Gam-Anon 170, 226, 232

Gamblers Anonymous (GA) 54–5, 56, 59, 64, 67, 71, 138, 176, 202; '20 Questions' 79, 85; availability-help seeking link 93–4; and the British Gambling Prevalence Survey 1999 170; drop-out rates 227; economic issues 216; on the Gambling Review Report 2001 245; helpline of 230; overcoming problem gambling 207; and the treatment of problem gambling 226–7, 230, 231, 232; and the unconscious wish to lose 112; and uncontrolled gambling 209, 211; and young people 61, 85
gambler's fallacy 118, 128, 132
Gambling Commission 236, 237, 238, 241, 243
Gambling Expectancy Effects Questionnaire (GEEQ) 125
gambling industry: and the British Gambling Prevalence Survey 1999 141; concerns regarding regulation 47–8; deregulation 32–9; and gambling research 258–9; and the Gambling Review Report 2001 xi, 234, 242–3, 248, 257; and government 253; growth in Britain 23–7; international growth 21–3; and problem gambling 64, 70, 258–9; profits 26; scale at the end of the twentieth century 23–5, **24**; and treatment of problem gambling 258–9
gambling machines 5, 11, 250; addiction potential 214; age limits for 236; alcohol and 136; all-cash 34, 237, 240; amusement-with-prizes (AWP) machines 34, 35, 36, 239; and arousal level 120; aura of 97; availability/accessibility of 91, 199, 207, 208, 209, 221, 222; backlash against the liberalisation of 255; and the British Gambling Prevalence Survey 1999 145, 146, 149, 150, 152, 153–4, 155, 165, 168; and casino deregulation 34–5; chasing losses with 133; and classical conditioning 122; deregulation 34–6; emotional responses to 192; expenditure/spend on 21, 150, 200–1, 202–3; as first gambling experience 182, 183, 184; and the Gambling Review Report 2001 237, 238–40, 241, 243, 244, 245,

246, 257, 260; gambling strategies for 187; and the illusion of control 130, 131, 132; international increase in 21, 22, 23; and internet gambling 37; jackpots 34; Japanese 22; liberal attitudes to 256; limiting the availability of 207, 208, 209; locations of 44, 239; names of 97–8; and near misses 97; and operant learning 118; participants 152, 153–4, 155; payouts 34, 240; and peer pressure 101; and problem gambling 60–2, 72, 81–4, 88, 165, 168, 213–14, 257; and the qualitative interview study of problem gambling 178, 182–4, 186–7, 192, 199–203, 207–9; regulation of 25, 47–8; and skill 97, 108–9, 116, 130; and social class 215; and the social functions of gambling 108–11; structural features of 96–8; and telephone helplines 230; turnover 25; types 239; and women 81–2; and young people 60–1, 62, 82–4, 88, 97, 116, 153–4, 239–40, 244, 257
Gambling Review Report 2001 x–xi, 30, 38, 48–9, 98, 234–48; Department of Culture, Media and Sport 235–6; failures of 257–60; and gambling machines 237, 238–40, 241, 243, 244, 245, 246, 257, 260; general principles 236; government welcoming of 247–8; and the National Lottery 235, 237, 238, 240–1, 242, 244; negative views of gambling in the face of 248; new freedoms in the provision of gambling 236–8; press response to 241–8, 257, 260; terms of reference 234–5
gambling sheds 244
Gambling Trust 258–9
GamCare x, xi, 140, 141, 170, 230, 232
Gaming Act 1968 19, 25, 33, 46, 254
Gaming Regulator 48
Gateshead Times 15
gender differences *see* sex differences
General Household Survey 232
general practitioners (GPs) 207
genetic studies 137–9
Gentleman's Magazine, The 7
Germany 7, 22, 23, 32, 58–9, 93, 106, 256
Gordon House Association 229–30, 232

government: abdication of responsibility 259; attitudes to gambling 253–5, 256; and the Gambling Review Report 2001 247–8
grandeur, fantasies of 112, 113
grandparents' gambling 99
group norms 107–8
Guardian, The 242, 243, 244, 247
guilt 112, 113, 193

habitual gambling 188, 190, 191
Hattersley, Roy 245, 257
heart rate (HR) 123
help-seeking 93–4, 169–70, 207, 230
hemispheric deregulation 137
hierarchical cluster analysis 146
Hilton Group 242, 243
Hispanics 105
Hoggart, David 50
Holland 93
Home Office x, 12, 20, 27, 140, 141, 258; and betting duties 17; and deregulation 33–4, 36; and the Gambling Review Report 2001 xi, 235, 237; and street betting 9
Horse Race Betting Levy Board 140
horse racing 2; and arousal level 120, *120*; attitudes to 6–7, 8; availability of 199; and biological explanations of gambling 136; and the British Gambling Prevalence Survey 1999 145, 146, 149, 150, 152, 155, 156, 165, 168, 172; effect of the National Lottery on 30; emotional responses to 192; expenditure/spend on 150, 201, 202, 203, 212; as first gambling experience 182, 184, 185; and income 215; and life pathways 195; National Anti-Gambling League's attack on 9; participants 152, 155, 156; preparation for 187, 188; and problem gambling 54, 82, 165, 168, 172, 212, 213, 214; and the qualitative interview study of problem gambling 178, 182, 184–8, 192, 195, 199, 201–3; regulation of 17–18; and social class 215; turnover 30; *see also* race courses

IG Group 39
illegal gambling 236
illogical beliefs 123–32
image 181–2, 220

imaginal desensitisation (ID) 228
impulsivity 116, 117, 124
incentive conditioning/learning 122–3
income 103–4, 215; disposable 2, 103, 196, 204, 206–7; household 156, *157*, 162, **164**, **165**; of lower-income groups 103–4, 108, 215–16; proportional spend on gambling 103–4, 215–16
Independent 242–4, 246–7
Independent on Sunday 245–6
Industrial Revolution 2
International Classification of Diseases (ICD) 62, 64, 69, 223
internet gambling 23; and the British Gambling Prevalence Survey 1999 141, 142, 145, 149; deregulation of 36–8; and the Gambling Review Report 2001 237, 238; Gaming Board's lack of knowledge of 26; on-line betting/gambling distinction 238; prevalence 232
interviews, cognitive 142, 143
Ireland 29
irrationality 126–32
Italy 29

Japan 22
Jazz Co-ordination Association 44
Jockey Club 48
Jowell, Tessa 247
judgement 186, 194; suspension of 97

'Kings' 108–9, 111
Kipling, Rudyard 4, 6

Labour Party 8, 9, 27, 33, 235
Ladbrokes 22, 140, 242, 243
legislation: 20th century 13–20; Betting Act 1853 2, 9, 13; Betting and Gaming Act, 1960 14, 18–19, 46; Betting, Gaming and Lotteries (Amendment) Act, 1984 19–20; Betting and Loans (Infants) Act 1892 15; Betting and Lotteries Act, 1934 17; Deregulation and Contracting Out Act 1994 33–4; Gaming Act, 1968 19, 25, 33, 46, 254; key dates **3**; National Lottery Act 1993 19, 27; Street Betting Act 1906 9, 13–14, 15–16
leisure, gambling as a harmless form of 44, 189, 248, 252–4, 256
Leisure Parcs 242, 243

liberalisation of gambling xi, 22, 32–9;
attitudinal liberalisation 252–3; and
the availability-prevalence link 90–1;
backlash against 255–6; in the
Gambling Review Report 2001
235–6, 236–8, 241–2, 244, 245–6,
247, 248, 257, 260; and internet
gambling 36–8; and problem
gambling 60, 63; and spread betting
38–9; use of stigma neutralization
techniques for 256; and young people
60
licensing 25, 28; casinos 35; internet
gambling 36, 38
licensing magistrates 19
Lie/Bet Questionnaire 79
life influences on gambling 195–200, **197**
life pathways 194–5; declining 194, 195;
fluctuating 194–5, 217–19, *218*; stable
194, 195
lithium carbonate 229
Littlewoods 4–5
local authorities 236
locus of control 115–16
logistic regression analysis 163–4, **165**
London Clubs International 140
losses: and the British Gambling
Prevalence Survey 1999 150–2, **151**,
156, *157*, 168, **169**; chasing 132–3,
136, 171, 210, 233; emotional
responses to 192–3, 194, 205; and first
experiences of gambling 185; influence
on other people's gambling 198; and
problem gambling 168, **169**; as a
proportion of income 156, *157*; and
risk-seeking behaviour 124;
unconscious wish to lose theory 63,
64, 112–13
lotteries 5; age factors 214, 236; and the
British Gambling Prevalence Survey
1999 145, 149, 150; expenditure/spend
on 150; and the Gambling Review
Report 2001 238; gambling systems
for 186–7; international expansion of
21–2, 23, 28–9; and internet gambling
37; 'keno' 32; legalisation 27; and
problem gambling 81, 213, 214; public
attitudes to 6, 251; and the qualitative
interview study of problem gambling
178, 186–7, 191; regulation of 17,
25–6; and sex differences 81, 214;
'speil games' 32; takings 28–9, 30;

video lotteries 32; *see also* National
Lottery
luck 128; beginner's 119, 185

MacDonald, Ramsey 8
'Machine Beaters' 110
machine gambling *see* gambling
machines
magnetic resonance imaging (MRI) 137
Mail on Sunday 244, 246
Manchester Evening News 11
mania 63; gambling as a form of 53, 63,
209
marital status 154, 162, **164**, **165**
Massachusetts Gambling Screen
(MAGS) 85
medical (illness) model of gambling
224–6, 250
Memorandum of the Roman Catholic
Church 5
men and gambling: expenditure/spend
of 150–2; participation in gambling
152; prevalence of problem gambling
in 81, 161–4, *162*, *163*;
underrepresentation in the British
Gambling Prevalence Survey 1999 144
Methodist church 244, 245, 248
middle classes 9, 11, 52–3
Mirror 242, 244
mood, positive, and risk taking 12
Moody, Gordon 10, 229
moral discourse on gambling: death of
256; sidelining 248, 252–3
Morning Post 5
motivations for gambling 188–91, 194,
222
multiple-interest gamblers 147, 154, 155,
156, 167, 172, 175, 213, 233
multiplier potential 96

naltrexone 229
National Bingo Game Association
(NBGA) 140, 141
National Centre for Social Research
(NatCen) x, xi, 49, 140, 141, 174, 177
National Council on Compulsive
Gambling (later National Council on
Problem Gambling) 64
National Council of Welfare 21
National Gambling Impact Study
Commission 74, 252
National Gambling Survey 90

National Greyhound Racing Club 48
National Lottery Act 1993 19, 27
National Lottery Commission (NLC)
    28, 140, 141, 241
National Lottery Distribution Fund
    (NLDF) 254
National Lottery (NL) 5, 10, 16, 26,
    27–31; addiction potential 213; age
    factors 84, 214; availability of 92, 93,
    199, 221; in betting offices 237, 244;
    and the British Gambling Prevalence
    Survey 1999 141, 145, 146, 147, 149,
    150, 155, 164, 165, 167, 168, 172;
    competitive advantage of 30; and
    education 104; and entrapment 128;
    expenditure/spend on 103–4, 150, 168,
    201, 203, 212, 216; freedom of 32–3;
    and the gambler's fallacy 128; and the
    Gambling Review Report 2001 235,
    237, 238, 240–1, 242, 244; gambling
    strategies/number selection 187, 223;
    Gaming board's ignorance of 25; and
    the illusion of control 129; and
    income group 103–4; influence of
    parental gambling on 100, 101; and
    the legitimisation of gambling 25,
    27–8, 32, 180, 181, 241, 246, 251, 254,
    256; lucky dips 129; and the
    Methodist church 248; and near
    misses 97; not seen as a gambling
    activity 180, 241, 254, 256; odds 126,
    127; participants 155; and peer
    pressure 101; and player sex
    differences 214; popularity of 145;
    and problem gambling 164, 165, 167,
    168, 212, 213; and the qualitative
    interview study of problem gambling
    178, 180, 181, 186, 187, 198, 199, 201,
    203; regulation 19, 28, 29, 241; spread
    of 23; stir caused by 141; success 28;
    takings 26, 28–9, 30; and telephone
    helplines 230; Thunderball 27
National Lottery scratchcards:
    expenditure/spend and income group
    103–4; influence of parental gambling
    on 100, 101; National Lottery
    Instants 27, 28, 30; and problem
    gambling 213; and young people 84,
    88
nationalisation of gambling 16
naturalisation of gambling 183
near misses 97, 125, 133

negative aspects of gambling 39–49,
    203–6, 210–11; psychological 56–8,
    67, 68, 205; see also financial
    problems/debt
The Netherlands 22–3, 29
neurosis, gambling as 63–4, 112–13
neurotransmitters 136–7, 229
New Statesman 246
New Zealand 27, 28–9, 75, 77, 90, 102,
    212
noradrenalin 136, 137
NORC DSM Screen for Gambling
    Problems (NODS) 74
norepinephrine 229
normalization of gambling 19
norms 107–8, 220
Norway 29

Oakley, Robin 48
Observer 246
obsessive gambling behaviour 190–1
odds 96; odds ratios 163–4
Oedipal Complex 112
off-course betting 22, 26, 230; see also
    betting offices; bookmakers
Office for National Statistics (ONS) 92,
    143–4, 236, 251, 258
omnipotence 112, 113
on-line gambling see internet gambling
OPCS survey of psychiatric disorders
    211
operant/Skinnerian conditioning
    117–19; fixed-interval (FI)/variable-
    ratio (VR)/random ratio (RR)
    schedules 120; fixed-ratio (FR)
    schedules 118; gradient of
    reinforcement 118; inconsistent
    reinforcement 118; probabilities 118;
    random ratio (RR) schedules 118–19;
    variable-ratio (VR) schedules 118, 119
opioids, endogenous 136
optimism 181
other people, influences on gambling
    221; discouragement 196–8;
    encouragement 196, 198; see also
    friends' gambling; parental gambling;
    partners
outlay 149
overcoming problem gambling 206–8;
    see also treatment/prevention of
    problem gambling

'pachinko' (Japanese gambling machines) 22
Palmer, William 50
parental discouragement of gambling 196
parental gambling 98–100; influence on first gambling experiences 183–4, 186; and problem gambling 162–3, 164, **165**, 219–20
Parents of Young Gamblers (self-help group) 61
Parliamentary Deregulation Committee 36
partners: discouragement of gambling 196–8; effects of problem gambling on 249, 250; effects of uncontrolled gambling on 205–6; overcoming problem gambling 206; and the treatment of problem gambling 226, 231–2
pathological gambling 62–7, **66**, 69–72, 72, 211, 223, 224; and age at which gambling started 105; and the availability-prevalence link 91, 92; biological explanations of 136–7, 138; and the British Gambling Prevalence Survey 1999 158, 160; classical conditioning of 123; DSM definitions of 225; and escapism 121; estimation of 73, 74, 76, 85, 86, 87; and ethnicity 105; and expectancies 125; expenditure/spend and income level 104; and impulsivity 116; and marginalisation of the family 250; and parental gambling 100; and personality disorders 113; and substance abuse 101–2
payment ratio 96
payout interval 96
peer pressure see friends' gambling
People's Lottery, The (White Paper) 27
person-centred theories 90
personal-social functions of gambling 106–11, 189
personality disorders 113–15
personality traits 115–17, 222
pharmacological treatment of problem gambling 226, 229
physical effects of gambling 56, 67, 68
pigeon racing 4, 5, 12
Pilgrim Trust 13

'pitch-and-toss' (game) 2–4, 51
play, gambling as 107
pleasure of gambling 189; replacement by the need to gamble 204
poker 107, 132
Poland 23
police: corruption 15; and slot-machine gambling 11; and street betting 9, 14–15; and working class gambling 12
Police Federation 15
Portugal 29
positive aspects of gambling 39–49, 106–11, 189, 222, 253–5, 260
positron emission tomography (PET) 137
postcode address file (PAF) 142
poverty 13, 50
premises 149; availability of 23; impact of gambling machines on 44; local authority power over 236; role of 221–2; see also specific premises
premium bonds 5–6, 10, 26
preparation for gambling 186–8, 194, 223
press: and the Gambling Review Report 2001 241–8, 257, 260; racing 10, 188
'pressure-relief' group 232
prevalence of gambling 144–57, **153**; and expenditure/spend 149–52, **151**; future research into 232; gambling last year and last week 144–9, **145**, *146*, **147**, *148*, 214
prevalence of problem gambling 72–88, **75**, 158–70, 211–12, 213, 214; and age 215; and availability/accessibility of gambling 90–3; estimate criticisms 77–80, **78**; false negatives 78, 79, 211; false positives 77, 78–9, 158, 211; lack of a gold standard 79; women gamblers 80–2; young people 82–8, **86**
prevention of problem gambling see treatment/prevention of problem gambling
primary sampling units (PSUs) 142
private betting 1; 17th century 2; and the British Gambling Prevalence Survey 1999 145, 146, 149, 152, 154, 155, 156–7, 168; Gaming Board's lack of knowledge of 26; history of 2; and income 215; participants 152, 154,

155, 156–7; and problem gambling 168, 213, 214; and the qualitative interview study of problem gambling 175, 180
prize fighting 2
pro-gambling discourses 254; backlash against 255–6
probability: lack of public understanding of 127–8, 223; in operant learning theory 118
problem gambling 41, 42, 44, 45, 50–88; as addiction 60–1, 62–72, 223–6; age factors 214–15; assessment tools for 72–3; and attitudes to gambling 168, **170**; and the British Gambling Prevalence Survey 1999 141, 142, 158–70; by type of gambling activity 164–8, *166*; effects of 53–4, 55–62, 249–53; and expenditure/spend 168, **169**; explaining 216–23; and the family 249–53; in fiction 52–3; and the Gambling Review Report 2001 236, 237, 241, 244, 245, 257–8, 260; as impulsive control disorder 116, 139; and income 215–16; and the liberalisation of gambling 237, 245; medical model of 224–6; overcoming 206–8; and parental gambling 162–3, 164, **165**, 219–20; prevalence 72–88, **75**, 158–70, **160**, **161**, *162*, *163*, **164**, 211–12, 213, 214, 215; criticisms of prevalence estimates 77–80, **78**; problems identifying 170–2, **170**; qualitative study of 49, 174–208; recognition of 53–9; regulation of 46–7; responsibility for 71; risks factors for 212–16; seeking help for 169–70; and sex 214–15; symptoms of 53, 56–7; thresholds 158, 170, 225; and women 80–2; and young people 59–62, 82–8, **86**, 105, 161, 214–15, 231, 233, 257–8; *see also* addiction to gambling; causes of problem gambling; compulsive gambling; obsessive gambling behaviour; pathological gambling; treatment/ prevention of problem gambling
problem gambling syndrome 56
productivity 7
profits, gambling industry 26
prohibition 251
Pronto 238

psy professions 62–3, 64, 207
psychiatrists 207
psychiatry 62–3
psychoanalysis 53, 63, 112–13
Psychoanalytic Review 52
psychodynamic/personality theories of gambling 112–17
psychological effects of problem gambling 56–8, 67, 68, 205; *see also* depression
psychosomatic symptoms 56
psychotherapy 226, 228
public debate/discourse 209, 224
public houses 23, 149, 187, 199, 221, 240
pull and push motives 121
punishment: self 112, 113; under the 1906 Street Betting Act 15, 16

qualitative interview study of problem gambling x, 49, 174–208, 209–11, 219–22, 225–6, 234; definitions of gambling 178–81, 182; downsides of gambling 203–6; financial issues 216; first gambling experiences 177, 182–6; image of gamblers 181–2; life influences 195–200, **197**; life pathways 194–5; and marginalisation of the family 250; participants 175–6, **175**; procedure followed 177–8; study design 175–8; topics covered 177, 178; uncontrolled gambling 201–3; variation in gambling control 200–2; variation in the preparation for gambling 186–8, 194; varied experiences and motivations 186–94; when gambling becomes a problem 200–8
Qualitative Research Unit 174, 177
questionnaires, for the British Gambling Prevalence Survey 1999 142–3, 144, 149–50

race courses 23; *see also* horse racing
racing press 10, 188
random ratio (RR) schedules 118–19
Rank Leisure Gaming Sector 140
'ratcheting up' effect 32
rationality 223
Reader's Digest magazine 112
rebellion 112–13
reels, knowing the 108–9
Reformation church leaders 6

regulation 46–8; at the end of the 20th century **47**; and the Gambling Review Report 2001 234–6; National Lottery (NL) 241; *see also* legislation; liberalisation of gambling
reinforcement, gradient of 118
reinforcement schedules 118–19, *120*
relationships: effects of uncontrolled gambling on 205–6; *see also* families, effects of gambling on; partners
remorse 110
'Rent-a-Spacers' 110
representativeness heuristic 127
research: biases in 254–5; funding 258–9; future 232–3; independence of 259
residential treatment 226, 229–30, 232
responsibility 71
Restoration 2
retired people 155
reward/reinforcement theories of gambling 117–23; classical conditioning 122–3; emotional rewards of gambling 119–22, *120*
risk factors *see* causes of problem gambling; social groups at risk
risk taking: attitudes to 124; as definition of gambling 178–9
risk-aversion 124
risk-seeking behaviour 124
riverboat casinos 32, 91
role dispossession 108
Rosebery, Lord 8
Rothschild, Lord 19
roulette: and the gambler's fallacy 128; and the illusion of control 129, 131; and the qualitative interview study of problem gambling 180; simplification of the rules of 34; 'touchbet roulette' (electronic) 34
Rowntree family 10
Rowntree, Seebohm 8
Royal Commission on Lotteries and Betting 1932–33 16, 17
Russia 23

Scale of Gambling Choices (SGC) 133
Scandinavia 36–7
scratchcards: addictiveness of 28; availability of 199, 207–8; and the British Gambling Prevalence Survey 1999 145, 147, 149, 153, 167, 168, 172; international expansion of 23; and near misses 97; participants 153; and problem gambling 167, 168; and the qualitative interview study of problem gambling 178, 199, 207–8; and sex differences 214; and telephone helplines 230; *see also* National Lottery scratchcards
seaside arcades 185, 221–2; availability of 199; and the Gambling Review Report 2001 239–40, 258, 260; liberalisation of attitudes to 256
Secretary of State at the Home Office 19, 25
Select Committee 1808 6
Select Committee 1902 7, 9
Select Committee 1918 10
Select Committee (Cautley Committee) 1923 16
Select Committee on Gaming 1844 4
self-depreciation 110
self-esteem 190
self-help 230
self-loathing 205
self-punishment 112, 113
selfishness 7
sensation-seeking 115, 117, 222
sensitivity 77, **78**
serotonin 136–7, 229
sex differences 80–2, 152, 161–4, *162*, *164*, **165**, 214–15; *see also* men and gambling; women and gambling
Sheffield gang wars 4
sicbo (card game) 34
single distribution theory 93, 221
skill 96, 181, 186, 194, 223, 233; and gambling machines 97, 108–9, 116, 130; and the illusion of control 129, 130; as part of the definition of gambling 180
skin conductance level (SCL) 123
smart cards 240
smoking 71, 101–3
Snowden, Lord 16
social class 1, 11–13; and bingo 215, 254; in the British Gambling Prevalence Survey 1999 155–6, 162, **164**, 215; and the qualitative interview study of problem gambling 181; *see also specific classes*
social functions of gambling 106–11, 189

social groups at risk 98–106; age at which gambling started 105–6; friends' gambling 100–1; future research into 232, 233; income, education and ethnic group 103–5; parental gambling 98–100; prevalence estimation of 74, 85; smoking, drinking and drug-taking 101–3

social impact of gambling: and the Gambling Review Report 2001 39, 40, **40**, 45, 234, 241, 245–7, 260; lack of government interest in 255

social roles 196

social science 253

South Asians 157

South Oaks Gambling Screen (SOGS) 41, 72–4, 76, 86, 90–2, 99, 102, 123, 125, 130, 132, 211, 214–16, 224; comparison with the DSM-IV 170–2, **170**; criticisms of 77–9, 211–12; false negatives 211; false positives 158, 211; lack of a gold standard 79; and the qualitative interview study of problem gambling 174, 175, 176–7; reliability 171–2; thresholds 225; use in the British Gambling Prevalence Survey 1999 158, **159**, 160–1, **160**, 162–72, *162*, **165**; and women gamblers 81; for young people (SOGS-RA) 85, 87

Spain 22, 29, 75, 102, 228, 256

specificity 77, **78**

Spectator, The 48

spend, gambling *see* expenditure/spend

Sporting League 9

sports betting 22, 25, 46, 81, 136; *see also specific sports*

spread betting: and the British Gambling Prevalence Survey 1999 141, 142, 145, 149, 150; deregulation of 38–9; expenditure/spend on 150; prevalence 232; turnover 39

stages of gambling 217; addiction 217; adoption 217; induction 217; promotion 217

stakes 96, 149, 150, 156, *157*, 168, **169**

Stakis Casinos 140

Steering Group 225

stigma 180–1; neutralization techniques 256

stock market betting 5, 81, 179

strategies, gambling 186–7, 223

street betting 9–10, 13–15

Street Betting Act 1906 9, 13–14, 15–16

structural characteristics 95–8

structural equation modelling 59

suicide 56–8, 205, 229, 230, 257

Sun 245

Sunday Express 243

Sunday Times 246

super pan 9 (card game) 34

support services 206, 207

Sweden 23, 75, 104, 105, 212

Swedish National Register 75

systems of gambling 186–7, 223

taxation, gambling 21, 22–3, 26, 42; cost benefit-analysis of 42, 44; and regulation 48; *see also* duties on gambling

Technical Casino Services 140

telephone betting 23, 199, 232

telephone hotlines 226, 229, 230, 232

telephone surveys 74, 77, 81, 250–1

television 188; interactive 21, 232

temperance movement 8

thinking-aloud experiment 130–2, **131**

Times, The 242, 243, 244, 245, 247, 257

tokens 97

tolerance 67, 69

toss the coin 182–3, 203

tossing rings 4

Tote 16, 17, 18, 140

tourism 43

transnational gambling companies 252–3

treatment/prevention of problem gambling 64, 226–32; cognitive behavioural therapy (CBT) 226, 228–9; counselling 226, 228; funding 229, 232, 258–9; future research 232, 233; GamAnon 226, 232; Gamblers Anonymous 226–7, 232; and the Gambling Review Report 2001 235; involving partners and other family members 226, 231–2; multi-modal 226; pharmacological 226, 229; psychotherapy 226, 228; residential forms 226, 229–30, 232; self-help 230; telephone hotlines 226, 229, 230, 232; unaided quitting 230–1; *see also* overcoming problem gambling

truancy 60, 83
turnover 21, 23, 26, 149; bingo 25, 30; casinos 25; football pools 29–30; gambling machines 25; horse racing 30; problems in estimating 25; sports betting 25; spread betting 39
twin studies 137–8; dizygotic (DZ) twins 137–8; monozygotic (MZ) twins 137–8
types of gambler 51, 108–11

unaided quitting 230–1
unconscious wish to lose theory 63, 64, 112–13
uncontrolled gambling 201–5, 209–12, 223–6; prevalence 211–12
unemployment 41, 43, 155
upper-class gambling 8, 11–12, 155
USA 7, 21–2, 27, 29, 216, 247; addictive nature of gambling 62, 63, 64–5; age at which gambling started 105; alcohol-problem gambling link 134; attitudes to gambling 251–3; availability/accessibility of gambling 91, 93–4, 221; backlash against pro-gambling discourse 255, 256; biological causes of problem gambling 138; casinos 39; cost-benefit analysis 39; ethnic groups 104–5; expectancy 125; help-seeking in 93–4; internet gambling 37; lotteries 32; peer pressure 101; personality disorders 113; problem gambling 12, 54–6, 62–5, 72–5, 81, 85–7, 91, 101–2, 104–5, 113, 134, 212; substance abuse and problem gambling 101, 102; treatment of problem gambling 226, 227, 228, 229, 231, 232; women gamblers 81; young gamblers 62, 85, 86, 87

variable-ratio (VR) schedules 118, 119
Vernons 5
video lottery terminals (VLTs) 121
video-poker games 132
vulnerability 232, 233, 257–8, 260

weightings 144
West Germany 22
white gamblers 157
William Hill 140, 199
Winner, Michael 245

winning: alcohol consumption and delusions of 199; early win hypothesis 119, 219, 220; emotional responses to 191–2, 193–4; fantasies of 188–9, 191; and first experiences of gambling 185; influence on other people's gambling 198
wish to lose theory 63, 64, 112–13
withdrawal symptoms 56, 67–9
within case analysis 178
women and gambling: bingo 81, 82, 214–15, 254; expenditure/spend of 150–2; overrepresentation in the British Gambling Prevalence Survey 1999 143–4; participation in gambling 152; prevalence of problem gambling in 80–2, 161–4, *162*, *163*; and street betting 15
working classes 1, 11–13, 52–3; and bingo 254; and the football pools 11; growing social acceptability of the gambling of 16–17; income levels 2, 103–4, 108, 215–16; influence of the upper classes on 11–12; and lotteries 6; and the qualitative interview study of problem gambling 181; seen as unfit to gamble 8, 12–13; specific laws against the gambling of 9–10; and street betting 9–10, 15; use of judgement in gambling 13
workplaces 149, 221
World Health Organisation 62, 64

young people: and the British Gambling Prevalence Survey 1999 152–4, 161; crime associated with gambling 60, 61–2, 83, 85, 110; and the early start hypothesis 105–6, 219, 220–1; ethnic minorities 105; and gambling machines 60–1, 62, 82–4, 88, 97, 116, 153–4, 239–40, 244, 257; in the Gambling Review Report 2001 236, 239–40, 241, 244, 257–8, 260; income of 104; and locus of control 116; and parental gambling 99–100; and peer pressure 100–1; and problem gambling 59–62, 82–8, **86**, 105, 161, 214–15, 231, 233, 257–8; and the social functions of gambling 108–11; substance abuse and gambling 101–2; treatment of problem gambling 231; vulnerability 257–8; *see also* children